The Doctrine of God

The Doctrine of God

Introducing the Big Questions

John C. Peckham

t&tclark
LONDON • NEW YORK • OXFORD • NEW DELHI • SYDNEY

T&T CLARK
Bloomsbury Publishing Plc
50 Bedford Square, London, WC1B 3DP, UK
1385 Broadway, New York, NY 10018, USA

BLOOMSBURY, T&T CLARK and the T&T Clark logo are trademarks
of Bloomsbury Publishing Plc

First published in Great Britain 2020

Copyright © John C. Peckham, 2020

John C. Peckham has asserted his right under the Copyright, Designs
and Patents Act, 1988, to be identified as Author of this work.

All rights reserved. No part of this publication may be reproduced or
transmitted in any form or by any means, electronic or mechanical, including
photocopying, recording, or any information storage or retrieval system,
without prior permission in writing from the publishers.

Bloomsbury Publishing Plc does not have any control over, or responsibility for,
any third-party websites referred to or in this book. All internet addresses given
in this book were correct at the time of going to press. The author and publisher
regret any inconvenience caused if addresses have changed or sites have
ceased to exist, but can accept no responsibility for any such changes.

A catalogue record for this book is available from the British Library.

A catalog record for this book is available from the Library of Congress.

ISBN:	HB:	978-0-5676-7787-7
	PB:	978-0-5676-7784-6
	ePDF:	978-0-5676-7786-0
	ePuB:	978-0-5676-7785-3

Typeset by Integra Software Services Pvt. Ltd.

To find out more about our authors and books visit www.bloomsbury.com
and sign up for our newsletters.

Contents

1 **Introducing the Doctrine of God** 1
2 **Does God Change? Does God Have Emotions?** 27
3 **Does God Have a Future?** 69
4 **Does God Know Everything? Does God Know the Future?** 109
5 **Can God Do Anything?** 145
6 **Is God Entirely Good?** 175
7 **How Can God Be One and Three?** 199

Epilogue: Concluding Reflections 239

Glossary 242
Index 253

1

Introducing the Doctrine of God

What is God like? How does God relate to the world? These questions are integrally related to all other theological questions. Theology refers to the study of God. Yet, theological study encompasses far more than the study of God alone. Theology extends to what theologians call the God–world relationship, which is the relationship between God and everything else.

This book introduces the big questions about God, including questions such as: Does God change? Does God have emotions? Can God do anything? Does God know the future? Does God always get what God wants? Is God entirely good? How can God be one and three? The answers to these questions hold massive implications for all other theological issues. As Thomas Aquinas put it, "A small mistake in the beginning is a great one in the end."[1] At the beginning of theology is how one conceives of God, which affects everything else. The theological path you set out on depends a great deal on your concept of God and how God relates to his creation (the world).

In systematic theology, the study of God's nature and attributes and how God relates to the world is known as the doctrine of God or theology proper. This book approaches the doctrine of God from the standpoint of Christian theism, defined as belief in the one, triune God who is the creator and sustainer of the world. Here, the "world" refers to *everything* other than God—the entire cosmos. As such, nothing exists beyond God and the world. Put differently, the God–world relationship encompasses everything that is. Accordingly, the doctrine of God holds implications for *everything* else.

---

[1] Thomas Aquinas, *On Being and Essence*, trans. Armand Maurer (Toronto: Pontifical Institute of Mediaeval Studies, 1949), 25.

This book aims to provide a clear and concise introduction to the doctrine of God, focusing on some big questions relative to divine attributes and the God–world relationship in recent Christian theology. Given the huge number of issues relative to the doctrine of God, this introduction is necessarily selective and is not meant to be taken as comprehensive. There are many nuanced views of the various issues, more than can be engaged in a short book like this. Accordingly, this introductory, issues-focused, textbook surveys some selected contemporary perspectives regarding each of the primary questions, briefly considering where each perspective locates itself relative to the classical Christian tradition, offering explanations of the technical issues involved, and including a brief survey of some relevant biblical data regarding each question. This chapter begins by introducing the crucial place of the doctrine of God and the framework for addressing the doctrine of God.

The nature of systematic theology

To understand the crucial place of the doctrine of God in systematic theology, it is important to have a basic understanding of the nature of theological systems. A system is a connected and organized group of working parts that contribute to and compliment the whole. For example, a properly functioning car requires a *system* of working parts that are properly organized and function harmoniously. If even one crucial component is missing, out of place, or disconnected, the vehicle will not work properly, if at all. Similarly, a coherent theological system requires that one has the right conceptual components and that those components be properly organized.

Articulating a coherent theological system is the task of systematic theology. Minimally defined, systematic theology is the study and articulation of an orderly and coherent account of theological beliefs. As such, Christian systematic theology might be defined as the study and articulation of an orderly and coherent account of Christian beliefs. Systematic theology has been practiced in various ways. Most systematic theologies are not only concerned with an orderly and coherent account of theistic beliefs, but they are also concerned with articulating such an account in a way that is shaped by and responsive to historical and contemporary philosophical issues. Further, the majority of Christians take Scripture to be normative regarding theological claims and many theologians hold that Christian theological claims should meet the standard of biblical warrant, which requires that one's claims are adequately grounded in Scripture. As Katherin Rogers puts it, "The God whom most of us *care* about is the one we associate with biblical revelation. So it is important to take the Bible seriously."[2] Accordingly, Christian systematic theology often overlaps with philosophical and biblical studies.

Theologians navigate the interrelationship of philosophy, systematic theology, and biblical studies in diverse ways, but all Christian approaches that take Scripture seriously navigate these three areas in some manner. For those seeking biblical warrant for theological claims, there are at least three levels of theological conceptualization at work. The micro-level is the interpretation of individual texts and passages of Scripture. The macro-level consists of the overarching philosophical presuppositions relative to the nature of reality (ontology), knowledge (epistemology), God, and the world, which impinge upon how one views and interprets everything else. In between the micro-level and macro-level are one's doctrinal commitments, which make up the meso-level.[3] Each of these levels affects the others. One's philosophical framework (macro) sets the overarching parameters within which theological doctrines (meso) are conceptualized and both one's philosophical framework (macro) and theological doctrines (meso) impinge upon the reading of individual texts and passages of Scripture (micro).[4] Conversely, insofar as one seeks to employ Scripture as normative regarding theological claims, the reading of Scripture should inform—and perhaps reform—one's doctrines (meso) and overarching philosophical framework (macro).

For example, those who adopt a philosophical framework in which God cannot experience emotional changes tend to read the passages of Scripture

---

[2]Katherin A. Rogers, *Perfect Being Theology* (Edinburgh: Edinburgh University Press, 2000), 8. Jay Wesley Richards adds, "commitment to biblical normativity" is itself "the norm among Catholic and Orthodox" and Protestant theologians. *The Untamed God: A Philosophical Exploration of Divine Perfection, Simplicity, and Immutability* (Downers Grove, IL: InterVarsity, 2003), 32.

[3]Fernando Canale articulates these levels in terms of micro-, meso-, and macro-hermeneutical principles of theological interpretation in *Back to Revelation-Inspiration: Searching for the Cognitive Foundation of Christian Theology in a Postmodern World* (Lanham, MD: University Press of America, 2001), 148–49.

[4]As Brevard Childs notes, "For systematic theologians the overarching categories are frequently philosophical. The same is often the case for biblical scholars even when cloaked under the guise of a theory of history." Brevard S. Childs, *Biblical Theology in Crisis* (Philadelphia, PA: Westminster, 1970), 158. Accordingly, Craig Bartholomew adds, "One ignores the role of philosophy in biblical interpretation at one's peril." *Introducing Biblical Hermeneutics: A Comprehensive Framework for Hearing God in Scripture* (Grand Rapids, MI: Baker Academic, 2015), 131.

that attribute emotional changes to God as metaphorical depictions of God *as if* he experienced emotional change. Conversely, some who believe God does experience emotional changes argue that such passages provide compelling evidence against the philosophical presupposition that God cannot experience emotional changes (this issue is discussed in Chapter 2). Regarding this and many other issues, much hinges upon how one navigates cases of tension between one's philosophical framework, doctrinal commitments, and the apparent meaning of Scripture.

In this and other respects, one's conception of God is bound up with one's view of the nature of reality (ontology), which is part and parcel of one's metaphysical framework. Put simply, one's metaphysical framework consists of one's views regarding the nature of ultimate reality, particularly relative to questions concerning existence, the nature of being, the nature and properties of beings, space and time, causality, and others. Each of us operates with a metaphysical framework whenever we think about any object. The way one views reality and the relationship between realities—one's metaphysical framework—dramatically affects the way one conceives of God and the God–world relationship; indeed, the way one conceives of every facet of reality.

There are various theological proposals regarding how to best navigate the interrelationship between one's metaphysical framework, doctrinal beliefs, and reading of Scripture. Since this is not a book on theological method, no attempt is made in this book to prescribe how the interrelationship of these areas *should* be navigated.[5] Rather, this book introduces (in a primarily descriptive manner) prominent philosophical and theological commitments and some of the oft-referenced biblical material that bears on the doctrine of God. Before engaging the big questions in the following chapters, however, it is important to first become oriented to the broad landscape of contemporary theology relative to the doctrine of God.

Classical theism

The contemporary debate is often framed as a discussion regarding the so-called classical conception of God, or classical theism. Generally

---

[5] For my proposal regarding theological method, see John C. Peckham, *Canonical Theology: The Biblical Canon, Sola Scriptura, and Theological Method* (Grand Rapids, MI: Eerdmans, 2016).

speaking, traditional classical theism holds that God, as the perfect being, is necessarily existent, self-sufficient, simple, eternal, immutable, impassible, omnipotent, omniscient, and omnibenevolent.[6] Each of these terms will be unpacked and explained throughout this book. For now, I will offer a brief explanation of these attributes and how they fit together in classical theism.

To say that God is the perfect being means more than to say God is without any faults or flaws. It typically conveys that God is the greatest being in every conceivable way and is thus uniquely worthy of worship. As Anselm (c. 1033–1109) put it, God is "whatever it is better to be than not to be."[7] This approach is often referred to as perfect being theology, which maintains that God is that which nothing greater can be conceived.[8] On this view, the perfect being "must have all great-making properties and must have them to an unlimited extent."[9] That is, whatever property would make a being great is possessed by God to the maximum extent possible.

This way of thinking about God as possessing anything great in an eminent fashion is sometimes called the "way of eminence" (*via eminentiae*). This way of approaching theology predicates of God every good attribute or "perfection" in an eminent fashion. This way is mirrored by the way of negation (*via negativa*), which operates by negating that which is thought to be limiting or in any way less than proper for a perfect being (e.g., change is

---

[6]For example, Brian Leftow describes the God of classical theism as: *a se*, simple, immaterial, not spatially extended, without accidents, immutable, impassible, eternal ["in the sense of timeless"], necessarily existent, omnipresent, having perfect intellect (including perfect knowledge) and perfect will, perfect power, and perfect goodness. "God, Concepts of," in *The Routledge Encyclopedia of Philosophy* (London: Taylor and Francis, 1998): Accessed June 10, 2018: https://www.rep.routledge.com/articles/thematic/god-concepts-of/v-1/sections/classical-theism. See, further, the similar list in Thomas Williams, "Introduction to Classical Theism," in *Models of God and Alternative Ultimate Realities*, ed. Jeanine Diller and Asa Kasher (New York: Springer, 2013), 95. Cf. Ronald Nash, *The Concept of God: An Exploration of Contemporary Difficulties with the Attributes of God* (Grand Rapids, MI: Zondervan, 1983), 20. Eleonore Stump, *The God of the Bible and the God of the Philosophers* (Marquette: Marquette University Press, 2016), 18; Veli-Matti Kärkkäinen, *The Doctrine of God: A Global Introduction*. 1st ed. (Grand Rapids, MI: Baker Academic, 2004), 54–55; Rogers, *Perfect Being Theology*, 19ff.

[7]Anselm, *Proslogion* 5. Anselm goes on: "Thus, then, truly are You perceptive, omnipotent, merciful, and impassible, just as You are living, wise, good, blessed, eternal, and whatever it is better to be rather than not to be." *Proslogion* 11. These and all other citations of Anselm's works in this book are from Anselm of Canterbury, *The Major Works*, ed. Brian Davies and G.R. Evans (New York: Oxford University Press, 1998).

[8]This premise is the core of Anselm's famous ontological argument for God's existence. See Anselm, *Proslogion* 2–3.

[9]Rogers, *Perfect Being Theology*, 13.

negated such that God is *im*mutable).¹⁰ Many forms of theology operate on the assumption that God is a perfect being, including approaches that are directly opposed to traditional classical theism—such as Charles Hartshorne's process theology (discussed further below). Vastly different conceptions of God as perfect being may be held because, Rogers notes, "in the past and today, the enumeration of great-making properties has proceeded largely on the basis of intuition."¹¹ Accordingly, "*That* God is the best [possible being] seems taken for granted. What that means is the subject of debate."¹²

Traditional Christian approaches typically suppose that the perfect or greatest being would possess the greatest possible power and the greatest possible knowledge. Accordingly, classical theists maintain that God is all-powerful (omnipotent) and all-knowing (omniscient). Divine perfection is also often thought to entail that God exists necessarily, on the supposition that a being who exists necessarily would be greater than a being who does not. If God is a necessary being, it is impossible that God not exist. Another way of saying this is that there is no possible world—i.e., no possible universe—in which God does not exist.¹³ Additionally, classical theism generally teaches that God's existence is not dependent upon or derived from anything else. God is self-existent. That is, God exists entirely of himself (*a se*).¹⁴ This is typically referred to as divine aseity or self-sufficiency (with regard to God's existence). As self-sufficient, God does not need anything relative to his existence or essential nature. Closely related to divine aseity, divine simplicity maintains that God is not composed of parts. That is, God is a non-composite being. Many classical theists have argued that if God had parts (including, in some views, attributes that are genuinely distinct from

---

¹⁰The contrast between negative ways and positive ways is sometimes called apophatic and cataphatic theology. The attributes derived from these ways are closely related to the distinction between incommunicable and communicable attributes, the latter being those that humans can possess in some lesser way than God. Notably, Karl Barth raises significant questions for the *via negativa*, asking: "How can our negation be a trustworthy transcending of the created world and as such a trustworthy description of God?" He finds this method "suspicious," particularly given his view of divine freedom as "just as operative in His relation to the world as in His being in Himself." Karl Barth, *Church Dogmatics*, ed. Geoffrey W. Bromiley and T. F. Torrance (Edinburgh: T&T Clark, 1957), 2/1, 347. Relative to the way of eminence, Barth adds, "the concepts by which, superlatively, we attempt to transcend this other, make shipwreck on the rock of this eternal self-existence of God." Barth, *Church Dogmatics* 2/1, 348.
¹¹Rogers, *Perfect Being Theology*, 4.
¹²Rogers, *Perfect Being Theology*, 2.
¹³See, for example, Richard Swinburne, *The Christian God* (New York: Clarendon, 1994), 144.
¹⁴As Leftow explains, to be *a se* is to be "wholly independent of all else." God, then, "must need or depend on nothing in any way other than himself (Aseity)." Leftow, "God, Concepts of."

one another) then God's being would depend in some way on those parts, undermining divine aseity (as some understand it).[15]

Classical theism further maintains that God is eternal, meaning God's existence has no beginning and no end. Additionally, many classical theists have traditionally held that God is timeless or atemporal, meaning that there is no "before" or "after" from God's perspective. Here, the "a" in atemporal is meant as a negation of temporality. On this view, God's being is incompatible with time (where time is conceived of in terms of the succession of moments or events). God, then, has no past and no future and can only be said to have a "present" euphemistically (the eternal "present").[16] This view of divine eternity is bound up with divine immutability and impassibility. Divine immutability means that God is changeless. Some Christian thinkers maintain the view (typically traced to Plato) that a perfect being could not change, supposing that if God changed he would thereby become better or worse. If he became better, he was not perfect in the first place. If he became worse, he would not be perfect after changing.[17] Apart from this, if God is timeless (as defined above), God cannot change because any change would require movement from one time to another. That is, any change requires an initial time (time 1) at which something was in one state and a later time (time 2) in which that something has changed (see Chapters 2 and 3).

If God cannot change in any way whatsoever, it follows that God cannot be affected by anyone or anything else. For many classical theists, this is what is meant by divine impassibility. On this view, God cannot be acted upon; God cannot be affected by any creaturely action or disposition. Taken in an unqualified sense, this means that God cannot have any *responsive, changing* emotions or, strictly speaking, become pleased or displeased by creatures or events.[18]

Those who affirm the above tenets are typically identified as classical theists. However, classical theism is not monolithic. There is more than one

---

[15] As Leftow explains it, God is "completely without parts. Whatever has parts depends on them for its existence and nature." Leftow, "God, Concepts of."

[16] Rogers explains, "God is eternal. He is outside of time. All of time is immediately present to God but He is not temporal." *Perfect Being Theology*, 21.

[17] Rogers, *Perfect Being Theology*, 20.

[18] As Nash explains, impassibility "suggests that God cannot be 'moved' in an emotional sense: God cannot be hurt, grieved, saddened, and so on." Nash, *Concept of God*, 21. Leftow adds, God is "unable to be affected by beings other than himself. For if we affected God—if, say, our suffering made him sorrowful—his emotional state would depend on us, and so God would not be wholly *a se*." Leftow, "God, Concepts of."

kind of classical theism and the basic tenets of classical theism (as described above) are not unique to Christian theology but have also been advocated by significant Jewish and Muslim thinkers.[19] Indeed, as Thomas Williams defines it, classical theism is "the name given to the model of God we find in Platonic, neo-Platonic, and Aristotelian philosophy and in Christian, Muslim, and Jewish thinkers who appropriate those traditions of classical Greek philosophy."[20] In its Christian forms, classical theism includes the all-important doctrine of the Trinity.

Yet, there is diversity even among Christians who adopt the label classical theist. Indeed, Veli-Matti Kärkkäinen notes, there is a "diversity and plurality of interpretations of God under the umbrella concept of classical theism."[21] Some identify as classical theists without maintaining all of the tenets described above or with considerable qualifications to some of them. For instance, whereas many think of divine immutability and impassibility as meaning that God cannot change in any way whatsoever and thus cannot be affected by anything outside of himself, others take a more moderate or qualified view, often alongside a view of divine eternity as other than strictly timeless.[22]

In this regard, John W. Cooper writes, "traditional classical theism is not a single, monolithic position. It has variations and nuances on many issues" such that "broad generalizations risk being caricatures."[23] Accordingly, Cooper distinguishes between "classical Christian theism, modified classical Christian theism," and "revised classical Christian theism."[24] He explains:

---

[19]See, for example, the work of the Muslim philosophers Avicenna (980–1037) and Averroes (1126–98) and the Jewish philosopher Maimonides (1153–1204). For some brief excerpts, see Avicenna, "God's Nature and Knowledge," in *The Philosophy of Religion Reader*, ed. Chad Meister (New York: Routledge, 2008), 93–99; Moses Maimonides, "Divine Simplicity, Negative Theology, and God-Talk," in *The Philosophy of Religion Reader*, ed. Chad Meister (New York: Routledge, 2008), 100–07.

[20]Williams, "Classical Theism," 95. Leftow adds, "Classical theism's ancestry includes Plato, Aristotle, Middle Platonism and Neoplatonism. It entered Judaism through Philo of Alexandria, reaching its apogee there in Maimonides. It entered Christianity as early as Irenaeus and Clement of Alexandria and became Christian orthodoxy as the Roman Empire wound down. Though more and more challenged after 1300, it remains orthodox." Leftow, "God, Concepts of."

[21]Veli-Matti Kärkkäinen, *The Doctrine of God: A Global Introduction*. 2nd ed. (Grand Rapids, MI: Baker Academic, 2017), 35.

[22]See, for example, the positions of Nicholas Wolterstorff, William Lane Craig, Bruce Ware, and Rob Lister, discussed in Chapter 2.

[23]John W. Cooper, *Panentheism: The Other God of the Philosophers* (Grand Rapids, MI: Baker Academic, 2006), 322.

[24]Cooper, *Panentheism*, 321. Cooper himself opposes panentheism, advocating "a fairly traditional version of classical theism," while being "open to minimal modifications concerning God's relation to time." *Panentheism*, 322.

All classical Christian theism maintains an unqualified Creator-creature distinction. The traditional version affirms God's [timeless] eternity. The modified version asserts that God is involved in time. It nuances his attributes accordingly but continues to affirm God's complete omniscience and omnipotence over all creatures, times, and places. If God responds to creatures temporally, it is by acting according to his sovereign knowledge and will. Revised classical theism goes further: it limits God's knowledge by time and limits his power relative to the choices and actions of creatures.[25]

What Cooper describes as revised classical theism is usually called open theism, so-called because it maintains that the future is open even to God and that it is therefore impossible for God to know the future free decisions of creatures. There are various versions of open theism, some of which will be discussed later in this book. There are also varieties of what Cooper calls modified classical theism, distinct from open theism most notably in affirming that God *does* know the future free decisions of creatures and providentially governs the world accordingly.[26] Forms of modified classical theism are so-called because they depart from stricter forms of classical theism relative to some classical divine attributes. For example, some forms of modified classical theism affirm a qualified form of divine impassibility and others affirm a qualified conception of divine passibility.

Some believe the label classical theism should be reserved for views that affirm a strict conception of the classical divine attributes.[27] To distinguish

---

[25]Cooper, *Panentheism*, 321.

[26]Cooper lists Richard Swinburne, Nicholas Wolterstorff, Alvin Plantinga, and William Lane Craig as modified classical theists. *Panentheism,* 321n2. For his part, Craig maintains divine necessity, aseity, incorporeality, omnipresence, eternity (omnitemporality), omniscience, (modified/weak) simplicity, qualified immutability, omnipotence, and utter goodness. J.P. Moreland and William Lane Craig, *Philosophical Foundations for a Christian Worldview* (Downers Grove, IL: IVP Academic, 2003), 502-29. Cf. Nash's "mediating concept of God that" seeks to avoid "the most serious difficulties of both the process and the Thomistic concepts of God." Nash, *Concept of God*, 36.

[27]In Cooper's view, modified classical theists can reject divine timelessness and still "be fully consistent with the classical Christian and Reformed doctrine of God, including God's aseity, the Trinity, creation, and the incarnation." Cooper, *Panentheism*, 343. Conversely, some pejoratively refer to modified classical theists such as William Lane Craig as theistic personalists or theistic mutualists, often focusing on the denial of strict simplicity by such thinkers. For example, Brian Davies labels Alvin Plantinga and Richard Swinburne "theistic personalists" because they depart from strict simplicity and, "unlike classical theism, they think it is important to stress that God is a person." Brian Davies, *An Introduction to the Philosophy of Religion*. 3rd ed. (New York: Oxford University Press, 2004), 9-10. Similarly, see Edward Feser, *Five Proofs of the Existence of God* (San Francisco, CA: Ignatius, 2017), 190-91; David Bentley Hart, *The Experience of God: Being, Consciousness, Bliss* (New Haven, CT: Yale University Press, 2013), 127-30. Similarly, James Dolezal has recently criticized and labeled a number of thinkers as theistic mutualists or revisionists because, he contends, they have rejected or revised the classical doctrine of divine simplicity (e.g., Bruce

it from so-called modified approaches, I will refer to this approach as strict classical theism—though many speak and write of this stricter approach simply as classical theism. A strict classical theist, for the purposes of this book, is one who subscribes to a strong or strict understanding of the divine attributes, often referred to as divine perfections. Accordingly, the strict classical theist is one who affirms, as a tightly connected package, divine perfection, necessity, *pure* aseity, *utter* self-sufficiency, *strict* simplicity, *timeless* eternity, *utter* immutability, *strict* impassibility, omnipotence, and omniscience.[28] The italicized modifiers in the previous sentence denote some ways in which strict classical theism affirms these attributes in a strong or strict sense, briefly explained below and taken up in further detail in later chapters.

First, whereas some understand and affirm divine aseity and self-sufficiency to mean that God's existence and *essential* nature are not dependent on or derived from anything else, strict classical theists tend to promote a stronger claim of *pure* aseity and self-sufficiency.[29] On this view, "God is wholly self-sufficient in all that he is and thus exists independently of all causal influence from his creatures."[30] As such, not only is God's essential nature not dependent on or derived from anything else, God is thought to be such that he has no contingent or accidental properties. That is, God has no properties that are dependent (in any way whatsoever) upon anything outside of himself. As John Webster puts it, "In every respect, God is of himself God."[31]

Ware, Rob Lister, John Frame, D.A. Carson, Ronald Nash, William Lane Craig, Alvin Plantinga, K. Scott Oliphint, Wayne Grudem, John Feinberg, and Kevin Vanhoozer). James E. Dolezal, *All That Is in God: Evangelical Theology and the Challenge of Classical Christian Theism* (Grand Rapids, MI: Reformation Heritage Books, 2017). Whereas some believe any departure from doctrines like simplicity renders one outside of classical theism and perfect being theology, Moreland and Craig contend: "Since the concept of God is underdetermined by the biblical data and since what constitutes a 'great-making' property is to some degree debatable, philosophers working within the Judeo-Christian tradition enjoy considerable latitude in formulating a philosophically coherent and biblically faithful doctrine of God." Moreland and Craig, *Philosophical Foundations*, 501.

[28]For one example of strict classical theism (from an Anselmian approach), see Rogers, *Perfect Being Theology*.

[29]This strict definition of aseity is often closely associated with the affirmation of God as pure actuality, discussed in Chapter 2.

[30]James E. Dolezal, "Strong Impassibility," in *Divine Impassibility: Four Views*, ed. Robert Matz and A. Chadwick Thornhill (Downers Grove, IL: IVP Academic, 2019), 18.

[31]John Webster, *God without Measure: Working Papers in Christian Theology*, vol. 1: God and the Works of God (New York: T&T Clark, 2016), 13.

Second, some classical theists adopt weaker views of divine simplicity, one of which allows that divine attributes such as love and power are *formally* distinct—genuinely distinct but inseparable. However, strict classical theism maintains that God is simple (non-composite) in a stronger sense, which maintains that there are *no* genuine distinctions in God relative to the divine attributes or otherwise (except, perhaps, relative to the persons of the Trinity).[32]

Third, strict classical theism maintains that God is *timelessly* eternal, meaning that God is not only without beginning or end but also without any temporal succession. This affirmation of atemporality is in contrast to the view of other Christian theists that God is *everlastingly* eternal. To say God is *everlastingly* eternal means that God is not atemporal or timeless but is everlasting (sometimes referred to as sempiternal); God has always existed and always will exist but does experience temporal succession.

Conversely, strict classical theists maintain, if God is *timelessly* eternal, God is *utterly* immutable (changeless). God cannot change in any way whatsoever. Accordingly, they maintain, God is also impassible in a strong sense, meaning God cannot be affected by anything else and thus cannot experience *responsive*, changing, emotions. This is in contrast to other classical theists who hold to a qualified kind of divine immutability, meaning that God is immutable relative to his essential nature but experiences other kinds of change in relationship to creatures.[33]

Summarizing what I have labeled strict classical theism, Thomas Williams explains:

> The God of classical theism is unqualifiedly perfect, where 'perfection' is conceived in ways congenial to the mind of Greek metaphysics: as requiring absolute unity, self-sufficiency, and immutability. The unqualifiedly perfect being is atemporal and immaterial—free from all limitations of time and place. It acts but is not acted upon, and so is said to be impassible. It is perfect in knowledge, perfect in power, and perfect in goodness.[34]

As such, Williams continues: "Classical theists thus typically understand God's perfection as requiring simplicity, eternity, immutability, and impassibility, and not merely his perfection in knowledge, power, and goodness."[35] As Michael Rea and Louis Pojman define it, "Classical

---

[32]See Chapter 7.
[33]See Chapter 2.
[34]Williams, "Classical Theism," 95.
[35]Williams, "Classical Theism," 97.

theism is perhaps best seen as what one gets when one does perfect-being theology under the influence of ancient Greek philosophical notions about perfection."[36] Thus, "when people speak of the 'God of the philosophers,' it is often the God of classical theism that they have in mind."[37]

In the eyes of many, the foremost example of strict classical theism is the scholastic theology of Thomas Aquinas, a kind of classical–scholastic theism that is sometimes called "Thomistic theism."[38] Apart from Scripture, Thomas Aquinas (1225–74) is the most influential theologian in history other than Augustine (354–430).[39] Aquinas is well known for, among many other things, articulating what many classical theists believe is the most elegant Christian systematic theology ever produced, the *Summa Theologiae*. To do this, Aquinas carefully synthesized elements of Aristotle's philosophical framework—which had recently become available in Latin translations and disrupted metaphysics in the academy—with the great tradition of Christian theology set forth by Augustine (and others).[40]

While it would be difficult to overstate Aquinas's influence, some advocates of strict classical theism describe their thought as most influenced by the perfect being theology of Anselm (*c.* 1033–1109) or Augustine and/or other church fathers. The strict classical theist need not subscribe to the entire system of Aquinas or another classical theologian. Many Protestants affirm strict classical theism while departing significantly from Augustine, Aquinas, and others relative to other points of doctrine (e.g., those within the Reformed scholastic tradition). In this regard, historian Richard A. Muller notes the significant influence of earlier Christian tradition on Protestant approaches to the doctrine of God, explaining that "the Reformation altered comparatively few of the major loci of theology: the doctrines of justification, the sacraments, and the church received the greatest emphasis, while the doctrines of God, the trinity, creation, providence, predestination,

---

[36]Michael Rea and Louis P. Pojman, "The Concept of God," in *Philosophy of Religion: An Anthology*. 7th ed, ed. Michael Rea and Louis P. Pojman (Stamford, CT: Cengage, 2015), 3.

[37]Rea and Pojman, "The Concept of God," 3.

[38]Nash, *Concept of God*, 19.

[39]Richards comments, "Thomas's thought is the high water mark and *locus classicus* of classical theism." *Untamed God*, 26. Rogers adds: "For the European intellectual tradition ... Augustine and Aquinas are the most influential philosophers of the Middle Ages" and "often we can treat their views on God as almost identical." Rogers, *Perfect Being Theology*, 7.

[40]See Jan A. Aertsen, "Aquinas's Philosophy in Its Historical Setting," in *The Cambridge Companion to Aquinas*, ed. Norman Kretzmann and Eleonore Stump (New York: Cambridge University Press, 1993), 20–22.

and the last things were taken over [from the medieval and patristics] by the magisterial Reformation virtually without alteration."[41]

Relative to the doctrine of God in general, many advocates maintain that strict classical theism *just is* the genuinely classical Christian view held by the patristics and others through the ages. For example, Rogers maintains that the strict classical theism she advocates comports with "the standard medieval view of the Augustinian Neoplatonists and the more Aristotelian thinkers as well."[42] In her view, "Both the Neoplatonism of Augustine and Anselm and the Aristotelianism of Aquinas provide all-encompassing frameworks within which to make sense of God and creation."[43]

Other proponents of the classical Christian tradition contend that the patristic fathers should be interpreted as holding more moderate or qualified conceptions of the divine attributes.[44] Given the differing understandings of just what constitutes the traditional, classical Christian understanding of the doctrine of God, those who differ from strict classical theism might prefer the label *moderate* classical theism instead of *modified* classical theism, since the latter may imply that strict classical theism is the standard, traditional view. Here, Kärkkäinen avers, there is considerable "diversity" within the Christian tradition, which "tests the limits of what is often taken as classical theism."[45]

Criticism of classical theism

In recent decades, classical theism—especially strict classical theism—has faced heavy criticism from many philosophers and theologians, including many Christian theists. As Fred Sanders puts it, "Sometime after the middle

---

[41]Richard A. Muller, *The Unaccommodated Calvin: Studies in the Foundation of a Theological Tradition*, Oxford Studies in Historical Theology (New York: Oxford University Press, 2000), 39. Jay Wesley Richards adds, "The so-called Protestant Scholastics who followed the Reformation adopted his [Aquinas's] doctrine of God, whether consciously or unconsciously, almost in its entirety." Richards, *Untamed God*, 26. D. Stephen Long adds: "Revising the doctrine of God was never part of the Reformation, and central to my argument in this work is that it should not be now." *The Perfectly Simple Triune God: Aquinas and His Legacy* (Minneapolis, MN: Fortress, 2016), 129.

[42]Rogers, *Perfect Being Theology*, 14.

[43]Rogers, *Perfect Being Theology*, 6.

[44]See, for example, the case in Paul L. Gavrilyuk, *The Suffering of the Impassible God: The Dialectics of Patristic Thought* (New York: Oxford University Press, 2006). See the further discussion in Chapter 2.

[45]Kärkkäinen, *The Doctrine of God*, 2nd ed., 59.

of the twentieth century, a number of related movements in academic theology began to call into question the God of classical theism."[46] While some objected on philosophical grounds, Sanders notes that many of the objections arose because "it seemed hard to reconcile this austere and metaphysically severe God with the biblical story. How could God be ontologically above distinctions, change, and suffering, when the Bible is the story of a God who has many distinct attributes, who becomes human and dies on the cross?"[47]

In this respect, the seminal theologian Jürgen Moltmann's critique of classical theism was highly influential in recent decades and continues to be so in some circles. In the main, Moltmann critiques classical theism for its conception of a God who "cannot suffer" and who cannot desire and who remains maximally blissful without any world.[48] Moltmann maintains instead that God takes suffering into God's very being: "God's being is in suffering and suffering is in God's being itself, because God is love."[49] For Moltmann, "Creation is a fruit of God's longing for 'his Other'" such that "God cannot find bliss in eternal self-love."[50] This suffering God, Moltmann avers, "is not in accord with the absolutism of pure power; for power is replaced by mutual friendship."[51]

Among many others, Moltmann has advocated the controversial claim that the Christian tradition was corrupted by a Hellenized conception of God (the so-called Hellenization thesis).[52] Some have claimed the classical Christian tradition was so influenced by Greek philosophy that the God of the Bible was replaced by the "god" of the philosophers. There is considerable disagreement on just how the influence of various streams

---

[46]Fred Sanders, "Classical Theism Makes a Comeback," *Didaktikos* 1/1 (November 2017): 47.

[47]Sanders, "Classical Theism," 47.

[48]Jürgen Moltmann, *The Crucified God: The Cross of Christ as the Foundation and Criticism of Christian Theology* (New York: Harper & Row, 1974), 215–16.

[49]Moltmann, *The Crucified God*, 227. Moltmann is especially concerned about the horrors of Auschwitz, saying: "God in Auschwitz and Auschwitz in the crucified God—that is the basis for a real hope which both embraces and overcomes the world, and the ground for a love which is stronger than death and can sustain death." *The Crucified God*, 278.

[50]Jürgen Moltmann, *The Trinity and the Kingdom*, trans. Margaret Kohl (Minneapolis, MN: Fortress, 1993), 106. This is in reference to what he calls "Christian panentheism," claiming that God "is eternally creative." *Trinity and the Kingdom*, 106.

[51]Moltmann, *Trinity and the Kingdom*, 106.

[52]See Moltmann, *Trinity and the Kingdom*, 22. See the further discussion in Chapter 2. Moltmann makes a more nuanced and sophisticated case than some, as noted by Gavrilyuk, *The Suffering of the Impassible God*, 178.

of Greek philosophy on the Christian tradition should be understood, addressed further in Chapter 2. Many advocates of classical theism have criticized the Hellenization thesis as a caricature and a straw man.[53] However, while advocates of the Hellenization thesis may often overstate their case, proponents and critics alike generally agree that streams of Greek philosophy such as Neoplatonism and Aristotelianism greatly influenced the church fathers. The debate, generally speaking, is over whether and to what extent such influence was received uncritically in the Christian tradition and whether such influence was a corrupting one.

Debates regarding just how the history should be understood aside, William Alston describes a "pervasive tension in Christian thought between 'the God of the philosophers and the God of the Bible,' between God as 'wholly other' and God as a partner in interpersonal relationships, between God as the absolute, ultimate source of all being and God as the dominant actor on the stage of history."[54] Here, Rea and Pojman note that an "important question" is "whether the so-called God of the philosophers has any real claim to being *the God of Abraham, Isaac, and Jacob*, or *God, the Father of Jesus*, or *God, the object of our ultimate concern*."[55] James Cone maintains, in this regard:

> Unlike the God of Greek philosophy who is removed from history, the God of the Bible is involved in history, and his revelation is inseparable from the social and political affairs of Israel .... To know him is to experience his acts in the concrete affairs and relationship of people, liberating the weak and the helpless from pain and humiliation.[56]

Sallie McFague adds, the "two images of God—one as the distant, all-powerful, perfect, immutable Lord existing in lonely isolation, and the other as the One who enters human flesh as a baby to eventually assume the alienation and oppression of all peoples in the world—do not fit together."[57]

As Katherin Rogers describes this line of criticism, which she denies: "It is often said that the God of Augustine, Anselm and Aquinas, the

---

[53] See Chapter 2.
[54] William Alston, *Divine Nature and Human Language* (Ithaca, NY: Cornell University Press, 1989), 147.
[55] Rea and Pojman, "Concept of God," 3.
[56] James Cone, *God of the Oppressed* (New York: Seabury Press, 1975), 62.
[57] Sallie McFague, *The Body of God: An Ecological Theology* (Minneapolis, MN: Fortress, 1993), 136.

immutable, eternal, transcendent source of all, cannot be the personal, loving God who acts as an agent in the world and takes an interest in individuals."[58] To some, the "perfect being Anselm describes, beyond time and space and quite unlike us, seems too distant to hear us or to care."[59] Rogers, however, argues that "the classic tradition would be surprised to learn of this 'pervasive tension,'" being "unwaveringly committed to a God who is both the eternal source of all and the one who answers prayers."[60] She recognizes that it is "an especially vexed question whether or how creatures can affect an omnipotent, absolutely independent [and timeless] creator," but asserts that "God's loving concern is as non-negotiable a perfection as omnipotence or omniscience in the classic tradition."[61] Similarly, Eleonore Stump notes:

> [contrasted with] biblical representations of God, to many people the God of classical theism seems unresponsive, unengaged, and entirely inhuman. That is because, on classical theism as it is often interpreted, God is immutable, eternal, and simple, devoid of all potentiality, incapable of any passivity, and inaccessible to human knowledge. So described, the God of classical theism seems very different from the God of the Bible.[62]

Yet, she argues, the "God of classical theism is the engaged, personally present, responsive God of the Bible."[63]

Conversely, Charles Hartshorne (1897–2000) set forth a sustained and influential philosophical critique of classical theism. At nearly every critical juncture, Hartshorne protests the classical–scholastic conception of God as incoherent or impoverished and promotes his version of process theology, which is in many respects the polar opposite of strict classical theism.[64] While critical of classical theism as out of step with the biblical portrayal of God, Hartshorne does not himself afford any normative authority to sacred religious texts such as the Bible but instead

---

[58] Rogers, *Perfect Being Theology*, 8.
[59] Rogers, *Perfect Being Theology*, 9.
[60] Rogers, *Perfect Being Theology*, 9.
[61] Rogers, *Perfect Being Theology*, 10.
[62] Stump, *The God of the Bible*, 18.
[63] Stump, *The God of the Bible*, 19.
[64] Hartshorne was heavily influenced by Alfred North Whitehead (1861–1947), his teacher. See Whitehead's seminal work, *Process and Reality: An Essay in Cosmology* (Cambridge: Cambridge University Press, 1929). For an introduction to process theology, see John B. Cobb Jr. and David Ray Griffin, *Process Theology: An Introductory Exposition* (Philadelphia, PA: Westminster Press, 1976).

approaches the doctrine of God by way of strictly natural theology, wherein God is conceived by what can be known of him through nature.[65]

Hartshorne's theology is an alternative kind of perfect being theology, drastically differing from classical theism with regard to what kind of characteristics a perfect being is thought to possess. For example, Hartshorne holds that a perfect being must be the most relational being; not impassible but the eminent feeler of the feelings of all others.[66] In Hartshorne's view, "divinity is not the privilege of escaping all sufferings but the exactly contrary one of sharing them all."[67] For some, the fact that one perfect being theologian might consider a particular characteristic (e.g., impassibility) to be a great-making property while another might consider it to be a deficiency manifests a practical problem relative to the methodology of perfect being theology (e.g., the ways of eminence and negation).

On the view that the most perfect being is the most relative being, Hartshorne holds that God and everything else is in continual process and the world itself is included in God as part of God's essential being. This is a form of panentheism, which literally means "all *in* God" and, generally speaking, refers to the view that the world (i.e., the universe) is *in* God but God is more than the world.[68] It is thus distinct from pantheism (literally, "all is God"), which claims God and the world are identical.

In Hartshorne's process panentheism, God is essentially related to the world such that God is in process and ever changing; the polar opposite of strict classical theism wherein God cannot change and is not *really* related to the world. In Hartshorne's process theism God is not timeless but temporal. God is not changeless (except ethically) but always changing. God is not impassible but is the supreme feeler of *all* feelings of others. God's knowledge is not independent but directly depends on the world. God is not causally independent but God and the world are interdependent. God cannot exist alone but the world necessarily and eternally exists in relation to God. God is not all-powerful (omnipotent) in the traditional sense but possesses maximal

---

[65]For Hartshorne, nature "is the real 'word of God' concerning the general structure of the cosmos." Charles Hartshorne, *Omnipotence and Other Theological Mistakes* (Albany: State University of New York Press, 1984), 73.

[66]God's universal sympathy is "relative in the eminent sense" and has "infinite sensitivity." Charles Hartshorne, *The Divine Relativity: A Social Conception of God* (New Haven, CT: Yale University Press, 1964), 76.

[67]Charles Hartshorne, *Man's Vision of God and the Logic of Theism* (Hamden, CT: Archon, 1964), xvi.

[68]There are numerous, varying, forms of panentheism. See Cooper, *Panentheism*.

persuasive power; the greatest power possible given the process axiom that individuals "can only be influenced, they cannot be sheerly coerced."[69]

More will be said about this approach, where relevant, later in this book. For now, we focus on Hartshorne's strident criticism of strict classical theism. "I am convinced," Hartshorne wrote, "that 'classical theism' (as much Greek as Christian, Jewish, or Islamic) was an incorrect translation of the central religious idea into philosophical categories."[70] Hartshorne further criticizes "classical theism" for what he characterizes as "metaphysical snobbery toward relativity, dependence, or passivity, toward responsiveness or sensitivity" and the "worship of mere absoluteness, independent, and one-sided activity or power."[71] Hartshorne contends, moreover, that classical theists "made God, not an exalted being, but an empty absurdity, a love which is simply not love, a purpose which is no purpose, a will which is no will, a knowledge which is no knowledge."[72]

In this and other ways, Hartshorne argued that Aquinas's "doctrine was shipwrecked on certain rocks of contradiction."[73] For example, Hartshorne wrote:

> Knowledge seems to imply an internal distinction between subject and object—but God is said to be simple. Volition seems to imply change—but God is changeless. Purpose seems to imply a present lack of something—but God is perfect; and for him there is no contrast between present intent and future realization. Love involves sensitivity to the joys and sorrows of others, participation in them—but we cannot infect God with our sufferings since he is cause of everything and effect of nothing, and our joys can add nothing to the immutable perfection of God's happiness. Though in religion one speaks of "serving" God, in reality, according to technical theology, one can do nothing for God, and our worst sins harm God as little as the finest acts of sainthood can advance him.[74]

Hartshorne's critique is echoed by many other process theologians. Perhaps most notably, David Ray Griffin offers his own strong criticism of classical theism, which is primarily directed against strict classical theism.[75]

---

[69]Hartshorne, *Man's Vision*, xvi.
[70]Hartshorne, *Divine Relativity*, vii.
[71]Hartshorne, *Divine Relativity*, 50.
[72]Hartshorne, *Omnipotence*, 31.
[73]Hartshorne, *Divine Relativity*, xii.
[74]Hartshorne, *Man's Vision*, 114.
[75]Griffin refers to this as "Thomistic theism." See David Ray Griffin, *God, Power, and Evil: A Process Theodicy* (Louisville, KY: Westminster John Knox, 2004), 73–77.

Likewise, many advocates of open theism—known for maintaining the future is open even for God and thus not exhaustively known by him—have offered similar critiques of classical theism, while differentiating themselves from many of the tenets of process theology, with many open theists emphasizing a view of the Creator-creature distinction that rules out panentheism and denies that there is an essential relation between God and the world.[76] Both process and open theists often frame their views in opposition to "Aristotle's Unmoved Mover, [which] was able to maintain a pristine motionlessness by always doing exactly the same perfect thing, thinking Itself."[77] In contrast, the open theist Clark Pinnock understands God as the "most moved Mover," holding a view distinct from process theism but similarly positioned over and against Aristotle's "unmoved Mover," which many claim is the God of classical theism.[78]

Hartshorne's biting criticism of strict classical theism and other criticisms like it have received a wide hearing and have been embraced in some circles while being met with strong rebuttals in others. Some charge that Hartshorne "systematically misunderstands" and caricatures the "classical"

---

[76] See, for example, Clark Pinnock, Richard Rice, John Sanders, William Hasker, and David Basinger, *The Openness of God: A Biblical Challenge to the Traditional Understanding of God* (Downers Grove, IL: InterVarsity Press, 1994); Clark Pinnock, *Most Moved Mover: A Theology of God's Openness* (Grand Rapids, MI: Baker Academic, 2001); Gregory A. Boyd, *God of the Possible: A Biblical Introduction to the Open View of God* (Grand Rapids, MI: Baker, 2000); John Sanders, *The God Who Risks: A Theology of Providence* (Downers Grove, IL: InterVarsity, 1998). While many open theists reject panentheism, one notable exception is Thomas Jay Oord, who describes himself as an open theist while also embracing a kind of panentheism that he calls essential kenosis. See Thomas Jay Oord, *The Nature of Love: A Theology* (St. Louis, MO: Chalice, 2010). On the clear distinction that many open theists make between their own views and process theology, see David Ray Griffin, John B. Cobb, Jr., and Clark H. Pinnock, eds. *Searching for an Adequate God: A Dialogue between Process and Free Will Theists* (Grand Rapids, MI: Eerdmans, 2000).

[77] Rogers, *Perfect Being Theology*, 48–49. For Aristotle, God is the unmoved mover. In his words, the "prime mover, which is immovable, is one both in formula and number." Aristotle, *Metaphysics* 12.8.18 (1074a. I am using the translation of Hugh Tredennick from the Loeb Classical Library). Further, the prime mover is the ultimate substance, separate from potentiality and materiality, "eternal and immovable" and "indivisible" and "impassive and unalterable." *Metaph.*, 12.7.12–13 (1073a). For Aristotle, the ultimate reality, the unmoved mover, is Mind (*nous*) and the mind is wholly unaffected and undetermined by external reality. *Metaph.*, 12.9.1–2 (1074b). It "does not change; for the change would be for the worse, and anything of this kind would immediately imply some sort of motion." *Metaph.*, 12.9.3 (1074b). The divine mind is entirely self-sufficient and thinks only itself: "Therefore Mind thinks itself, if it is that which is best; and its thinking is a thinking of thinking." *Metaph.*, 12.9.4 (1074b).

[78] See Pinnock, *Most Moved Mover*. Pinnock claims, however, that while "Augustine's model of God," which is "called classical by some conservatives today," is "a legitimate, neo-Platonic pattern of interpretation, … Augustine was in many ways the innovator here, while the open view connects with more ancient traditions." *Most Moved Mover*, 105.

view that he criticizes.[79] Further, classical theists such as Rogers charge that "process theology does not claim to adhere to a biblical conception of God and has moved far outside the field of orthodoxy."[80] Further, while some have abandoned classical theism in light of such criticisms, "classical theism" has also made something of a "comeback."[81] Fred Sanders notes: "In [much] recent work ... there has been a glad embrace of these classic doctrines of divine simplicity, aseity, impassibility, and immutability," as demonstrated in many recent publications.[82]

The framework and approach of this book

Framing the discussion

This brief survey of the debate regarding classical theism may serve to frame some of the most prominent contemporary positions regarding the doctrine of God. The purpose of this survey is not to render judgment on either classical theism or its critics but to illuminate the background of the contemporary discussion that will be engaged throughout this book. Whatever one thinks of classical theism, the magnitude of its programmatic influence on Christian systematic theology is unmatched. Conversely, whatever one thinks of the critiques of classical theism, such as those of Hartshorne and others, the contemporary discussion has been shaped significantly by such critiques.

Indeed, contemporary Christian approaches to the doctrine of God are often framed as either an endorsement, modification, or rejection of classical theism of some variety. Many of the most prominent contemporary positions *frame themselves* either as (1) supporting or sympathetic to classical theism, in its strict forms or otherwise, (2) offering modifications or qualifications

---

[79]W. Norris Clarke, "Charles Hartshorne's Philosophy of God: A Thomistic Critique," in *Charles Hartshorne's Concept of God: Philosophical and Theological Responses*, ed. S. Sia (Dordrecht, The Netherlands: Kluwer, 1990), 103.
[80]Rogers, *Perfect Being Theology*, 9.
[81]Sanders, "Classical Theism," 47.
[82]Sanders, "Classical Theism," 47. In addition to the many sources engaged in this book, a couple of recent, more popular, presentations of classical theism include Dolezal, *All That Is in God* and Peter Sanlon, *Simply God: Recovering the Classical Trinity* (Nottingham: Inter-Varsity Press, 2014).

relative to classical–scholastic conceptions of God, or (3) criticizing or rejecting the strict, classical–scholastic, conception of God. Whether or not the doctrine of God should be approached in this way is a discussion for another book. This book is aimed at introducing the discussion and debates within contemporary Christian theism and does so according to the form the discussion typically takes.

On one end of the spectrum, as we have seen, the classical–scholastic conception of God offered by strict classical theism affirms divine perfection, necessity, *pure* aseity, *utter* self-sufficiency, *strict* simplicity, *timeless* eternity, *utter* immutability, *strong* impassibility, omnipotence, and omniscience. Near the other end of the spectrum, Hartshorne's process theism maintains that God is perfect in a maximally relational sense, interdependent upon and inclusive of the world, temporally everlasting, always changing and growing in process, the supremely passible feeler of all others' feelings, possessing maximal persuasive power rather than all power, and knowing all there is to know at present.

While these views function as nearly polar opposites in the contemporary debate, it would be a mistake to think that classical and process theism are equally prominent among Christian theologians. The majority of Christian theological views fall within some form of classical theism, broadly construed, or some revision thereof. Jay Wesley Richards maintains that "there has been a common core of beliefs about God" for "most of Christian history" wherein "classical theists [understood broadly] understand God to be a supremely perfect, free, transcendent and sovereign Being who freely created the world and upon whom the world depends for its existence."[83] Thomas Morris also offers a broad definition, in this regard, saying: "Traditional theists typically characterize God as, among other things, an all-powerful, all-knowing, perfectly good, eternal and transcendent being who has created our entire universe and preserves its existence moment to moment."[84] For the sake of discussion, this might be called the common core of classical theism or core classical theism.

As such, strict classical theism and process theism are by no means the only options. It is not true that the doctrine of God must take either the form of strict classical theism or some form of process theism. There are numerous other perspectives in the contemporary Christian debate. In

---

[83] Richards, *Untamed God*, 24.
[84] Thomas V. Morris, *Our Idea of God: An Introduction to Philosophical Theology* (Notre Dame, IN: University of Notre Dame Press, 1991), 17.

addition to various forms of open theism, there are also various forms of moderate classical theism, which maintains the common core of classical theism as described by Morris above, but qualifies or departs from some tenets of strict classical theism in ways that will be introduced throughout this book. Still other approaches (particularly those favorable to dialectical theology) think the framing of the debates on respective "sides" is too restrictive and largely unhelpful.[85] There is a real danger here, but, given the trajectory of the conversation, it cannot be avoided in this discussion.

The simplest way to introduce the issues is to frame the discussion along the lines of the traditional categories as they are framed in the contemporary debate, with the caveat that the categories and questions themselves are sometimes criticized and rejected. Given the massive scope of the topic and the relative brevity of this book, some framework for, and limitations to, the discussion must be chosen. In this book, I have chosen to focus on contemporary views that frame themselves relative to classical theism of some kind (broadly construed).[86]

The approach of this book

Accordingly, each of the following six chapters consists of a discussion of contemporary views relative to the big questions about the doctrine of God and a brief survey of some of the relevant biblical data. A book like this continually runs the risk of oversimplification. There are always more views

---

[85]With respect to discussion framed around classical theism, Bruce McCormack thinks Karl Barth's doctrine of God "is not to be found anywhere on this spectrum—for the simple reason that he rejects the metaphysics embodied in all of the approaches belonging to it. His is a strictly *christological* approach—which means that it constitutes a fairly radical departure from all other existing options." Bruce L. McCormack, "The Actuality of God: Karl Barth in Conversation with Open Theism," in *Engaging the Doctrine of God: Contemporary Protestant Perspectives*, ed. Bruce L. McCormack (Grand Rapids, MI: Baker Academic, 2008), 188. However, other interpreters of Barth (e.g., George Hunsinger and Paul Molnar) interpret him as a fairly traditional classical theist in many respects. Regarding the debate over how to understand Barth, see Kevin W. Hector, "God's Triunity and Self-Determination: A Conversation with Karl Barth, Bruce McCormack and Paul Molnar," *International Journal of Systematic Theology* 7/3 (2005): 246–61.

[86]The scope of this book requires that we largely leave aside many of the modern, liberal approaches to the doctrine of God, engaging process theology as an example of one notable approach in this stream. To engage other liberal approaches and trajectories would take us far beyond the scope of this book. It is notable, however, that Friedrich Schleiermacher (1768–1834), often called the father of modern/liberal theology, articulated a conception of God that corresponds strikingly to the metaphysics of strict classical theism (e.g., with respect to divine timelessness, causality, immutability and impassibility, and so on). See, for example, Schleiermacher, *The Christian Faith*, ed. H.R. Mackintosh, trans. J.S. Stewart (Edinburgh: T&T Clark, 1948), 204.

with further nuances that could be discussed. To try to cover all the views that are worth considering would require more than a single book and would not serve well as an introduction. Accordingly, as an introduction, this book must be selective with regard to which views and authors are engaged. Further, toward the goal of avoiding caricatures of the various views, I seek to allow proponents of the various positions to speak in their own voice and thus quote often from selected exemplars.

Each of the following six chapters is organized around some prominent contemporary views that frame themselves relative to classical theism of some kind, whether as an endorsement, modification, or rejection thereof. Given this framework and the issue-oriented approach of this book, each chapter focuses primarily on the contemporary discussion of a big question or questions, only briefly addressing the historical backgrounds and roots of the issues as relevant to the way the contemporary views frame themselves.[87] Accordingly, each chapter will provide a survey of some of the most prominent live options in Christian theism relative to the big questions considered in this book.

Each chapter will also offer a brief discussion of some biblical data that is relevant to the issues at hand, without attempting to lay out a single view as "biblical," pointing instead to some pertinent biblical data and (as space permits) interpretations of that data that may support, or challenge, the various positions under discussion. The biblical texts and passages referenced demand much more close study in their own contexts. The passages cited in this book are not cited as proof texts but as an orientation to some of the data that is most prominently referenced and relevant to the issues discussed in this book. This will serve to orient the reader not only to the theological issues involved, but also to some of the most prominent ways such issues are treated relative to Christianity's most sacred text. Overall, my aim in this book is not to prescribe the way forward relative to the questions and issues but to map out the contemporary landscape in a way that provides an introductory entry point to these discussions that can be useful to students of theology regardless of which answers one prefers.

The following chapter takes up the debates over divine immutability and impassibility, addressing questions such as Does God change? Does God have emotions? Does God repent or change his mind? Does God truly care about and respond to humans? Chapter 3 continues by taking up related

---

[87]For a brief introduction to the historical theology and background of the doctrine of God see Kärkkäinen, *The Doctrine of God,* 2nd ed.

debates over how to understand divine eternity and divine presence, addressing questions such as What is God's relationship to time and history? Does God have a future? Is God timelessly eternal, everlastingly eternal, or something else? Does God occupy space? Is God actually always with us? Chapter 4 continues on to the issue of divine omniscience, particularly relative to contemporary debates about divine knowledge of the future (foreknowledge), addressing questions like Does God know everything? Does God know the future? Chapter 5 moves to the issues of divine omnipotence and providence, addressing a number of questions about the extent and exercise of divine power, including Can God do anything and everything? Is omnipotence a coherent idea? What does it mean to say God is all-powerful (omnipotent)? Does God cause everything? Does God always get what he wants? Against the background of this discussion, Chapter 6 takes up the complex issue of God's goodness, particularly in light of the kind and amount of evil in this world (the problem of evil), addressing questions such as Is God entirely good and loving? If so, why is there so much evil in the world?

Chapter 7 turns to the all-important doctrine of the Trinity along with a brief discussion of the doctrine of divine simplicity, addressing questions such as: How can God be one *and* three? How should Christians understand the doctrine of the Trinity? Here, it is important to note that the Trinity doctrine is taken up after the other questions for pedagogical reasons. How one views the Trinity doctrine is closely related to one's perspective on the questions and issues addressed in Chapters 2–6. As such, I have found that students typically have an easier time grasping the issues and debates relative to the Trinity doctrine after they've become familiar with the issues and debates over the classical attributes of God. Finally, the concluding epilogue offers some concluding reflections relative to the contemporary discussion of the doctrine of God in Christian theism and where the discussion might go from here.

Study questions

1. What is the significance of the doctrine of God in the context of systematic theology?
2. Why does it matter how one conceives of the nature of God, divine attributes, and the God–world relationship?

3. Is classical theism too broad of a category? Do you think the label classical theism should be restricted to those who affirm strict classical theism?
4. What are the primary criticisms of classical theism and who gives voice to them? Do you think such criticisms are fair or unfair, valid or invalid?
5. Do you think the God of the Bible and the so-called God of the philosophers are the same God? Why or why not?

Suggestions for further reading

Selected premodern sources

Aristotle, *The Metaphysics* Book XII.
Augustine, *The Trinity* Book XV.
Anselm, *Proslogion* 2–20.
Thomas Aquinas, *Summa Theologiae* I.3–11, I.19–25.
John Calvin, *Institutes of the Christian Religion* 1.10–18.

Selected modern/contemporary sources

Barth, Karl. *Church Dogmatics*, ed. Geoffrey W. Bromiley and T. F. Torrance (Edinburgh: T&T Clark, 1957), 2/1, 257–677.
Hartshorne, Charles. *Man's Vision of God and the Logic of Theism* (Hamden, CT: Archon, 1964).
Kärkkäinen, Veli-Matti. *The Doctrine of God: A Global Introduction.* 2nd ed. (Grand Rapids, MI: Baker Academic, 2017).
Kenny, Anthony. *The God of the Philosophers* (Oxford: Clarendon, 1979).
Moltmann, Jürgen. *The Trinity and the Kingdom.* Translated by Margaret Kohl (Minneapolis, MN: Fortress, 1993).
Moreland, J.P. and William Lane Craig. *Philosophical Foundations for a Christian Worldview* (Downers Grove, IL: IVP Academic, 2003), 502–29.
Morris, Thomas V. *Our Idea of God: An Introduction to Philosophical Theology* (Notre Dame, IN: University of Notre Dame Press, 1991).
Nash, Ronald. *The Concept of God: An Exploration of Contemporary Difficulties with the Attributes of God* (Grand Rapids, MI: Zondervan, 1983).
Oden, Thomas C. *The Living God* (San Francisco, CA: Harper & Row, 1987).

Rogers, Katherin A. *Perfect Being Theology* (Edinburgh: Edinburgh University Press, 2000).

Stump, Eleonore. *The God of the Bible and the God of the Philosophers* (Marquette: Marquette University Press, 2016).

Swinburne, Richard. *The Christian God* (New York: Clarendon, 1994).

Webster, John. *God without Measure: Working Papers in Christian Theology*, vol. 1: God and the Works of God (New York: T&T Clark, 2016).

2

Does God Change?
Does God Have Emotions?

Does God change? Does God have emotions? Does God truly care about humans? Does God repent or change his mind? These questions are at the heart of understanding the God–world relationship. Underlying these questions is the issue of whether God can be affected by the actions of creatures or experience change of any kind.

The view that God cannot change is typically referred to as divine immutability. To say God is immutable is to say that God is changeless or unchangeable. Yet, what does it mean to say that God does not or cannot change? Does divine immutability mean that God cannot change in any way whatsoever? Some answer yes to this question, whereas others maintain that God is unchangeable in many respects but does experience change in other respects (e.g., relationally).

Closely related to the view that God cannot change is the view that God cannot be affected by creatures, which is typically referred to as divine impassibility. Impassibility is often taken as the denial that God has passions of any kind. Yet, language of divine impassibility is sometimes employed in a qualified fashion that does not rule out God being affected by creatures but qualifies the way in which divinity might be affected. In this discussion, much hinges upon how the terms "passible" and "impassible" are defined. Some distinguish between external, sensational, and internal impassibility. Whether or not God can "be acted upon from without" is a question of external impassibility or passibility.[1] Whether or not God can feel "pleasure"

---

[1] "Impassibility of God," in *The Oxford Dictionary of the Christian Church*, 3rd rev. ed, ed. Frank L. Cross and E. A. Livingstone (New York: Oxford University Press, 2005), 828. Cf. Richard Creel's distillation of the "core definition" of impassibility: "That which is impassible is that which cannot be affected by an outside force. Hence, impassibility is imperviousness to causal influence from external factors." *Divine Impassibility: An Essay in Philosophical Theology* (Cambridge: Cambridge University Press, 1986), 11.

or "pain caused by the action of another being" is a question of sensational impassibility or passibility.[2] Finally, whether or not God can change his own "emotions from within" is a question of internal impassibility or passibility.[3]

Advocates of strong impassibility tend to affirm external, sensational, *and* internal impassibility. Numerous advocates of qualified impassibility, conversely, affirm that God cannot *be changed* from without but changes his own emotions from within. Others contend instead that God is passible, maintaining that God experiences genuinely changing, responsive emotions that God does not self-determine. This chapter introduces these prominent contemporary views on these questions, followed by a brief discussion of some biblical data relevant to the issues as well as a brief discussion of the so-called Hellenization hypothesis.

Utter immutability and strict impassibility

Strict classical theism maintains that God is utterly immutable and strongly impassible. That is, God cannot change in any way and God cannot be affected by the world or experience emotional change. On this view, impassibility is a subcategory of immutability. As Katherin Rogers puts it:

> In the classic tradition of Augustine, Anselm and Aquinas God is immutable. Really immutable! His essential nature does not change. His will does not change. His knowledge does not change. Since God is simple, so that His will and intellect are identical with His essence, if He were to change in any way at all this would involve a change in His essence.[4]

One traditional argument for utter immutability goes like this: if God were to change he would become better or worse. If he became better, he was not perfect in the first place. If he became worse, he would not be perfect after changing. A perfect being, therefore, cannot change. Critics of this view have contended, however, that some changes do not increase or decrease value, for instance changing the color of one's shirt (i.e., value-

---

[2]"Impassibility of God," 828.
[3]"Impassibility of God," 828.
[4]Katherin A. Rogers, *Perfect Being Theology* (Edinburgh: Edinburgh University Press, 2000), 46.

neutral changes) and, thus, it does not follow that one who changes must thereby become better or worse.

This argument aside, utter immutability is closely tied to the wider conception of strict classical theism, particularly relative to divine timelessness, strong simplicity, and a particular view of *pure* aseity. For strict classical theists, divine aseity requires not only that God is self-existent but also that God does not depend—in any way—on anything else. As James Dolezal writes, divine aseity "teaches that God is wholly self-sufficient in all that he is and thus exists independently of all causal influence from his creatures."[5]

In this regard, strict classical theists often affirm that God is pure act (*actus purus*), drawing on Aristotle's (384–322 BC) understanding of the nature of being (ontology), particularly as articulated by Thomas Aquinas (1225–74).[6] This view depends on Aristotle's distinction between actuality and potentiality. On this view, creatures are substances that possess actuality and potentiality. The potentiality of a creature refers to the potential of a substance to change or become in some way. To say God is pure act, among other things, denies that God has any potentiality; it excludes any possibilities or contingencies relative to God's being or life. However, change requires potentiality. As such, if God is pure act, God cannot change. Accordingly, on the view of Aquinas, as Rogers explains it: "If God is full and unlimited being, perfect act, there is in Him no potentiality. Change involves the actualization of some potentiality. So there is no change in God."[7] In this vein, Steven Duby maintains: "Divine aseity entails first that God is *actus purus*" (pure act), God is without any "capacity to be moved" and without any "passive potency" because "God is fully in act."[8]

The claim that God is pure act entails that God cannot have any accidental or contingent properties. On this view, creatures are substances that have some essential properties and some accidental or contingent properties. Essential properties refer to those properties that something must possess, without which that thing would not exist or be the kind of being that it is. Accidental or contingent properties are properties that something might

---

[5]James E. Dolezal, "Strong Impassibility," in *Divine Impassibility: Four Views*, ed. Robert Matz and A. Chadwick Thornhill (Downers Grove, IL: IVP Academic, 2019), 18.

[6]See James E. Dolezal, *God Without Parts: Divine Simplicity and the Metaphysics of Divine Absoluteness* (Eugene, OR: Pickwick, 2011), 34–37.

[7]Rogers, *Perfect Being Theology*, 46. Cf. Thomas Aquinas, *Summa Theologiae* I.9, trans. Fathers of the English Dominican Province (Albany, OR: Ages, 1997).

[8]Steven J. Duby, *Divine Simplicity: A Dogmatic Account* (London: Bloomsbury T&T Clark, 2016), 121.

possess or not possess or might possess at one time and not possess at another. For example, the color of a motorcycle is an accidental property. A motorcycle might be painted many colors and still be a motorcycle. However, possessing a motor might be thought of as an essential property of a motorcycle because without a motor, it would not be a *motorcycle*.[9] Whereas creatures have both essential and accidental properties, if God is pure act, God has no potentiality and thus cannot have any accidental or contingent properties. God is, in this view, the perfect being to whom nothing could be added or taken away.

Such a God is absolutely simple, that is, not consisting of any parts (non-composite) and thus not (strictly speaking) possessing properties in addition to, or genuinely distinct from, the divine essence. On this view, what humans refer to as God's power or goodness or love are merely different descriptions of God's one, indivisible, essence. An absolutely simple God cannot change because this would require a distinction between what was previously true of God and what is later true of God (see the further discussion in Chapter 7).

Accordingly, strict classical theism maintains that God is timeless; there is no before and after for God, no succession of events or moments in God's life (see Chapter 3). Yet, change requires the possibility that something be different than it previously was—a change from what something is at one time to what something is at another time. Accordingly, Thomas Williams explains, "Because there is no before and after in God, God cannot undergo change, and so the doctrine of divine [timeless] eternity leads directly to the claim that God is immutable."[10]

As pure actuality, then, God must be utterly immutable. Any change or experience ascribed to God in Scripture or elsewhere does not describe a real change in God but is understood as metaphorical language that depicts God in human terms. In this regard, following Aquinas (1225–74), Gilles Emery maintains that passions like compassion "are attributed to God due to the effects they denote."[11] However, God does not feel any "sensible affections"

---

[9]Of course, one might refer to a motorcycle that is currently lacking a motor. However, while lacking a motor it would not be, strictly speaking, a *motor*cycle (if actually being a motorcycle requires having a motor).

[10]Thomas Williams, "Introduction to Classical Theism," in *Models of God and Alternative Ultimate Realities*, ed. Jeanine Diller and Asa Kasher (New York: Springer, 2013), 96.

[11]Gilles Emery, "The Immutability of the God of Love and the Problem of Language Concerning the 'Suffering of God,'" in *Divine Impassibility and the Mystery of Human Suffering*, ed. James Keating and Thomas Joseph White (Grand Rapids, MI: Eerdmans, 2009), 67.

like compassion but only "acts" in a way that might metaphorically be deemed compassionate.[12] As Anselm (1033–1109) put it, God is beyond passion or "impassible" and thus God does "not have any compassion," that is, God's "heart is not sorrowful from compassion with the sorrowful, which is what being merciful is."[13] Yet, Anselm maintains that God is both "merciful and not merciful" in that God is "merciful in relation to us and not in relation to" himself, that is, God is "merciful because" he "save[s] the sorrowful and pardon[s] sinners against" him but God is "not merciful because" he does "not experience any feeling of compassion for misery."[14]

On this view, strong impassibility follows from utter immutability, since being affected by a creature would be a kind of change and, according to Anselm, "nothing may be predicated of the supreme and immutable nature which might suggest that it is mutable."[15] As Thomas Williams puts it, "God is impassible: that is, God cannot be acted upon by anything outside himself. If something other than God were able to affect God, God would undergo change."[16] God, then, cannot be passible. God is without passions. Accordingly, divine impassibility is often defined "as an aspect of immutability" such that "God cannot be changed, in particular he cannot be changed from without."[17] For example, Paul Helm reasons, "(1) God is timelessly eternal. (2) Whatever is timelessly eternal is unchangeable. (3) Whatever is unchangeable is impassible. (4) Therefore, God is impassible."[18] Put differently, "a timelessly eternal God is immutable and so impassible in a very strong sense; he *necessarily* cannot change *for* change takes time, or is in time, and a timelessly eternal God by definition is not in time, and so his actions cannot take time, nor can he experience fits of passion or changes in mood."[19] Dolezal adds: "If temporal succession of life is denied to God, so

---

[12]Emery, "The Immutability of the God of Love," 66.
[13]Anselm, *Proslogion*, ed. Brian Davies and G.R. Evans (New York: Oxford University Press, 1998), 8.
[14]Anselm, *Proslogion* 8. Compare Augustine's view that God "lovest souls far more purely than do we, and" is "more incorruptibly compassionate," yet "wounded by no sorrow." Augustine, *Confessions* 3.2.3 (*NPNF1* 1:61).
[15]Anselm, *Monologion*, ed. Brian Davies and G.R. Evans (New York: Oxford University Press, 1998), 25.
[16]Williams, "Classical Theism," 96.
[17]Paul Helm, "B. B. Warfield on Divine Passion," *Westminster Theological Journal* 69 (2007): 101.
[18]Helm, "The Impossibility of Divine Passibility," in *The Power and Weakness of God: Impassibility and Orthodoxy*, ed. Nigel M. de S. Cameron (Edinburgh: Rutherford, 1990), 119.
[19]Paul Helm, "Divine Timeless Eternity," in *God and Time: Four Views*, ed. Gregory Ganssle (Downers Grove, IL: InterVarsity, 2001), 38–39.

then must be all those experiences, such as emotional change, that require time."[20]

In this regard, Thomas Williams adds that a strict kind of "aseity" also "entail[s] impassibility: for if God could be acted upon by something other than himself, he would in some respect depend on something other than himself to be what he is, in violation of aseity."[21] Brian Leftow likewise states, "if we affected God—if, say, our suffering made him sorrowful—his emotional state would depend on us, and so God would not be wholly *a se*."[22] Put more positively by John Webster, "God is fully actual, possessing no potency whose realization would extend or complete his being. God is immutable—already infinitely sufficient and complete and therefore beyond alteration or acquisition—and impassible—inexhaustibly alive, stable and entire in himself and so beyond the reach of any agent or act of contestation or depredation."[23]

Indeed, as pure act, God cannot have any "passive potency," which Aquinas defined as "the principle of being acted upon by something else."[24] As pure act, then, Thomas Weinandy maintains, God cannot have anything "analogous to human feelings."[25] God cannot experience "inner emotional changes of state, either of comfort or discomfort, whether freely from within or by being acted upon from without."[26] As such, God is not "capable of freely changing his inner emotional state in response to" creatures.[27] Rather, "God simply loves himself and all things in himself in the one act which he himself is."[28]

Accordingly, strict classical theism affirms external, sensational, *and* internal impassibility. That is, God cannot "be acted upon from without"

---

[20]James E. Dolezal, "Still Impassible: Confessing God without Passions," *Journal of the Institute of Reformed Baptist Studies* 1 (2014): 131.

[21]Williams, "Classical Theism," 97.

[22]Leftow, "God, Concepts of," in *The Routledge Encyclopedia of Philosophy* (London: Taylor and Francis, 1998): Accessed June 10, 2018: https://www.rep.routledge.com/articles/thematic/god-concepts-of/v-1/sections/classical-theism

[23]*God without Measure: Working Papers in Christian Theology*, vol. 1: God and the Works of God (New York: T&T Clark, 2016), 120.

[24]Aquinas, *Summa Theologiae* I.25.1. Here and elsewhere in this book, I am using the translation of the Fathers of the English Dominican Province.

[25]Weinandy, *Does God Suffer?* (Notre Dame, IN: University of Notre Dame Press, 2000), 39.

[26]Weinandy, *Does God Suffer?* 39. For a far different form of unqualified impassibility, see Friedrich Schleiermacher, *The Christian Faith*, trans. H.R. Mackintosh (Edinburgh: T&T Clark, 1948), 206.

[27]Weinandy, *Does God Suffer?* 39.

[28]Weinandy, *Does God Suffer?* 39.

(external impassibility), God cannot feel "pleasure" or "pain caused by the action of another being" (sensational impassibility), and God cannot change "emotions from within" (internal impassibility).[29] Yet, Helm maintains, this should not be taken to mean that God "is like a withdrawn, sadly incapacitated human being. Impassibility in God is not a defect but a perfection; it signals fullness, not deficiency."[30] As "pure act," Helm argues, God "has fullness of being" such that "far from being psychologically or spiritually impoverished, an 'impassible,' timelessly eternal God may have a fullness of character of which our fitful human emotions are but inadequate shadows."[31]

In this regard, Weinandy maintains, "God is supremely passionate, not in the sense of being acted upon but in a way that is unchangeably constant, as appropriate to a God who is *actus purus*."[32] However, Gary Culpepper contends, it is "not at all clear what the term 'passionate' adds" to such an understanding of "God as purely actualized love."[33] In this regard, Dolezal agrees with Weinandy's overall view but thinks speaking of God as "passionate" or "impassioned," as Weinandy and Helm do, is "somewhat malapropos." By such language Dolezal takes Weinandy and Helm to "mean nothing more than that God is eternally and purely actual in his love, compassion, and the like" while denying "that God is 'affected by his creatures.'"[34]

A number of contemporary theologians claim that this conception of strict impassibility is the traditional Christian view. For instance, Thomas Weinandy cites the *Oxford Dictionary of the Christian Church*'s conclusion that "orthodox theology has traditionally denied God's subjection to" external, sensational, and internal "passibility."[35] According to Rogers, further, "Augustine and Aquinas even seem to hold that God is not at all affected by human activities."[36] Dolezal adds that divine impassibility, meaning "that God cannot undergo emotional changes" and thus "cannot suffer" or be affected, "was the orthodox Christian consensus for nearly two

---

[29]"Impassibility of God," 828.
[30]Helm, "Divine Timeless Eternity," 39.
[31]Helm, "Divine Timeless Eternity," 39, 40.
[32]Weinandy, *Does God Suffer?* 127.
[33]Culpepper, "'One Suffering, in Two Natures': An Analogical Inquiry into Divine and Human Suffering," in *Divine Impassibility and the Mystery of Human Suffering*, ed. James Keating and Thomas Joseph White (Grand Rapids, MI: Eerdmans, 2009), 83.
[34]Dolezal, "Still Impassible," 144n 30.
[35]Weinandy, *Does God Suffer?* 38, quoting from "Impassibility of God," 828.
[36]Rogers, *Perfect Being Theology*, 20.

millennia."[37] Others maintain a different view of how the tradition should be understood in this regard, discussed later in this chapter.

Critics maintain that this view seems to contradict the biblical portrayal of God and that it seems an utterly immutable being could not know or otherwise be genuinely related to a temporal, changing universe (the question of divine knowledge will be taken up in Chapter 5). Advocates of strict impassibility, however, recognize that Scripture frequently portrays God as experiencing some kinds of change and that "many passages of the Bible" do indeed "speak of God as undergoing affective changes."[38] However, many advocates of strict impassibility argue that such passages of Scripture should not be taken to mean that God actually experiences any change or is actually affected by creaturely causes. Helm maintains, it "is because God wishes people to respond to him that he *must* represent himself to them as one to whom response is possible, as one who acts in time." Yet, God does not temporally respond to humans or experience emotions as "affect."[39] Rather, God's very relation to the world is only a "relation of reason," that is God is not really related to the world but the world is related to God.

On this view, God "does not feel sorrow Himself."[40] Yet, as Rogers understands it, God is not "entirely free from emotions" but God experiences "the 'positive' emotions, love and joy, to an infinite degree."[41] Here, though, "divine joy and love are the simple act of God's willing Himself and willing other things as the manifold reflections of His perfect goodness."[42] To make clear, in this regard, that such divine "emotions" are strictly impassible and "non-affective" and thus do not involve any change in God's emotional state, inwardly or outwardly, Helm suggests replacing language of divine emotion with that of "*themotion*," defined as that which is "as close as possible to the corresponding human emotion X except that it cannot be an affect."[43]

---

[37] Dolezal, "Still Impassible," 125. Further, see the arguments in Ronald S. Baines, Richard C. Barcellos, James P. Butler, Stefan T. Lindblad, and James M. Renihan, eds. *Confessing the Impassible God: The Biblical, Classical, & Confessional Doctrine of Divine Impassibility* (Palmdale, CA: RBAP, 2015).

[38] Dolezal, "Still Impassible," 134.

[39] Helm, "The Impossibility of Divine Passibility," 133–34.

[40] Rogers, *Perfect Being Theology*, 51.

[41] Rogers, *Perfect Being Theology*, 51.

[42] Rogers, *Perfect Being Theology*, 51. Here, she paraphrases the conclusion of Norman Kretzmann in his *The Metaphysics of Theism: Aquinas's Natural Theology in Summa Contra Gentiles I* (New York: Clarendon, 1997), 236–37.

[43] Helm, "The Impossibility of Passibility," 140 (emphasis original).

For strict classical theists, God cannot actually become pleased or displeased by humans (or anything else) for that would not only compromise the nature of the divine being (in the ways described above) but would also interrupt the divine tranquility or blessedness—God's immutable state of perfect bliss. Rogers explains, "God is infinitely happy and we can do nothing to lessen it, nor can we (even logically) add to infinity."[44] God, then, "cannot be enriched but always remains the enricher."[45] Saying otherwise, in this view, suggests that God is imperfect and acts "to expedite his own fulfillment."[46] Critics maintain that strict impassibility would render God incapable of love and compassion and is difficult, if not impossible, to square with the God of the Bible. In response, strict classical theists maintain that a passible God would be imperfect and thus God's love and compassion must be impassible. On this view, a suffering, passible God would be deficient and needy. As such, the perfect being *must be* utterly immutable and strictly impassible.

Ethical immutability and strong or essential passibility

Near the other end of the spectrum, advocates of strong passibility maintain that God is essentially passible in relation to the world. For example, Hartshorne's process theism maintains that the most perfect being is not utterly immutable or impassible but is maximally and universally sympathetic, meaning that God is the feeler of all others' feelings.[47] Here, relational sensitivity and compassion are seen not as defects but as strengths such that God is supremely passible.

Hartshorne's process theism is a form of panentheism wherein the world is *in* God but God is more than the world.[48] For Hartshorne, the basic form of reality is becoming—the continual process of change. Because the world

---

[44] Rogers, *Perfect Being Theology*, 51.
[45] John Piper, "How Does a Sovereign God Love? A Reply to Thomas Talbott," *The Reformed Journal* 33/4 (1983): 11.
[46] Carl F. H. Henry, *God, Revelation, and Authority*, 6 vols. (Wheaton, IL: Crossway, 1999), 6:289.
[47] See Charles Hartshorne, *Man's Vision of God and the Logic of Theism* (Hamden, CT: Archon, 1964), 116.
[48] Hartshorne, *Man's Vision of God*, 89.

is part of God's being, Hartshorne maintains, God is continually in process, constantly growing as the world grows, and God internally and immediately feels the feelings of all creatures and changes accordingly. As the cosmos evolves and grows, God evolves, becoming greater and greater. God is essentially related to the world and thereby dependent on it. The world is essential to God's existence and nature.[49] God is, then, not the unmoved mover of strict classical theism but is the most moved mover; the eminently moved mover of all. On this view, God is the supreme, perfect being in the sense that God is "the self-surpassing surpasser of all."[50]

While God is ever changing and growing along with the world, Hartshorne maintains, God necessarily feels the feelings of all others according to God's "infinite sensitivity."[51] As such, God's disposition of perfect sympathy and desire for the well-being of all (love) never changes and indeed cannot change; it is immutable. In other words, God is *ethically* immutable.[52] Thus, "God is perfect in love, but never-completed" and "ever growing (partly through our efforts) in the joy, the richness of his life."[53]

For Hartshorne, if God were strictly impassible, "God could not love in a real sense, for to love is to find joy in the joy of others and sorrow in their sorrows" but the "wholly perfect could neither gain nor lose."[54] Further, "Since love involves dependence upon the welfare of the beloved, and in so far is a passion," the strict classical theist "God, being passionless, wholly active, is necessarily exempt from it."[55] Daniel Day Williams adds: "Impassibility makes love meaningless."[56] Indeed, Hartshorne avers "to love a being yet be absolutely independent of and unaffected by its welfare or suffering seems nonsense."[57]

Further, Hartshorne argues, "The idea that God equally and solely experiences bliss in all his relations is once for all a denial of the religiously essential doctrine that God is displeased by human sin and human

---

[49]Hartshorne, *Man's Vision of God*, 108.

[50]Hartshorne, *Reality as Social Process: Studies in Metaphysics and Religion* (New York: Hafner, 1971), 116.

[51]Hartshorne, *The Divine Relativity: A Social Conception of God* (New Haven, CT: Yale University Press, 1964), 76.

[52]Hartshorne, *Man's Vision of God*, 36, 165.

[53]Hartshorne, *Reality as Social Process*, 156. Cf. Hartshorne, *Divine Relativity*, 17.

[54]Hartshorne, *Reality as Social Process*, 156.

[55]Hartshorne, *Man's Vision of God*, 115.

[56]*The Spirit and the Forms of Love* (New York: Harper & Row, 1968), 127.

[57]Hartshorne, *Reality as Social Process*, 40.

misfortune" and "without such displeasure, the words 'just' and 'loving' seem mockeries."[58] Indeed, Hartshorne contends impassibility makes God a "heartless benefit machine."[59] As such, if God "can receive value from no one, then to speak of serving him is to indulge in equivocation."[60] Conversely, Hartshorne argues, the meaning of life is "to serve and glorify God, that is, literally to contribute some value to the divine life which it otherwise would not have."[61]

Process theists like Hartshorne are not the only advocates of strong passibility. Any theologian who maintains that God's essence is such that, in order to be perfect God must be involved in passible relationship with some world is an advocate of strong passibility. That is, strong passibility maintains that God is essentially passible *or* that God would somehow be incomplete without passible relationship with some world. Critics target this as a reason that strong passibility should be rejected, claiming that such a view makes God dependent on the world, undermines divine sovereignty and freedom relative to creation and otherwise, and might make God indiscriminately subject to mood swings proportionate to the good and evil in the world. Advocates of strong passibility, however, think these objections assume classical theism of a kind that strong passibilists are willing to reject in favor of a God who is essentially related to the world in love relationship.

Jürgen Moltmann promotes an alternative form of strong passibility, distinct from process theism. In Moltmann's highly influential view, "God's being is in suffering and the suffering is in God's being itself, because God is love."[62] For Moltmann, God is profoundly emotional and creatures may contribute to "an increase of his riches and his bliss."[63] Indeed, Moltmann believes, "a God who cannot suffer is poorer than any human. For a God who is incapable of suffering is a being who cannot be involved. Suffering

---

[58]Hartshorne, *Man's Vision of God*, 195.

[59]Hartshorne, *Omnipotence and Other Theological Mistakes* (Albany: State University of New York Press, 1984), 29.

[60]Hartshorne, *Divine Relativity*, 58.

[61]Hartshorne, *Divine Relativity*, 133.

[62]Moltmann, *The Crucified God: The Cross of Christ as the Foundation and Criticism of Christian Theology* (New York: Harper & Row, 1974), 227. Cf. Sallie McFague, *Models of God: Theology for an Ecological, Nuclear Age* (Philadelphia, PA: Fortress, 1987), 134.

[63]Moltmann, *The Trinity and the Kingdom: The Doctrine of God*, trans. Margaret Kohl (San Francisco, CA: Harper & Row, 1981), 121. Paul S. Fiddes adds: "To love is to be in a relationship where what the loved one does alters one's own experience." *The Creative Suffering of God* (Oxford: Oxford University Press, 1988), 50.

and injustice do not affect him. And because he is so completely insensitive, he cannot be affected or shaken by anything"; thus, "he is a loveless being."[64] Eberhard Jüngel adds, "The God who is love must be able to suffer and does suffer beyond all limits in the giving up of what is most authentically his for the sake of mortal man."[65] Kazoh Kitamori also comments, "God is the wounded Lord, having pain in himself."[66] Indeed, Kitamori believes, "God in pain is the God who resolves our human pain by his own."[67]

In contrast to Hartshorne, Moltmann maintains that God does not suffer in the sense of internal relatedness but in voluntary identification. God "opens himself to the suffering which is involved in love."[68] This involves "the voluntary laying oneself open to another and allowing oneself to be intimately affected by him; that is to say, the suffering of passionate love."[69] As such, Moltmann maintains that God "does not suffer out of deficiency of being, like created beings."[70] In Moltmann's view, God "creates by withdrawing himself" and creation "is also a self-humiliation on God's part, a lowering of himself into his own impotence."[71] This involves "an emptying of himself" to open "up the space, the time and the freedom" of the world.[72]

While speaking of God's relationship to the world as voluntary, Moltmann also maintains that "love has to suffer" and "God 'needs' the world and man. If God is love, then he neither will nor can be without the one who is his beloved."[73] Indeed, Moltmann maintains, "the lack of any creative movement would mean an imperfection in the Absolute."[74] Further, "Freedom can only be made possible by suffering love. The suffering of God with the world, the suffering of God from the world, and the suffering of God for the world are the highest forms of his creative love."[75]

---

[64]Moltmann, *The Crucified God*, 222. Cf. Moltmann, *Trinity and the Kingdom*, 23, 51–52.

[65]Jüngel, *God as the Mystery of the World* (Grand Rapids, MI: Eerdmans, 1983), 373.

[66]Kazoh Kitamori, *A Theology of the Pain of God: The First Original Theology from Japan*, 5th ed. (Richmond, VA: John Knox, 1965), 20.

[67]Kitamori, *Theology of the Pain of God*, 20.

[68]*The Crucified God*, 230. Cf. Moltmann, *Trinity and the Kingdom*, 51–56; Marcel Sarot, *God, Passibility and Corporeality* (Kampen: Kok Pharos Pub. House, 1992).

[69]Moltmann, *Trinity and the Kingdom*, 23.

[70]Moltmann, *Trinity and the Kingdom*, 23.

[71]Moltmann, *Trinity and the Kingdom*, 110.

[72]Moltmann, *Trinity and the Kingdom*, 111.

[73]Moltmann, *Trinity and the Kingdom*, 33, 58. See, further, *Trinity and the Kingdom*, 32–34, 52–60.

[74]Moltmann, *Trinity and the Kingdom*, 45.

[75]Moltmann, *Trinity and the Kingdom*, 60.

To take one other example, Thomas Jay Oord, who is sympathetic to process theism but does not identify himself as a process theologian, advocates what he calls essential kenosis theology. On Oord's view, "being affected by others is a necessary attribute of God's nature. God doesn't voluntarily choose to be affected; God is necessarily affected."[76] This is God's "essential relatedness."[77] In this view, which Oord calls "theocosmocentrism," God neither existed without the universe nor created "the universe out of nothing," but "always and necessarily relates with creatures."[78] As such, Oord's essential kenosis theology maintains that God could *not* have remained unchanged and unaffected but must be in passible relationship with some world. On this view, the perfect being must be essentially passible and thus cannot be strictly immutable.

Qualified immutability and qualified impassibility

Many Christian theologians, from varying perspectives, consider strong passibility to be unsatisfactory while also criticizing strict impassibility.[79] One alternative taken by many philosophers and theologians is to adopt the view that God is immutable and impassible in qualified senses. Bruce Ware, for example, departs from strict immutability but affirms a qualified kind of immutability, holding a view that falls within the broad category of modified or moderate classical theism (see Chapter 1).[80] Ware maintains that "the immutability proper to God must not be conceived so as to allow any threat to God's free and active love, as is the case when immutability

---

[76]Oord, "Strong Passibility," in *Divine Impassibility: Four Views*, ed. Robert Matz and A. Chadwick Thornhill (Downers Grove, IL: IVP Academic, 2019), 145.

[77]Oord, "Strong Passibility," 129.

[78]Oord, "Strong Passibility," 146. See, further, Thomas Jay Oord, *The Nature of Love: A Theology* (St. Louis, MO: Chalice, 2010), 139–40.

[79]See, among many others, Vincent Brümmer, *The Model of Love: A Study in Philosophical Theology* (Cambridge: Cambridge University Press, 1993), 160, 227; H. Ray Dunning, *Grace, Faith, and Holiness: A Wesleyan Systematic Theology* (Kansas City, MO: Beacon Hill, 1988), 195; Abraham Heschel, *The Prophets* (New York: Perennial, 2001), 286.

[80]See Bruce Ware, "A Modified Calvinist Doctrine of God," in *Perspectives on the Doctrine of God: Four Views*, ed. Bruce Ware (Nashville, TN: B & H, 2008), 76–120; Bruce Ware, *God's Greater Glory: The Exalted God of Scripture and the Christian Faith* (Wheaton, IL: Crossway, 2004).

is seen as immobility."[81] In Ware's view, God is really related to the world; his relation to the world is not merely a "relation of reason." Yet, God is not determined by his relation to the world but God causally determines history. Further, Ware contends, any "appropriate conception of God's changelessness provides full and unwavering assurance that the God who shows himself in free and sacrificial love always was, is, and will be the same in and through all changes. Thus, a qualified immutability, not an abstract or absolute immutability, is proposed as that conception proper to God."[82]

In Ware's view, then, Scripture presents God as "relationally mutable" such that God may "'change' in relation to" human action "in ways called forth by his immutable character and promise."[83] At the same time, Ware affirms "the absolute changelessness of God's character and essential nature."[84] As such, the "relational mutability of God" is "a change not of his essential nature, nor of his word or promise, but of his attitude and disposition toward his moral creatures in ways that are commensurate to changes that happen in them."[85] That is, God is unchanging in his essential attributes but changing in his contingent attributes, contrary to the view of God as pure act. God is immutable (in himself) and mutable (in relation to the world), in different senses. Thus, God's relationship and disposition toward humans can *really* change but always in accordance with God's immutable character and essential nature.

Similarly, John Cooper believes, "Classical Christian theism must affirm an element of contingency in God's life." Yet, Cooper thinks this should be "quite apart from the issue of [God's] involvement in temporal change" and "consistent with a strong notion of the immutability of God's nature and his unchanging will."[86] Bruce Demarest adds:

---

[81]Bruce Ware, "An Evangelical Reexamination of the Doctrine of the Immutability of God" (Ph.D. diss., Fuller Theological Seminary, 1984), 240. Cf. Millard Erickson's view that there are problems with the historical views of immutability because they "have actually drawn heavily on the Greek idea of immobility and sterility. This makes God inactive. But the biblical view is not that God is static but that he is stable. He is active and dynamic." Erickson, *Christian Theology*, 3rd ed. (Grand Rapids, MI: Baker Academic, 2013), 250. Yet, Richard Muller contends, "The scholastic notion of God as *immobile* does not translate into English as 'immobile' … but as 'unmoved.' This is, doubtless, the Aristotelian conception of an 'unmoved Mover,' but it is not a conception which in and of itself implies stasis or incapability of relation with externals. Rather it indicates a being who has not been 'moved' or brought into being by another." Muller, "Incarnation, Immutability, and the Case for Classical Theism," *Westminster Theological Journal* 45 (1983): 27.

[82]Ware, "Evangelical Reexamination," 240.

[83]Ware, *God's Greater Glory*, 28.

[84]Ware, *God's Greater Glory*, 141.

[85]Ware, "Modified Calvinist Doctrine of God," 91.

[86]John Cooper, *Panentheism: The Other God of the Philosophers* (Grand Rapids, MI: Baker Academic, 2006), 327.

The God of the Jewish-Christian tradition is changeless in being, attributes and purposes, but in His dealings with the creation God does enter into changing relations. Thus, the divine immutability in no wise implies that God is unconcerned, inactive, or unrelated.... Biblical faith unhesitatingly affirms that the perfection of God includes creative interaction consistent with His changeless character and purposes.[87]

While critics thinks the conception of qualified immutability is too weak to apply to the perfect being, Jay Wesley Richards makes a case for a qualified kind of immutability that he claims "upholds [the] classical motivation [of immutability] as well as much of [its] traditional content."[88] In Richards's view, "God has certain essential properties by virtue of being perfect [including omnipotence, omniscience, perfect goodness, freedom and faithfulness]; so he cannot change in those respects."[89] Here, "immutability is the very quality that distinguishes God's essential properties from his accidental ones."[90] For Richards, "this sense of immutability seems to capture most of the concerns of classical theists."[91] Richards maintains further that "God could have done otherwise" than create this world and there thus must be "contingent properties concerning God's relation to a contingent creation," which "are the expression of his freedom, as are all his contingent properties; so they do not imply any significant ontological dependence of God on the world."[92] As Richards understands it, then, a qualified doctrine of immutability "preserves the contrast between Creator and creation, it simultaneously expresses the doctrines of creation, divine aseity and sovereignty."[93]

With regard to the question of impassibility, Ware criticizes views of "divine immutability" that view God as "distant, unfeeling, uncaring, static, and in every way unchanged and unaffected by the human condition."[94] Ware believes that "Scripture indicates clearly ... the reality of variable emotions in God."[95] Accordingly, Ware and his former student Rob Lister adopt a

---

[87]Demarest, "Process Trinitarianism," in *Perspectives on Evangelical Theology*, ed. Kenneth S. Kantzer and Stanley N. Gundry (Grand Rapids, MI: Baker, 1979), 29.
[88]Jay Wesley Richards, *The Untamed God: A Philosophical Exploration of Divine Perfection, Simplicity, and Immutability* (Downers Grove, IL: InterVarsity, 2003), 195.
[89]Richards, *Untamed God*, 199.
[90]Richards, *Untamed God*, 199.
[91]Richards, *Untamed God*, 199.
[92]Richards, *Untamed God*, 202.
[93]Richards, *Untamed God*, 196.
[94]Ware, "Evangelical Reexamination," 11.
[95]Ware, *God's Greater Glory*, 147.

view wherein God experiences genuine changing emotions but remains impassible in a qualified sense. As Lister explains qualified impassibility, God is both "impassible and impassioned."[96] That is, God is emotionally "affected by his creatures" (analogically) but "in ways that accord rather than conflict with his will" such that God is transcendently and voluntarily "responsive, but never passive" or "manipulated, overwhelmed, or surprised."[97] That is, God can be "emotionally" affected by creatures but emotions are defined in a way that they remain impassible in a qualified sense. On this view, "God is *both* invulnerable to *involuntarily* precipitated emotional vicissitude *and* supremely passionate about his creatures' practice of either obedience or their experience of either joy of affliction."[98] That is, God's emotions are non-passive, voluntary, and self-determined.

Other views also retain the language of impassibility but attribute, or come very close to attributing, what many consider to be passible emotions (e.g., suffering) to God. In this regard, Michael Horton contends that he has "revised" impassibility to refer to "incapacity for being overwhelmed by suffering, not inability to enter into it."[99] He contends that we must maintain that God "is the transcendent *Lord* of the covenant who is never a passive victim" and does not respond "in the same way we respond to each other," while "we must avoid the conclusion that God is untouched or unmoved by creaturely suffering."[100] Horton thus criticizes what he calls "a Stoic thread that runs from Origen to Maimonides to Spinoza and Kant that denies that God experiences joy or sorrow: he neither loves nor hates."[101] For Horton, "God is affected by us but is not determined in his being, will, or actions by us."[102] Kevin Vanhoozer adds:

> Impassibility means not that God is unfeeling but that God is never *overcome* or *overwhelmed* by passion. Though certain feelings may *befall* God, he will not be subject to them. In this strict sense, then, it is no contradiction to say

---

[96] Rob Lister, *God Is Impassible and Impassioned: Toward a Theology of Divine Emotion* (Wheaton, IL: Crossway, 2013), 143.

[97] Lister, *God Is Impassible and Impassioned*, 36, 230. Lister notes that this view might make him a passibilist under Creel's definition. *God Is Impassible and Impassioned*, 150.

[98] Lister, *God Is Impassible and Impassioned*, 153.

[99] Michael Horton, *Lord and Servant: A Covenant Christology* (Louisville, KY: WJK, 2005), 195.

[100] Michael Horton, *The Christian Faith: A Systematic Theology for Pilgrims on the Way* (Grand Rapids, MI: Zondervan, 2011), 248, 247.

[101] Horton, *The Christian Faith*, 247–248.

[102] Horton, *The Christian Faith*, 249.

that God experiences human sorrow yet is nevertheless apathetic (because this experience does not compromise his reason, will or wisdom).[103]

That is, Vanhoozer explains, "God feels the force of the human experience without suffering change in his being, will or knowledge."[104]

Donald Bloesch goes further. While opposing process theology, Bloesch states that "the modern process conception of God who shares our suffering is probably closer to the Biblical view than the Hellenistic conception of a God who is wholly self-contained, who is removed from temporality and exempt from vulnerability."[105] He contends, the "classical idea of perfection as all-sufficiency and completeness had indubitably penetrated Christian thinking and prevented the church through the ages from giving due justice to the biblical idea of God sharing the pain and suffering of his people."[106] At the same time, Bloesch maintains, "the notion of impassibility can be retained so long as it does not mean that God is impassive and unfeeling."[107]

For his part, Lister's view of qualified impassibility is grounded in the "Creator/creature distinction," the "transcendence/immanence balance, incorporeality, self-sufficiency, eternality, omniscience, exhaustive sovereignty, immutability, [and] intra-Trinitarian love and holiness," all of which he considers to be derived from Scripture.[108] Yet, Lister advocates an "adjustment of the Augustinian stance on divine eternity, such that the eternal God is capable of having actual in-time [and responsive] relations with his creatures."[109] Dolezal strongly criticizes this view, which he characterizes as a voluntarist account of impassibility or neo-impassibilism, for "speak[ing] of impassibility as if it simply means God *controls* all the changes in his emotions rather than the more austere [strict] understanding that he undergoes no emotive change whatsoever."[110] Dolezal thinks this contradicts the Christian tradition and contradicts God's pure actuality.

---

[103]Kevin J. Vanhoozer, *First Theology: God, Scripture, and Hermeneutics* (Downers Grove, IL: IVP Academic, 2002), 93(emphasis original). See, further, Kevin J. Vanhoozer, *Remythologizing Theology* (New York: Cambridge University Press, 2010).

[104]Vanhoozer, *First Theology,* 93.

[105]Bloesch, "Process Theology and Reformed Theology," in *Process Theology,* ed. Ronald H. Nash (Grand Rapids, MI: Baker, 1987), 53. Cf. John Frame's rejection of impassibility insofar as it refers to the absence of divine emotion. *The Doctrine of God* (Phillipsburg, NJ: P&R, 2002), 608–16.

[106]"Process Theology and Reformed Theology," 51.

[107]Donald Bloesch, *God the Almighty: Power, Wisdom, Holiness, Love* (Downers Grove, IL: InterVarsity, 1995), 94.

[108]Lister, *God Is Impassible and Impassioned,* 184.

[109]Lister, *God Is Impassible and Impassioned,* 184.

[110]Dolezal, "Still Impassible," 126.

Conversely, Lister argues that qualified impassibility is consonant with the Christian tradition and criticizes the concept of God as pure act, saying, "God as *actus purus* (or pure actuality), while seemingly guaranteeing that God is never passive, also ensures that God is never, properly speaking, responsive either."[111] Further, Lister charges, strict impassibility is a "more extreme version of divine impassibility than is biblically required or historically warranted."[112] He notes that the Christian tradition includes some "extreme impassibilists" who promote(d) a "hyper-transcendent" perspective that excludes God's being affected by creatures (e.g., Justin Martyr, Clement of Alexandria), which he believes "proved an impediment to accounting for divine involvement with creation."[113] However, Lister argues the patristic tradition also includes many qualified impassibilists, who dually affirm "divine impassibility and divine passion," affirming "voluntary affections" but excluding unexpected or "involuntary passions."[114]

Many others have also recently argued that many patristics held a *qualified* form of impassibility, claiming the Christian tradition has been misunderstood and caricatured on this issue (see the discussion later in this chapter).[115] Taking this view, Paul Gavrilyuk contends that *both* "unrestricted divine passibility" and "unrestricted divine impassibility" are "fraught with many difficulties."[116] Yet, Gavrilyuk believes, it is important to maintain the language of impassibility as a "marker of the unmistakably divine identity."[117] However, Gavrilyuk maintains, God is not only "impassible inasmuch as he is able to conquer sin, suffering, and death" but "God is also passible (in a carefully qualified sense) inasmuch as in the incarnation God has chosen to enter the human condition in order to transform it."[118]

Katherine Sonderegger also wants to say that God is somehow both immutable and mutable, impassible and yet passionate, in a way that is consonant with what she calls "the 'Greek metaphysical tradition,'"

---

[111] Lister, *God Is Impassible and Impassioned*, 157.
[112] Lister, *God Is Impassible and Impassioned*, 152.
[113] Lister, *God Is Impassible and Impassioned*, 95.
[114] Lister, *God Is Impassible and Impassioned*, 101, 122.
[115] See, for example, Gavrilyuk, *The Suffering of the Impassible God: The Dialectics of Patristic Thought* (New York: Oxford University Press, 2006), 21–63. Weinandy, *Does God Suffer?* 83–113; Lister, *God Is Impassible and Impassioned*, 41–122.
[116] Gavrilyuk, *Suffering of the Impassible God*, 5.
[117] Gavrilyuk, *Suffering of the Impassible God*, 15, 173.
[118] Gavrilyuk, "God's Impassible Suffering in the Flesh: The Promise of Paradoxical Christology," in *Divine Impassibility and the Mystery of Human Suffering*, ed. James Keating and Thomas Joseph White (Grand Rapids, MI: Eerdmans, 2009), 146.

maintaining that God "is eternal, not temporal."[119] She thus speaks of what she calls "the Lord's perfect mutable Immutability and passionate Impassibility."[120] As she puts it, "Deity is itself immutable, impassible, yet in such a surpassing manner that mutability and passibility are caught up in its own Perfection."[121] Whereas some "assume that emotion or passion entails embodiment," Sonderegger contends that "emotion might be a matter of mind or spirit, rather than flesh. It may be that emotion is largely, perhaps even predominately, an intellectual state, even in human beings."[122] Further, she contends, "emotion or passion need not imply mutuality or dependence or succession."[123] Rather, Scripture affirms "emotion" as a "fitting term for the wholly intellectual and spiritual …. The Bible does not depict the Lord God of Sinai as embodied or material … yet as unmistakably passionate, dynamic, alive."[124] In Sonderegger's view, the "impassible God of tradition is the passionate God of Scripture," though we cannot "fully explicate how this is so," how God's "fiery Life can remain transcendent, free from suffering, yet wholly near His creature."[125] For her, God's is "a passionate, holy Love that is without suffering passion or need."[126]

Daniel Castelo also affirms both divine impassibility and passibility, advocating divine impassibility as an "apopathic qualifier and indicator of divine transcendence" such that "God 'cannot be affected against his will by an outside force.'"[127] At the same time, Castelo is willing to maintain divine passibility, at least in Christ.[128] As such, Castelo questions the very "categories [of impassibility and passibility] and the weight they place on the formulation of a spectrum because the use of dyadic categories in particular—as necessary as they typically appear to be—often occludes as it reveals."[129] He even goes so far as to state: "It could very well be the case that

---

[119]Katherine Sonderegger, *Systematic Theology: The Doctrine of God* (Minneapolis, MN: Fortress, 2015), 493.
[120]Sonderegger, *Systematic Theology*, 524.
[121]Sonderegger, *Systematic Theology*, xiii.
[122]Sonderegger, *Systematic Theology*, 491–92.
[123]Sonderegger, *Systematic Theology*, 494.
[124]Sonderegger, *Systematic Theology*, 492.
[125]Sonderegger, *Systematic Theology*, 494.
[126]Sonderegger, *Systematic Theology*, 495.
[127]Daniel Castelo, *The Apathetic God: Exploring the Contemporary Relevance of Divine Impassibility*. Paternoster Theological Monographs (Colorado Springs, CO: Paternoster, 2009), 124, 16.
[128]Castelo, *Apathetic God*, 3–4.
[129]Daniel Castelo, "Qualified Impassibility," in *Divine Impassibility: Four Views*, ed. Robert Matz and A. Chadwick Thornhill (Downers Grove, IL: IVP Academic, 2019), 70.

the language of divine impassibility has run its course and that new terms need to replace it."[130]

Castelo is not alone in this regard. Some dialectical theologians have advocated for a view of God that breaks the traditional, bifurcating, mold. Some have understood Karl Barth in this way, though others interpret Barth as more in line with traditional classical theism in this and other respects. In one place, Barth states that the God of the Bible "can feel, and be affected. He is not impassible" yet "He cannot be moved from outside by an extraneous power" but "is moved and stirred" by "His own free power."[131] On Bruce McCormack's reading, Barth is "neither an impassibilist [in the strict sense of non-affectivity] nor a passibilist."[132] McCormack argues that Barth's mature view of divine constancy actually rejects any "doctrine of divine impassibility" and that his "position would take us beyond that rather unfortunate set of alternatives."[133] According to McCormack, "impassibility and passibility constitute an altogether this-worldly dialectic" and the "truth is that God transcends this dialectic."[134] For his part, T. F. Torrance maintains that "in Christ God both suffered and did not suffer: through the eternal tranquility of his divine impassibility he took upon himself our passibility." Torrance thus excludes "any thought of God as impassible in the Greek or Stoic sense, and any thought of God as passible in the way human beings are."[135]

Qualified immutability and qualified passibility

Other theologians affirm qualified immutability while maintaining a qualified conception of passibility. On this view, God is immutable in that

---

[130]Castelo, *Apathetic God*, 68.

[131]Karl Barth, *Church Dogmatics*, ed. Geoffrey W. Bromiley and T. F. Torrance (Edinburgh: T&T Clark, 1957), 2/1, 370.

[132]McCormack, "Divine Impassibility or Simply Divine Constancy? Implications of Karl Barth's Later Christology for Debates over Impassibility," in *Divine Impassibility and the Mystery of Human Suffering*, ed. James Keating and Thomas Joseph White (Grand Rapids, MI: Eerdmans, 2009), 186. Cf. Barth, *Church Dogmatics*, 2/1, 495–96.

[133]McCormack, "Divine Impassibility or Simply Divine Constancy?" 186.

[134]McCormack, "Divine Impassibility or Simply Divine Constancy?" 182.

[135]Torrance, *The Christian Doctrine of God: One Being Three Persons* (New York: T&T Clark, 2001), 251.

God's essential nature and character do not change. However, God voluntarily enters into real relationship with creatures and changes (relationally). As Stephen Davis puts it, God is "immutable in the sense of remaining ever true to his promises and purposes and eternally retaining his essential nature" but God is not "immutable in other stronger [strict] senses."[136] Further, Alan Padgett explains, "God is immutable relative to essential divine attributes, those powers and properties that constitute a perfect Being. God changes only in relational ways, in order to create and care for that creation. The ability to change in response to others is part of what makes God a perfect Being."[137] Thomas Oden adds, "It is precisely because God is unchanging in the eternal character of his self-giving love that God is free in responding to changing historical circumstances, and versatile in empathy."[138] In Oden's view, the "biblical narrative views God not as immobile or static, but as consistent with his own nature, congruent with the depths of his own essential goodness, stable, not woodenly predictable."[139]

In Nicholas Wolterstorff's view, "God the Redeemer is a God who changes." While recognizing "there is an important sense in which God as presented in Scripture is changeless," Wolterstorff believes "God is steadfast in God's redeeming intent and ever faithful to God's children. Yet, ontologically, God cannot be a redeeming God without there being changeful variation among God's states."[140] Richard Swinburne, further, considers the view that "God is completely changeless" to be "an unnecessary dogma," which is not "implicit in the Old or New Testaments" and, he thinks, not a view "to which very many modern theists are committed, unless they have absorbed Thomism fairly thoroughly."[141] Similarly, John Feinberg rejects what he characterizes as "the static view of God that so many within the classical Christian tradition have held."[142] Instead, Feinberg adopts what he calls

---

[136]Stephen T. Davis, "Temporal Eternity," in *Philosophy of Religion: An Anthology*. 7th ed, ed. Michael Rea and Louis P. Pojman (Stamford, CT: Cengage, 2015), 89. Cf. Stephen T. Davis, *Logic and the Nature of God* (Grand Rapids, MI: Eerdmans, 1983), 24.

[137]Padgett, "Eternity as Relative Timelessness," in *God and Time: Four Views*, ed. Gregory Ganssle (Downers Grove, IL: InterVarsity, 2001), 109. See also Alan Padgett, *God, Eternity, and the Nature of Time* (Eugene, OR: Wipf & Stock, 2000), 131.

[138]Thomas Oden, *Classic Christianity: A Systematic Theology* (San Francisco, CA: HarperOne, 2009), 68.

[139]Oden, *Classic Christianity*, 68.

[140]Wolterstorff, *Inquiring about God: Selected Essays*, vol. 1 (New York: Cambridge University Press, 2010), 134.

[141]Swinburne, *The Coherence of Theism* (Oxford: Oxford University Press, 1977), 215.

[142]John S. Feinberg, *No One Like Him: The Doctrine of God* (Wheaton, IL: Crossway, 2001), 266.

a nuanced definition of immutability wherein God does not change with respect to his "person [his being and attributes], purposes, will, and ethical rules," but does experience "changes in relationships" with creatures.[143]

Along these lines, J.P. Moreland and William Lane Craig reject strict or "radical immutability" and maintain that "God is immutable in the biblical sense of being constant and unchangeable in his character. Moreover, [God] is immutable in his existence (necessity, aseity, eternity) and his being omnipresent, omniscient and omnipotent. These essential attributes are enough to safeguard God's perfection without freezing him into immobility."[144] Clark Pinnock notes, further, "God is immutable in essence and in his trustworthiness over time, but in other respects God changes."[145] However, in contrast to Craig and other moderate classical theists who advocate qualified immutability, Pinnock ties this to the open theist belief that "God learns new facts when they occur and changes plans in response to what humans do."[146] That is, Pinnock maintains, "God is unchanging in nature and essence but not in experience, *knowledge* and action."[147] On this controversial open theist view of divine knowledge, see Chapter 4.

While rejecting open theism, Ronald Nash also affirms qualified immutability, stating, "even an immutable and perfect God can change. Human beings can make a difference to God."[148] For Nash:

> God must be immutable with regard to His nature and character [yet] immutability should not exclude the possibility of God's acting and interacting with His creation in an interpersonal way. The paradigm of an impersonal immutability is Aristotle's Unmoved Mover who was incapable of doing anything other than contemplating his own perfection. The change that necessarily accompanies God's interpersonal relations with His creatures is not a sign of imperfection. On the contrary, a personal God would lack perfection if He were incapable of such relations.[149]

---

[143]Feinberg, *No One Like Him*, 271.
[144]Moreland and Craig, *Philosophical Foundations for a Christian Worldview* (Downers Grove, IL: IVP Academic, 2003), 527.
[145]Clark Pinnock, "Systematic Theology," in *The Openness of God: A Biblical Challenge to the Traditional Understanding of God* (Downers Grove, IL: InterVarsity, 1994), 117.
[146]Pinnock, "Systematic Theology," 118.
[147]Pinnock, "Systematic Theology," 118 (emphasis mine).
[148]Nash, *The Concept of God: An Exploration of Contemporary Difficulties with the Attributes of God* (Grand Rapids, MI: Zondervan, 1983), 105.
[149]Nash, *Concept*, 101.

Indeed, Nash avers, "Any person, including God, who could not enter into mutual relations of love would be imperfect."[150] Advocates claim this view consistently affirms *both* the biblical testimony that God does not change with respect to his essential nature and character (e.g., Mal 3:6), *and* the biblical testimony that God does actually experience (analogically) the kinds of relational "changes" attributed to God throughout Scripture.

Relative to the question of divine impassibility, a number of theologians maintain that God is passible but are dissatisfied with both impassibility and extreme or strong passibility. For instance, Wayne Grudem, an Evangelical proponent of (modified) classical theism, states, "the idea that God has no passions or emotions *at all* clearly conflicts with much of the rest of Scripture, and for that reason I have not affirmed God's impassibility" for "the opposite is true," God "certainly does feel emotions."[151] Further, John Feinberg maintains: "In light of the nuanced understanding of divine immutability" he adopts (see above), "it is necessary to reject divine impassibility. The king who cares experiences real emotions; he sympathizes with our pains and can rejoice over our joys."[152] Whereas some see divine passibility as a defect, Alvin Plantinga maintains that "God's capacity for suffering" is "proportional to his greatness."[153] Accordingly, "God does not stand idly by, coolly observing the suffering of his creatures. He enters into and shares our suffering."[154] Similarly, while commenting that there are "serious problems with an unreflective passibilism," Charles Taliaferro writes, "I believe theistic passibilism is defensible insofar as we can understand God's sorrow, not as an imperfection, but an aspect of what it is for God to be supremely good."[155]

Nicholas Wolterstorff adds, "God's love for his world is a rejoicing and suffering love. The picture of God as Stoic sage, ever blissful and nonsuffering, is in deep conflict with the biblical picture."[156] He goes on: "In the light of" the cross, "I think it grotesque to suggest that God's valuing of our human predicament was so mildly negative as to cause God no suffering."[157] In this

---

[150] Nash, *Concept*, 102.

[151] Grudem, *Systematic Theology: An Introduction to Biblical Doctrine* (Grand Rapids, MI: Zondervan, 1994), 166.

[152] Feinberg, *No One Like Him*, 277.

[153] Alvin Plantinga, "Self-Profile," in *Alvin Plantinga*, ed. James E. Tomberlin and Peter van Inwagen (Dordrecht: D. Riedel, 1985), 36.

[154] Plantinga, "Self-Profile," 36.

[155] Taliaferro, *Consciousness and the Mind of God* (New York: Cambridge University Press, 1994), 323.

[156] Wolterstorff, *Inquiring about God*, 219.

[157] Wolterstorff, *Inquiring about God*, 220.

regard, John Stott comments, love makes itself "vulnerable to pain, since it exposes itself to the possibility of rejection and insult."[158] He goes on: "In the real world of pain, how could one worship a God who was immune to it?"[159] As Dietrich Bonhoeffer famously wrote, "only the suffering God can help."[160] In this regard, James Cone maintains: "God is not indifferent to suffering and not patient with cruelty and falsehood."[161] Further, "The King is a *Servant* who suffers on behalf of the people. He takes their pain and affliction upon himself, thereby redeeming them *from* oppression and *for* freedom."[162] Thus, Cone emphasizes, "The pain of the oppressed is God's pain."[163]

In a similar vein, Justo L. González argues: "Nowhere does the Bible say that God is impassible. On the contrary, there are repeated references to divine anger, love, and even repentance!" Further, "God wrestles with Jacob and haggles with Abraham" and "God is love. Thus if there is any sense in which the God of the Bible can be described as 'immutable,' this has nothing to do with impassibility or ontological immobility, but rather with the assurance that God's 'steadfast love endureth forever.'"[164] Further, R. T. Mullins contends that Scripture depicts God as:

> entering into an intimate relationship that implies a type of vulnerability. In Exodus 3, God is freely choosing to identify with the suffering of the Hebrew people in order to redeem them and the world. This is not an impassible God who exists in a timeless present. This is a God with a history and a future. This is a God who is active in the present, and willing to suffer with His beloved children.[165]

As Amos Yong puts it, further, "God can enter into the pathos of the human condition" and "it is precisely such pathic openness that enables reception of God's redemptive work."[166]

Many impassibilists claim that divine passibility undermines the Creator–creature distinction and makes God dependent on the world. In response,

---

[158] *The Cross of Christ* (Downers Grove, IL: IVP, 2006), 323.

[159] *Cross of Christ*, 326.

[160] Bonhoeffer, *Letters and Papers from Prison*, Dietrich Bonhoeffer Works, vol. 8 (Minneapolis, MN: Fortress, 2009), 479.

[161] James Cone, *God of the Oppressed* (New York: Seabury Press, 1975), 8–9.

[162] Cone, *God of the Oppressed*, 75 (emphasis original).

[163] Cone, *God of the Oppressed*, 175.

[164] *Mañana: Christian Theology from a Hispanic Perspective* (Nashville, TN: Abingdon, 1990), 92.

[165] Mullins, *The End of the Timeless God* (New York: Oxford University Press, 2016), 202.

[166] Amos Yong, *Spirit of Love: A Trinitarian Theology of Grace* (Waco, TX: Baylor University Press, 2012), 84.

advocates of qualified divine passibility maintain that God is voluntarily passible in relation to the world, meaning God freely decided to create this world and freely opened himself up to being affected by the world in a way that upholds the Creator–creature distinction[167] and affirms divine aseity and self-sufficiency, understood to mean that God's existence and essential nature are not dependent on or derived from anything outside of himself.[168] Against critics who sometimes allege otherwise, qualified passibilists further affirm divine transcendence, omnipotence, and omniscience, maintaining that God is not involuntarily vulnerable but freely created the world ex nihilo and freely enters into relationship with creatures. Qualified passibility thus significantly differs from the strong passibility view that God is *essentially* passible in relation to the world, maintaining instead that God does not need the world and is voluntarily, rather than essentially, related to the world.[169] Some strong passibilists claim that this view requires that God's love relationship with the world is arbitrary. In contrast, advocates of qualified passibility maintain that while God is free in relationship to the world, God's decisions to create the world and sustain relationship with it are rooted in God's essential nature and character of love; the perfect love which God eternally enjoys in Trinitarian relationship.[170]

Because God has voluntarily opened himself up to love relationship with creatures, God may be emotionally affected by creatures. Although God is voluntarily passible such that no creature could affect God if God had not enabled them to do so, according to advocates of qualified passibility, God feels emotions responsive to creaturely actions that he does not causally determine.[171] As such, God can be "acted upon from without" such that he can feel joy, delight, pleasure, displeasure, pain, or grief "caused by the action" of humans (external and sensational passibility).[172] Yet, God also affects his own "emotions from within" (internal passibility, e.g., Ps 78:38) as appropriate in response to creaturely actions and relative to his overarching

---

[167]Moreland and Craig comment, "God could have remained changeless had he wished to; the fact that he did not is testimony to both his love and freedom." *Philosophical Foundations*, 527.
[168]See the fuller definitions and discussion in Mullins, *End of the Timeless God*, 139, 62–63.
[169]See John C. Peckham, "Qualified Passibility," in *Divine Impassibility: Four Views*, ed. Robert Matz and A. Chadwick Thornhill (Downers Grove, IL: IVP Academic, 2019), 102.
[170]See the discussion between Oord and Peckham in *Divine Impassibility: Four Views*, ed. Robert Matz and A. Chadwick Thornhill (Downers Grove, IL: IVP Academic, 2019).
[171]See Peckham, "Qualified Passibility," 98.
[172]"Impassibility of God," 828.

purpose.[173] In this way, divine emotions are affected, but not determined, by external stimulus in a way that does not exclude or override divine volition and evaluation. God's love for the world thus includes profoundly passible emotions. Yet, divine love is not merely emotional. Divine love is also volitional and evaluative (among other aspects).[174]

Many who affirm qualified passibility maintain that God cannot be "manipulated, overwhelmed, or surprised."[175] Open theists like Pinnock, however, depart from this relative to surprise, maintaining that God is voluntarily passible in relation to the world but that God lacks exhaustive knowledge of the future and thus can be surprised.[176] Apart from disagreement relative to God's knowledge, discussed in Chapter 4, qualified passibilists agree that God experiences emotions in a flawless way and that God's emotions are thus significantly different than human emotions.[177] Humans are often overcome and defeated by suffering but God is never overcome or defeated. Rather, God ultimately defeats suffering through voluntarily and temporarily taking on suffering, without divesting himself of any divine attributes (contra some kenoticist approaches, which maintain God empties himself of some divine attributes).[178] On this view, God is unconquerable and indomitable but not impassible.

Strict classical theists criticize both qualified impassibility and qualified passibility for denying that God is pure actuality, timeless (in the classical-scholastic sense), and utterly immutable. Conversely, advocates of both qualified impassibility and qualified passibility maintain it is sufficient to instead uphold the immutability of God's essential being and divine aseity and self-sufficiency relative to God's existence and essential nature. For qualified passibilists specifically, although God is *voluntarily* passible in relation to the world, God's essential nature is independent and not contingent on anything else. Advocates believe this view is advantageous since it maintains that God possesses essential attributes that are independent of the world

---

[173]"Impassibility of God," 828.

[174]See John C. Peckham, *The Love of God: A Canonical Model* (Downers Grove, IL: IVP Academic, 2015), 89–247. Here, I employ a working definition of *passible* emotions, defined as conscious, changing, feelings affected by and responsive to external stimulation.

[175]Lister, *God Is Impassible and Impassioned*, 36. Many qualified passibilists thus agree with Lister's qualified impassibility in this respect.

[176]Some who self-identify as open theists (e.g., Oord) hold to an essential God–world relationship instead.

[177]As Pinnock puts it, "God is beyond certain modes of suffering, just as he is beyond certain modes of change." "Systematic Theology," 119.

[178]See Peckham, "Qualified Passibility," 100.

and unchanging while also being able to freely enter into mutual, responsive relationship with the world.

Some biblical data relevant to the discussion of divine immutability and impassibility

We now turn to a consideration of some relevant biblical data. There is too much biblical data to provide anything like an adequate survey here so this section will only seek to highlight some prominent biblical data in the discussion. Two texts stand out as the most commonly cited in support of divine immutability. The first is Malachi 3:6, which states, in part: "For I, the LORD, do not change."[179] The second text is James 1:17: "Every good thing given and every perfect gift is from above, coming down from the Father of lights, with whom there is no variation or shifting shadow."

Some cite these texts as support for strict immutability. For example, after quoting Malachi 3:6, Aquinas states: "Hence it is evident that it is impossible for God to be in any way changeable."[180] Others maintain that these verses actually indicate divine responsiveness of a kind that is incompatible with strict immutability. For example, Wolterstorff contends that James 1:17 is likely saying "that God is unchangeable in that God is never the source of evil" but "only and always of good."[181] Many likewise understand Malachi 3:6 as a reference to God's *moral* changelessness rather than a reference to strict immutability. They argue that the full text of Malachi 3:6 indicates relational responsiveness, saying: "I, the LORD, do not change; *therefore you, O sons of Jacob, are not consumed*" (Mal 3:6, emphasis added). Further, Malachi 3:7—"Return to Me, and I will return to you"—suggests God's relationship to the people may change based on the people's action. Wolterstorff notes: "Surely the prophet is not here affirming God's ontological immutability but instead saying that God's fidelity to the covenant he has made with his people remains unalterable. The passage affirms covenantal fidelity, not ontological immutability."[182]

---

[179] Unless otherwise noted, all Scripture quotations are from the NASB.
[180] Aquinas, *Summa Theologiae* I.9.1.
[181] Wolterstorff, *Inquiring about God*, 163.
[182] Wolterstorff, *Inquiring about God*, 161.

In this regard, Moreland and Craig contend, "the biblical authors did not have in mind the radical changelessness contemplated by Aristotle nor the immutability required by the doctrines of essential divine timelessness or simplicity. They were speaking primarily of God's unchanging character and fidelity."[183] Wolterstorff concurs, adding, "there are no passages in Scripture which can be cited as supporting the doctrine" of "ontological [strict] immutability."[184] Ronald Nash similarly maintains: "If God is [strictly] immutable, He cannot be the religiously available God of the Scriptures. But if God is religiously available, He cannot be the unchanging God of the philosophers."[185] Indeed, Nash asks, "If God cannot change, how can He enter into the kinds of interpersonal relations attributed to Him in Scripture? How can He love and care? How can the world and human beings make any difference at all to Him? How can such a God be religiously available?"[186] Conversely, James Dolezal maintains, "the classical understanding of immutability argues that God's ethical immutability requires his [strict] ontological immutability as its foundation."[187] Given strict classical theism, God does not love and care in the way that humans do but God's love is unilateral beneficence consistent with utter immutability and pure actuality.[188]

However the verses above are understood, parties to the discussion generally agree that Scripture teaches the constancy of God's faithful character. Scripture directly affirms God's moral immutability (e.g., Deut 32:4; Ps 100:5) and the "unchangeableness of His purpose" such that God's promises are always trustworthy (Heb 6:17–18). God is eternally faithful (Ps 100:5; 117:2) and always acts in "perfect faithfulness" (Isa 25:1). Further, Scripture teaches that God remains the same (in some sense) throughout all ages: "You are the same, And Your years will not come to an end" (Ps 102:27).

At the same time, numerous texts suggest that God changes in relationship to humans. The OT repeatedly portrays God as moved by human suffering (Judg 10:16; cf. Luke 19:41) and responsive to entreaty (Ex 33:12–34:10; Judg 2:18; Isa 30:18–19). In this regard, Walter Brueggemann states, the

---

[183] Moreland and Craig, *Philosophical Foundations*, 526.
[184] Wolterstorff, *Inquiring about God*, 163.
[185] Nash, *Concept of God*, 100.
[186] Nash, *Concept of God*, 100.
[187] Dolezal, "Still Impassible," 129.
[188] See the discussion in Peckham, *The Love of God*, 16–26.

"immutable God" of "scholastic theology" that maintains God's utter imperviousness to being affected by the world "stands in deep tension with the biblical presentation of God."[189]

Here, one of the most oft-discussed issues is the question of whether God can "repent" or "relent." Numbers 23:19 states, "God is not a man, that He should lie, nor a son of man, that He should repent [*nāḥam*, hitpael]; Has He said, and will He not do it? Or has He spoken, and will He not make it good?" Likewise, 1 Samuel 15:29 states, God "will not lie nor relent [*nāḥam*, niphal]. For He is not a man, that He should relent [*nāḥam*, niphal]" (NKJV). Proponents of strict immutability often appeal to these texts as evidence that God does not repent.

On the other hand, many instances in Scripture portray God as relenting or repenting (*nāḥam*, e.g., Gen 6:6; Ex 32:14; 2 Sam 24:16; Ps 106:45; Jer 18:7–10; Joel 2:13–14; Jonah 3:9–10; 4:2; cf. Ps 81:13–14). Twice in 1 Samuel 15 itself, God is depicted as relenting or repenting (*nāḥam*, niphal, 1 Sam 15:11, 35). Critics of strict immutability point to this as evidence that 1 Samuel 15:29 and Numbers 23:19 should not be taken to mean God never relents but that he does not relent in the way humans do. John T. Willis comments, Scripture "nowhere indicates that the idea that God does not repent [*nāḥam*] is a universal principle, but always with relation to a specific event or situation."[190] Bruce McCormack thinks opposing sides in this debate make a choice between those sets of texts that speak of God as immutable on one hand and relenting on the other and that the "choice of either is predicated finally upon a presupposed metaphysical construct (in the one case, the metaphysics of pure being and, in the other case, the metaphysics of love)."[191] However, many theologians do not believe one must choose between sets of texts but maintain both sets can be understood harmoniously.

In this regard, how one views Scripture relative to immutability has significant implications relative to impassibility. While advocating qualified impassibility, Rob Lister notes that "Scripture never makes a direct assertion

---

[189] Brueggemann, "The Book of Exodus: Introduction, Commentary, and Reflections," in *The New Interpreter's Bible* (Nashville, TN: Abingdon Press, 1994), 1:932. Cf. Oden, *Classic Christianity* (New York: HarperCollins, 2009), 68.

[190] John T. Willis, "The 'Repentance' of God in the Books of Samuel, Jeremiah, and Jonah," *HBT* 16 (1994): 168.

[191] Bruce L. McCormack, "The Actuality of God: Karl Barth in Conversation with Open Theism," in *Engaging the Doctrine of God: Contemporary Protestant Perspectives*, ed. Bruce L. McCormack (Grand Rapids, MI: Baker Academic, 2008), 194.

of a metaphysical doctrine of divine impassibility."[192] Indeed, "Scripture itself does not explicitly supply" this "theological category."[193] Yet, many impassibilists maintain that "impassibility is simply a subset of divine immutability."[194] Trent Pomplun explains, "theologians took it for granted that the Most High was impervious to any pathos external to his own nature" because they believed "God was immutable (Mal. 3:6) and invariable (James 1:17)."[195] Some further claim that divine impassibility is entailed by other biblical teachings, such as divine aseity and self-sufficiency.[196] However, while some opponents agree that Scripture teaches a kind of aseity and self-sufficiency such that God does not need anything (Acts 17:25), they argue that Scripture does not teach aseity or self-sufficiency of the kind that would entail impassibility.

Passibilists highlight numerous biblical depictions of God as changing emotionally in a way responsive to creatures, including divine pleasure and displeasure, joy and suffering, delight and grief.[197] For example, Proverbs 15:8 states, "the sacrifice of the wicked is an abomination to the LORD, But the prayer of the upright is His delight" (Prov 15:8; cf. 11:20; 12:22). Further, Israel "provoked the LORD" to "wrath in the wilderness" (Deut 9:7) and on many other occasions (e.g., Ps 78:40–41). Scripture also frequently depicts God as deeply displeased, vexed, suffering, provoked, angered by human evil, and "grieved in His heart" (Gen 6:6).

Further, God is said to be the "passionate" God (*'ēl qannā'*, Deut 4:24; cf. Ex 34:14) and the "compassionate God" (*'ēl raḥûm*, Deut 4:31; cf. Ex 34:6–7). Scripture describes God as repeatedly provoked to jealousy/passion (*qānā'*) by his people's unfaithfulness (Deut 32:21; Ps 78:58), grounded in his intense passion for exclusive relationship with his people (see Hos 1–3; Isa 62:4; Jer 2:2; 3:1–12; Ezek 16, 23; Zech 8:2; cf. 2 Cor 11:2). Further, divine compassion is often depicted in visceral terms. "Can a woman forget her nursing child and have no compassion [*rāḥam*] on the son of her womb (*reḥem*)? Even these may forget, but I will not forget you" (Isa 49:15). The verb *rāḥam*, used

---

[192]Lister, *God Is Impassible and Impassioned*, 190.
[193]Lister, *God Is Impassible and Impassioned*, 173.
[194]Dolezal, "Still Impassible," 129.
[195]Trent Pomplun, "Impassibility in St. Hilary of Poitiers's *De Trinitate*," in *Divine Impassibility and the Mystery of Human Suffering*, ed. James Keating and Thomas Joseph White (Grand Rapids: Eerdmans, 2009), 187.
[196]See, for example, Dolezal, "Strong Impassibility."
[197]See Peckham, *The Love of God*, 147–89.

here and elsewhere of God's compassion, is believed to be based on the noun *reḥem* ("womb").[198] In Hosea 11:9, further, God states, "My heart is turned over within Me, all my compassions [niḥumîm] are kindled."

The NT also portrays the "tender mercy of God" (Luke 1:78) in terms of visceral compassion, frequently using the NT counterpart of *rāḥam* (*splangchnizomai*) to depict Christ's feelings of compassion, moved by the sight of people in distress (Matt 9:36; 14:14; Mark 1:41; 6:34; Luke 7:13; cf. Mark 10:21; Luke 15:20; Heb 4:15). Here, the biblical data regarding the incarnation complicates matters and has been the subject of extended discussion. As Mullins portrays the conceptual difficulty, regarding which there are numerous understandings on all sides: "An impassible God cannot suffer, but the Son of God became incarnate and suffered on the cross."[199]

Impassibilists recognize that, as Dolezal states, "many passages of the Bible" do "speak of God as undergoing affective changes."[200] Indeed, Lister states, "the biblical portrayal of divine emotion is both powerful and pervasive. One cannot read Scripture and come away with the conclusion that God is affectionless."[201] D.A. Carson believes that "God is impassible in the sense that he sustains no 'passion,' no emotion, that makes him vulnerable from the outside, over which he has no control, or which he has not foreseen" but that God's love "is clearly a vulnerable love that feels the pain and pleads for repentance."[202] Indeed, Carson maintains, viewing God as "emotionless" is "profoundly unbiblical and should be repudiated."[203]

Some advocates of qualified impassibility (e.g., Lister) maintain that God really does have the emotions Scripture portrays, viewing those emotions however as non-passive and self-determined.[204] In contrast, strict impassibilists typically maintain that such texts should be understood as anthropopathic, that is, as accommodative depictions of God *as if* he

---

[198]See H.J. Stoebe, "רחם," Theological Lexicon of the Old Testament. Ed. Ernst Jenni and Claus Westermann. Translated by Mark E. Biddle. 3 vols. (Peabody, MA: Hendrickson, 1997). Cf. *HALOT* 1217–1218; Butterworth, *NIDOTTE*, 3:1093. John Goldingay explains, *rāḥam* is a "feelings word" that "denotes strong emotion," the "strong feelings of love and concern" that result in "action." *Daniel*, WBC (Dallas, TX: Word, 1989), 243, 244.

[199]Mullins, *End of the Timeless God*, 64.

[200]Dolezal, "Still Impassible," 134.

[201]Lister, *God Is Impassible and Impassioned*, 195.

[202]Carson, *The Difficult Doctrine of the Love of God* (Wheaton, IL: Crossway, 2000), 60, 59.

[203]Carson, *Difficult Doctrine*, 48.

[204]Cf. Horton, *The Christian Faith*, 250.

experienced emotions as humans do.[205] For instance, Dolezal maintains that God "communicates the truth about his infinite and unchanging existence under the form of what is finite and changeable."[206] Similarly, Helm contends, "the impression we may form, reading the biblical narrative, that God changes is [an] illusion."[207] Helm argues "the metaphysical or ontological or strictly literal data must control the anthropomorphic and anthropopathic data, and not vice versa."[208] Yet, opponents ask, how might one know which language, if any, is "strictly literal" and which is not? Further, many impassibilists argue that biblical language of emotion is often closely connected to anatomical imagery. Presupposing the traditional doctrine that God has no body (incorporeality), they argue that language of divine emotions should no more be taken to mean God actually has emotions then language of divine body parts should be taken to mean that God actually has such body parts.[209]

Emphasizing that biblical language accommodates primitive human understanding, strict impassibilists tend to argue that passibilists mistakenly interpret Scripture univocally, that is, as if language applies to God and creatures in *exactly* the same way. Rogers notes that the "Bible speaks of God feeling joy and love and compassion, anger and hate, jealousy and sorrow."[210] Yet, she maintains, the "Bible also says that God forgets things and regrets things He has done, but perhaps these terms do not mean just what they do when we use them of our fellow human beings. Perfect being theology will deny that God has the sorts of feelings which are tied to creaturely limitations."[211]

Setting aside for now disputes over whether Scripture actually maintains "that God forgets things and regrets things He has done" (discussed in Chapter 4), many passibilists *and* qualified impassibilists agree with strict impassibilists that Scripture should be understood as analogical, that is, language relative to God should be understood as holding some similarity to

---

[205]See, for example, John Calvin's interpretation of Hosea 11:8–9 along these lines in *Commentaries on the Twelve Minor Prophets* (Grand Rapids, MI: Eerdmans, 1950), 400–40. Cf. John Calvin, *Institutes of the Christian Religion* 1.17.13, trans. Ford Lewis Battles, ed. John T. McNeill (Philadelphia, PA: Westminster Press, 1960), 1:227; Martin Luther, *Luther's Works*, ed. J. Pelikan, et al. (Philadelphia, PA: Fortress Press, 1999), 17:358.

[206]Dolezal, "Still Impassible," 135.

[207]Helm, "Divine Timeless Eternity," 46.

[208]Helm, "The Impossibility of Divine Passibility," 131.

[209]See Rogers, *Perfect Being Theology*, 52. Cf. Aquinas *Summa Theologiae* I.20.

[210]Rogers, *Perfect Being Theology*, 50.

[211]Rogers, *Perfect Being Theology*, 50–51.

how God actually is in some respects but also very dissimilar to how God is in himself.[212] However, many passibilists *and* qualified impassibilists maintain that understanding Scripture as analogical should not be employed to negate the exegetical import of texts relative to divine emotions; doing so may err in the direction of treating biblical language as equivocal (holding an entirely different meaning). On this view, understanding that language about God is analogical should caution us to remember that divine emotions are not the same as human emotions, without leading us to negate the exegetical import of biblical language about God.

Further, some passibilists maintain that, while biblical language is accommodative, so is all other language. They also warn that impassibilists may impose a preconception of divine impassibility onto Scripture. Further, passibilists (and some qualified impassibilists) maintain that body language relative to God is demonstrably idiomatic in a way the language and depictions of divine emotion are not. Such body language is often used metaphorically (of both God and humans) to depict something true about someone independent of reference to literal anatomy (e.g., "arm" represents "power," "eyes" represent knowledge/awareness). Passibilists maintain that language of divine emotion also should be taken as portraying something true about God. As Ware puts it, "Unlike in the case of Scripture's references to God's bodily parts, where other Scriptures tell us that God transcends those bodily qualities, understood literally, in the case of emotions we have no Scripture that would lead us to think that God actually transcends the emotions Scripture ascribes to him."[213] Further, Ware contends, "it seems there is no basis for calling such emotions mere anthropomorphisms."[214] Here, Wolterstorff adds: "The fact that the biblical writers speak of God as rejoicing and suffering over the state of creation is not a superficial eliminable feature of their speech. It expresses themes deeply embedded in the biblical vision."[215] As such, he thinks writing off such text as anthropopathic renders them "misleadingly metaphorical."[216] Further, whereas some impassibilists argue that emotions or "passions" require a body, passibilists tend to deny

---

[212]Lister, *God Is Impassible and Impassioned*, 106. Distinguishing between univocal, analogical, and equivocal language has a long history. See Thomas Aquinas's influential treatment (utilizing Aristotle's treatment) in *Summa Theologiae* I.1.13.

[213]Ware, *God's Greater Glory*, 146.

[214]Ware, "An Evangelical Reformulation of the Doctrine of the Immutability of God," *Journal of the Evangelical Theological Society* 29/4 (1986): 445.

[215]Wolterstoff, *Inquiring about God*, 219.

[216]Wolterstoff, *Inquiring about God*, 152.

this, asking: if God can have a will—as Christian theologians generally agree he does—without having a body, why could God not have emotions without having a body?

In all this, many opponents of strict impassibility and strict immutability believe biblical texts portraying passible divine emotions—that is, conscious, changing feeling(s) affected by and responsive to external stimulation—should be understood to mean that God in reality experiences passible emotions. Conversely, those who are convinced that there is sufficient biblical warrant for strict immutability contend that immutability entails strict impassibility as well. In contrast to strict impassibilists, advocates of qualified immutability and impassibility are open to real divine emotion and change being depicted in Scripture, but understand such as non-passive and self-determined. In contrast to strong passibilists, who maintain that God's nature necessitates passible relation to some world and tend to reject the view that God freely creates ex nihilo, advocates of qualified passibility believe that Scripture provides evidence that God voluntarily created the world ex nihilo and entered into passible relationship with the world, while maintaining that God's nature does not necessitate that God do so.

The Hellenization hypothesis and dispute over the classical view(s)

Before leaving this chapter behind, it is important to consider two related matters of considerable dispute: the Hellenization hypothesis and the dispute over differing interpretations of the classical tradition. With regard to the former, many have charged that the strict conception of divine immutability and impassibility (as well as timelessness, simplicity, and others) have been unduly influenced by Platonic, Aristotelian, and other streams of Greek philosophy.[217] For example, Pinnock argues: "The idea of God's impassibility arises more from Plato than from the Bible."[218] Further, Wolterstorff

---

[217]This is often traced back to "Adolf von Harnack's (1851–1930) theory of the development of dogma in terms of chronic Hellenization," which "has come under devastating criticism in many areas." Gavrilyuk, *Suffering of the Impassible God*, 3, 4. However, Gavrilyuk notes, "a version of this [Hellenization] theory was not unknown to the early Fathers and had been around since Hippolytus of Rome (170–235), who argued that the heretics did not derive their doctrines from the scriptures and apostolic tradition, but rather from Greek philosophers." Gavrilyuk, *Suffering of the Impassible God*, 3.
[218]Pinnock, "Systematic Theology," 118.

maintains, "the Augustinian God turns out to be remarkably like the Stoic sage: devoid of passions, unfamiliar with longing, foreign to suffering, dwelling in steady bliss, exhibiting to others only benevolence. Augustine fought free of the Stoic (and neo-Platonic) vision when it came to humanity; when it came to God, he succumbed."[219] Many thinkers have questioned whether strict classical theism more broadly is unduly influenced by some streams of classical Greek metaphysics. For example, Moltmann maintains:

> Christian theology acquired Greek philosophy's ways of thinking in the Hellenistic world; and since that time most theologians have simultaneously maintained the passion of Christ, God's Son, and the deity's essential incapacity for suffering—even though it was at the price of having to talk paradoxically about "the sufferings of the God who cannot suffer." But in doing this they have simply added together Greek philosophy's "apathy" axiom and the central statements of the gospel. The contradiction remains— and remains unsatisfactory.[220]

Closely related to this issue, there are competing interpretations of the classical tradition relative to the attributes of God, highlighted by considerable disagreement regarding just what constitutes the patristic view of divine impassibility. Many advocates of strict impassibility maintain the view "that God cannot undergo emotional changes," and thus "cannot suffer" or be affected, "was the orthodox Christian consensus for nearly two millennia."[221] Conversely, many others have argued the patristics actually held a *qualified* form of impassibility and the Christian tradition has been misunderstood and caricatured, particularly relative to claims that the classical conception of God was corrupted by the influence of Greek philosophy (i.e., the Hellenization hypothesis).[222]

Leading the way for the latter view, Paul Gavrilyuk argues that "modern passibilists" have incorrectly alleged that the Patristic view of divine impassibility amounts to "God's emotional apathy."[223] Gavrilyuk

---

[219]Wolterstoff, *Inquiring about God*, 199.

[220]Moltmann, *Trinity and the Kingdom*, 22. See also Richard J. Plantinga, Thomas R. Thompson, and Matthew D. Lundberg, *An Introduction to Christian Theology* (Cambridge: Cambridge University Press, 2010), 83–91, 99–108; John Sanders, "Historical Considerations," in *The Openness of God: A Biblical Challenge to the Traditional Understanding of God* (Downers Grove, IL: IVP, 1994), 59–91.

[221]Dolezal, "Still Impassible," 125. So, also, Weinandy, *Does God Suffer?* 38n21.

[222]See, for example, Gavrilyuk, *Suffering of the Impassible God*, 21–63; Lister, *God Is Impassible and Impassioned*, 41–122. Cf. Weinandy, *Does God Suffer?* 83–113. There is also dispute over whether the patristic view comports with the scholastic view of Aquinas and others.

[223]Gavrilyuk, "God's Impassible Suffering," 139.

maintains that, rather than being understood as "a psychological term," for the orthodox Patristics, "divine impassibility is primarily a metaphysical term, marking God's unlikeness to everything in the created order."[224] Gavrilyuk claims it was the heretical "Docetists, Arians, and Nestorians" who "deployed divine impassibility in an unqualified sense, as a property that categorically excluded God's participation in any form of suffering."[225] Lister takes a similar view, claiming that a few of "the earliest Church fathers" were "extreme impassibilists" (e.g., Justin Martyr and Clement of Alexandria) who "succumbed to Hellenistic influence" and promoted a flawed "hyper transcendent" perspective, but the mainstream understanding of "impassible" did not exclude "emotionally laden" language of God.[226] Accordingly, Gavrilyuk maintains, for the Patristic fathers "divine impassibility functioned as an apophatic qualifier of all divine emotions and as the marker of the unmistakably divine identity."[227]

Gavrilyuk recognizes that Aristotle and "later Platonism" advanced strong conceptions of impassibility but downplays the influence of both on the early fathers. Significantly, however, Augustine (354–430) himself—the most influential Christian theologian outside of Scripture—wrote of the great influence "the Platonists" had upon his thinking.[228] Further, Aquinas's seminal system was heavily influenced by the Augustinian tradition and by Aristotle's metaphysical framework, including Aristotle's conception of the Unmoved Mover, who cannot be acted upon. As Castelo notes while advocating qualified impassibility: "Although the matter becomes much more systematized in later iterations, one initially can see that the roots of impassibility lie within several strands of Hellenistic philosophy."[229]

---

[224] "God's Impassible Suffering," 139.

[225] Gavrilyuk, "God's Impassible Suffering," 143.

[226] Lister, *God Is Impassible and Impassioned*, 95–96, 102. In this regard, Plantinga, Thompson, and Lundberg maintain that "many early Christian thinkers held that Platonic theism was actually a divine preparation for the Christian gospel—sometimes inspired by the example of Philo of Alexandria (c.25 BCE–45 CE)." They cite Clement of Alexandria, who, "along with Justin Martyr and many others … even held that Plato himself had been instructed by Moses and the prophets" and wrote that "philosophy … was given to the Greeks, as a covenant peculiar to them—being, as it is, a stepping-stone to the philosophy which is according to Christ." *An Introduction to Christian Theology*, 85. Cf. Clement of Alexandria, *Stromata*, Book 6, ch. 8.

[227] Gavrilyuk, *Suffering of the Impassible God*, 173.

[228] Augustine, *Confessions* 7.9.13 (NPNF1 1:107).

[229] Castelo, *Apathetic God*, 42.

In this regard, Gavrilyuk argues, the picture in the patristic age was far more complicated than is sometimes recognized. On the one hand, Gavrilyuk maintains, "among educated pagans, whose philosophical views tended toward later Platonism, the divine impassibility [in the sense of being "supremely transcendent" and "above passions"] did acquire the status of a universally shared opinion."[230] Yet, Gavrilyuk emphasizes, Hellenistic thought on these matters was by no means monolithic.[231] Further, he maintains, to the extent that Christians adopted some language and thought patterns from Greek thinking, they did not do so *uncritically* or uniformly. Rather, the "Fathers had to find an adequate language to express the truth of divine revelation, carving out their distinctive account of divine agency in the midst of passion and dispassion narratives of the Hellenistic world, and proposing their own understanding of the divine possibility and impassibility."[232] As such, Gavrilyuk maintains: "Impassibility was not baptized without conversion."[233]

While Gavrilyuk criticizes and rebuts overstated versions of the Hellenization hypothesis, Gavrilyuk's work itself seems to provide support for a moderate or qualified Hellenization hypothesis. For instance, Gavrilyuk notes that "by calling the Christian God impassible the Fathers sought to distance God the creator from the gods of mythology" and those gods' "unworthy passions."[234] Further, the Fathers faced a "Greek speaking-world" wherein "*pathe* had a negative connotation" and "divine impassibility" was the "universally shared opinion" of "educated pagans."[235] Accordingly, Gavrilyuk writes, "it must be admitted that the Bible ascribes to God a much wider range of human emotions than any philosophically minded pagan of the Hellenistic period would ever find appropriate."[236] Unsurprisingly, some Christian apologists sought to depict God in a way that might assuage the concerns of Christianity's cultured despisers who thought, in the Bible, "God was described in the most naïve, anthropomorphic, and anthropopathic terms" and "whose understanding of God did not allow for the possibility

---

[230]Gavrilyuk, *Suffering of the Impassible God*, 34.
[231]Gavrilyuk, *Suffering of the Impassible God*, 34.
[232]Gavrilyuk, *Suffering of the Impassible God*, 36.
[233]Gavrilyuk, *Suffering of the Impassible God*, 15.
[234]Gavrilyuk, *Suffering of the Impassible God*, 48.
[235]Gavrilyuk, *Suffering of the Impassible God*, 28, 34.
[236]Gavrilyuk, *Suffering of the Impassible God*, 37.

that God could empty himself, assume the human condition, and suffer the consequences."[237]

Many other critics of the Hellenization hypothesis also recognize the significant influence of streams of Greek philosophy. Katherin Rogers, an advocate of strict classical theism, comments: "When Augustine and later thinkers who were committed to the God of biblical revelation came to approach their faith in the light of Greek thought the result was what we can call the 'classical God of the Philosophers.'"[238] Gerald Bray notes, further, needing "to address their contemporaries," there "is no doubt that the early Christians were influenced by the philosophical currents surrounding them."[239] Similarly, Lister comments, while "the Fathers sought to defer to biblical authority," it "is obvious to all that the Patristic theologians borrowed Greek language and made use of Greek concepts."[240] Likewise, Castelo comments, given "the double testimony of the Hebrew Scriptures and the gospels' depiction of a suffering Christ, there is no question that divine impassibility as it existed in the wider Hellenistic world is untenable for Christians."[241] He adds, further, "the early Christians drew from their pagan neighbors in significant ways. Had Christianity not emerged within the Greco-Roman world, it could very well be the case that the terminology of divine impassibility would not have been prominent within the tradition and so not an issue for systematics today."[242]

---

[237]Gavrilyuk, *Suffering of the Impassible God*, 51, 18. In this regard, scholars have long noted that the Septuagint (LXX)—the ancient Greek translation of the Old Testament—often downplays the portrayal of divine emotions (e.g., Jer 31:20 [LXX 38:20]). For a discussion of many examples, see Charles T. Fritsch, *The Anti-Anthropomorphisms of the Greek Pentateuch* (Princeton, NJ: Princeton University Press, 1943), 17–18. Albrecht Stumpff explains that, although the LXX depicts passion as a positive divine attribute, out of "fear of any kind of anthropomorphising" the idea of passion or jealousy came to be considered inappropriate to God among some Jewish scholars. *TDNT*, 2: 879–880. Cf. Philo of Alexandria's presentation of divine impassibility in "On the Unchangeableness of God," in *The Works of Philo* (Peabody, MA: Hendrickson, 1995), XIII.60–61 (Yonge 163).

[238]Rogers, *Perfect Being Theology*, 6. She notes, further, that "Plotinus, embracing both Platonic and Aristotelian doctrines, constructed a unified philosophical/religious system which would exercise a double impact on the medieval synthesis of reason and revelation; first through the work of Augustine, undoubtedly the most influential thinker in Western Christendom, and in a second reincarnation when his work, mistakenly attributed to Aristotle, was rediscovered by the great Islamic philosophers who had such a profound impact on European thought in the later Middle Ages." Rogers, *Perfect Being Theology*, 6.

[239]"Has the Christian Doctrine of God Been Corrupted by Greek Philosophy?" in *God under Fire*, ed. Douglas S. Huffman and Eric L. Johnson (Grand Rapids, MI: Zondervan, 2002), 112.

[240]Lister, *God Is Impassible and Impassioned*, 61. Cf. the *Oxford Dictionary of the Christian Church*'s position that divine impassibility's "foundation in Christian sources is probably due to direct Greek influences." "Impassibility of God," 828.

[241]Castelo, *Apathetic God*, 124.

[242]Castelo, *Apathetic God*, 64.

This debate over the extent and impact of Greek philosophies on the Christian tradition extends far beyond the issue of divine impassibility, encompassing the discussion of classical theism as a whole, particularly of the strict variety. Here, however, the extent to which church fathers were dependent on Greek philosophies cannot by itself determine whether and to what extent their conceptions of divine impassibility specifically, or classical theism more broadly, are valid. Thus, what one concludes regarding divine impassibility, and relative to the other elements of classical theism, does not depend upon how one views the extent of Greek influence.

In this regard, while many advocates of the Hellenization hypothesis have overstated their case, proponents and critics alike generally agree that streams of Greek philosophy such as Neoplatonism and Aristotelianism greatly influenced the church fathers. The ongoing debate, which I will not attempt to settle here, is generally about whether such influence was received and employed *uncritically* in the Christian tradition and whether and/or to what extent such influence was a *corrupting* one.[243]

This discussion is complicated significantly by the fact that different scholars come to widely diverging interpretations of the views of the church fathers individually and in general. Many make a compelling case that there was no single, monolithic, patristic view of impassibility. Castelo notes "the multivalent ways in which divine impassibility functioned for numerous ancient writers."[244] Gavrilyuk also testifies to "the range of meanings that patristic authors give to the term 'impassible,'" including meaning merely "resilient in the face of suffering."[245] He contends that some fathers "resorted to paradoxical affirmations," using "boldly theopaschite terms" yet "without abandoning divine impassibility,"[246] while others (e.g., Augustine) were "by no means consistent on this point."[247]

---

[243] See the further discussion of this in Michael Allen, "Exodus 3 after the Hellenization Thesis," *Journal of Theological Interpretation* 3/2 (2009): 180–82; Peter W. Martens, "Embodiment, Heresy, and the Hellenization of Christianity: The Descent of the Soul in Plato and Origen," *Harvard Theological Review* 108/4 (2015): 620.

[244] Castelo, *Apathetic God*, 41.

[245] Gavrilyuk, *Suffering of the Impassible God*, 11n.29.

[246] Gavrilyuk, *Suffering of the Impassible God*, 89. For instance, regarding divine anger, some offered "a purely subjectivist interpretation" wherein God is not actually angry but humans only perceive him to be and others claimed that God "indeed experiences anger" but "in a carefully qualified sense." *Suffering of the Impassible God*, 56.

[247] Specifically, Gavrilyuk maintains, Augustine affirmed, but not consistently, a subjectivist account of divine anger. *Suffering of the Impassible God*, 57. See, for example, Augustine, *Contra Faustum*, 22.18; Augustine, *De Patientia*, 1. Cf. Augustine, *Confessions* 3.2.3.

Whereas numerous advocates of both strong and qualified impassibility claim their view is supported by the tradition, Gavrilyuk maintains that there was such diversity regarding im/passibility that even qualified passibility may find significant support in the tradition, particularly relative to the (qualified) theopaschite terminology used by many fathers.[248] For instance, Tertullian maintained that God has "the same emotions and sensations" as humans but "they are not of the same kind" since "God alone" is "perfect" and has them according to his "property of incorruptibility."[249] Thus, divergent positions relative to impassibility—and relative to other debates over classical theism—may find some support within the broad Christian tradition, depending on how the tradition is interpreted and what aspect(s) of the tradition are considered. Here, whatever one concludes, many philosophers and theologians agree that, in Castelo's words, "at some level the need for an accounting is obvious: the God-talk … of the Bible and that of the ancient church repeatedly sound at odds with each other."[250]

Conclusion

This chapter introduced some prominent contemporary views regarding the issues of divine immutability and impassibility, briefly discussed some biblical data relevant to the issues, and briefly discussed the so-called Hellenization hypothesis. The next chapter moves on to the closely related questions of God's relationship to time and space.

---

[248]Indeed, even "the orthodox" used "theopaschite expressions" in "reference to Christ's crucifixion as freely as did the Arians." *Suffering of the Impassible God*, 127.

[249]Tertullian, *Against Marcion*, 2.16 (*ANF* 3:309). Accordingly: "Angry He will possibly be, but not irritated, nor dangerously tempted. He will be moved, but not subverted." Rather, God is appropriately "moved" to "affections" such as "anger," "indignation," "jealousy," "mercy," and "patience," yet in "all these affections He is moved by that peculiar manner of His own." Tertullian, *Against Marcion*, 2.16 (*ANF* 3:309). Cf. Cyril of Alexandria's view that "the Word suffered impassibly" or "the impassible suffered." Gavrilyuk, *Suffering of the Impassible God*, 147. As Cyril put it, "Even if he [the Son] is said to suffer in the flesh, even so he retains his impassibility insofar as he is understood as God." As such, Cyril maintains, "the same one suffers and does not suffer." Cyril of Alexandria, *On the Unity of Christ*, trans. J.A. McGuckin (Crestwood, NY: St. Vladimir's Seminary Press, 1995), 117. Thus, in Cyril's view (according to Gavrilyuk) "both qualified divine impassibility and qualified divine passibility were necessary for a sound theology of incarnation." Gavrilyuk, *Suffering of the Impassible God*, 150.

[250]Castelo, "Qualified Impassibility," 81.

Study questions

1. How do you understand the relationship between divine aseity, timelessness, immutability, and impassibility? Do you think each of these entail the others or can one consistently affirm some and deny others? How much of this discussion hinges on definitions?
2. How do you evaluate the various perspectives on whether God changes? Do you think God has changing emotions? Does God repent or change his mind? Why do the answers to these questions matter?
3. How do you think one should decide between various perspectives on the questions raised in this chapter? What role does the data from Scripture play in the way you think of these issues? What do you make of differing interpretations of the Christian tradition relative to divine immutability and divine impassibility? What are some of the implications for Christian theism regarding how these questions are answered?
4. What are some of the strengths of each view? What are some weaknesses of each view? Can you think of any further difficulties with any of the views discussed in this chapter? Can you think of any further advantages of views discussed in this chapter?
5. How do you think the controversy over the so-called Hellenization hypothesis should be approached? Must one either accept or reject the theory or do you think there might be some truth on both sides of the debate?

Suggestions for further reading

Selected premodern sources

Philo of Alexandria. "On the Unchangeableness of God," in *The Works of Philo*. Translated by C.D. Jonge (Peabody: Hendrickson, 1995).

Tertullian, *Against Marcion* 2.16.

Cyril of Alexandria. *On the Unity of Christ*. Translated by J.A. McGuckin (Crestwood, NY: St. Vladimir's Seminary Press, 1995), 101–20.

Anselm, *Proslogion* 8.
Thomas Aquinas, *Summa Theologiae* I.3, I.9. I.25.1.
John Calvin, *Institutes of the Christian Religion* 1.17.12–14.

Selected modern/contemporary sources

Castelo, Daniel. *The Apathetic God: Exploring the Contemporary Relevance of Divine Impassibility*. Paternoster Theological Monographs (Colorado Springs, CO: Paternoster, 2009).

Cone, James. *God of the Oppressed* (New York: Seabury Press, 1975).

Creel, Richard. *Divine Impassibility: An Essay in Philosophical Theology* (Cambridge: Cambridge University Press, 1986).

Gavrilyuk, Paul L. *The Suffering of the Impassible God: The Dialectics of Patristic Thought* (New York: Oxford University Press, 2006).

Kitamori, Kazoh. *A Theology of the Pain of God: The First Original Theology from Japan*. 5th ed. (Richmond, VA: John Knox, 1965).

Lister, Rob. *God Is Impassible and Impassioned: Toward a Theology of Divine Emotion* (Wheaton, IL: Crossway, 2013).

Matz, Robert and A. Chadwick Thornhill, eds. *Divine Impassibility: Four Views* (Downers Grove, IL: IVP Academic, 2019).

McFague, Sallie, *Models of God: Theology for an Ecological, Nuclear Age* (Philadelphia, PA: Fortress, 1987).

Moltmann, Jürgen. *The Crucified God: The Cross of Christ as the Foundation and Criticism of Christian Theology* (New York: Harper & Row, 1974).

Richards, Jay Wesley. *The Untamed God: A Philosophical Exploration of Divine Perfection, Simplicity, and Immutability* (Downers Grove, IL: InterVarsity, 2003).

Vanhoozer, Kevin J. *Remythologizing Theology* (New York: Cambridge University Press, 2010).

Ware, Bruce. "An Evangelical Reformulation of the Doctrine of the Immutability of God," *Journal of the Evangelical Theological Society* 29/4 (1986): 431–46.

Weinandy, Thomas. *Does God Suffer?* (Notre Dame, IN: University of Notre Dame Press, 2000).

Wolterstorff, Nicholas. *Inquiring about God: Selected Essays*, volume 1 (New York: Cambridge University Press, 2010).

3

Does God Have a Future?

Does God have a future? What does "eternity" mean relative to God? Christian theists continue to debate the relationship between God and time. They generally agree that God has no beginning and no end. God is eternal. However, there is disagreement about whether God is timelessly eternal or everlastingly eternal or something else. This disagreement has massive ramifications regarding how one conceives of God and the God–world relationship. As Nicholas Wolterstorff puts it, "What one says about God's relation to time involves a very great deal of the rest of one's theology."[1]

Strict classical theism maintains that God is timelessly eternal, that is, atemporal. On this view, God's life has no succession of moments. There is no before or after for God. God does not experience one moment then another or do one thing, then another. If God is timeless, then God's being is *incompatible* with temporal succession (the succession from one moment to the next). Many theists, however, maintain that the Christian God does experience temporal succession and does act sequentially. The God of the Bible, some argue, has not only a present but also a past and a future. There are various nuanced positions opposed to divine timelessness, some of the most prominent of which will be discussed in this chapter.

Beyond the issue of God's relationship to time is God's relationship to space. Does God occupy space? Is God everywhere or nowhere or something else? Is God always "with us"? Christian theists generally agree that God is omnipresent but just what this means is sometimes unclear. This chapter introduces some prominent contemporary perspectives on divine eternity and omnipresence, followed by a brief discussion of selected biblical data relevant to both issues.

---

[1]Nicholas Wolterstorff, *Inquiring about God: Selected Essays*, vol. 1 (New York: Cambridge University Press, 2010), 181.

Divine timelessness

Strict classical theists contend that God exists without beginning, without end, and without temporal succession. There is no before or after for God; no succession of moments or passage of time. God is timeless or atemporal, meaning that God has no temporal location and God's being is incompatible with temporal succession. God cannot experience one moment after another. God cannot do one thing and then another. God is not located at any time; "a timeless God experiences His life all at once."[2] Accordingly, in the view of some atemporalists, the Exodus, the cross, and the second coming are all equally present to God in what some call God's "eternal now."[3]

As John W. Cooper defines this view, "Eternity is the enduring, simultaneous presence of the infinite divine life without any succession."[4] Thus, Katherine Sonderegger explains, God "is eternal, not temporal."[5] Thomas Williams adds, "God is eternal, not in the sense that he exists at every moment of time, but in the sense that his life is not characterized by succession at all. For God there is no before and after."[6] Paul Helm explains, "as timeless," God "cannot have temporal relations with any of his creation. He is time-less in the sense of being time-free."[7] Katherin Rogers maintains, further, God's timeless "eternity has no duration."[8] Yet, Rogers explains, "the nature of divine eternity" is that "all of time is 'present' to God."[9] Divine timelessness is very difficult for us to conceive because "we are temporal beings and cannot envision a timeless existence."[10]

Strict classical theists maintain that divine timelessness entails, and/or is entailed by, a number of other elements of strict classical theism. For example,

---

[2] R.T. Mullins, *The End of the Timeless God* (New York: Oxford University Press, 2016), xvi.
[3] Gregory E. Ganssle, "Introduction: Thinking about God and Time," in *God and Time: Four Views*, ed. Gregory Ganssle (Downers Grove, IL: InterVarsity, 2001), 12.
[4] John W. Cooper, *Panentheism, the Other God of the Philosophers: From Plato to the Present* (Grand Rapids, MI: Baker Academic, 2006), 330.
[5] Katherine Sonderegger, *Systematic Theology: The Doctrine of God* (Minneapolis, MN: Fortress, 2015), 493.
[6] Thomas Williams, "Introduction to Classical Theism," in *Models of God and Alternative Ultimate Realities*, ed. Jeanine Diller and Asa Kasher (New York: Springer, 2013), 96.
[7] Paul Helm, *Eternal God: A Study of God without Time* (New York: Oxford University Press, 1998), 39.
[8] See Katherin Rogers, "Eternity Has No Duration," *Religious Studies* 30/1 (1994): 1–16.
[9] Katherin A. Rogers, *Perfect Being Theology* (Edinburgh: Edinburgh University Press, 2000), 59.
[10] Rogers, *Perfect Being Theology*, 57.

Helm maintains that in "Perfect Being theology, [timeless] eternality implies and is implied by divine simplicity (the view that though we are able to think of distinctions in the Godhead it is actually uncompounded, without parts, including temporal parts)."[11] Further, Rogers avers, "it is only by postulating divine eternity that God's immutability can be preserved, and with it His simplicity."[12] Edward Feser similarly maintains that "strict *timelessness* … follows from both [God's] immutability and his simplicity."[13] Williams adds, "The doctrine of divine eternity leads directly to the claim that God is immutable."[14] As Eleonore Stump explains, "God is outside time; but change requires succession, which is characteristic of time, and so nothing that is outside time can change."[15]

In this regard, as seen in the previous chapter, Helm argues that "a timelessly eternal God is immutable and so impassible in a very strong sense; he *necessarily* cannot change for change takes time."[16] Helm also affirms the reverse, maintaining that "only a God who is immutable in a particularly strong sense can (logically) perform all that Scripture claims that God performs, and a God can only be immutable in this strong sense if he exists timelessly."[17] If God is timeless, "there is no change or succession possible in the timeless eternity of God's life."[18] If so, God cannot experience successive events and can neither enter into time nor temporally interact with creatures. God cannot be affected by any other (strong impassibility) and cannot change in any way whatsoever (utter immutability), relationally or otherwise.

Yet, some ask, how could such a timeless God act in relation to the world? How could God "act" at all if God lacks temporal succession? Atemporalists generally maintain the Augustinian position that God "does all He does in one, perfect, eternal and immutable act."[19] In other words, God's singular

---

[11] Paul Helm, "Divine Timeless Eternity," in *God and Time: Four Views*, ed. Gregory Ganssle (Downers Grove, IL: InterVarsity, 2001), 34.
[12] Rogers, *Perfect Being Theology*, 55–56.
[13] Edward Feser, *Five Proofs of the Existence of God* (San Francisco, CA: Ignatius, 2017), 200 (emphasis original).
[14] Williams, "Classical Theism," 96.
[15] Eleonore Stump, *The God of the Bible and the God of the Philosophers* (Marquette, MI: Marquette University Press, 2016), 26.
[16] Helm, "Divine Timeless Eternity," 38–39 (emphasis original).
[17] Helm, *Eternal God*, 21–22.
[18] Helm, "Divine Timeless Eternity," 54.
[19] Rogers, *Perfect Being Theology*, 54.

timeless "act" causes the entire series of events in history. As Hugh McCann puts it, "In a single *fiat* [God] produces the entire universe, in all of its history, all of it with equal directness and absolute control."[20] Put another way: "All actions ever truly ascribed to God are just manifestations in time of one atemporal act."[21]

In this regard, many classical theists adopt Aquinas's view that God relates to the world via a relation of reason such that "though the universe is really related to God, God is not really related to the created universe."[22] As Aquinas puts it, "Since all creatures depend on God but He does not depend on them, there are real relations in creatures, referring them to God. The opposite relations in God to creatures, however, are merely conceptual relations," that is, the "relation [of God to the world] is merely one of reason."[23] Put simply, Webster explains, there is a "non-reciprocity of the creator-creature relation, which is not real on the side of the creator."[24] Yet, since "all of time is [timelessly] 'present' to God," God can timelessly cause anything to occur at any time he wills. Indeed, on this view, God "knows and causes all things at all times because all of time is immediately present to Him."[25]

A number of disputed issues arise relative to timelessness and divine action. First, many critics contend that we have "no acceptable conception of atemporal causation," that is, "of what it is for a timeless cause to produce a temporal effect."[26] As such, "it is not clear how a timelessly eternal being can be the creator of this temporal universe."[27] Likewise, critics question how a timeless, immutable being could know a temporal, changing universe

---

[20] Hugh J. McCann, "The God beyond Time," in *Philosophy of Religion: An Anthology*, 7th ed, ed. Michael Rea and Louis P. Pojman (Stamford, CT: Cengage, 2015), 91. So, also, Feser, *Five Proofs*, 201; Helm, "Divine Timeless Eternity," 53.

[21] Thomas V. Morris, *Our Idea of God: An Introduction to Philosophical Theology* (Notre Dame: University of Notre Dame Press, 1991), 132.

[22] Helm, "Divine Timeless Eternity," 48. Helm does not defend this view in this essay, however.

[23] Thomas Aquinas, *Truth* 4.5, trans. Robert W. Mulligan (Indianapolis, IN: Hackett, 1994), 191. Aquinas explains: "Whenever two things are related to each other in such a way that one depends upon the other but the other does not depend upon it, there is a real relation in the dependent member, but in the independent member the relation is merely one of reason." Aquinas, *Truth* 4.5 (Mulligan, 190–91). Indeed, Aquinas contends: "The relation of God to creatures can be only that of a cause to an effect." *Truth* 4.5 (Mulligan, 189).

[24] John Webster, *God without Measure: Working Papers in Christian Theology*, vol. 1: God and the Works of God (New York: T&T Clark, 2016), 93.

[25] Rogers, *Perfect Being Theology*, 56.

[26] Stephen T. Davis, "Temporal Eternity," in *Philosophy of Religion: An Anthology*. 7th ed, ed. Michael Rea and Louis P. Pojman (Stamford, CT: Cengage, 2015), 86.

[27] Davis, "Temporal Eternity," 86. Cf. Mullins, *End of the Timeless God*, 106–7.

(see Chapter 5 for more on this). Some advocates of timelessness elude these problems by maintaining the world is not actually temporal but only seems to be so (see the discussion of eternalism below).

Second, some classical theists (and others) believe this understanding of God entails causal determinism, meaning that creatures are determined by external causes to act just as they do. As Helm puts it, "The existence of an omniscient, timelessly eternal God is logically inconsistent with the libertarian freedom in any of his creatures."[28] However, some reject this conclusion. For instance, Katherin Rogers maintains strict divine timelessness, immutability, and impassibility and yet affirms human libertarian freedom (the kind of free will that is incompatible with causal determinism). This will be discussed further in Chapter 5.

Third, some think that if all of history is eternally "present" to God, then it seems events that occur in 586 BC and AD 70 would be simultaneous with one another and "with the whole of eternity," which seems intuitively false.[29] In this regard, Hugh McCann, himself an advocate of divine timelessness, thinks atemporalists should "drop the idea that history is 'present' to God, in any sense other than being given to him timelessly in experience or awareness." He contends, "God creates and is aware of all history neither simultaneously nor at different times, but eternally."[30] Some advocates of timelessness argue that such evaluations of the traditional view regarding God's "eternal present" depend on diverging views of the nature of time (see the discussion below) and/or may not account for the difference between divine and human perspectives (see the discussion of divine knowledge in Chapter 5). Nevertheless, critics claim, if all of history is eternally present to God, then it would seem that all evil events in history are eternal. Stephen T. Davis cites this as one "reason that I do not affirm the timelessness of either God or heaven. I hope events like the Holocaust recede further and further into the past rather than remain an aspect of an 'eternal present moment.'"[31] See the discussion of the problem of evil in Chapter 6.

Fourth, questions arise regarding the compatibility of divine timelessness with the incarnation of Christ. R.T. Mullins notes, "Many of the early

---

[28] Helm, *Eternal God*, 144.

[29] Anthony Kenny, *The God of the Philosophers* (Oxford: Clarendon, 1979), 38. See also Davis, "Temporal Eternity," 87; Richard Swinburne, *The Coherence of Theism* (Oxford: Oxford University Press, 1977), 220–21.

[30] McCann, "God beyond Time," 94.

[31] Davis, "Temporal Eternity," 107. Cf. R.T. Mullins, "Four-Dimensionalism, Evil, and Christian Belief," *Philosophia Christi* 16/1 (2014): 127–28.

Christological heresies were motivated by the prima facie incompatibility of divine timelessness, immutability, impassibility, and the incarnation."[32] Mullins himself makes a case that "divine timelessness is not compatible with the ecumenical model of the incarnation."[33] Helm, conversely, understands the incarnation as "a unique case of God's acting in time," maintaining that "if God the Son is timelessly eternal and yet incarnate in Jesus Christ, there is no time in his existence when he was not incarnate, though since he became incarnate at a particular time in our history there were times in that history before the incarnation, and times since."[34] In Helm's view, "God did not exist and then at some later *point decide* to become incarnate, for there is no change or succession *possible in the* timeless eternity of God's life."[35] As such, the "incarnation is the 'projection' of the eternal God."[36]

Fifth, some think a timeless God cannot genuinely respond to creatures, as Scripture repeatedly portrays God as doing. Yet, Rogers contends, while "God thinks or wills or loves in a single, eternal act," this is not incompatible with an atemporal kind of divine response.[37] She maintains that, since the current and fourth "centuries are equally present" to God, one could pray today for a fourth-century person and, if God "in His single, immutable act of being, gives" that person "strength in part (very small part) because of" one's prayer, then, "he has responded" to that prayer.[38] As Eleonore Stump explains, "an eternal, immutable God cannot do anything *after* something happens in time. But such a God can certainly act *because of* something that happens in time."[39] Helm argues, similarly, that "not only may such a [timeless] God act within time but he may also be said to act in response to what happens in time."[40] Richard Creel contends that it is more accurate to call these "presponses" rather than responses.[41]

---

[32] Mullins, *End of the Timeless God*, 158.

[33] Mullins, *End of the Timeless God*, 194. For an argument that the incarnation and timelessness can be held compatibly, see Douglas K. Blount, "On the Incarnation of a Timeless God," in *God and Time: Essays on the Divine Nature*, ed. Gregory E. Ganssle and David M. Woodruff (New York: Oxford University Press, 2002), 236–48.

[34] Helm, "Divine Timeless Eternity," 54.

[35] Helm, "Divine Timeless Eternity," 54.

[36] Helm, "Divine Timeless Eternity," 54.

[37] Rogers, *Perfect Being Theology*, 65.

[38] Rogers, *Perfect Being Theology*, 66.

[39] Stump, *God of the Bible*, 76.

[40] Helm, "Divine Timeless Eternity," 53.

[41] Richard Creel, *Divine Impassibility: An Essay in Philosophical Theology* (Cambridge: Cambridge University Press, 1986), 22–23.

Others question, however, whether such timeless action should be considered genuinely responsive at all. For instance, Nelson Pike argues, "a timeless being could not be affected or prompted by another" nor "respond to needs, overtures, delights or antagonisms of human beings" but must be "immutable in the strong sense of 'immutable'" such that the "actions of a timeless being could not be interpreted as a *response* to something else. Responses are located in time after that to which they are responses."[42] Stephen Davis adds, similarly: "To respond is to be affected by events that have occurred in the past."[43] On this definition, if God is atemporal, God could not respond to creatures. Thus, Rob Lister contends, a "commitment to an atemporal view of God" would preclude consistently holding "that God is ever actually *re*-sponsive."[44]

The atemporalist, however, might define a divine "response" as God "eternally will[ing] his own reactions in time to some human action."[45] The strict classical theist will then have to understand "reaction" in some way that does not conflict with pure aseity and strict impassibility and also, for those who affirm it, divine determinism. That is, if "the concept of a response requires that there be a certain sort of causal connection such that," say, a "prayer 'prompts' the response, and the response 'answers' the prayer," it is difficult (if not impossible) to reconcile pure aseity, strict impassibility, and determinism with divine responsiveness.[46] The critic will contend that, even if one rejects determinism, it is not clear that a timeless God can *react* and if a timeless God can do so it is not clear what *reaction* then means. Whatever it may mean, many classical theists believe divine timelessness is not compatible with God having the *kinds of reactions* that Scripture describes and portrays such as emotional changes in response to creaturely actions (i.e., temporally responsive emotions). As James Dolezal puts it,

---

[42]Nelson Pike, *God and Timelessness* (London: Routledge & Kegan Paul, 1970), 128 (emphasis original). William Lane Craig avers, in response, that only mere changelessness must be true of a timeless being rather than a lack of ability to change. On his view, a timeless God could create time and become temporal and thus change. See Craig, *God, Time and Eternity: The Coherence of Theism II: Eternity* (Dordrecht: Kluwer, 2001), 53.

[43]Davis, "Temporal Eternity," 86–87.

[44]Rob Lister, *God Is Impassible and Impassioned* (Wheaton, IL: Crossway, 2013), 230.

[45]Helm, "Divine Timeless Eternity," 54.

[46]Rogers, *Perfect Being Theology*, 66. For her part, Rogers rejects determinism and upholds divine response. Further, though she thinks God is impassible, she elsewhere maintains: "Any systematic philosophy of God which incorporated free choice on the part of creatures would have to hold that God is somehow affected by and responsive to something outside Himself." Rogers, *Perfect Being Theology*, 37–38.

"If temporal succession of life is denied to God, so then must be all those experiences, such as emotional change, that require time."[47] As John Cooper puts it, then, "Biblical assertions of God's reactions are anthropopathic."[48] Rob Lister concludes, in this regard, if God is "pure actuality," then "God is never, properly speaking, responsive."[49]

In this and other regards, atemporalists such as Helm contend that divine timelessness is "the classical Christian view of God's relation to time"; it is "the 'mainstream' view represented by Augustine, Anselm, Aquinas, Calvin, and hosts of others."[50] According to Rogers, "It was Augustine's doctrine of divine eternity which shaped the theology of Western Christendom."[51] In her view, "Criticisms of the tenseless view of time are not powerful enough to necessitate abandoning the venerable tradition of an eternal God."[52] Indeed, she claims, "Only through the Augustinian move to eternity can God's perfection be reconciled with His living agency in our world."[53]

According to Augustine (354–430) himself, "In eternity nothing moves into the past: all is present …. eternity, in which there is neither past nor future, determines both past and future time."[54] Further, "Should the present be always present, and should it not pass into time past, time truly it could not be, but eternity."[55] In this regard, Augustine maintains that God "made time itself" and "no times are co-eternal with" God who, as eternal, "remainest for ever."[56] In this vein, Boethius (*c.* 480–524) wrote: "Eternity, then, is the whole, simultaneous and perfect possession of boundless life" in contrast to "temporal things" that live "in time."[57] Further, Boethius wrote:

> Whatever therefore comprehends and possesses at once the whole fullness of boundless life, and is such that neither is anything future lacking from it, nor

---

[47]James E. Dolezal, "Still Impassible: Confessing God without Passions," *Journal of the Institute of Reformed Baptist Studies* 1 (2014): 131.

[48]Cooper, *Panentheism*, 332.

[49]Lister, *God Is Impassible and Impassioned*, 157.

[50]Helm, "Divine Timeless Eternity," 28.

[51]Rogers, *Perfect Being Theology*, 54.

[52]Katherin A. Rogers, "Omniscience, Eternity and Freedom," *International Philosophical Quarterly* 36/4 (1996): 408.

[53]Rogers, *Perfect Being Theology*, 55.

[54]Augustine, *Confessions* XI, 11, quoted from Pine-Coffin translation in Rogers, *Perfect Being Theology*, 66. Cf. the alternate translation in *Confessions* 11.11.13 (*NPNF1* 1:167).

[55]Augustine, *Confessions* 11.14.17 (*NPNF1* 1:168).

[56]Augustine, *Confessions* 11.14.17 (*NPNF1* 1:168).

[57]Boethius, *The Consolation of Philosophy* 5.6, trans. H.F. Stewart, E.K. Rand, and S.J. Tester. Loeb Classical Library 74 (Cambridge, MA: Harvard University Press, 1973), 423.

has anything past flowed away, that is rightly held to be eternal, and that must necessarily both always be present to itself, possessing itself in the present, and hold as present the infinity of moving time.[58]

Centuries later, Anselm (c. 1033–1109) also maintained divine timelessness, arguing that "in eternity a thing has no past or future but only an (eternal) present, though in the realm of time things move from past to future without any contradiction arising."[59] If God were not eternal in this fashion, Anselm claims, the "supreme essence ... would be cut up into parts along the divisions of time" and have "past, present, and future" and thus would not be "supremely simple and supremely unchangeable."[60] As such, Anselm wrote: "You [God] exist neither yesterday nor today nor tomorrow but are absolutely outside all time."[61] Similarly, Thomas Aquinas (1225–74) stated that God is "bereft of movement" and as "always the same, there is no before or after. As therefore the idea of time consists in numbering before and after in movement [succession]; so likewise in the apprehension of the uniformity of what is outside movement, consists the idea of eternity." Further, "whatever is wholly immutable can have no succession" such that "what is eternal is interminable" and "eternity has no succession, being simultaneously whole."[62]

Indeed, while noting exceptions such as John Duns Scotus (c. 1266–1308) and William of Ockham (c. 1287–1347), Rogers claims that divine timelessness was held by "almost every philosopher or theologian in the Latin West from Augustine at least through Aquinas, that is to say from the fourth century for the next thousand years."[63] According to Rogers, then, divine timelessness "is the standard medieval view of the Augustinian Neoplatonists and the more Aristotelian thinkers as well."[64] In this regard, Garrett DeWeese claims: "Since Augustine's arguments for God's atemporality depend heavily on the Neoplatonic understanding of

---

[58] Boethius, *The Consolation of Philosophy* 5.6 (LCL 423–25).
[59] Anselm, *De Concordia: The Compatibility of God's Foreknowledge, Predestination, and Grace with Human Freedom* 1.5.
[60] Anselm, *Monologion* 21.
[61] Anselm, *Proslogion* 19.
[62] Thomas Aquinas, *Summa Theologiae* I.10.1.
[63] Rogers, *Perfect Being Theology*, 54.
[64] Rogers, *Perfect Being Theology*, 14.

immutability and simplicity, his view of an atemporal God is as strong or as dubious as the Neoplatonic foundations."[65]

In this regard, many philosophers and theologians note that, as Thomas Morris puts it, the view of divine timelessness "derives ultimately from pre-Christian philosophical sources," such as "Parmenides" and later, "Plotinus" and "the Neo-Platonists."[66] According to Michael Rea and Louis P. Pojman, "The notion of timeless eternity first appears in Parmenides's poem 'The Way of Truth.'" Parmenides "denied the reality of time" and "the concept of the timeless eternal was further developed by Plato in the dialogue *Timaeus*," which "deeply influenced the early Church, and through Augustine and Boethius the doctrine of eternity (as timelessness) made its way into Christian thought" and was "embraced by Anselm, Aquinas, Luther, Calvin, and the vast majority of theologians."[67]

Rogers notes, in this regard, "some contemporary philosophers of religion accuse the doctrine" of divine timelessness "of being 'non-biblical' and, even worse, 'Greek' or 'Platonic'" (see the discussion in Chapter 2).[68] Helm maintains, however, that though "it is undoubtedly true that the classical formulas of orthodox trinitarianism owe much to the language of Greek metaphysics" and "perhaps Neo-Platonism influenced the way *eternalism* is formulated and expressed, it would be hasty to suppose that the use of such language signals a takeover of biblical ideas by pagan ideas."[69] The dispute regarding divine timelessness in relation to the biblical data is briefly surveyed later in this chapter.

In keeping with the traditional views surveyed above, many classical theists maintain that God must be atemporal because, in Roger's words, "being temporal is being limited" and, thus, imperfect.[70] She avers, "a God who is temporal and mutable" cannot be a maximally perfect being.[71] Whereas humans "cannot 'possess' all of our lives at once," God can.[72] Yet, if God were

---

[65]Garrett DeWeese, *God and the Nature of Time* (Burlington, VT: Ashgate, 2004), 133. DeWeese believes that Augustine's commitment to divine "atemporality" is "rooted not in biblical exegesis, but in the doctrines of divine simplicity and immutability." *God and the Nature of Time*, 110.
[66]Morris, *Our Idea of God*, 122.
[67]Rea and Pojman, "Classical Theistic Attributes: Introduction," in *Philosophy of Religion: An Anthology*, 7th ed, ed. Michael Rea and Louis P. Pojman (Stamford, CT: Cengage, 2015), 79. See, also, Alan Padgett, *God, Eternity, and the Nature of Time* (Eugene, OR: Wipf & Stock, 2000), 38–55. For a brief, helpful introduction to the relationship between classical philosophy and theology, see Diogenes Allen and Eric O. Springsted, *Philosophy for Understanding Theology*, 2nd ed. (Louisville, KY: Westminster John Knox, 2007), 1–112.
[68]Rogers, *Perfect Being Theology*, 64.
[69]Helm, "Divine Timeless Eternity," 32.
[70]Rogers, *Perfect Being Theology*, 58.
[71]Rogers, *Perfect Being Theology*, 54–55.
[72]Rogers, *Perfect Being Theology*, 56.

temporal, even "though God may infallibly and vividly remember his past, those bits of his life that he remembers are over."[73] Such a view, Helm avers, "is incompatible with God's fullness and self-sufficiency" as well as with "divine sovereignty" and "divine perfection."[74] Indeed, Helm comments that "all" of "the theological attractions of timelessness" might "be said to rest" on an "intuition," namely "the idea of the divine fullness or self-sufficiency."[75]

Debating the nature of time

In this and other regards, much of the debate hinges on the nature of time itself, especially regarding "what moments of time exist."[76] Does the present alone exist? Do the past and/or future also exist? People tend to intuitively believe that only the present exists. The past is gone—it no longer exists—and the future does not yet exist. This view is known as presentism. On this view, things may come into existence and pass out of existence but "the only objects that exist are the ones that presently exist."[77]

This view stands in contrast to eternalism, which holds that the past, present, and future all exist and there is no privileged time that is objectively "now." Here, the past, present, and future "are all equally real."[78] Time is typically thought of as a "four-dimensional spacetime manifold" or block; time being the fourth dimension added to the three spatial dimensions (height, length, and width). In this space–time block, there is "no privileged moment that marks the present."[79] Further, on this block theory of time, "there is no real passage of time because all moments of time exist. Nothing ever comes into existence nor ceases to exist."[80] The human experience of the succession of time as past, present, and future is "usually explained as just a subjective illusion of human consciousness."[81]

---

[73]Helm, "Divine Timeless Eternity," 30.
[74]Helm, "Divine Timeless Eternity," 30, 31.
[75]Helm, "Divine Timeless Eternity," 29.
[76]Mullins, *End of the Timeless God*, 25.
[77]Mullins, *End of the Timeless God*, 26.
[78]Mullins, *End of the Timeless God*, 26.
[79]Mullins, *End of the Timeless God*, 27.
[80]Mullins, *End of the Timeless God*, 27.
[81]William Lane Craig, "Timelessness and Omnitemporality," in *God & Time: Four Views*, ed. Gregory E. Ganssle (Downers Grove, IL: InterVarsity Press, 2001), 133. Cf. Mullins, *End of the Timeless God*, 27.

Alternatively, some affirm the growing block theory of time. On this version of the spacetime block theory, the present *and* past exist, but the future does not yet exist. Here, time "is dynamic in the sense that new things really do come into existence as new time slices are added to the four-dimensional spacetime manifold."[82]

Relative to theology, the debate usually focuses on presentism versus eternalism. The debate is rather complex but, for the purposes of this book, it is sufficient to note that much of the debate between presentists and eternalists hinges upon whether "tensed" statements express something that is a genuine feature of reality that cannot be expressed by "tenseless" statements.[83] That is, there has been considerable debate over whether the so-called tensed statement, "today John is writing on theories of time" expresses something that is a genuine feature of reality that cannot be expressed by the so-called tenseless statement, "on January 24, 2018 John writes on theories of time."

Further, "Most contemporary discussions on God and time hold that presentism is incompatible with divine timelessness, whereas eternalism is compatible with timelessness."[84] As such, contemporary advocates of divine timelessness tend to adopt eternalism. As Katherin Rogers puts it, the claim that "all of time is 'present' to God entails a particular theory of time." Indeed, she maintains, the "classic doctrine of eternity" entails "eternalism," which is "the view that the past and future are as real as the present, as opposed to presentism, the view that only the present actually exists."[85]

Rogers might be right that divine timelessness entails eternalism. However, Mullins maintains that whereas the classical Christian tradition affirms divine timelessness, the common claim that "classical theologians" affirmed "eternalism" is "anachronistic."[86] On the contrary, Mullins argues, "Presentism is the classical Christian position."[87] According to Mullins,

---

[82] Mullins, *End of the Timeless God*, 27.

[83] Sometimes presentism is conflated with what is called the "A" or "tensed" theory of time and eternalism is identified with the so-called "B" or "tenseless" theory of time. However, Mullins argues that these should not be conflated because the A and B theories do not entail a particular ontology of time. See Mullins, *End of the Timeless God*, 19–30. Cf. J. M. E. McTaggart, "Time," in *Metaphysics: Contemporary Readings*, ed. Michael J. Loux, 2nd ed. (New York: Routledge, 2008), 350–61.

[84] Mullins, *End of the Timeless God*, 30. However, Mullins himself argues that even eternalism is incompatible with timelessness. See below.

[85] Rogers, *Perfect Being Theology*, 59.

[86] Mullins, *End of the Timeless God*, 75.

[87] Mullins, *End of the Timeless God*, 75. Cf. DeWeese, *God and the Nature of Time*, 114–16.

presentism was the "traditional" view "amongst Christian theologians throughout Church history," held by such luminaries as Augustine, Boethius, Anselm, Thomas Aquinas, and others.[88] Indeed, Mullins maintains, "It is not clear that anyone prior to the nineteenth century actually held the view that all times are literally present to God."[89] If Mullins is right about the history and if divine timelessness is incompatible with presentism—as even most contemporary advocates of divine timelessness believe it is—there is an apparent contradiction in the (majority) traditional view.[90] If this is so, the Christian theist who wishes to maintain internal coherence will have to break with the tradition with respect to divine timelessness or presentism (or both).

Beyond the typical atemporalist position, some thinkers have attempted to find a way to coherently maintain what they believe is the traditional medieval view of the eternal present as "not instantaneous but extended."[91] Eleonore Stump and Norman Kretzmann argue for something they called E-T simultaneity, wherein God's eternal existence is characterized as "a duration without succession."[92] This view distinguishes between what Stump and Kretzmann call eternal simultaneity and temporal simultaneity and articulates divine timelessness "in terms of presentness that is in some sense simultaneous with the events of the creation."[93] Here, God somehow has an "atemporal" and yet "extensive mode of existence."[94]

Rogers argues, however, "It is not possible to make sense of a timeless duration."[95] In later work, Stump and Kretzmann have clarified that they mean "duration" only as an analogy. Yet, even so, many have wondered just how to make sense of this position. The arguments in this regard are rather technical and sometimes opaque so, for our purposes, it suffices to note that some defend this option or something like it, but many advocates and critics of divine timelessness believe arguments in this direction are unpersuasive, and

---

[88]Mullins, *End of the Timeless God*, 74.
[89]Mullins, *End of the Timeless God*, 84.
[90]Mullins, *End of the Timeless God*, 30.
[91]Eleonore Stump and Norman Kretzmann, "Eternity," in *The Concept of God*, ed. Thomas V. Morris (New York: Oxford University Press, 1987), 225.
[92]Stump and Kretzmann, "Eternity," 225.
[93]Helm, "Divine Timeless Eternity," 36. That is, "any eternal event is ET-simultaneous with any temporal event." Helm, "Divine Timeless Eternity," 36.
[94]Stump-Kretzmann, "Atemporal Duration: A Reply to Fitzgerald," *Journal of Philosophy* 84 (1987): 215.
[95]Rogers, *Perfect Being Theology*, 58. Cf. Rogers, "Eternity Has No Duration," 1–16.

perhaps incoherent.[96] Mullins claims, for instance, that Stump and Kretzmann's "ET-Simultaneity model" is "widely regarded as explanatorily vacuous."[97]

God as timeless *and* not timeless?

Some maintain that God is somehow both atemporal and temporal. On this view, God is conceived as being outside of time, or timeless, and yet entering into time (temporal). This view is often set forth in popular conceptions of the relationship between God and time. As William Lane Craig notes, "Oftimes laypeople, anxious to affirm both God's transcendence and God's immanence, assert that God is both timeless and temporal. But in the absence of some sort of model or explanation of how this can be the case, this assertion is flatly self-contradictory and so cannot be true. One cannot affirm both."[98]

Although Craig and many others contend that atemporality and temporality are contradictory, some theologians do affirm both, apparently motivated by a desire to affirm the traditional language relative to divine timelessness while also affirming that God enters into time and space. For instance, Bruce Ware asks: "Must God be viewed exclusively as timeless or exclusively as temporal?"[99] He contends that there may be "good reason to consider a model of God's relation to time in which both, in different senses, are true."[100] Ware maintains that "we can understand God's relation to time as comprising both his atemporal existence in himself *(in se)* apart from creation, and his 'omnitemporal' existence in relation to the created order he has made *(in re)*."[101]

---

[96]Brian Leftow offers an alternative view of atemporal duration, which he calls quasi-temporal eternity (QTE). See Leftow, *Time and Eternity* (Ithaca, NY: Cornell University Press, 1991), 120–22. On Leftow's proposal, the "life of a being with QTE is an extension in which positions are ordered as earlier and later. Yet none of it 'passes away' or is 'yet to come,' as we think happens with temporal lives." Leftow, *Time*, 120. However, some consider Leftow's view "self-contradictory," particularly the claim that "QTE is an extension that has no proper parts and is indivisible, but is nevertheless an extension in which points are ordered as earlier and later." Helm, "Divine Timeless Eternity," 37.

[97]Mullins, *End of the Timeless God*, 107n12. This is the judgment of William Lane Craig in "Timelessness and Omnitemporality," 142. Further, Helm writes: "Not only are these ideas of Stump and Kretzmann difficult to grasp, there is reason to think that the modification they propose to the classical idea of divine timelessness is not actually coherent." Helm, "Divine Timeless Eternity," 37.

[98]Craig, "Timelessness and Omnitemporality," 129.

[99]Bruce Ware, "A Modified Calvinist Doctrine of God," in *Perspectives on the Doctrine of God: Four Views*, ed. Bruce Ware (Nashville, TN: B & H, 2008), 87.

[100]Ware, "Modified Calvinist," 87.

[101]Ware, "Modified Calvinist," 88. Cf. Lister, *God Is Impassible and Impassioned*, 226–30.

In Ware's view, "At creation God became both omnipresent and omnitemporal, while remaining, in himself and apart from creation, fully nonspatial and timelessly eternal."[102] Ware contends that God might be "both transcendent in his eternal nonspatial and atemporal existence independent of everything created, and immanent in his omnipresent and omnitemporal inhabiting of everything created."[103] Similarly, Horton maintains that "God is omnitemporal in the way that he is omnipresent." That is, "God's transcendence of time is the very presupposition of his presence in every creaturely moment."[104] Further, while "God transcends time and space, he enters both freely," though "even enters must be understood analogically, since God is already present in every moment and permeates every place."[105]

John Frame makes a similar case for what he calls "temporal omnipresence," maintaining that God is present in all space and time.[106] As Frame puts it, "God not only *works* in time, but is also *present* in time, at all times."[107] For Frame, divine eternity "does not primarily mean that God is 'outside' time (though it is better to say that he is 'outside' than that he is 'inside'), but rather that he is present in time as the Lord, with full control over the temporal sequence."[108] Frame argues that "God is indeed temporal in his immanence, but that he is (most likely) atemporal in his transcendence. He exists in time as he exists throughout creation. But he also (I say with some reservations) exists beyond time, as he exists beyond creation."[109] On this view, God is both "immanent in time" and "also transcendent over time, in the sense of having an atemporal existence."[110] That is, "God is the Lord *in* time as well as the Lord *above* time."[111] So, Frame avers, "God is temporal after all, but not merely temporal. He really exists in time, but he also transcends time in such a way as to exist outside it."[112]

Distinct from views like those of Ware, Horton, and Frame, some would classify Karl Barth as holding a view that transcends the dichotomy

---

[102] Ware, "Modified Calvinist," 89.
[103] Ware, "Modified Calvinist," 89.
[104] Michael Horton, *The Christian Faith* (Grand Rapids, MI: Zondervan, 2011), 255.
[105] Horton, *Christian Faith*, 256.
[106] John Frame, *The Doctrine of God* (Phillipsburg, NJ: P&R, 2002), 547.
[107] Frame, *Doctrine of God*, 558 (emphasis original).
[108] Frame, *Doctrine of God*, 543.
[109] Frame, *Doctrine of God*, 549.
[110] Frame, *Doctrine of God*, 551.
[111] Frame, *Doctrine of God*, 559 (emphasis original).
[112] Frame, *Doctrine of God*, 559.

of temporality and timelessness. According to Christophe Chalamet, for instance, Karl Barth maintains that God is "both timeless *and* temporal" in a way that is unique to God.[113] However, as is the case with most significant theological issues, Barthian scholars disagree on how to understand Barth's dialectical view.[114] For his part, Mullins thinks Barth's view is inconsistent, what he calls "the Barthian blunder." He interprets Barth as "explicitly reject[ing] the doctrine of divine timelessness" and yet "affirm[ing] a doctrine of divine eternality that is indistinguishable from divine timelessness."[115]

Others have also advocated for a third way between timelessness and temporality, though just what this means is often unclear. For instance, F. LeRon Shults wants to move beyond the "antinomy of divine timelessness" and beyond claims that God is "essentially outside of time or inside of time."[116] Yet, Mullins contends: "When it comes to whether God is temporal or atemporal, there simply is no third way. The two positions are logically contradictory."[117] If timelessness or atemporality means to lack temporal succession and temporality means to have temporal succession then to hold both that God is atemporal and temporal is contradictory. "God cannot have succession in His life and lack succession in His life. That is a straightforward contradiction. Further, we can see that there is not a third way between having succession and lacking succession."[118]

Some theologians who seem to affirm both divine atemporality and temporality might mean by such language that God is not related to time as creatures are and not temporal in the way that creatures are. Yet, this is distinct from what strict classical theists mean by divine atemporality and timelessness and using such terms of negation introduces confusion. One way that might be less confusing—and might avoid what many see as a self-contradictory position—is to say that God is *neither* atemporal nor temporal

---

[113]See, for example, Christophe Chalamet, "No Timelessness in God. On Differing Interpretations of Karl Barth's Theology of Eternity, Time, and Election," *Zeitschrift für Dialektische Theologie* 4 (2010): 26. Cf. Karl Barth, *Church Dogmatics*, ed. Geoffrey W. Bromiley and T. F. Torrance (Edinburgh: T&T Clark, 1957), 2/1, 608–40.

[114]See, for example, Chalamet, "No Timelessness in God. On Differing Interpretations of Karl Barth's Theology of Eternity, Time, and Election," 21–37.

[115]Mullins, *End of the Timeless God*, xvii. See Karl Barth, *Church Dogmatics*, ed. Geoffrey W. Bromiley and T. F. Torrance (Edinburgh: T&T Clark, 1960), 3/2, 438–39.

[116]F. LeRon Shults, *Reforming the Doctrine of God* (Grand Rapids, MI: Eerdmans, 2005), 267. Cf. 267–73. Cf. Eunsoo Kim, *Time, Eternity, and the Trinity: A Trinitarian Analogical Understanding of Time and Eternity* (Eugene, OR: Pickwick, 2010).

[117]Mullins, *End of the Timeless God*, xvi.

[118]Mullins, *End of the Timeless God*, xvi.

in the way that creatures are, meaning that God's being is not incompatible with entering into time and space (without being encompassed by it)—and thus not atemporal—and that God's being is also not restricted by time or temporal in the way that humans are (i.e., God is not univocally temporal). Yet, this would seem to amount to a denial of timelessness as strict classical theism understands it and would seem to amount to some species of divine temporality, understood analogically.

Divine temporality

Many contemporary theologians and philosophers maintain that God is not timeless but is everlasting, or sempiternal. On this view, God has always existed and always will exist. God experiences temporal succession and interacts with the world in a temporal fashion. Here, it is crucial to distinguish between that which is "temporal" and that which is "temporary." On this view, God is not temporary but everlastingly eternal. There is, however, a diversity of views regarding the nature of divine temporality, situated in various approaches to the doctrine of God. Proponents of some form of divine temporality include process theists, open theists, and many moderate classical theists, which depart significantly from one another regarding the doctrine of God more broadly.

Despite their differences, the advocates of divine temporality discussed here agree that God is everlastingly eternal. That is, God has no beginning and no end, but God does experience temporal succession. As R.T. Mullins puts it, the "life of a temporal God is characterized by a succession of moments. In other words, a temporal God has a before and after in His life. He experiences one moment of time after another." Here, "God is temporal if and only if God exists (i) without beginning, (ii) without end, and (iii) with succession."[119]

Process theists summarily reject divine timelessness and maintain that God is utterly temporal. The world itself is an eternal part of God's being and all reality is a temporal process wherein the future does not yet exist. Open theists likewise reject divine timelessness, maintaining—along with process theists—that such a view "offers a static, inert, and aloof God who in no way resembles the dynamic, personal God of the Bible."[120] As the influential

---

[119]Mullins, *End of the Timeless God*, xvi.
[120]Mullins, *End of the Timeless God*, 22. See, further, the discussion between process and open theists in David Ray Griffin, John B. Cobb, and Clark H. Pinnock, eds., *Searching for an Adequate God: A Dialogue between Process and Free Will Theists* (Grand Rapids, MI: Eerdmans, 2000).

open theist Clark Pinnock put it: "The God of the Bible is not timeless."[121] However, many open theists sharply distinguish their concept of God from that of process theology. Whereas process theists and open theists agree that God cannot know the future free decisions of creatures (see Chapter 4), many open theists depart from process theism by maintaining (among other things) that God is not *essentially* related to the world, the world is not eternal but God freely chose to create the world out of nothing (ex nihilo), and God is omnipotent in the traditional sense (see Chapter 5).[122]

Distinct from process and open theism, Ronald Nash has noted that numerous "classical theists" have found "a reinterpretation of God's relationship to time compatible with other elements of their conception of God." For instance, Stephen Davis argues, a temporal God "can still be immutable in the sense of remaining ever true to his promises and purposes and eternally retaining his essential nature" and, contrary to process and open theism, God "can still have complete knowledge of all past, present and future events" (see the discussion of this last point in the next chapter).[123] So many theists affirm divine temporality that Helm even claimed at the turn of the century that "most theologians and philosophers of religion think that God is in time," affirming "temporalism."[124]

Among these, Davis maintains that God "is a temporal being. Past, present and future are real to him; he has simultaneity and succession in his states, acts and knowledge."[125] On Davis's view, God "has temporal location" and "he has temporal extension."[126] Conversely, Davis argues, "a timeless being cannot be the Christian God" and "the notion of a timeless being is probably incoherent."[127] Whether incoherent or not, Davis believes "a timeless being cannot be the personal, caring, involved God we read about in the Bible. The God of the Bible is, above all, a God who cares deeply about what happens in history."[128]

---

[121] Clark Pinnock, "Systematic Theology," in *The Openness of God: A Biblical Challenge to the Traditional Understanding of God* (Downers Grove, IL: InterVarsity, 1994), 121.

[122] See, for example, Richard Rice, "Process Theism and the Open View of God: The Crucial Difference," in *Searching for an Adequate God*, 163–200. One notable exception is Tom Oord, who is closer to process theism than open theists such as Clark Pinnock, William Hasker, Greg Boyd, John Sanders, and Richard Rice.

[123] Davis, "Temporal Eternity," 89.

[124] Helm, "Divine Timeless Eternity," 28.

[125] Davis, "Temporal Eternity," 89.

[126] Davis, "Temporal Eternity," 89.

[127] Davis, "Temporal Eternity," 84.

[128] Davis, "Temporal Eternity," 86.

William Lane Craig similarly argues that "God is (present tense) in time."[129] That is, "God, as a personal being, has experientially a past, a present, and a future."[130] Indeed, Craig maintains, "In virtue of his real, causal relation to the temporal world, God must minimally undergo extrinsic change and therefore be temporal—at least since the moment of creation."[131] That is, "If God is really related to the world," as Craig affirms, then "simply in virtue of his being related to changing things ... there would exist a *before* and *after* in God's life."[132] John Feinberg adds, "A God who changes his relationship with a repentant sinner incorporates a sequence in his handling of that person, but that sequence necessitates time and so rules out atemporalism."[133]

Richard Swinburne has also made a case that God is everlasting. On Swinburne's view, God "exists now, he has existed at each period of past time, he will exist at each period of future time."[134] This, he believes, is "the view explicit or implicit in Old and New Testaments and in virtually all the writings of the Fathers of the first three centuries."[135] In this regard, temporalists often note that Scripture portrays God as acting sequentially. As Tom Morris puts it, God "speaks to Abram, and then later he speaks to Moses. He sends his Son, becoming incarnate in the world, and later he pours out his Spirit. He creates and then he saves. This is sequence and succession. If it is succession *within* the life of God, God is a temporal being."[136]

Similarly, Nicholas Wolterstorff argues that "God is represented in Scripture as One who has a history of acting and responding."[137] The "God of Scripture is One of whom a narrative can be told" and "an implication of this

---

[129] William Lane Craig, "Response to Nicholas Wolterstorff," in *God and Time: Four Views*, ed. Gregory Ganssle (Downers Grove, IL: InterVarsity, 2001), 222.

[130] William Lane Craig, "Divine Eternity," in *The Oxford Handbook of Philosophical Theology*, ed. Thomas P. Flint and Michael C. Rea (New York: Oxford University Press, 2009), 146.

[131] J.P. Moreland and William Lane Craig, *Philosophical Foundations for a Christian Worldview* (Downers Grove, IL: IVP Academic, 2003), 527.

[132] Moreland and Craig, *Philosophical Foundations*, 512.

[133] John S. Feinberg, *No One Like Him: The Doctrine of God* (Wheaton, IL: Crossway, 2001), 432. For this and many other reasons, Feinberg adopts temporalism.

[134] Richard Swinburne, *The Christian God* (New York: Clarendon, 1994), 37. Cf. other advocates of divine temporality such as J.R. Lucas, *The Future: An Essay on God, Temporality, and Truth* (Cambridge, MA: Blackwell, 1989), 213; Garrett DeWeese, *God and the Nature of Time* (Burlington, VT: Ashgate, 2004); Dean Zimmerman, "God inside Time and before Creation," in *God and Time: Essays on the Divine Nature*, ed. Gregory E. Ganssle and David M. Woodruff (New York: Oxford University Press, 2002), 75-94.

[135] Swinburne, *The Christian God*, 138.

[136] Morris, *Our Idea of God*, 125-126.

[137] Wolterstorff, *Inquiring about God: Selected Essays*, 157.

is that God is in time. If something has a history then perforce that being is in time."[138] It is "typical of Scripture's representation of God" that "God responds to what transpires in human affairs by performing a succession of actions, including actions of speaking."[139] This implies "that there's change in God's life; if a person does one thing at one time and a different thing at a later time, then there's change in that person's life."[140] A striking example of this is the incarnation, "an orthodox understanding of" which Wolterstorff believes is not "compatible" with timelessness.[141]

Wolterstorff argues that "God the Redeemer is a God who changes. And any being that changes is a being among whose states there is temporal succession."[142] Despite atemporalist claims to the contrary, Wolterstorff believes that it follows from divine timelessness "that none of God's actions is a response to what we human beings do; indeed, not only is none of God's *actions* a response to what we do, but nothing at all in God's life is a response to what occurs among God's creatures."[143] This hinges upon what "constitutes genuine response on God's part."[144] As Wolterstorff defines it: "If I respond to what someone does, then I do something later than, and on account of, another person's having done something."[145]

Put simply, Wolterstorff argues, "God does have a history" and "God *accordingly is* not timeless."[146] Alan Padgett concurs, saying: "The biblical God has a history, and this means that God is temporal."[147] Given this, Wolterstorff believes, "A theology that opts for God as [timelessly] eternal cannot be a theology faithful to the biblical witness."[148] In this regard, Wolterstorff maintains, "The patterns of classical Greek thought are incompatible with the pattern of biblical thought."[149]

---

[138] Wolterstorff, *Inquiring about God*, 158.
[139] Wolterstorff, *Inquiring about God*, 158.
[140] Wolterstorff, *Inquiring about God*, 158.
[141] Wolterstorff, *Inquiring about God*, 178.
[142] Wolterstorff, *Inquiring about God*, 134.
[143] Wolterstorff, *Inquiring about God*, 174 (emphasis original).
[144] Nicholas Wolterstorff, "Response to Critics," in *God and Time: Four Views*, ed. Gregory Ganssle (Downers Grove, IL: InterVarsity, 2001), 232.
[145] Wolterstorff, "Response to Critics," 232.
[146] Wolterstorff, *Inquiring about God*, 163.
[147] Alan Padgett, "Response to Wolterstorff," in *God and Time: Four Views*, ed. Gregory Ganssle (Downers Grove, IL: InterVarsity, 2001), 219.
[148] Wolterstorff, *Inquiring about God*, 134.
[149] Wolterstorff, *Inquiring about God*, 134.

Temporalists tend to agree that "a proper understanding of God's action vis-a-vis the creation implies that God is temporal," and "that a proper understanding of God's knowledge implies that God is temporal."[150] Regarding this, William Lane Craig argues that if God "is Creator of a temporal world," as Craig believes he is, then God "is temporal."[151] This is because: "If God is creatively active in the temporal world, God is really related to the temporal world." And, "If God is really related to the world, God is temporal."[152] This hinges, however, on whether there is a *temporal* world. Temporalists typically affirm presentism—the view that only the present exists—and most believe that "God is a temporal being who endures through time."[153] Given presentism, William Lane Craig avers, "it follows from God's creative activity in the temporal world and his complete knowledge of it that God is temporal. God quite literally exists now." That is, if God is presently and continually sustaining a temporal world and possesses knowledge of a continually changing world as it changes, it follows that God is temporal.

In this vein, R. T. Mullins makes an extensive case that "the Christian God cannot be timeless" and develops "an account of God's temporality from a presentist ontology of time."[154] On his view, "God does have a before and after in His life."[155] Yet, Mullins maintains, "even if eternalism is the correct theory of time, God cannot be regarded as timeless."[156] Mullins argues (among other things) that "divine timelessness is metaphysically impossible given that God has created a temporal universe. It does not matter which theory of time one holds. We know that God has created a temporal universe and that He causally sustains this universe and interacts in it, and as such God must be temporal."[157] Further, he argues that "divine timelessness is not compatible with the ecumenical model of the incarnation. One must pick either divine timelessness or the incarnation."[158] Relative to these and other issues, Mullins contends that "theologians and philosophers should abandon the divine timeless research program because it is unworkable and

---

[150] Wolterstorff, "Response to William Lane Craig," in *God and Time: Four Views*, ed. Gregory Ganssle (Downers Grove, IL: InterVarsity, 2001), 171.
[151] Craig, "Timelessness and Omnitemporality," 141.
[152] Craig, "Timelessness and Omnitemporality," 141.
[153] Mullins, *End of the Timeless God*, 31.
[154] Mullins, *End of the Timeless God*, 195, 196.
[155] Mullins, *End of the Timeless God*, 32.
[156] Mullins, *End of the Timeless God*, 196.
[157] Mullins, *End of the Timeless God*, 155.
[158] Mullins, *End of the Timeless God*, 194.

devastating to Christian theology."¹⁵⁹ In his view, "Christians should feel no worries about giving up divine timelessness in order to be faithful to the explicit teachings of scripture."¹⁶⁰

Critics of temporalism, however, often argue that to say God is temporal is to limit God. For instance, Thomas Williams contends that, as timeless, God's "life is not marked by gain and loss in the way that a time-bound being's life is, part of his life having slipped away into an unrecoverable past" and "only this tiny sliver of a 'now' present and accessible to him."¹⁶¹ However, Craig asks, why should we assume that "timeless life" is "the most perfect mode of existence of a perfect person"?¹⁶² Craig maintains there is some evidence that temporal succession enriches one's life, for example, the temporal passage required in music. Further, since God's life has no beginning and no end and God can perfectly and vividly recall the past such that "his experience of the past remains as vivid as ever," the assumption that God might experience some undesirable longing for the past seems unwarranted.¹⁶³ As Ganssle notes, human "regrets about the passage of time are closely tied to our finitude" and mortality, including "dim and inaccurate" memory and the ubiquity of death, which would not be the case for God.¹⁶⁴

Whereas some critics contend that a temporal God is somehow a "prisoner" of time, Swinburne avers, "although God and time exist together—God is a temporal being—those aspects of time which seem so threatening to his sovereignty only occur through his own voluntary choice. To the extent to which he is time's prisoner, he has chosen to be so. It is God, not time, who calls the shots," such that God is not a "prisoner" of time at all.¹⁶⁵

Further, some temporalists maintain that the timeless view itself limits God in significant ways. Davis comments, "Not even a timelessly eternal God is free of all temporal limitations, for he is actually unable to experience 'before' or 'after.' His nature [as timeless] limits him; he is unable to experience such things, for if he did experience them he would be temporal. There is temporal limitation whichever view we take."¹⁶⁶ If God is atemporal,

---

[159] Mullins, *End of the Timeless God*, 209.
[160] Mullins, *End of the Timeless God*, 194.
[161] Williams, "Classical Theism," 96.
[162] Craig, "Timelessness and Omnitemporality," 136.
[163] Craig, "Timelessness and Omnitemporality," 135.
[164] Ganssle, "Introduction," 23.
[165] Swinburne, *The Christian God*, 140.
[166] Davis, "Temporal Eternity," 89.

he cannot know that *today* is May 3, 2018 or that the crucifixion is *now* in the past, but a temporal God can. Further, an atemporal God is limited by being incompatible with succession and thus unable to do or enjoy anything that requires temporal succession. As Clark Pinnock puts it, "Timelessness limits God. If he were timeless," then God would "have no real relationship with people."[167]

Yet, God's relation to time is different than that of creatures. To distinguish God's temporality from that of creatures some theologians refer to divine temporality as *analogical* temporality.[168] In this regard, Pinnock maintains, "God is not temporal as creatures are."[169] God "can enter into time and relate to sequence and history," yet God is not "exhaustively in time" but "God transcends our experience of time, is immune from the ravages of time, is free from our inability to remember, and so forth."[170] Morris adds, "To say that God is a temporal being is not to say that he exists within the bounds of Eastern Standard Time or Daylight Savings Time. It is only to say that he is a being whose life encompasses successive states."[171] Here, time is not thought of as a container that envelopes God but as a (partial) descriptor of God's dynamic life, including God's experiences such as pleasure and displeasure, delight and grief, joy and sorrow, passion and compassion. A temporal God can experience new things such that, as T.F. Torrance states, "the creation of the world out of nothing is something *new even for God*. God was always Father, but he *became* Creator."[172] In Torrance's view, "far from being a static or inertial Deity like some 'unmoved mover,'" God "is absolutely free to do what he had never done before, and free to be other than he was eternally: to be Almighty Creator, and even to become incarnate as a creature within his creation, while nevertheless remaining eternally the God that he always was."[173]

In this regard, many temporalists emphasize a distinction between created and uncreated time and/or between physical and metaphysical time. For example, Torrance distinguishes "the uncreated Time of God and the created

---

[167]Pinnock, "Systematic Theology," 121.
[168]See, for example, Fernando Canale, *Basic Elements of Christian Theology* (Berrien Springs, MI: Andrews University Lithotech, 2005), 71. Cf. Thomas F. Torrance, *The Christian Doctrine of God: One Being Three Persons* (London: T&T Clark, 2016), 220, 241.
[169]Pinnock, "Systematic Theology," 121.
[170]Pinnock, "Systematic Theology," 121, 120.
[171]Morris, *Our Idea of God*, 125–26.
[172]Torrance, *The Christian Doctrine of God*, 208.
[173]Torrance, *The Christian Doctrine of God*, 208.

time of our world."[174] Mullins defines created, or physical time, as having the following features: "physical time began to exist" at creation, "physical time can be measured," and "the physical time of one universe cannot relate to a separate physical universe and its time series."[175] Conversely, uncreated or "metaphysical time never came into existence."[176] On some understandings, physical time is temporal succession as creatures know and experience it and metaphysical time is God's time apart from the physical world.

Here, some temporalists maintain that "metaphysical time cannot be measured because it lacks an intrinsic metric."[177] On this view: "Prior to the creation of the world God exists without beginning and end in an unmetricated time."[178] On this view, there is a genuinely temporal "before" creation but it is temporality of a kind that is not temporality as humans experience it. Padgett, along with a number of philosophers associated with Oxford (sometimes called the Oxford school of divine temporality), argues extensively for this view.[179] As Padgett puts it, "God is the Lord of Time" and "God is beyond space-time, beyond time as we know it."[180] As such, "God is both transcendent relative to time and immanent within time. God both transcends history, providing the very possibility of historical existence; and is within history, especially but not only in the incarnation of the Word."[181]

In this regard, Padgett states "Anything that has a history is temporal" but "not everything that is temporal has a history."[182] Despite explicitly affirming that God is temporal, Padgett refers to his view, somewhat confusingly, as "relative timelessness." By "relative timelessness," he means that "God is the Creator of our (physical, measured) time; that in contrast to our time, God's eternity is infinite and immeasurable and finally that God's time is dependent on God's Being, not the other way around."[183] As such, divine eternity "cannot be measured by our time."[184] Rather, "Our time takes place

---

[174] Torrance, *The Christian God*, 220.
[175] Mullins, *End of the Timeless God*, 33.
[176] Mullins, *End of the Timeless God*, 35.
[177] Mullins, *End of the Timeless God*, 35.
[178] Mullins, *End of the Timeless God*, 35.
[179] Padgett, *God, Eternity, and the Nature of Time*, 122–36. Cf. Swinburne, *The Christian God*, 72–95.
[180] Padgett, "Response to Wolterstorff," 220.
[181] Padgett, "Response to Wolterstorff," 220.
[182] Padgett, "Response to Wolterstorff," 220.
[183] Alan Padgett, "Eternity as Relative Timelessness," in *God and Time: Four Views*, ed. Gregory Ganssle (Downers Grove, IL: InterVarsity, 2001), 108.
[184] Padgett, "Eternity," 107. Cf. Zimmerman, "God inside Time and before Creation," 75–94.

within (and only because of the prior existence of) God's own time."[185] This view explicitly protects the transcendence of God, the sovereignty of God, and the Creator–creature distinction, maintaining that "nothing takes place outside of the divine will," that God "is not limited or changed in any fundamental way by the passage of time, and that God is a metaphysically necessary Being who lives forever and ever."[186]

While agreeing in many respects, Craig differs from Padgett's view that time is intrinsic to the divine life. Craig maintains instead that God created time and that "'before' creation," God was "atemporal."[187] On his view: "With the creation of the universe, time began, and God entered into time at the moment of creation in virtue of his real relations with the created order."[188] As such, God "is timeless without creation and temporal subsequent to creation."[189] Craig calls this view omnitemporality (not to be confused with Ware and Frame's use of the term referenced earlier) because it maintains that "God exists at every time that ever exists."[190]

Craig thinks divine omnitemporality is preferable to other views of divine temporality because it avoids the problem "of an infinite, empty time prior to creation," which he thinks amounts to absurdity because it would be impossible to traverse an infinite amount of time to arrive at today.[191] Padgett thinks this problem is overcome if God's time is "amorphous" or "unmetricated" time.[192] However, Craig thinks this view does not work to avoid "the difficulties of an infinite past" because he thinks it still requires an infinite number of "temporal intervals."[193] Padgett, conversely, thinks that Craig's "criticisms" are "wide of the mark" and that in "unchanging, perfect eternity" as Padgett views it, before the first change, "*there cannot be temporal intervals*."[194]

In contrast to some process and other views wherein the world is eternally part of God's being, Padgett and Craig are representative of many temporalists who maintain that *physical* time is not intrinsic to God's being.

---

[185]Padgett, "Eternity," 107.
[186]Padgett, "Eternity," 108.
[187]Craig, "Timelessness and Omnitemporality," 132.
[188]Craig, "Timelessness and Omnitemporality," 156.
[189]Moreland and Craig, *Philosophical Foundations*, 515.
[190]Craig, "Timelessness and Omnitemporality," 153.
[191]Craig "Timeless and Omnitemporality," 153.
[192]See Padgett, "Response to Craig," 166–69.
[193]Craig, "Timelessness and Omnitemporality," 157.
[194]Padgett, "Response to Craig," 167.

Both admit, however, that their views about *how* this is so involve speculation and go beyond what is explicitly supported by Scripture. Accordingly, some temporalists refrain from confident judgments regarding God's relationship to time (or lack thereof) "prior to" or without the world. In this regard, Wolterstorff notes that he, Padgett, and Craig all agree "that God's existence *with crea*tion is temporal."[195] Padgett maintains that, though God created *physical* time, "God is temporal" in a uniquely divine, non-metricated and immeasurable fashion prior to and without the world.[196] Craig maintains that God was "timeless without the universe" and now is "temporal with the universe."[197] Wolterstorff, however, holds "no settled view" regarding God's relationship to time prior to creation and "find[s] the considerations either way indecisive."[198] There is, then, considerable agreement among many Christian theists that God is temporal but, among moderate classical theists and others who maintain that God is *not* essentially related to the world, there is a diversity of views regarding God's relation to time without the world.

Some biblical data relevant to the issue of God and time

Christian theists agree that Scripture teaches God is eternal in the minimal sense that God has no beginning or end. Psalms 90:2 states, "Before the mountains were born or You gave birth to the earth and the world, even from everlasting to everlasting, You are God." Further, Psalm 102:27 asserts, "You [God] are the same, And Your years will not come to an end" (cf. Heb 1:12). Likewise, Isaiah 40:28 calls God "the Everlasting God, the LORD, the Creator of the ends of the earth." Isaiah 57:15, further declares that God "lives forever" (NASB) or "inhabits eternity" (NKJV, NRSV). Romans 16:26 refers to "the eternal God." 1 Timothy 1:17 speaks of "the King eternal, immortal, invisible, the only God." Christian theists also generally agree that Scripture indicates that God does not relate to time just as humans do, citing

---

[195] Wolterstorff, "Response to Craig," in *God and Time: Four Views*, ed. Gregory Ganssle (Downers Grove, IL: InterVarsity, 2001), 170.
[196] Padgett, "Response to Wolterstorff," 219.
[197] Craig, "Timelessness and Omnitemporality," 156.
[198] Wolterstorff, "Response to Craig," 170.

texts like Psalm 90:4, "a thousand years in Your sight are like yesterday as it passes by" (cf. 2 Pet 3:8; Job 10:4–5; 36:26).

The primary debate among Christian theists, however, is over whether God is timelessly eternal or everlastingly eternal (or something else). Those on all sides of the issue tend to agree that Scripture seems to portray God as temporal, including many advocates of divine timelessness. For instance, Helm states, "Any reader of Scripture is forcefully struck by the language of time and change as applied to God."[199] Likewise, McCann summarizes how the "God of the Bible" is portrayed as interacting with people and "*reacting* to the behavior of humankind."[200] From this, he concludes: "There is no denying that such an interactive God is more easily understood as temporal."[201] Further, Rogers states, "There certainly are scriptural passages which *prima facie* imply that God is temporal."[202] Yet, she claims, the Bible "never addresses the question of the metaphysical nature of time."[203]

In this regard, numerous advocates on both sides also believe that, as Helm puts it, Scripture is "somewhat underdetermined" on the matter, meaning "the language of Scripture about God and time is not sufficiently precise so as to provide a definitive resolution of the issue one way or the other."[204] Morris adds: "The most natural reading of most biblical texts about God is one on which God is seen as a temporal being. He is talked about in temporal language and there is not any clear nonpoetic passage to the contrary."[205] Yet, he goes on, "it is very difficult to resolve a disputed point concerning a fairly esoteric matter in theistic metaphysics by just consulting biblical passages. As they were written for very different purposes, their content will often fail to settle such an issue."[206]

William Lane Craig agrees, noting, "it is indisputable that the biblical writers typically portray God as engaged in temporal activities, including foreknowing the future and remembering the past, and when they speak directly of God's eternal existence they do so in terms of beginningless and endless temporal duration" (Ps 90:2; Rev 4:8).[207] However, Craig maintains,

---

[199] Helm, "Divine Timeless Eternity," 42.
[200] McCann, "God Beyond Time," 91.
[201] McCann, "God Beyond Time," 91 (emphasis original).
[202] Rogers, *Perfect Being Theology*, 64.
[203] Rogers, *Perfect Being Theology*, 64.
[204] Helm, "Divine Timeless Eternity," 31.
[205] Morris, *Our Idea of God*, 135.
[206] Morris, *Our Idea of God*, 135.
[207] Craig, "Timelessness and Omnitemporality," 129–30.

Scripture is often "anthropomorphic" and "there is just no reason to invest such portrayals with metaphysical significance."[208] He thus concurs with James Barr's influential conclusion that "if such a thing as a Christian doctrine of time has to be developed, the work of discussing it and developing it must belong not to biblical but to philosophical theology."[209]

Helm appeals even more strongly to the accommodative nature of Scripture, writing: "If a timelessly eternal God is to communicate to embodied intelligent creatures who exist in space and time and to bring about his purposes through them, and particularly to gain certain kinds of responses from them, then he must do so by representing himself to them in ways that are not literally true."[210] McCann similarly argues that, in Scripture, "God is [also] presented as a spatial being: as having a head, hands and feet, as dwelling in cities and tabernacles, as moving from place to place. If it is fair to take this kind of talk as metaphorical, then surely passages that portray God as temporal can in principle be so taken as well."[211] McCann then refers to Scriptures such as God calling himself "I am" in Exodus 3:14, the language of God being "from everlasting to everlasting" in Psalm 90:2, and Christ saying, "before Abraham was, I am" in John 8:58 and concludes: "It is not unreasonable to think passages like this aim at an atemporal conception."[212]

Helm concurs, saying the biblical "data are compatible with [timeless] eternalism but do not require it."[213] Yet, he believes, "Eternalism is a better approach to the relevant scriptural data than any of its rivals."[214] For Helm, "Eternality has two main sources: the data of Scripture coupled with a priori reflection on the ideas of the divine fullness and aseity and on the Creator-creature distinction."[215] That is, Helm understands the biblical texts on divine eternity in light of the metaphysical framework he believes to be true, that of strict classical theism.

Temporalists also recognize that Scripture is accommodative and contains anthropomorphisms but some contend that this does not provide sufficient

---

[208]Craig, "Response to Wolterstorff," 223.
[209]James Barr, *Biblical Words for Time* (London: SCM Press, 1969), 149. Many have followed Barr in concluding that one cannot make any judgment on the matter by reference to the terminology of time in Scripture.
[210]Helm, "Divine Timeless Eternity," 46.
[211]McCann, "God beyond Time," 91–92.
[212]McCann, "God beyond Time," 92.
[213]Helm, "Divine Timeless Eternity," 32.
[214]Helm, "Divine Timeless Eternity," 33.
[215]Helm, "Divine Timeless Eternity," 34.

basis to maintain that portrayals of God lack "metaphysical significance" (see the discussion in Chapter 2). In this regard Wolterstorff worries that "if we don't take Scripture as speaking literally about God unless we have good reason in a given case to conclude otherwise," then "everything" might be "up for grabs in interpretation" and "Scripture loses all authoritative function."[216]

In this regard, *some* temporalists think not only that temporalism is the best interpretation of Scripture but that atemporalism is inconsistent with Scripture. Wolterstorff argues, "There are no passages in Scripture which can be cited as supporting the doctrine" of "God's timelessness."[217] On the contrary, it is "typical of Scripture's representation of God" that "God responds to what transpires in human affairs by performing a succession of [temporally responsive] actions."[218] As such, "Scripture represents God as having a history [of successively 'acting and responding'], from which it is to be concluded that God is not timeless."[219] Padgett adds: "As a theologian and philosopher; I agree with" Wolterstorff "about accepting the priority of Scripture in our understanding of God, and I agree with his reading of Scripture. The biblical God has a history, and this means that God is temporal."[220]

In a similar vein, R.T. Mullins quotes Psalm 90:2, "Before the mountains were brought forth, or ever you had formed the earth and the world, from everlasting to everlasting you are God" [cf. Ps 103:15], then states:

> The from/to formula in this passage is a common formula in scripture used to denote a span of time. In this instance, the Hebrew word *olam*—sometimes translated as eternity depending on context—is used twice here to refer to the span of God's life. It quite literally means from perpetual duration in the indefinite past to perpetual duration in the indefinite future. This is a deeply temporal portrayal of God.[221]

Temporalists sometimes argue similarly regarding Psalm 102:24–27, which says of God:

---

[216] Wolterstorff, "Response to Critics," in *God and Time: Four Views*, ed. Gregory Ganssle (Downers Grove, IL: InterVarsity, 2001), 228.
[217] Wolterstorff, *Inquiring about God*, 163.
[218] Wolterstorff, *Inquiring about God*, 158.
[219] Wolterstorff, *Inquiring about God*, 164.
[220] Padgett, "Response to Wolterstorff," 219.
[221] Mullins, *End of the Timeless God*, 33.

Your years are throughout all generations. Of old You founded the earth, And the heavens are the work of Your hands. Even they will perish, but You endure; And all of them will wear out like a garment; Like clothing You will change them and they will be changed. But You are the same, And Your years will not come to an end. (Ps 102:24–27; cf. Job 36:26; Heb 1:10–12)

Further, the temporalist may point to texts that seem to indicate God himself has a future. Zephaniah 3:16–17, often understood as a reference to the eschatological day of the Lord, states, "In that day," God "will exult over you with joy, He will be quiet in His love, He will rejoice over you with shouts of joy" (Zeph 3:16–17; cf. Isa 65:19; Jer 32:41; Rev 21:4). Mullins further points to the temporal language used to describe God in Revelation as "the Alpha and the Omega … who is and who was and who is to come" (Rev 1:8; cf. 1:4; 4:8) as further evidence of divine temporality.[222]

Some temporalists argue further that:

an atemporal being never changes, and the sort of actions ascribed to the biblical God require that he be doing one thing at one time (creating), and something else at a later time (calling Abram), and yet again something different at a still later time (speaking to Moses). A being who does different things at different times is a being in time. Thus, God's eternity must be understood to be one of everlasting temporal duration.[223]

Atemporalists respond that what are portrayed as many divine actions are just the effects of God's one timeless act. Temporalists reply that the consistent narrative of Scripture might be undermined by such a reading. The God of the Bible is consistently portrayed as involved in dynamic covenant relationships, making covenants and interacting with people according to them, being pleased by faithfulness but angered by evil (see Chapter 2), active in creating (Gen 1–3) and sustaining creation, appearing to people in theophanies (Exod 3), relenting in response to human repentance (Jer 18:7–10), doing new things (Isa 43:19), "making all things new" (Rev 21:5), and *will* create a new heaven and a new earth.

The temporalist may also appeal to the biblical data referenced in Chapter 2 regarding divine passibility. If Helm is right that "a timelessly eternal God is immutable and so impassible in a very strong sense" such that "he *necessarily*

---

[222]Mullins, *End of the Timeless God*, 201.

[223]Morris, *Our Idea of God*, 130–31. Morris suggests this as a possible argument, without endorsing it, and goes on to point out that atemporalists counter this by appealing to God's singular timeless action.

cannot change *for* change takes time," then, if Scripture is rightly taken as teaching that God does experience emotional change, for example, it follows that God is not timeless.[224] One's understanding of God's relation to time is closely related to one's view regarding divine immutability and impassibility.

One final issue worth noting is the data raised relative to the competing temporalist positions regarding God's relation to time without the world. Without claiming the evidence of Scripture is sufficient to settle the matter, Craig maintains that Genesis 1:1 "speaks of an absolute beginning" and "may very well be intended to teach *that the* beginning was not simply the beginning of the physical universe but the beginning of time itself."[225] He thinks this might be taken to mean that "God, as least 'before' creation, must therefore be atemporal."[226] Further, Craig thinks that "certain New Testament passages also seem to affirm a beginning of time" such as Jude 25, which "ascribes glory to God 'before all time and now and forever.'"[227] Colossians 1:17 adds, God is "before all things" (Col 1:17). Further, Scripture speaks of a "before" the foundation of the world (*cosmos*; John 17:5, 24; Eph 1:4; 1 Pet 1:20; Rev 13:8 cf. Ps 90:2; Col 1:16–17; Rev 10:6) and a "before the ages" (*pro + aiōn* in 1 Cor 2:7; cf. Eph 3:9; Col 1:26 and *pro chronōn aiōniōn* in Tit 1:2–3; 2 Tim 1:9 [NRSV]; cf. Rom 16:25–26).

However, these texts may be variously interpreted; the root *aiōn* is translated variously as "ages," "world," "eternal/eternity," and others. Further, while Craig takes such texts as evidence that God was timeless "before" he created time itself, others take such texts as referring to uncreated or metaphysical time such that there was a temporal "before" for God himself prior to creation. Wolterstorff suggests: "If God existed *before* time and issued his decrees *before* the ages, then it appears that the writers were thinking of *God* as *temporally* preceding this present age, or something like that."[228] Mullins goes further, maintaining that "Psalm 90 not only portrays God in temporal terms, it also speaks of God existing alone before creation. One would be hard pressed to say that this is not a temporal *before* since the language employed is explicitly temporal."[229] In this and other regards, the debate about just how to understand Scripture on God and time continues.

---

[224] Helm, "Divine Timeless Eternity," 38.
[225] Craig, "Timelessness and Omnitemporality," 130.
[226] Craig, "Timelessness and Omnitemporality," 132.
[227] Craig, "Timelessness and Omnitemporality," 131.
[228] Wolterstorff, "Response to Critics," 237.
[229] Mullins, *End of the Timeless God*, 33.

Perspectives on divine omnipresence

Much less will be said here about divine presence and omnipresence because, while Christian theists generally agree that God is omnipresent, meaning that God is present everywhere, there is considerable mystery with respect to just how to understand divine presence and omnipresence. As such, there are multiple perspectives on divine omnipresence.

In process theism, God is spatially present to the world and the world is spatially present to God because the world is in God and part of God's being.[230] Since every physical location is in God's being, God is physically extended everywhere. While God has an abstract pole, God's concrete (physical) pole occupies all space. Most Christian theists, however, reject this (panentheistic) view of the God–world relation. Christian theists generally maintain that, whatever omnipresence means, it does not mean that the physical world is either part of God's being (panentheism) or identical with God's being (pantheism).

Most Christian theists wish to affirm divine omnipresence, defined as "God's being present at every point in space," while also maintaining that God is not "locally circumscribed" and is not "universally extended."[231] That is, God is not contained in, or encompassed by, space and it is not the case that parts of God are spread out through space. In the latter regard, Ganssle explains: "We do not think [God] is spread out in space the way I am spread out when I lie down for a nap on the couch. It is not that part of God is here at the foot of the couch and a different part of God is at the head of the couch."[232] As such, many Christian theists would affirm the way Anselm speaks of divine omnipresence when he writes: "Since, then, nothing is greater than You, no place or time confines You but You exist everywhere and always."[233]

In this regard, some maintain that God is "spatially located but not spatially extended" such that God is "wholly present at every point in the universe."[234]

---

[230]For a distinct view, similar in understanding the world as God's body, see Sallie McFague's feminist panentheism in *The Body of God: An Ecological Theology* (Minneapolis, MN: Fortress, 1993).
[231]Moreland and Craig, *Philosophical Foundations*, 515.
[232]Ganssle, "Introduction," 9.
[233]Anselm, *Proslogion* 13.
[234]Moreland and Craig, *Philosophical Foundations*, 515.

Others maintain that God is "not spatially located in the universe at all but cognizant of and causally active at every point in it."[235] Such understandings complement the traditional notion that God is incorporeal, meaning that God is not a bodily (corporeal) being. However, this can be understood in more than one way. One could maintain that God is incorporeal in a way that is *incompatible* with God occupying space or taking any bodily form whatsoever, as strict classical theists do. Or, one could maintain that God is not *essentially* corporeal, meaning God is not *restricted to* any bodily form or indeed any physical characteristics because God is spirit and the omnipotent creator of the physical universe. For example, Swinburne believes "God is essentially bodiless," meaning that, "although he may sometimes have a body, he is not dependent on his body in any way."[236]

While most Christian theists agree that God cannot be *contained* or *encompassed* by space, strict classical theists and others adopt the stronger claim that God *cannot* occupy space because, just as God's being is incompatible with temporal succession, God's being is incompatible with the limitations of spatial location. As Rogers puts it, "God is neither spatial nor temporal … Space and time are not categories which apply to God, but all spatial and temporal things are immediately known and caused by God."[237] Further, Rogers maintains: "Almost all Judeo-Christian philosophers of religion, past and present, have agreed that God is not spatial, and that nonetheless He is 'present' to all of space and it to Him."[238]

Mullins, however, maintains that what he calls the "weak notion of omnipresence" wherein "God is aspatial, and so not actually located in space" is "not the traditional doctrine of omnipresence."[239] Rather, "Traditionally, omnipresence holds that the entire being of God is wholly located in every point or region of space."[240] In support of this claim, Mullins cites Robert Pasnau, who writes: "Medieval Christian authors, despite being generally misread on this point, are in complete agreement that God is literally present, spatially, throughout the universe. One simply does not find anyone wanting to remove God from space, all the way through to the end of the

---

[235] Moreland and Craig, *Philosophical Foundations*, 515.
[236] Swinburne, *The Christian God*, 127.
[237] Rogers, *Perfect Being Theology*, 59.
[238] Rogers, *Perfect Being Theology*, 59. Cf. the view of Joshua Hoffman and Gary S. Rosenkratz that "God is a nonphysical spirit, or soul" and such "a soul cannot literally be omnipresent." *The Divine Attributes* (Malden, MA: Blackwell, 2002), 53.
[239] Mullins, *End of the Timeless God*, 38.
[240] Mullins, *End of the Timeless God*, 38.

seventeenth century."[241] Whether it is the traditional view or not, even some who are critical of classical theism, such as Wolterstorff, maintain that "God does not have a spatial location."[242]

Yet, how can God be omnipresent without having spatial location? For some, whether or not God *can* occupy space, God's omnipresence is "thought of as a function of his knowledge and power. God is thought to be present everywhere in the sense that his perfect knowledge and power extend over all."[243] For example, Swinburne thinks God *can* occupy space but that God "is omnipresent in the sense of being able to act intentionally anywhere without intermediary" and in "knowing what is happening everywhere without intermediary."[244] Moreland and Craig add that "God literally exists spacelessly but is present at every point in space in the sense that he is [immediately] cognizant of and causally active at every point in space."[245] That is, God "knows what is happening at every spatial location in the universe and he is causally operative at every such point."[246] In their view, "God brings space into being at the moment of his creation of the universe. Without creation, therefore, God exists spacelessly. But the creation of space would do nothing to 'spatialize' God, that is to say, to draw him into space."[247]

Bruce Ware, on the other hand, maintains both that "God is nonspatial in himself *(in se)* apart from creation, and God is everywhere spatially present in relation to creation *(in re)*—and without conflict or contradiction."[248] In this and other ways, some Christian theists wish to maintain that God is present everywhere in some way that is more than merely with respect to God's knowledge of everything and power to act everywhere, while maintaining that God cannot be *contained* in space. Further, some wish to maintain that God is not restricted by physical form or spatial location, but God is able to occupy space and sometimes take physical form and acts and interacts within space without needing physical form to act in the world and without being encompassed or bound by space. Thus, while Christian

---

[241] Pasnau, "On Existing All at Once," in *God, Eternity, and Time*, ed. Christian Tapp and Edmund Runggaldier (Farnham: Ashgate, 2011), 19, quoted in Mullins, *End of the Timeless God*, 38.
[242] Wolterstorff, *Inquiring about God*, 177.
[243] Morris, *Our Idea of God*, 155.
[244] Swinburne, *The Christian God*, 127.
[245] Moreland and Craig, *Philosophical Foundations*, 511.
[246] Moreland and Craig, *Philosophical Foundations*, 510.
[247] Moreland and Craig, *Philosophical Foundations*, 510.
[248] Ware, "Modified Calvinist," 87. Cf. Horton, *The Christian Faith*, 256.

theists generally agree that God is omnipresent, there are various ways of understanding and describing omnipresence.

Some biblical data relevant to the issue of omnipresence

Christian theists understand many biblical passages as indicating divine omnipresence. Among the most prominent is Psalm 139:7–10:

> Where can I go from Your Spirit? Or where can I flee from Your presence? If I ascend to heaven, You are there; If I make my bed in Sheol, behold, You are there. If I take the wings of the dawn, If I dwell in the remotest part of the sea, Even there Your hand will lead me, And Your right hand will lay hold of me. (cf. Job 11:7–9)

Further, "'Can a man hide himself in hiding places so I do not see him?' declares the LORD. 'Do I not fill the heavens and the earth?'" (Jer 23:24). Such texts imply that God is somehow present everywhere. Wherever one might go, God is somehow there.

Yet, just what God's "presence" means is variously understood. Some interpret texts like these in non-spatial ways. For instance, Ganssle comments on Psalm 139: "Everywhere we go, he is there. He is there in that he has direct knowledge and access to every place we could go."[249] To speak of God's omnipresence in terms of God's awareness of everything seems congruent with, but not required by, texts like Proverbs 15:3, which states: "The eyes of the LORD are in every place, Watching the evil and the good" (cf. Job 34:21; Ps 139:1–3).

In Matthew 18:20, Jesus speaks of some sense in which he will be with his followers even though they are scattered across the earth: "For where two or three have gathered together in My name, I am there in their midst" (cf. John 14:19; 16:7). Elsewhere, Jesus promised, "lo, I am with you always, even to the end of the age" (Matt 28:20; cf. Heb 13:5; Rev 3:20). This may echo OT promises of divine presence, even amid tribulation (whether of God's power to sustain or in other ways), such as Deuteronomy 31:6: "Be strong and courageous, do not be afraid or tremble at them, for the LORD

---

[249]Ganssle, "Introduction," 10.

your God is the one who goes with you. He will not fail you or forsake you" (cf. 31:8). Likewise, in Isaiah 43:2 God states: "When you pass through the waters, I will be with you." In Isaiah 57:15, God states further, "I dwell on a high and holy place, and also with the contrite and lowly of spirit." These and other passages indicate that God is by no means restricted to one location.

Indeed, Scripture suggests God cannot be contained in spatial locations at all. Solomon states: "But will God indeed dwell on the earth? Behold, heaven and the highest heaven cannot contain You, how much less this house which I have built?" (1 Kings 8:27; cf. 2 Chron 6:18; Isa 66:1; Acts 7:49). In reference to whether God can be properly worshiped in Jerusalem or at Mt. Gerizim, Jesus proclaims, "God is Spirit" (John 4:24), seemingly indicating that God is not physically restricted and can be worshiped anywhere.

At the same time, Michael Horton notes, "God's dwelling in the midst of his people is a prominent motif from Genesis to Revelation."[250] God manifests his presence in Solomon's temple and Scripture speaks as if God's presence is concentrated in the Most Holy Place of the sanctuary (cf. Ex 25:8). Further, God's presence in the Most Holy Place appears to be both special and conditional; the presence of God (shekinah glory) is depicted as departing before Babylon destroyed the temple (Ezek 11:22; cf. Ezek 9; 10). Yet, the return of God's glory is also promised. Here, Horton notes "God's presence and absence in the covenantal drama," distinguishing between what he calls God's "*ontological omnipresence*" and God's "*covenantal-judicial presence*."[251] That is, "God is omnipresent in his essence, but the primary question in the covenantal drama is whether God is present for us, and if so, where, as well as whether he is present in judgment or in grace."[252]

In this regard, Scripture speaks of humans as if they might come into God's presence in some special way: "Let us come before His presence with thanksgiving" (Ps 95:2). Conversely, Adam and Eve are depicted as hiding "themselves from the presence of the LORD" (Gen 3:8), Cain "went out from the presence of the LORD" (Gen 4:16; cf. 1 Sam 26:20), and Satan is also said to have "departed from the presence of the LORD" (Job 1:12; cf. 2:7; Jon 1:3, 10).

Further, many texts depict encounters between God and humans in specific places. Moses encounters God, who "called to him from the midst of

---

[250] Horton, *The Christian Faith*, 255.
[251] Horton, *The Christian Faith*, 255 (emphasis original).
[252] Horton, *The Christian Faith*, 255.

the bush" and told him "the place on which you are standing is holy ground" (Ex 3:4–5; cf. 33:11; Gen 26:24). 1 Kings 19:11 speaks of God "passing by" Elijah and "a great and strong wind" that "was rending the mountains and breaking in pieces the rocks before the LORD." Neither these nor other encounters with God entail that God was or is contained in one place. Yet, such texts do depict God as specially manifesting his presence in particular places. This motif reaches its zenith in the incarnation itself: "And the Word became flesh, and dwelt among us, and we saw His glory, glory as of the only begotten from the Father, full of grace and truth" (John 1:14). Here, while Sonderegger maintains God is "not a visible God" and "not a local or explicit presence," she notes: "Of course God does have these modes as well! He can be and has been incarnate."[253]

Some might infer from the data surveyed here that God is everywhere but God is not everywhere in the same sense. God is omnipresent in some way, at least relative to the biblical evidence that nothing escapes divine knowledge or power (on the latter, see Chapter 5) and, yet, some texts suggest that God sometimes specially manifests his presence in specific locations—perhaps specially localizing his presence without being restricted to, or *contained* in, any spatial location. That is, some hold, God transcends spatial limitations ("the highest heaven cannot contain" him, 1 Kings 8:27) yet God is not incompatible with spatial location such that can occupy space.

With regard to this and other potential views, considerable mystery remains. Most Christian theists take Scripture to explicitly affirm that God is omnipresent in some sense without providing an explanation of precisely *how* God is omnipresent.

Conclusion

This chapter has introduced some prominent contemporary views on divine eternity and omnipresence, followed by a brief discussion of biblical data relevant to both issues. The next chapter moves on to a discussion of divine knowledge, with emphasis on the question of whether God knows the future.

---

[253]Sonderegger, *Systematic Theology*, 526.

Study questions

1. How do you evaluate the various perspectives on whether God is timeless or temporal? Does one have to choose between divine timelessness and temporality or do you think some mediating view is possible? Do you think God has a future? What difference does it make?
2. How do you understand the relationship between God's relationship to time and God's relationship to space? Does one's view of God's relationship to time determine one's view of God's relationship to space and/or vice versa? What are some implications of the differing views on the nature of time?
3. How do you think one should decide between competing views of the relationship between God and time and God and space? What role does the data from Scripture play in the way you think of these issues? What do you make of differing interpretations of the Christian tradition relative to God and time and God and space? What are some of the implications for Christian theism regarding how these questions are answered?
4. What are the strengths and weaknesses of divine timelessness? What are the strengths and weaknesses of divine temporality? Do you think one conception of divine temporality is preferable to others? What are the strengths and weaknesses of views that attempt to hold both (or something like both) together? Can you think of any further difficulties with any of these views?
5. Which view of God's relationship to space do you find the most compelling? What are the advantages and drawbacks of various views in this regard? Do you think God can occupy space? Why or why not?

Suggestions for further reading

Selected premodern sources

Parmenides, "The Way of Truth."
Augustine, *Confessions* 1.1–3; 11.10–28.

Boethius, *The Consolation of Philosophy* 5.6
Anselm, *Monologion* 18–24.
Anselm, *Proslogion* 18–20.
Thomas Aquinas, *Summa Theologiae* I.8; I.10.
William Ockham, *Predestination, God's Foreknowledge, and Future Contingents*. 2nd ed. Translated with Introduction, notes, and appendices, by Marilyn McCord Adams and Norman Kretzmann (Indianapolis, IN: Hackett, 1983).

Selected modern/contemporary sources

Barth, Karl. *Church Dogmatics*, ed. Geoffrey W. Bromiley and T. F. Torrance (Edinburgh: T&T Clark, 1957), 2/1, 461–90, 608–40.
Callender, Craig, ed. *The Oxford Handbook on the Philosophy of Time* (New York: Oxford University Press, 2011).
Canale, Fernando Luis. *A Criticism of Theological Reason: Time and Timelessness as Primordial Presuppositions* (Berrien Springs, MI: Andrews University Press, 1987).
Craig, William Lane. "Divine Eternity," in *The Oxford Handbook of Philosophical Theology*, ed. Thomas P. Flint and Michael C. Rea (New York: Oxford University Press, 2009), 145–66.
Craig, William Lane. *Time and Eternity* (Wheaton, IL: Crossway, 2001).
Davis, Stephen T. *Logic and the Nature of God* (Grand Rapids, MI: Eerdmans, 1983), 8–24.
DeWeese, Garrett. *God and the Nature of Time* (Burlington, VT: Ashgate, 2004).
Frame, John. *The Doctrine of God* (Phillipsburg, NJ: P&R, 2002), 543–99.
Ganssle, Gregory E, ed. *God and Time: Four Views* (Downers Grove, IL: InterVarsity, 2001).
Ganssle, Gregory E. and David M. Woodruff, eds. *God and Time: Essays on the Divine Nature* (New York: Oxford University Press, 2002).
Helm, Paul. *Eternal God: A Study of God without Time* (New York: Oxford University Press, 1998).
Hudson, Hud. "Omnipresence," in *The Oxford Handbook of Philosophical Theology*, ed. Thomas P. Flint and Michael C. Rea (New York: Oxford, 2009), 199–216.
Leftow, Brian. *Time and Eternity* (Ithaca, NY: Cornell University Press, 1991).
Mullins, R.T. *The End of the Timeless God* (New York: Oxford University Press, 2016).
Padgett, Alan. *God, Eternity, and the Nature of Time* (Eugene, OR: Wipf & Stock, 2000).
Stump, Eleonore and Norman Kretzmann. "Eternity," in *The Concept of God*, ed. Thomas V. Morris (New York: Oxford University Press, 1987), 219–52.

4

Does God Know Everything? Does God Know the Future?

This chapter introduces the debate over God's knowledge, addressing questions like: Does God know everything? Does God know the future? If so, does that mean humans have no free will? Christian theists generally agree that God is omniscient, which means all-knowing and is generally taken to mean that God knows (at least) "all truths and believes no falsehoods."[1] Put differently, God knows all there is to know and does so infallibly; God cannot be wrong. Most Christian theists maintain that divine omniscience includes knowledge of the future decisions of creatures (foreknowledge). However, some maintain that divine omniscience does not include foreknowledge of creatures' future free decisions because they consider such knowledge impossible. Omniscience is thus defined as possessing all knowledge that is possible. The omniscient God knows everything there is to know.

Much of the debate over God's knowledge hinges upon the debate over creaturely free will, discussed further in Chapter 5. In this chapter, the pivotal question is whether humans have what is called libertarian free will. That is, free will of the kind that is incompatible with theistic determinism, which is the view that God causally determines history. Determinists maintain that creatures do not have libertarian free will and God can thus know the "future" free decisions of creatures because those decisions are causally determined. Among those who reject determinism (indeterminists) and affirm that creatures have libertarian free will, there are various views regarding foreknowledge. While some argue that human libertarian freedom is incompatible with God exhaustively knowing the future, others believe

---

[1]David Hunt, "The Simple Foreknowledge View," in *Divine Foreknowledge: Four Views*, ed. James K. Beilby and Paul R. Eddy (Downers Grove, IL: InterVarsity, 2001), 65.

there is no incompatibility between exhaustive divine foreknowledge and human libertarian freedom. Those of the latter view offer various models that, they claim, elude contradiction. This chapter introduces some examples of these prominent contemporary approaches to divine omniscience, focusing on the debate over divine foreknowledge, followed by a brief discussion of some biblical data relevant to the debate.

The determinist solution: God knows the future because he determines it

Many Christian theists maintain that God knows everything, including the future decisions of creatures, because God causes everything to happen as it does. That is, God knows the future because he knows what he has willed or decreed with regard to the future. This position affirms causal determinism, which means that every event is caused by "prior" external factors to occur just as it does.[2] The view that God causally determines every event is typically called theistic determinism. However, some theistic determinists (e.g., Paul Helm) attempt to nuance this view, holding that God causally determines many things to happen and others are causally determined by the chain of cause and effect.

Given determinism, humans are causally determined to act just as they do and cannot do otherwise. As such, creatures cannot have libertarian free will, the kind of free will that is incompatible with causal determinism.[3] Many determinists, however, maintain that humans possess a kind of free will that is compatible with causal determinism. This is called compatibilist free will, often defined as the freedom to do what one wants to do.[4] However, given determinism, what one wants to do is itself determined by prior factors (see Chapter 5).

---

[2] See Kevin Timpe, *Free Will in Philosophical Theology* (New York: Bloomsbury Academic, 2014), 8.
[3] Freedom to do otherwise is not the only kind of libertarian free will. Nevertheless, determinism rules out this and all other kind of libertarian free will.
[4] According to Steven B. Cowan and James S. Spiegel, one has compatibilist free will if one "has the ability to do what she wants to do" and is "not coerced by external forces against her will." *The Love of Wisdom: A Christian Introduction to Philosophy* (Nashville, TN: B&H, 2009), 237.

Given determinism, God knows the future exhaustively and definitely *because* he has determined the future, whether he has causally determined every event itself or causally determined some things and left others to be causally determined by other prior factors.[5] Either way, God knows every decision creatures will make by knowing what he has determined to be the case. This view is maintained by many strict classical theists. For example, Paul Helm characterizes his view as the "Augustinian-Calvinist" view regarding divine foreknowledge, holding that "it is reasonable to believe that divine foreknowledge and human freedom are consistent, where this freedom is understood in a compatibilist sense, in a sense that is consistent with causal determinism."[6]

On this view, God is sometimes said to foreknow all events because he foreordains all events, that is, ordains all events beforehand. However, for the many theistic determinists who affirm divine timelessness, God does not actually know or ordain anything *beforehand* but *timelessly* knows and ordains events. As Helm puts it, the "timelessly eternal God does not, strictly speaking, foreknow anything."[7] Rather, as Michael Horton explains, "Given his eternity, [God] knows the end from the beginning in one simultaneous act. God knows all things because he has decreed the end from the beginning and 'works all things according to the counsel of his will'" (Eph 1:11).[8]

However, as briefly noted in Chapter 3, some maintain that divine timelessness compromises divine omniscience because a timeless God could not know things that humans know such as today is May 7, 2018 or I am *now* writing this book. A timeless God could know that John Peckham is writing this book on May 7, 2018 but could not know that day is *today*.[9] Yet, defenders of timelessness maintain, this is only problematic if there is an objective moment that is "now," as presentism claims. If eternalism is true, this objection does not work. The objection, Rogers argues, "simply

---

[5]Helm takes the latter view in an attempt to avoid God being the author of evil. See the further discussion of this move, which some see as a distinction without a significant difference, in Chapters 5 and 6.
[6]Helm, "The Augustinian-Calvinist View," in *Divine Foreknowledge: Four Views*, ed. James K. Beilby and Paul R. Eddy (Downers Grove, IL: InterVarsity, 2001), 189.
[7]Helm, "Augustinian-Calvinist," 186.
[8]Michael Horton, *The Christian Faith* (Grand Rapids, MI: Zondervan, 2011), 260.
[9]See, for example, Arthur Prior, "The Formalities of Omniscience," *Philosophy* 37/140 (1962): 114–29; Norman Kretzmann, "Omniscience and Immutability," *Journal of Philosophy* 63 (1966): 409–21; Nicholas Wolterstorff, *Inquiring about God: Selected Essays*, vol. 1 (Cambridge: Cambridge University Press, 2010), 134–45. Cf. William Hasker, *God, Time, and Knowledge* (Ithaca, NY: Cornell University Press, 1989), 169.

begs the question against the traditional doctrine of eternity," which she believes is eternalism.[10] Here, some maintain that every tensed statement (e.g., John Peckham is writing *now*) can be put into a tenseless version (e.g., John Peckham is writing on May 7, 2018) without losing anything that is genuinely true about reality. As Helm puts it, "God can know that some event *E* is before another event *F*" but "cannot know that one of these events is occurring now, because it isn't true, as far as he is concerned, that one of these events is occurring now."[11]

Yet, even if one rejects the appeal to eternalism, Helm maintains that the advocate of divine timelessness could just "give up strict omniscience" and maintain that there are some things we know that God does not know.[12] Helm contends this would be no more problematic for divine omniscience than the widely accepted claim that God does not know *just as* each limited human knows. For instance, Helm writes, "I know that it is I who is typing this paper .... but you [or God] cannot know that fact *as I know it*."[13] Questions regarding whether and to what extent God can know *just as* each human subject knows relate to the question of divine omnisubjectivity.[14] On this issue, Katherin Rogers contends that "if 'complete knowledge' means knowledge from all perspectives as if one were every knower such knowledge is not possible. I cannot see things from a perspective which is not *my* perspective."[15] In this regard, Rogers and others argue that a perfect being cannot know the kinds of things that can only be known in a limited fashion and this might include tensed knowledge like today is May 7, 2018. As Rogers puts it, "God cannot know things from the perspective of a limited perceiver. He can know what I mean when I use the terms 'here' or 'now'" and, she believes, this is sufficient for perfect knowledge appropriate to a perfect being.[16]

---

[10]Katherin A. Rogers, *Perfect Being Theology* (Edinburgh: Edinburgh University Press, 2000), 68. Cf. the alternative strategy of Brian Leftow, *Time and Eternity* (Ithaca, NY: Cornell University Press, 1991), 332–37.

[11]Helm, "Divine Timeless Eternity," in *God and Time: Four Views*, ed. Gregory Ganssle (Downers Grove, IL: InterVarsity, 2001), 40.

[12]Helm, "Divine Timeless Eternity," 41. Cf. Leftow, *Time and Eternity*, 321–33.

[13]Helm, "Divine Timeless Eternity," 42.

[14]An adequate discussion of this issue is beyond the scope of this chapter. For more on this, see Linda Zagzebski, *Divine Omnisubjectivity: A Defense of a Divine Attribute* (Marquette, WI: Marquette University Press, 2013). Cf. Katherine Sonderegger, *Systematic Theology: The Doctrine of God* (Minneapolis, MN: Fortress, 2015), 359–61.

[15]Rogers, *Perfect Being Theology*, 89. This is sometimes called *de se* ("of oneself") knowledge.

[16]Rogers, *Perfect Being Theology*, 68.

Another objection that arises is the claim that a timeless God could not know a contingent, temporal world, particularly if God is pure actuality and simple (in the strict sense, see Chapter 7). Many advocates of strict classical theism who embrace determinism maintain that this is not a problem because "God's knowledge is the cause of his creatures."[17] That is, God causes everything he knows such that God does not depend on the world and has no real relation with the world. God's knowledge is not "determined and measured by things," it "is the *cause of things*." As such, the "divine intellect cannot derive any knowledge from things."[18] God's knowledge cannot be dependent on creation because, strict classical theists generally believe, there can be no "passivity" in God, including relative to knowledge (cf. Chapter 2).[19]

This view is often attributed to Thomas Aquinas, influenced by Aristotle's view of the Unmoved "Prime Mover" as "perfect in knowledge" by only knowing the "most perfect object of knowledge, namely, itself," alongside the view that "knowing the world of lesser things," subject to "change" and "imperfection" would be "a derogation from its supreme perfection."[20] This understanding of Aquinas's view is sometimes supported by statements of Aquinas such as "God knows things not by receiving anything from them, but, rather, by exercising His causality on them."[21] Elsewhere, Aquinas writes: "God knows other things in the same way as an effect is known through a knowledge of the cause. By knowing his essence, therefore, God knows all things to which his causality extends."[22]

---

[17] Roland J. Teske, "Omniscience, Omnipotence, and Divine Transcendence," *The New Scholasticism* 53/3 (1979): 280.

[18] Reginald Garrigou-LaGrange, *God: His Existence and His Nature*, 5th ed., trans. Dom Bede Rose (St. Louis, MO: Herder, 1936), 2:66. Garrigou-Lagrange appeals to Aquinas, in this regard, who writes God's "knowledge must be the cause of things, in so far as His will is joined to it." *Summa Theologiae* I.14.8. Cf. Garrigou-Lagrange, *God: His Existence and His Nature*, 2:538.

[19] In this regard, Garrigou-Lagrange contends "every Thomist will always reject the Molinist theory" because it posits "a *passivity in the pure Act*. If the divine causality is not predetermining with regard to our choice," then "the divine knowledge is fatally *determined* by it." Garrigou-Lagrange, *God: His Existence and His Nature*, 2:538 (emphasis original). On his view, "God is either *determining* or *determined*, there is *no* other alternative." Garrigou-Lagrange, *God: His Existence and His Nature*, 2:546 (emphasis original).

[20] Thomas Williams, "Introduction to Classical Theism," in *Models of God and Alternative Ultimate Realities*. ed. Jeanine Diller and Asa Kasher (New York: Springer, 2013), 95. Cf. Teske, "Omniscience"; Garrigou-Lagrange, *God: His Existence and His Nature*, 2:66–67, 538–39, 546–47.

[21] Aquinas, *Summa contra Gentiles* 1.70.2. Here and elsewhere in this book, I am using the translation of Anton C. Pegis in *Summa Contra Gentiles: Book One: God* (Notre Dame, IN: University of Notre Dame Press, 1975).

[22] Aquinas, *Summa contra Gentiles* 1.68.3.

However, whereas some take Aquinas to mean that "God knows a state of affairs just because he causes it to be," others such as Eleonore Stump maintain that "it is clear from many passages in Aquinas's work that Aquinas supposes God knows future contingents in virtue of their being present to him in his eternity."[23] Stump thinks Aquinas cannot have meant that "God's will is a cause of everything in creation," because this would make God "the ultimate cause, and so the ultimate agent, of morally wrong human actions, just in virtue of knowing them."[24] Regarding this issue, Anselm writes, "If everything that exists derives its existence from God's knowledge, then God is the Creator and author also of evil works and, by inference, unjustly punishes the wicked—a conclusion that is unacceptable."[25] The debate over whether determinism makes God culpable for evil will be taken up in Chapters 5 and 6.

With respect to Aquinas's view of divine knowledge, there is considerable disagreement regarding whether Aquinas was a determinist. Likewise, although Helm calls his view the "Augustinian-Calvinist view," there is also considerable debate regarding Augustine's view (regarding both, see Chapter 5). Some consider the views of both Augustine and Aquinas to be congruent with indeterminism and simple foreknowledge, discussed below. Further, although John Calvin explicitly affirmed determinism, he maintained: "I will freely admit that foreknowledge alone imposes no necessity upon creatures, yet not all assent to this."[26]

Apart from claims regarding the traditional view, Helm maintains that "only" a compatibilist "account of human freedom is logically consistent with divine efficacious grace."[27] Further, he believes determinism "does full justice to divine omniscience and is simpler than its closest rivals."[28] While some reject determinism because they think it undermines human responsibility and freedom, Helm maintains that if one adopts the "compatibilist sense" of "free" will, then human responsibility and deterministic foreknowledge

---

[23]Eleonore Stump, *The God of the Bible and the God of the Philosophers* (Marquette, WI: Marquette University Press, 2016), 24n14.

[24]Stump, *God of the Bible*, 25, 24n14. See, further, Eleonore Stump and Norman Kretzmann, "Eternity and God's Knowledge: A Reply to Shanley," *American Catholic Philosophical Quarterly* 72/3 (1998): 439–45.

[25]Anselm, *De Concordia: The Compatibility of God's Foreknowledge, Predestination, and Grace with Human Freedom* 1.7.

[26]John Calvin, *Institutes of the Christian Religion* 3.23.6, trans. Ford Lewis Battles, ed. John T. McNeill (Philadelphia, PA: Westminster Press, 1960), 2:954.

[27]Helm, "Augustinian-Calvinist," 188.

[28]Helm, "Augustinian-Calvinist," 188.

can be consistently maintained.[29] Determinists like Helm thus maintain that determinism is the best option to make sense of divine omniscience, including exhaustive knowledge of the "future." The debate over theistic determinism itself will be addressed in Chapter 5.

The open solution: God knows all there is to know

Some philosophers and theologians agree with those determinists who believe libertarian freedom is incompatible with exhaustive definite foreknowledge but, instead of denying libertarian freedom, they deny the view that God possesses exhaustive definite foreknowledge. On this view, foreknowledge is considered logically impossible without determinism and determinism is rejected. Therefore, the future is uncertain or open. God cannot know the future exhaustively and definitely because, the claim goes, knowledge of humans' future free decisions (in a libertarian sense) is impossible.[30]

This view is typically associated with process and open theists. Both, generally speaking, believe that creaturely libertarian free will is an axiomatic feature of reality and that the future does not yet exist (i.e., they reject eternalism). However, in the ways noted in the previous chapter (and other ways), process theism and open theism should not be conflated or confused. For one thing, as Clark Pinnock puts it, open theists (with some exceptions) differ from process theology in holding that "God is ontologically other than the world, which is not necessary to God—the world exists only because God wills it."[31] Both open and process theists affirm, however, that the future is open such that God himself does not know exactly how things will turn out. Many argue that it is logically impossible for God to know the future because the future does not exist. That is, the future is "not there to be known."[32]

---

[29]Helm, "Augustinian-Calvinist," 162.
[30]See, for example, Clark Pinnock, Richard Rice, John Sanders, William Hasker, and David Basinger, *The Openness of God: A Biblical Challenge to the Traditional Understanding of God* (Downers Grove, IL: InterVarsity Press), 1994; Hasker, *God, Time, and Knowledge*.
[31]Clark Pinnock, "Systematic Theology," in *The Openness of God: A Biblical Challenge to the Traditional Understanding of God* (Downers Grove, IL: InterVarsity, 1994), 194n49.
[32]Richard Rice, *God's Foreknowledge and Man's Free Will* (Minneapolis, MN: Bethany House, 1985), 54.

A number of prominent philosophers and theologians have advocated this view in recent decades, many of which hold numerous things in common with classical theism in contrast to process theism—such as divine omnipotence, creation ex nihilo, and God's freedom to create or not create—while departing from some forms of classical theism by affirming divine temporality, commitment to libertarian free will, and a kind of relational responsiveness that requires both temporality and libertarian free will.

For example, William Hasker maintains that "the future is genuinely open" such that "it is possible for a free agent to act in any of several different ways" and it is therefore "not possible for God to have complete and exhaustive knowledge of the entire future."[33] Similarly, Richard Swinburne has argued that "if humans are sometimes free in the [libertarian] sense that sometimes their choice at a time as to how they will act is not determined by any prior cause," then "no one can be guaranteed to have true beliefs in advance about the actions of [libertarian] free agents."[34] This is so because: "Whatever proposition I believe in advance about what you will do, if you act freely in this sense, you have it in your power to make my belief false."[35] Accordingly, "the universe may indeed contain the occasional surprise for God."[36]

Clark Pinnock adds: "Total knowledge of the future would imply a fixity of events. Nothing in the future would need to be decided. It also would imply that human freedom is an illusion, that we make no difference and are not responsible."[37] Similarly, Greg Boyd takes issue with the claim that "God eternally knows reality as one settled story," which he calls "the classical understanding of divine foreknowledge."[38] Boyd contends, instead, that "God knows all of reality perfectly" in that "he knows the possible aspects as possible and knows the settled aspects as settled."[39] This understanding, open theists claim, is the view most consistent with the kinds of things God

---

[33] William Hasker. "An Adequate God," in *Searching for an Adequate God: A Dialogue between Process and Free Will Theists*, ed. John B. Cobb Jr. and Clark Pinnock (Grand Rapids, MI: Eerdmans, 2000), 218.

[34] Swinburne, *The Christian God* (New York: Clarendon, 1994), 131. See, further, the arguments of Joshua Hoffman and Gary S. Rosenkratz that "divine omniscience would not include foreknowledge of human choices and actions that are free in the libertarian sense." *The Divine Attributes* (Malden, MA: Blackwell, 2002), 20. See the argumentation in *The Divine Attributes*, 126–35.

[35] Swinburne, *The Christian God*, 131.

[36] Swinburne, *The Christian God*, 143.

[37] Pinnock, "Systematic Theology," 121.

[38] Boyd, "The Open-Theism View," in *Divine Foreknowledge: Four Views*, ed. James K. Beilby and Paul R. Eddy (Downers Grove, IL: InterVarsity, 2001), 13.

[39] Boyd, "Open-Theism View," 14.

says and does in Scripture, particularly instances where, Boyd believes, God appears to change his mind, have regrets, ask questions about the future, and speak "of the future in conditional terms."[40]

Critics claim that this view cannot adequately account for the many predictions that God makes in Scripture, particularly long-term predictions. If God does not know with certainty the future decisions of creatures, yet God's knowledge is infallible such that he could not be wrong, how could God make the kinds of predictions he makes in Scripture? Some open theists respond to this objection by positing that God might selectively determine what he predicts and some appeal instead (or additionally) to a settled character hypothesis.[41] The settled character hypothesis maintains that, in some cases, God might know with certainty what a person will do on the basis of what he presently knows about that person's character. Yet, although God "anticipates all possibilities—he is nevertheless occasionally surprised at the improbable behavior of people."[42] Accordingly, Swinburne notes, while God might "predict human behavior correctly most of the time," if humans have libertarian free will, there is always "the possibility that men may falsify those predictions."[43]

With regard to selective determinism, some divine predictions might refer to things God sovereignly determines. For instance, seeking to explain how God foretold the very names and some acts of Josiah and Cyrus long before they were born (Isa 44:28–45:1; 1 Kings 13:1–2), Boyd comments: "These examples certainly show that Yahweh is the sovereign Lord of history and can predetermine and thus foreknow whatever he pleases. But they do not justify the conclusion that he desires to predetermine or foreknow the whole of the future."[44] In Boyd's view, "God determines whatever he sees fit and leaves as much of the future open as he sees fit."[45] In all, as Boyd puts it, "*God possesses perfect knowledge of the past and* present" and "some of the future is settled, either by present circumstances (Peter's character) or by God's sovereign design."[46]

---

[40] Boyd, "Open-Theism View," 23.
[41] In Boyd's words, "Future actions might also be settled not only because the Lord has decided them beforehand, but also because a person's character settles them." Boyd, "Open-Theism View," 20. Not all open theists, however, affirm these approaches.
[42] Boyd, "Open-Theism View," 24.
[43] Swinburne, *The Coherence of Theism*, 176. Check.
[44] Boyd, "Open-Theism View," 20.
[45] Boyd, "Open-Theism View," 19.
[46] Boyd, "Open-Theism View," 21.

Yet, some object, if God does not know the future exhaustively, how could God be omniscient? Hunt maintains that "the traditional doctrine" of omniscience maintains that "God has complete and infallible foreknowledge of the future."[47] This is "the overwhelming consensus of the Church's leading thinkers."[48] For instance, Augustine writes, "To confess that God exists, and at the same time to deny that he has foreknowledge of future things, is the most manifest folly."[49] Indeed, Augustine believes, "One who is not prescient of all future things is not God."[50] Accordingly, Helm refers to the open view as "weak omniscience."[51]

Many open theists respond to this objection by arguing that God is omniscient in the sense that God knows everything that is possible to know, given the way God has ordered the world. As William Hasker defines it, "God is omniscient" means that "God knows all [true] propositions which are such that God's knowing them is logically possible."[52] Hoffman and Rosenkrantz add, "Omniscience is not to be understood as knowing every truth, but rather as knowing as much as any being could know."[53] This view, open theists maintain, does not diminish divine omniscience because even God cannot do something that involves a logical contradiction.[54]

This hinges on the disputed claim that it is logically impossible for God to know the future free decisions of creatures. While open theists often maintain that God cannot know the future because the future is not yet there to be known, critics respond that this depends on a perceptualist account of knowledge; assuming that God's knowledge must depend on perception, as if "God looks and sees what is there."[55] Instead, Craig argues, one might adopt a "conceptualist model of divine knowledge," wherein "God does not acquire his knowledge of the world by anything like perception" and

---

[47] Hunt, "Simple Foreknowledge View," 65.
[48] Hunt, "Simple Foreknowledge View," 69. Hunt cites, in this regard, Justin Martyr, Augustine, Boethius, Anselm, Thomas Aquinas, Martin Luther, John Calvin, Jacob Arminius, and John Wesley.
[49] Augustine, *The City of God* 5.9.1 (NPNF1 2:90).
[50] Augustine, *The City of God* 5.9.4 (NPNF1 2:92).
[51] Helm, "Augustinian-Calvinist," 174. Similarly, see Hunt, "Simple Foreknowledge," 66.
[52] William Hasker, "A Philosophical Perspective," in *The Openness of God: A Biblical Challenge to the Traditional Understanding of God* (Downers Grove, IL: InterVarsity Press, 1994), 136. Similarly, see Swinburne, *The Christian God*, 133.
[53] Hoffman and Rosenkrantz, *The Divine Attributes*, 5.
[54] See Boyd, "Open-Theism View," 42.
[55] Craig, "The Middle-Knowledge View," in *Divine Foreknowledge: Four Views*, ed. James K. Beilby and Paul R. Eddy (Downers Grove, IL: InterVarsity, 2001), 133.

"God has essentially the property of knowing all truths" including "all truths concerning future events."[56]

Critics also object that the open view of divine omniscience compromises divine sovereignty and undermines a strong model of divine providence. Open theists often respond to this by arguing that God is like a master chess player in which "God neither predestines nor foreknows everything as settled but is nevertheless certain of victory because of his divine wisdom."[57] This shall be further discussed in Chapter 5.

The Ockhamist solution: God's knowing the future does not necessitate it

In contrast to the two previous views, many philosophers and theologians maintain that there is no logical or ontological incompatibility between the assertion that God knows the future exhaustively and that humans possess libertarian free will. One prominent approach to maintaining the compatibility of God's exhaustive definite foreknowledge and human libertarian freedom is often referred to as Ockhamism, named after the medieval philosopher William of Ockham (c. 1287–1347).[58] On Ockham's view, propositions about the future are either true or false—including propositions about creatures' future free choices. On the view that God's omniscience entails the knowledge of all true propositions, it follows that God has exhaustive knowledge of all true propositions about the future, including knowledge of the creatures' future free decisions.

While denying that "future contingents" are "present to" God, Ockham maintains that "God has evident cognition of all future contingents."[59] Ockham adds that this conclusion "cannot be proved *a priori* by means of the natural reason available to us, nevertheless [it] can be proved by means

---

[56]Craig, "Middle-Knowledge View," 133.
[57]Boyd, "Open-Theism View," 45.
[58]See, for example, Alvin Plantinga, "On Ockham's Way Out," *Faith and Philosophy* 3 (1986): 235–69.
[59]William Ockham, *Predestination, God's Foreknowledge, and Future Contingents*, 2nd ed. Translated with Introduction, notes, and appendices, by Marilyn McCord Adams and Norman Kretzmann (Indianapolis, IN: Hackett, 1983), 89, 90.

of the authorities of the Bible and the Saints, which are sufficiently well known."[60] Further, instead of attempting to offer an account of just how God possesses such knowledge, Ockham maintains: "I do not know how to describe the way [in which God has foreknowledge]."[61] Ockham maintains, further, that God's knowledge regarding "all future contingents" does not render what God knows itself to be "necessary." Rather, even though God foreknows something, "it is still possible that it will never have been true. And in that case there is a capacity for its opposite."[62] This view denies the common intuition that if God knows with certainty what I will do tomorrow, then I am not free (in a libertarian sense) with respect to what I will do tomorrow.

Here, the intuition that there is some contradiction between exhaustive definite foreknowledge and creaturely libertarian freedom, the Ockhamist argues, depends upon the fallacy of confusing different kinds of necessity, namely (1) necessity of consequence and (2) necessity of the thing consequent.[63] With respect to God's knowledge, the first kind of necessity—necessity of consequence—corresponds to the truth that, given the view that God's knowledge is infallible, it is necessarily true that whatever God believes about the future will come to pass. However, Ockhamists stress, this is very different from the claim that whatever God believes about the future will *necessarily* come to pass; a claim Ockhamists reject.

The conclusion that God's knowledge of humans' future free decisions renders those free decisions themselves necessary rests on a fairly common logical fallacy—the fallacy of necessity. The mistaken reasoning goes something like this:

(1) Necessarily, if God foreknows that I will work on this book tomorrow, then I will work on this book tomorrow.
(2) God foreknows that I will work on this book tomorrow.
(3) Therefore, I will *necessarily* work on this book tomorrow.[64]

Yet, the Ockhamist maintains, it is not true that I will *necessarily* work on this book tomorrow. I could decide not to work on this book tomorrow.

---

[60]Ockham, *Predestination*, 90.
[61]Ockham, *Predestination*, 90.
[62]Ockham, *Predestination*, 90.
[63]See Ockham, *Predestination*, 91.
[64]See J.P. Moreland and William Lane Craig, *Philosophical Foundations for a Christian Worldview* (Downers Grove, IL: IVP Academic, 2003), 519.

The mistake in the reasoning is in premise 3. The third premise should simply be:

(3')   Therefore, I will work on this book tomorrow.

It is true that God's belief cannot be wrong but the fact that God believes it does not make it such that a given event will *necessarily* happen. I *could* decide not to work on the book tomorrow and, if I do so, the Ockhamist argues, God would not have believed that I will work on this book tomorrow. As Craig puts it, "From God's knowledge that I shall do *x*, it does not follow that I must do *x* but only that I shall do *x*. That is in no way incompatible with my doing *x* freely."[65]

For an easier way to see the fallacy in the earlier argument, consider the following example. The three premises below are formally equivalent to the first three premises above. But, as you can see, the argument below is obviously flawed. Notice how moving the word "necessarily" results in an obviously false conclusion:

(1)   *Necessarily*, if Henry is a bachelor, Henry is unmarried.
(2)   Henry is a bachelor.
(3)   Therefore, Henry is *necessarily* unmarried.

Yet, Henry is not *necessarily* unmarried! Henry *could* become married. It just is the case that if Henry were to become married he would no longer be a bachelor. Here, what is necessarily true is the conjunction of (a) Henry is a bachelor and (b) Henry is unmarried. The error in the argument relates to moving "necessarily" from the conjunction of Henry being a bachelor and Henry being unmarried to Henry being unmarried itself.[66] As Alvin Plantinga explains, "*If I know that Henry is a bachelor, then Henry is a bachelor* is a necessary truth" but "it does not follow that" it "is necessarily true" that "Henry is a bachelor."[67]

Similarly, the Ockhamist argues, what is necessarily true with regard to God's knowledge is the conjunction of (a) God foreknows some event *x* and (b) event *x* will happen. Yet, it does not follow from this that event *x must* happen. The Ockhamist solution maintains that the common intuition that

---

[65] Craig, "Middle-Knowledge View," 127.
[66] As Craig puts it, "The fatalist illicitly transfers the necessity of the *inference* to the conclusion *itself.*" Craig, "Middle-Knowledge View," 127.
[67] Alvin Plantinga, *God, Freedom, and Evil* (Grand Rapids, MI: Eerdmans, 1977), 66 (emphasis original).

there is some contradiction between the assertions that God knows the future exhaustively and humans possess libertarian free will depends upon the fallacy of confusing necessity of consequence with necessity of the thing consequent. As Alvin Plantinga puts it, "The claim that divine omniscience [including exhaustive foreknowledge] is incompatible with human freedom seems to be based upon confusion."[68]

Although divine omniscience entails that God cannot hold incorrect beliefs, the Ockhamist maintains that God's belief about what an agent will do does not determine or necessitate what that agent does. Here, Craig explains, it is crucial not to confuse "certainty with necessity."[69] If God knows with certainty that Jones will mow his lawn on Saturday, it does not render it necessary that Jones will mow his lawn on Saturday.

To refute the oft-cited claim that God's belief that Jones will mow his lawn on Saturday entails that Jones could not do otherwise than mow his lawn on Saturday, one need only affirm the additional premise that, if Jones were to do otherwise than mow his lawn on Saturday, God would not have believed that Jones would mow his lawn on Saturday.[70] Thus, Craig maintains, "what is impossible is the *conjunction* of God's belief" that x will happen and x *not* happening.[71] However, Jones has the power to act in a different way, and if he *were* to act in that way, God *would have* believed differently.[72] That is, Jones "can do something different in such a way that God would have held a belief different from the belief he in fact holds."[73]

Some argue that this is impossible because one cannot change the past and thus cannot change God's past belief. However, the claim above is not that God's past belief could be changed but that God *would have* believed differently.[74] Yet, someone might argue that while there may be no logical necessity here, there is still some kind of "accidental necessity" of the past,

---

[68] Plantinga, *God, Freedom, and Evil*, 67.

[69] Craig, "Middle-Knowledge View," 127.

[70] See Plantinga, *God, Freedom, and Evil*, 67–73. Cf. Nelson Pike, "Divine Omniscience and Voluntary Action," *Philosophical Review* 74 (1965): 27–46.

[71] Craig, "A Middle-Knowledge Response," in *Divine Foreknowledge: Four Views*, ed. James K. Beilby and Paul R. Eddy (Downers Grove, IL: InterVarsity, 2001), 109.

[72] This is often argued further via a distinction between hard and soft facts, which I leave aside here in order to not further complicate the present discussion. See, for example, Swinburne, *The Christian God*, 132.

[73] William Lane Craig, *The Only Wise God: The Compatibility of Divine Foreknowledge and Human Freedom* (Grand Rapids, MI: Baker, 1987), 70.

[74] See Plantinga, *God, Freedom, and Evil*, 70–71.

or "temporal necessity."[75] That is, they believe it is just impossible that my decision could be free in a way that were I to do B instead of A, God would have known that I would do B instead of A and if I were to do A instead of B, God would have known that instead. Yet, Ockhamists claim, there is no conclusive argument demonstrating the impossibility of this kind of assertion. If so, the objection breaks down to an inability to conceive of how God's knowledge might be this way.

Here, Ockhamists tend to argue, in order to affirm *that* God knows the future free decisions of creatures, one need not claim to know *how* he does so (any more than one needs to know *how* God is omnipotent, eternal, etc. in order to affirm that he is so). One need only be able to affirm that God does so without any contradiction. Here, the basic argument is that one's freedom is not constrained simply by "God's merely knowing about it."[76] As Jacob Arminius (1560-1609) put it, "a thing does not come to pass because it has been foreknown or foretold; but it is foreknown and foretold because it is yet (*futura*) to come to pass."[77] While this perspective leaves many questions unanswered and is deemed inadequate by some, the Ockhamist maintains that the common claim that exhaustive divine foreknowledge is incompatible with creaturely libertarian freedom lacks support. Other accounts go beyond this, however, and we now turn to two such prominent approaches.

The Boethian solution: God knows the "future" directly

Some attempt to reconcile God's exhaustive definite foreknowledge and creaturely libertarian free will by maintaining that "God knows the future … via a direct apprehension of the future itself."[78] On this view, divine foreknowledge and human freedom are thought to be reconciled by

---

[75]See, on this, Edward Wierenga, "Omniscience," in *The Oxford Handbook of Philosophical Theology*, ed. Thomas P. Flint and Michael C. Rea (New York: Oxford, 2009), 138-39.
[76]Craig, "Middle-Knowledge View," 130.
[77]*The Writings of James Arminius*, trans. James Nichols (Grand Rapids, MI: Baker, 1977), 2:70 (Disputation 28.14). Notably, however, a number of prominent historians and theologians believe Arminius himself affirmed middle knowledge. See the discussion of middle knowledge below.
[78]Hunt, "Simple Foreknowledge," 67. Hunt, here, describes a view other than his own.

maintaining that God does not know "beforehand." Rather, all "times" are thought to be eternally present to God.[79] As such, God's knowledge of all events is eternal and "is not located *before* the free choice in question."[80]

On this view, God knows all of history as present to him, or *as if it were* present to him. This is sometimes called the atemporalist solution or the Boethian solution, advocated by many prominent thinkers in the tradition, including Boethius (*c*. 477–524), Anselm (1033/34–1109), and Aquinas (1225–74). For Boethius, eternity "is the whole, simultaneous and perfect possession of boundless life," in contrast to "temporal things."[81] As such, Boethius maintains, God, "embracing all the infinite spaces of the future and the past, considers them in his simple act of knowledge as though they were now going on."[82] This, Boethius maintains, is "not foreknowledge as it were of the future but knowledge of a never-passing instant."[83] Thus, via "divine foreknowledge," God "sees" things "present to him just such as in time they will at some future point come to be."[84] Things "are present indeed to him [God] but future with reference to imposed conditions of time" such that God knows that "something is going to happen," yet that something "lacks all necessity of happening."[85] That is, Boethius argues, the "same future event, when it is related to divine knowledge, is necessary, but when it is considered in its own nature it seems to be utterly and absolutely free."[86]

Although there is some dispute about whether Boethius (and others in the tradition) maintained a view compatible with eternalism (see Chapter 3), many contemporary proponents understand this view as presupposing eternalism. Further, Katherin Rogers maintains that "*only* the doctrine of divine [timeless] eternity allows an adequate reconciliation between divine foreknowledge and [libertarian] human freedom."[87] Given this view, she

---

[79]See Rogers, *Perfect Being Theology*, 67.

[80]Gregory E. Ganssle, "Introduction: Thinking about God and Time," in *God and Time: Four Views*, ed. Gregory Ganssle (Downers Grove, IL: InterVarsity, 2001), 20.

[81]Boethius, *The Consolation of Philosophy* 5.6, trans. H.F. Stewart, E.K. Rand, and S.J. Tester. Loeb Classical Library 74 (Cambridge, MA: Harvard University Press, 1973), 423.

[82]Boethius, *Consolation of Philosophy*, 5.6 (LCL 427).

[83]Boethius, *Consolation of Philosophy*, 5.6 (LCL 427).

[84]Boethius, *Consolation of Philosophy*, 5.6 (LCL 427).

[85]Boethius, *Consolation of Philosophy*, 5.6 (LCL 429).

[86]Boethius, *Consolation of Philosophy*, 5.6 (LCL 429). Cf. Anselm's discussion of this issue, in which he concludes "no impossibility is involved in the coexistence of God's foreknowledge and our free choices." Anselm, *De Concordia: The Compatibility of God's Foreknowledge, Predestination, and Grace with Human Freedom* 1.7.

[87]Rogers, *Perfect Being Theology*, 57.

contends, "God's knowledge of the 'future' does not render human choices unfree any more than does the historian's knowledge of the past."[88]

If the problem of reconciling divine foreknowledge and libertarian human freedom is a "time" problem, the supposed problem being that God knows what I will do *before* I do it, the problem evaporates on the atemporalist or Boethian solution. This is because, it is claimed, God knows timelessly rather than, strictly speaking, knowing "beforehand." In other words, Rogers explains, "If God is not in time at all then He knows things in eternity, not at a given time. But then the issue about the fixity of the past [the time problem] does not arise."[89] Hunt adds: "Since God's knowledge of Adam's sin does not precede the sin, it's not part of a fixed past dictating how Adam's future decisions and actions must go."[90] As Leftow puts it, "If God's knowledge is wholly outside time, it cannot have the sort of temporal relation to our actions which would let it determine them."[91]

A famous analogy of God's direct present knowledge of all events in history is that of "a circle where the center point represents eternity and the circumference represents time," used by Plotinus (*c.* 204/5–270), Boethius, and Aquinas.[92] As Aquinas puts it, "Something can be present to what is eternal only by being present to the whole of it, since the eternal does not have the duration of succession. The divine intellect, therefore, sees in the whole of its eternity, as being present to it, whatever takes place through the whole course of time."[93] Boethius also offers another analogy, writing that God "looks forward on all things as though from the highest peak of the world."[94] Similarly, Aquinas employs an analogy of a road, wherein one "who goes along the road, does not see those who come after him" but one "who sees the whole road from a height, sees at once all travelling by the way."[95]

Helm, however, contends such analogies are unsatisfactory because, in "the hilltop analogy of Boethius," the "person at the top of the hill and those beneath

---

[88]Rogers, *Perfect Being Theology*, 64.
[89]Rogers, *Perfect Being Theology*, 84. She, however, does not consider this "an adequate solution." Rogers, *Perfect Being Theology*, 85.
[90]Hunt, "Simple-Foreknowledge View," 78.
[91]Leftow, *Time and Eternity*, 251. Leftow claims that the "theory of time and eternity" he develops vindicates "Boethius' response to the freedom-foreknowledge problem." Leftow, *Time and Eternity*, 246. Cf. Brian Leftow, "Timelessness and Foreknowledge," *Philosophical Studies* 37/140 (1991): 309-25.
[92]Rogers, *Perfect Being Theology*, 57–58.
[93]Aquinas, *Summa contra Gentiles* 1.66.7.
[94]Boethius, *Consolation of Philosophy* 5.6 (LCL, 427).
[95]Aquinas, *Summa Theologiae* I.14.13.

her are all in time."⁹⁶ Further, the circle analogy "is also defective, because of course the temporal order is linear and not circular."⁹⁷ Further, these and other analogies rely heavily on time being sufficiently analogous to space, a matter of considerable dispute. Further, Edward Wierenga maintains, "whatever the merits of the doctrine of divine eternity, it does not by itself solve the [time] problem raised" because "an exactly analogous argument [to the one thought to be problematic for temporal foreknowledge] can be constructed in terms of the past truth of God's eternal knowledge of propositions about our future."⁹⁸

Moreover, even if positing an unextended divine vantage point would resolve the time problem relative to divine foreknowledge, some contend the time problem would remain relative to events prophesied to humans in advance. If God prophesies some event, then the human recipient of that prophecy would know the certainty of that event beforehand, amounting to "a version of the same problem we would have if we held that God is in time and foreknows my choice of breakfast."⁹⁹ Some eternalists might reply that if eternalism is true, the human recipient of such prophecy does not actually exist "before" in a genuine temporal sense, resolving the time problem.

Yet, some think, eternalism itself would render libertarian human freedom impossible because, on eternalism, the "future is 'already' *there*. It exists as much as what we call past and present."¹⁰⁰ If so, it seems the future is just as "unalterable" as the past. "Whatever I 'will' choose is 'already' chosen. My 'future' choice is eternally 'present' to God, and so I cannot do otherwise."¹⁰¹ Paul Helm even maintains that "the existence of an omniscient, timelessly eternal God is logically inconsistent with the libertarian freedom in any of his creatures."¹⁰² However, Rogers thinks such a conclusion is mistaken.¹⁰³

---

⁹⁶Helm, "Divine Timeless Eternity," in *God and Time: Four Views*, ed. Gregory Ganssle (Downers Grove, IL: InterVarsity, 2001), 38.

⁹⁷Helm, "Divine Timeless Eternity," 38.

⁹⁸Wierenga, "Omniscience," 140. So, also, Plantinga, "On Ockham's Way Out," 239–40. Linda Zagzebski thinks Plantinga's way of forming the objection fails because it is based on claims of "the past truth of propositions" whereas the Boethian solution posits the *timeless* rather than *past* truth of propositions. Nevertheless, she thinks the view that God timelessly believes that I do *x* at a given time raises a "dilemma exactly parallel to the" purported necessity of the past. Zagzebski, *The Dilemma of Freedom and Foreknowledge* (New York: Oxford University Press, 1991), 61. See Zagzebski, *Dilemma*, 44–46, 60–61.

⁹⁹Ganssle, "Introduction," 20. Cf. Helm, "Augustinian-Calvinist View," 187.

¹⁰⁰Rogers, *Perfect Being Theology*, 68.

¹⁰¹Rogers, *Perfect Being Theology*, 68. Rogers does not herself agree with this objection but gives voice to it.

¹⁰²Paul Helm, *Eternal God: A Study of God without Time* (New York: Oxford University Press, 1998), 144.

¹⁰³Rogers, *Perfect Being Theology*, 68–69.

She maintains that, while "God's eternal knowledge that I will choose *x* renders my choice for *x* necessary," this is a "*non-causal* sort of necessity which follows from, rather than determines the event in question" such that libertarian freedom is preserved. She explains: "If I know that you are walking it is necessary that you be walking," but "you may be walking quite freely since my knowledge neither caused you to walk, nor precluded the possibility that you might choose not to walk."[104] Further, she maintains, it is not a problem "that God knows what I will do *before* I do it," because the "reason God knows what I will choose is that I do in fact choose it. It is my choice which causes God's knowledge."[105]

Some critics maintain, further, that if God knows the entire "future" directly—"at a glance"—it seems that God cannot act providentially, except by causal determinism because the "future" would already include the presence or absence of divine action. If so, as William Hasker argues, "The doctrine of divine foreknowledge, in its most widely held form, is of *no importance whatever* for the religiously significant concerns about prayer, providence, and prophecy."[106] This objection, Hunt avers, requires that (1) "God can't put his foreknowledge to use without generating an explanatory circle" and that (2) "such circles are impossible."[107] However, Hunt thinks both of these premises can be challenged, while recognizing that this "Problem of Divine Providence presents a scenario that is every bit as tangled as the most complex time-travel story."[108] Somewhat parallel to this is the equally "tangled" and challenging problem of divine agency, which maintains that, if God foreknows everything, he must foreknow his own "future" decisions, perhaps undermining divine freedom.[109]

For his part, Hunt finds the Boethian view "very natural and attractive," but maintains an "agnostic" position regarding the "mechanism of divine foreknowledge." In his view, the Boethian account "simply exempts God from involvement in the puzzle" relative to foreknowledge "without doing anything to solve it."[110] Apart from a mechanism, Hunt offers an account

---

[104]Rogers, *Perfect Being Theology*, 85.
[105]Rogers, *Perfect Being Theology*, 86. She categorizes her view as the concomitance theory, but thinks it only works if God is timeless and knows all history directly and thus—despite similarities here—differentiates it from Ockhamism.
[106]Hasker, *God, Time, and Knowledge*, 55.
[107]Hunt, "Simple-Foreknowledge View," 97. Cf. Hasker, *God, Time, and Knowledge*, 57–58.
[108]Hunt, "Simple-Foreknowledge View," 101.
[109]We do not have space here to adequately discuss the debates over these potential problems. See the discussion in Hunt, "Simple-Foreknowledge View," 91–101.
[110]David Hunt, "Response to Helm," in *Divine Foreknowledge: Four Views*, ed. James K. Beilby and Paul R. Eddy (Downers Grove, IL: InterVarsity, 2001), 196.

of "simple foreknowledge" that does not hinge on direct apprehension. By "'simple' foreknowledge," Hunt means that "the *simple* affirmation" of foreknowledge ... is by itself wholly compatible with human freedom, divine agency and enhanced providential control."[111] However, while rejecting determinism, Hunt adopts the view that "Divine foreknowledge" does deprive us of "alternatives, but we just can't believe that it deprives [us] of free will."[112] Here, Hunt argues that "given exhaustive foreknowledge. it follows that the future is *epistemically* settled in the divine mind: but it does *not* follow that the future is *causally* settled in any way that conflicts with human freedom."[113]

The Molinist solution: God knows the future via middle knowledge

The Molinist solution attempts to reconcile God's exhaustive definite foreknowledge and creaturely libertarian free will by maintaining that God knows the future via middle knowledge. To say that God possesses "hypothetical" or "middle knowledge" means that God knows not only what any creature *might* do but also what any creature *would* freely do in any given circumstance. What an agent would freely do in some given circumstance is typically called a "would counterfactual" or a "counterfactual of creaturely freedom."[114] For example, in Charles Dickens's *A Christmas Carol*, what is revealed to Scrooge about the future is what *would* occur if Scrooge did not change course. Scrooge was not merely shown what "could" or "might" be, nor was he shown simply what "will be," but what "would be" if Scrooge maintained the course he was on.[115] Philosophers refer to knowledge of what "would be" as "counterfactual knowledge."[116] "Counterfactuals are conditional statements in the subjunctive mood."[117] We often speak and

---

[111] Hunt, "Simple-Foreknowledge View," 67.
[112] Hunt, "Simple-Foreknowledge View," 88.
[113] Hunt, "Response to Helm," 53.
[114] For an introduction to middle knowledge, see Thomas P. Flint, *Divine Providence* (Ithaca, NY: Cornell University Press, 2006), 11–71. See, further, Ken Perszyk, ed. *Molinism: The Contemporary Debate* (New York: Oxford University Press, 2011).
[115] Craig, "Middle-Knowledge View," 120.
[116] Craig, "Middle-Knowledge View," 120.
[117] Craig, "Middle-Knowledge View," 120.

think using counterfactuals. For example, "If I pulled out into traffic now, I wouldn't make it."[118]

If God knows what any creature *would* freely do in any given circumstances (middle knowledge), then God could factor that into his own decisions. By "adding" his own decisions to his knowledge of what any creature would do (along with his knowledge of all other factors), God could know and indeterministically plan the entire history of the world.[119] As Craig puts it, "Given middle knowledge and the divine decree [God's own decisions of what he will do], foreknowledge follows automatically as a result."[120]

The concept of middle knowledge can be traced back to the namesake of Molinism, Luis de Molina (1535–1600), and is now believed by many scholars to have been held by Arminius (1560–1609) as well.[121] Craig explains, "Luis de Molina developed his view precisely in response to the theological determinism of Calvin and Luther, and the brilliance of his achievement is that he did so without sacrificing divine sovereignty."[122] Middle knowledge is so-called because it refers to a kind of knowledge supposed to be in-between what scholastic thinkers referred to as natural knowledge and free knowledge; natural knowledge being divine knowledge of necessary truths—truths that could not be otherwise such as "all bachelors are unmarried"—and free knowledge being God's knowledge of contingent truths—truths that God freely determines to be true. God's knowledge of counterfactuals (middle knowledge), including what creatures would freely do in any given circumstances, is neither knowledge of necessary truths (natural knowledge) nor knowledge that is determined by God's will (free knowledge); it is knowledge of that which is contingently true, but not determined by God's will. In this regard, Molina himself maintained: "It is clear from Sacred Scripture that the supreme God has certain cognition of some future contingents that depend on human free choice, but that neither

---

[118]Craig, "Middle-Knowledge View," 120.

[119]See Flint, *Providence*.

[120]Craig, "Middle-Knowledge View," 133.

[121]On Molina's view, see Luis de Molina, *On Divine Foreknowledge: Part IV of the Concordia*, trans. Alfred J. Freddoso (Ithaca, NY: Cornell University Press, 1988). Cf. Kirk R. MacGregor, *Luis de Molina: The Life and Theology of the Founder of Middle Knowledge* (Grand Rapids, MI: Zondervan, 2015), 79–104. On Arminius and middle knowledge, see Richard Muller, *God, Creation and Providence in the Thought of Jacob Arminius* (Grand Rapids, MI: Baker, 1991), 155–66. See also Keith D. Stanglin and Thomas H. McCall, *Jacob Arminius: Theologian of Grace* (New York: Oxford University Press, 2012), 64–69.

[122]Craig, "Response to Boyd," in *Divine Foreknowledge: Four Views*, 59.

have existed nor ever will exist in reality and that hence do not exist in eternity either."[123]

Craig argues that middle knowledge holds many advantages, calling it "the single most fruitful theological concept I have ever encountered."[124] For one thing, he believes it is compatible with Scripture in a way the other theories are not. Further, he thinks Molinism provides a superior account of divine providence that can coherently explain "divine sovereignty over the affairs of" humans while maintaining libertarian human freedom (see, further, Chapter 5).[125]

Boyd claims, further, that Molinism entails that the future is settled in a way that excludes human freedom.[126] Craig argues, however, "Boyd equates God's *settling* something with God's *determining* or *controlling* it. But on the Molinist view God does *not* decree how free agents behave in the circumstances in which he places them" and thus they are genuinely free.[127] On Molinism, there is "the real possibility that the events foreknown by God will fail to happen; but if they were to fail to happen, God would have known that instead. Thus, this sense of being 'settled' does not exclude possibilities from *reality* but on the contrary, *affirms them*."[128] Craig explains, further: "The Molinist is quite glad to admit that nothing I can do now will cause or bring about the past. But he will insist that it does lie within my power to freely perform some action *a*, and if *a* were to occur, then the past [relative to God's knowledge] would have been different than it in fact is."[129]

Critics contend, further, that middle knowledge is utterly mysterious, particularly relative to how God could know future contingents. Craig replies:

> Molinists could respond either that God knows the individual essence of every possible creature so well that he knows just what each creature would [freely] do under any set of circumstances he might place him in, or that God, being omniscient, simply discerns all the truths there are and, prior to the divine decree, there are not only necessary truths but counterfactual

---

[123]Molina, *On Divine Foreknowledge*, Disputation 49.9 (Freddoso, 116).
[124]Craig, "Middle-Knowledge View," 125.
[125]Craig, "Middle-Knowledge View," 134.
[126]See Boyd, "Response to Craig," in *Divine Foreknowledge: Four Views*, 145–46.
[127]Craig, "Response to Boyd," in *Divine Foreknowledge: Four Views*, 57 (emphasis original).
[128]Craig, "Response to Boyd," in *Divine Foreknowledge: Four Views*, 57 (emphasis original).
[129]Craig, "Middle-Knowledge View," 131.

truths, and therefore God possesses not only natural knowledge but middle knowledge as well.[130]

In this regard, perhaps the most serious objection to Molinism is the so-called grounding objection. This objection maintains that, absent determinism, there appears to be no ground or "truth-maker" of "'would' counterfactuals of creaturely freedom."[131] If determinism is false, counterfactuals of creaturely freedom cannot be grounded in God's will. Yet, Boyd argues (assuming presentism), it seems that such counterfactuals cannot be grounded in creatures because God knows counterfactuals of creaturely freedom prior to those creatures' existence. Thus, Boyd criticizes, "To embrace classical Molinism, one must accept that the facts about what every conceivable free agent would do in every conceivable circumstance simply exist, from all eternity, as an ungrounded, metaphysical surd."[132] Craig responds to this objection by arguing that it is not clear that counterfactuals of creaturely freedom require "truth-makers" and, even if they do, "no reason has been given why their truth-makers cannot be the facts or state of affairs which are disclosed by the disquotation principle" such that "what makes it true that 'If I were rich, I would buy a Mercedes,' is the fact that if I were rich I would buy a Mercedes."[133]

As Plantinga puts it, "It seems to me much clearer that some counterfactuals of freedom are at least possibly true than that the truth of propositions must, in general, be grounded" via a truth maker.[134] Here, much hinges upon the principle of bivalence, which states: "For any proposition p, p is either true or

---

[130] Craig, "Middle-Knowledge View," 133.

[131] Greg Boyd, "Response to Craig," in *Four Views on Divine Providence*, ed. Dennis W. Jowers (Grand Rapids, MI: Zondervan, 2011), 131. Cf. Scott A. Davison, "Craig on the Grounding Objection to Middle Knowledge," *Faith and Philosophy* 21/3 (2004): 365–9; Timothy O'Connor, "The Impossibility of Middle Knowledge," in *Oxford Readings in Philosophical Theology*, ed. Michael C. Rea (New York: Oxford University Press, 2009), 2:45–67.

[132] Boyd, "Response to Craig," in *Four Views on Divine Providence*, 131. Cf. Paul Helm and Terrance L. Tiessen, "Does Calvinism Have Room for Middle Knowledge? A Conversation," *WTJ* 71 (2009): 437–54.

[133] William Lane Craig, "Middle Knowledge, Truth-Makers, and the 'Grounding Objection,'" in *Oxford Readings in Philosophical Theology*, 2:83, 81. See also Thomas Flint's response that "for every version of the grounding objection of which I am aware, some elaboration of the 'Are So!' or of the 'So What?' response can be made by a Molinist." "Divine Providence," in *The Oxford Handbook of Philosophical Theology*, ed. Thomas P. Flint and Michael C. Rea (New York: Oxford University Press, 2008), 281. Cf. William Lane Craig, "Ducking Friendly Fire: Davison on the Grounding Objection," *Philosophia Christi* 8/1 (2006): 161–66.

[134] Alvin Plantinga, "Self-Profile," in *Alvin Plantinga*, ed. James E. Tomberlin and Peter van Inwagen (Dordrecht: D. Riedel, 1985), 374.

false."[135] On the "standard definition," Craig argues, an "agent is omniscient if and only if he knows all truths and believes no falsehoods."[136] This "entails that if there are counterfactual truths, then an omniscient being must know them."[137] Craig thinks the principle of bivalence indicates there are indeed counterfactual truths, including counterfactuals of creaturely freedom regarding what any person would freely do in any situation.[138] Further, Craig believes "Scripture itself gives example of such true counterfactuals," supporting Molinism. This brings us to the debate over the biblical data.[139]

Biblical data relevant to the debate over divine omniscience

Christian theists generally agree that God is omniscient. Many texts are offered to support this view, including Psalm 147:5, which states that God's "understanding is infinite." Further, "Have you not known? Have you not heard? The LORD is the everlasting God, the Creator of the ends of the earth. He does not faint or grow weary; his understanding is unsearchable" (Isa 40:28, NRSV). The NT declares, "God is greater than our heart and knows all things" (1 John 3:20) and "there is no creature hidden from His sight, but all things are open and laid bare to the eyes of Him with whom we have to do" (Heb 4:13).

Scripture also frequently speaks of God's exhaustive and intimate knowledge of humans. God "knows the secrets of the heart" (Ps 44:21). Later, Psalm 139:1–5 declares:

> O Lord, You have searched me and known me. You know when I sit down and when I rise up; You understand my thought from afar. You scrutinize my path and my lying down, And are intimately acquainted with all my ways. Even before there is a word on my tongue, Behold, O Lord, You know it all. You have enclosed me behind and before, And laid Your hand upon me. (Psalm 139:1–5).

---

[135] Craig, "Response to Boyd," in *Divine Foreknowledge: Four Views*, 56.
[136] Craig, "Middle-Knowledge View," 138.
[137] Craig, "Middle-Knowledge View," 137.
[138] Craig, "Middle-Knowledge View," 139.
[139] Craig, "Middle-Knowledge View," 140.

Does God Know Everything?

Likewise, Jesus affirms, "your Father knows what you need before you ask Him" (Matt 6:8; cf. 10:30) and "God knows your hearts" (Luke 16:15; cf. Acts 15:8).

However, as seen above, the primary debate among Christians relative to divine omniscience is about whether God knows the future free decisions of creatures. In this regard, Isaiah 46:9–10 proclaims: "Remember the former things long past, for I am God, and there is no other; I am God, and there is no one like Me, Declaring the end from the beginning, and from ancient times things which have not been done, saying, 'My purpose will be established, And I will accomplish all My good pleasure.'" Determinists take these verses to mean that God knows the future because he determines it. Many indeterminists, however, understand this as a reference to God knowing the future without determining it.

Open theists like Boyd, however, contend this passage—and others like it—only requires that God predetermines *some* things, while leaving others unsettled. Boyd claims, "Neither this nor any other passage in Scripture says that God foreknows or declares *everything* that is going to occur. This passage specifies that God declares *'the end* from the beginning.'"[140] Exhaustive foreknowledge advocates, however, contend the phrase "the end from the beginning" is a merism that encompasses not just the "end" and the "beginning" but also *everything* in between. To support this interpretation, advocates point out that the broader context of this passage includes God repeatedly appealing to his knowledge of the future as evidence that he is the only true God, in contrast to the false gods that cannot "declare to us what is going to take place" (Isa 41:22). Indeed, God taunts the false gods, saying, "announce to us what is coming. Declare the things that are going to come afterward, that we may know that you are gods" (Isa 41:22–23; cf. 48:3–5). Hunt comments, Isaiah makes "God's ability to know what will happen before it happens … the chief mark by which the true God may be distinguished from false gods."[141]

Further, advocates of exhaustive definite foreknowledge believe Psalm 139:16 evinces God's exhaustive foreknowledge of the author's life. It states: "Your eyes have seen my unformed substance; And in Your book were all written the days that were ordained for me, When as yet there was not one of them." Exhaustive foreknowledge advocates also appeal to many other texts. For example, 1 Peter 1:20 states of Christ: "He was foreknown

---

[140] Boyd, "Open-Theism View," 16.
[141] Hunt, "Simple-Foreknowledge View," 68.

[*proginosko*] before the foundation of the world, but has appeared in these last times for the sake of you." Acts 2:23 also uses the word *proginosko*, which literally means to know beforehand, stating, "this Man, delivered over by the predetermined plan and foreknowledge [*proginosko*] of God, you nailed to a cross by the hands of godless men and put Him to death" (Acts 2:23; cf. 4:27–28; 15:16–18).

Among the most prominent references, Romans 8:29 declares: "For those whom He foreknew, He also predestined to become conformed to the image of His Son, so that He would be the firstborn among many brethren" (cf. 1 Pet 1:1–2). Determinists take this to mean that God foreknew what he determined but indeterminist foreknowledge advocates maintain that the text distinguishes foreknowledge from predestination, with some taking the word "predestination" here to refer to God's plan or purpose that takes into account things he indeterministically foreknows. In this regard, Ephesians 1:11 refers to those who "have obtained an inheritance, having been predestined according to His purpose who works all things after the counsel of His will." Exhaustive foreknowledge advocates view this—and texts like it—as teaching that God's plan or purpose is all-encompassing.

Foreknowledge advocates also point to many specific examples that suggest God knows the future free decisions of humans, including prophecies regarding Cyrus (Isa 44:28–45:1) and Josiah (1 Kings 13:1–2), which call each by name and state some things they would do long before they were born. To explain such texts, open theists sometimes appeal to selective determinism. Boyd states: "These decrees obviously established parameters around the parents' freedom to naming these individuals (cf. Luke 1:18–22, 59–64) and also restricted the scope of freedom these individuals could exercise regarding *particular foreordained activities*."[142] Yet, critics ask, if God selectively determined things like this, why did God not also selectively determine that horrendous evils be prevented? Craig further states: "Ironically, open theology is forced to revert to Calvinistic determinism to account for God's providence and thus actually winds up destroying [consistently granted] human freedom."[143]

Another potential example of exhaustive definite foreknowledge appears in the Joseph narrative, wherein God reveals "Pharaoh's future decision to restore the chief butler and condemn the chief baker" and "foretell[s]

---

[142] Boyd, "Open-Theism View," 19–20.
[143] Craig, "Response to Boyd," in *Divine Foreknowledge: Four Views*, 58.

seven years of plenty and seven years of famine"[144] (see Gen 41). Elsewhere, Scripture contains long-term, large-scale prophecies about the rising and falling of kingdoms (e.g., Daniel 2, Daniel 7) and even, some believe, about the timing of Christ's ministry and death on the cross (Daniel 9). If these and/or other passages are taken as genuinely foretelling events, the foreknowledge advocate maintains, they are exceedingly difficult to explain without extensive foreknowledge of future human decisions.

Foreknowledge advocates point to numerous other examples. Two of the most prominent are the cases of Jesus predicting Peter's denial and Judas's betrayal. Regarding the former, after Peter protests that he will not "fall away," Jesus correctly predicts: "Truly I say to you, that this very night, before a rooster crows twice, you yourself will deny Me three times." (Mark 14:27–30; cf. 14:13–15). To explain this, Boyd appeals to the settled character hypothesis, saying "the Father knew and revealed to Jesus one solidified aspect of Peter's character that was predictable in the immediate future."[145] Paul Helseth contends, however, that Peter's character was not yet irreversibly "solidified" when he denied Christ (as evinced by Peter's later repentance and other decisions).[146] Craig adds, even if "Jesus could infer that Peter would fail him, how could he infer that Peter's failure would come in the form of denials, rather than, say, flight or silence, and how could he infer *three* denials before the cock crowed *twice*?"[147] Craig contends, further: "In the absence of middle knowledge, Boyd's claim that God 'orchestrated' the circumstances implies that God took away the freedom of the servant girl and all the others in the courtyard of the high priest's house, as well as those at the arrest of Jesus."[148]

Regarding Judas's betrayal, John 6:64 states, "Jesus knew from the beginning who they were who did not believe, and who it was that would betray Him." Boyd takes this text to "mean that Jesus knew who would betray him *early on*."[149] Yet, exhaustive foreknowledge advocates emphasize that Jesus quotes Psalm 41:9—written centuries earlier—as a prophecy of Judas's betrayal and characterizes it as a fulfillment of this Scripture (John 13:18). However, regarding Judas and other "individuals who played foreordained

---

[144] Hunt, "Simple-Foreknowledge View," 68.

[145] Boyd, "Open-Theism View," 20.

[146] Paul Kjoss Helseth, "Response to Boyd," in *Four Views on Divine Providence*, ed. Dennis W. Jowers (Grand Rapids: Zondervan, 2011), 57.

[147] Craig, "Response to Boyd," in *Divine Foreknowledge: Four Views*, 57 (emphasis original).

[148] Craig, "Response to Boyd," in *Divine Foreknowledge: Four Views*, 57.

[149] Boyd, "Open-Theism View," 21.

roles in the death of Jesus" (Acts 2:23), Boyd contends, "Scripture never suggests that these specific individuals were destined or foreknown to carry out these wicked deeds. It only teaches that these specific deeds were destined and foreknown to take place."[150] Yet, exhaustive foreknowledge advocates contend, phrases like "he who eats my bread" (John 13:18; cf. Ps 41:9) is rather specific and many other predictions include specific details. Further, exhaustive foreknowledge advocates maintain that Jesus's statement in John 13:19—"From now on I am telling you before it comes to pass, so that when it does occur, you may believe that I am He"—appeals to divine foreknowledge to undergird faith regarding who Christ is, mirroring God's claim against the false gods in Isaiah 41:22–23. Hunt comments, in Matthew 26:

> We find Jesus predicting, in quick succession, that he will be betrayed on the feast of the Passover (v. 2) by a disciple (v. 21) 'who has dipped his hand into the bowl with me' (v. 23); that it is Judas in particular who will betray him (v. 25); that his other disciples will desert him (v. 31); and that Peter will deny him three times before morning (v. 34)—none of which looks like it could be foreknown with certainty in the absence of some supernatural insight into the future.[151]

The biblical data above is understood by both determinist and indeterminist advocates of exhaustive definite foreknowledge as supporting their respective views (I leave aside the debate over determinism here because it is the topic of the following chapter). Such data, however, is more difficult for the open theist to explain. Boyd argues that "while the Bible certainly celebrates God's foreknowledge and control of the future, it does not warrant the conclusion that the future is *exhaustively* controlled or foreknown as settled by God."[152] Exhaustive foreknowledge advocates such as Rogers believe, however, "The Bible expresses, clearly and often, the view that God knows the future" and knows it exhaustively.[153]

Many open theists, however, claim that some biblical passages indicate that God does not know the future exhaustively. For his part, Boyd acknowledges what he calls the foreknowledge "motif" of Scripture and states that he would believe it teaches that "the future is *exhaustively* settled" if it were not for "other biblical material that depicts the future as partly open."[154] For

---

[150] Boyd, "Open-Theism View," 22.
[151] Hunt, "Simple-Foreknowledge View," 68.
[152] Boyd, "Open-Theism View," 14.
[153] Rogers, *Perfect Being Theology*, 64.
[154] Boyd, "Open-Theism View," 15–16.

example, Boyd maintains, "God asks questions about the future, speaks of the future in conditional terms, regrets the outcome of decisions he has made, changes his mind in response to changing situations, and so on."[155]

Some maintain, in this respect, that Boyd's view is "guilty of naïve literalism," which, if applied consistently, would lead him to "believe not only that God literally changes his mind, but also that God literally lacks present knowledge; literally has eyes, arms and a mouth; and literally travels to and from earth."[156] Boyd responds that, of course, "all God's revelatory language is 'accommodated' to our human condition" and "God sometimes uses metaphors, symbols and anthropomorphisms to accomplish this task. But this nonliteral language accomplishes this task because it communicates *something truthful about God.*"[157] He contends, further, that "reinterpreting the passages that constitute the motif of future openness as 'metaphorical' does not *clarify* these passages: it *undermines* them."[158] Boyd alleges that critics unwarrantedly take "the entire openness motif of Scripture" as anthropomorphic.[159] He contends this is based on "philosophical presupposition[s]," indebted to "Ancient Greek philosophers," that are not based on "the plain meaning of Scripture."[160]

Apart from the debate over which language should be identified as anthropomorphic and how such language should be understood, some exhaustive foreknowledge advocates contend that, even if read straightforwardly, the texts Boyd and other open theists employ do not indicate that God lacks knowledge about the future. For example, Boyd contends that God tests Abraham in Genesis 22 because God "wants to know whether Abraham will choose to obey him or not."[161] However, interpreting God's declaration in Genesis 22:12—"now I know that you fear God"—as meaning that God did not already know Abraham feared God seems to deny divine omniscience relative to the *present* state of Abraham's mind. In this text and elsewhere (e.g., Gen 3:9–13), God's questions may have a different purpose than seeking information, analogous to when a mother—already knowing the answer—asks her toddler with cookie crumbs on his face, did

---

[155] Boyd, "Open-Theism View," 23.
[156] Boyd, "Response to Helm," 192. Cf. Bruce Ware, *God's Lesser Glory: The Diminished God of Open Theism* (Wheaton, IL: Crossway, 2000), 76–77.
[157] Boyd, "Response to Helm," 192 (emphasis original).
[158] Boyd, "Response to Helm," 192.
[159] Boyd, "Response to Helm," 193.
[160] Boyd, "Open-Theism View," 39–40.
[161] Boyd, "Open-Theism View," 33.

you get into the cookies? Tom Morris contends: "When God asks a question, he seeks to teach, not to be taught. We are not to infer that his knowledge is incomplete, requiring augmentation."[162]

Boyd also argues that expressions of divine frustration—such as God's searching for an intercessor but not finding any (Ezek 22:30–31)—and claims that God desires that all be saved indicate that God does not know the future.[163] However, critics respond, one can be frustrated by something one has certain prior knowledge about—a mother in child custody court might be frustrated by false claims made by her ex-husband, even if she knew in advance precisely what those claims would be. Further, critics of open theism argue, even on Boyd's view that God possesses all knowledge of the present, God would have known already that no suitable intercessor would be "found" and God could desire that all be saved even if he knows that some will reject his free offer of salvation.

Open theists also often appeal to instances that they interpret to mean that God changes his mind. Boyd claims, "God sometimes expresses in Scripture disappointment with the results of decisions *he himself made*."[164] After citing Genesis 6:6—"The LORD was sorry [*nāḥam*] that He had made man on the earth, and He was grieved in His heart"—Boyd comments, "If God truly wished he had never made humans—to the point of his wanting to destroy them and start over—shouldn't we conclude that the extent of their depravity *wasn't* a foregone conclusion at the time he created them?"[165] Yet, exhaustive foreknowledge advocates argue, one should not take Genesis 6:6 to mean that God regretted creating humans, particularly given God's action to save humans in the ark and later to save humans via the cross. God might be genuinely sorrowful over and regret the evil that occurred without indicating lack of foreknowledge of the outcome or that he would not create humans if he had it to do over again. In this regard, the exhaustive foreknowledge advocate argues, *nāḥam* (in the niphal stem as in Gen 6:6) basically means "suffer emotional pain," sometimes "extended to describe the release of emotional tension" via God's "retracting a declared action" such as "punishment" or "blessing" (cf. Jer 18:7–10).[166] It thus typically

---

[162]Thomas V. Morris, *Our Idea of God: An Introduction to Philosophical Theology* (Notre Dame, IN: University of Notre Dame Press, 1991), 85.
[163]Boyd, "Open-Theism View," 28.
[164]Boyd, "Open-Theism View," 26.
[165]Boyd, "Open-Theism View," 26.
[166]H. Van Dyke Parunak, "A Semantic Survey of *Nhm*," *Biblica* 56 (1975): 532. Cf. John C. Peckham, *The Concept of Divine Love* (New York: Peter Lang, 2014), 266–68.

depicts divine "sorrow" but, exhaustive foreknowledge advocates maintain, need not indicate lack of foreknowledge or be a "suggestion of regret" for God's own actions.[167]

Another oft-raised example of divine *nāḥam* is 1 Samuel 15:11, wherein God says "I regret [*nāḥam*] that I have made Saul king, for he has turned back from following Me and has not carried out My commands." Boyd comments, if God "was eternally certain that Saul would 'turn back' when he made him king, how can God regret making him king because he 'turned back?'"[168] Foreknowledge advocates may respond that God did not want to make anyone king of Israel in the first place (at least at that time) and warned Israel what would happen if they had a king (1 Sam 8:6–22). It is thus not surprising that God would be sorrowful that he made Saul king and does not indicate any lack of foresight.

Further, Boyd cites Isaiah 5:4, where God says of his vineyard: "Why, when I expected it to produce good grapes did it produce worthless ones?" Boyd asks: "How can the Lord say that he 'expected' one thing to occur, only to discover something else occurred instead, if he is eternally certain of all that shall ever occur?"[169] In response, the exhaustive foreknowledge advocate notes that this is a rhetorical question and that the Hebrew term translated "expected" (*qāvāh*) does not connote lack of knowledge but literally means "waited." Hunt comments that even in English the term "expect" often does not refer to a belief about the future but refers to a standard or expectation that one "expects" others to meet (even if one knows they will not fully meet it).[170]

Boyd also raises texts that are translated as God saying things like "I thought [*āmar*]" Israel "'will return to me'; but she did not return" (Jer 3:7). Yet, in Jeremiah 3:7 and elsewhere (e.g., 3:19), the word translated "I thought" is the verb *āmar*, which simply means "to say." This connotes nothing about God's knowledge but again may refer to a command (as NKJV, NASB, and others render it) or an expectation in the above-referenced sense of a standard that ought to be met. In this and other regards, Hunt argues, Boyd's "own readings can be turned against him, since they implicate God in various *mistaken beliefs*."[171]

---

[167]Parunak, "A Semantic Survey of *Nhm*," 513n.1.
[168]Boyd, "Open-Theism View," 26.
[169]Boyd, "Open-Theism View," 24.
[170]Hunt, "Response to Boyd," 50.
[171]Hunt, "Response to Boyd," 51.

Boyd also contends, "Three times in Jeremiah the Lord expresses his surprise at Israel's behavior by saying his children were doing things 'which I did not command or decree, *nor did it enter my mind*' (Jer 19:5; cf. 7:31; 32:35)."[172] Opponents argue that these passages do not express surprise but might be akin to saying of some despicable behavior, that is "unheard of." Boyd himself claims that God "anticipates all possibilities," so it could not be literally true that the possibility had never "entered God's mind." Further, given the immediately preceding words that God "did not command" such things, a likely reading is that it never entered God's mind *to "command" them to do* such horrible things like child sacrifice.

Further, some exhaustive foreknowledge advocates maintain there is considerable biblical evidence for middle knowledge. Craig comments, "Biblically speaking, it is not difficult to show that God possesses counterfactual knowledge" (see, for example, 1 Sam 23:8–13; Matt 11:23; 1 Cor 2:8; cf. Exod 3:19).[173] That God has counterfactual knowledge, Craig argues, is especially evident in texts like 1 Samuel 23:8–13 (cf. Jer 38:17–18). Therein, David asks God if the men of Keilah will surrender him to Saul and whether Saul will come down and God says, "He will come down" and "They will surrender you" (1 Sam 23:11–12). Then, David and his men leave Keilah and Saul "gave up the pursuit" (1 Sam 23:13). Here, God reveals to David "what *would* happen under certain circumstances," but which did not occur because David did not stay at Keilah.[174]

However, Craig notes, the textual evidence for counterfactual knowledge does not settle the question in favor of Molinism since determinists have also traditionally maintained that God possesses counterfactual knowledge.[175] The difference is that determinists believe God possesses such knowledge on the basis of his decree regarding what he will do and Molinists believe God possesses such knowledge logically prior to his decree. The Molinist argues, "If there are true counterfactuals of creaturely freedom, God must know them."[176] Scripture teaches that there are true counterfactuals of creaturely freedom. Therefore, if determinism is false, God possesses middle knowledge.

---

[172] Boyd, "Open-Theism View," 24 (emphasis original).
[173] Craig, "Middle-Knowledge View," 123.
[174] Craig, "Middle-Knowledge View," 123 (emphasis mine).
[175] Craig, "Middle-Knowledge View," 125.
[176] Craig, "Middle-Knowledge View," 139.

The debate over determinism is taken up in Chapter 5. For now, many (on all sides of the issue) agree with Helm that "we are constrained by the biblical witness" as "a set of fixed points" such that "we must reflect upon the cogency or coherence of the several parts of that witness."[177] Further, even if in the end we have to "draw the conclusion that we cannot at present see how these parts cohere," we might "have to be content with showing the ideas are not inconsistent. However, it is not open to us to amend or modify that witness in any way in the interests of greater comprehensibility."[178]

Conclusion

This chapter has introduced some prominent contemporary approaches to divine omniscience, with special attention to the debate over divine foreknowledge and a discussion of some relevant biblical data. The next chapter turns to the related issues of divine omnipotence and providence.

Study questions

1. What is the relationship between divine omniscience and divine foreknowledge? Could a God who does not know the future free decisions of creatures still be considered omniscient? What role does one's understanding of God's relation to time play in how one answers these questions?
2. What do you think of the various views of divine omniscience, particularly relative to whether God knows the future free decisions of creatures? Do you think it is possible that God could know the future without undermining genuine free will?
3. What difference does it make whether God knows the future exhaustively or not? Does it matter whether God can predict the future exhaustively? What is lost if God does not know the future exhaustively?

---

[177]Helm, "Augustinian-Calvinist View," 164.
[178]Helm, "Augustinian-Calvinist View," 164.

4. How do you think one should decide between proposed solutions to the problem of divine foreknowledge and human freedom? What role does the data from Scripture play in the way you think of these issues? What do you make of views in the Christian tradition relative to this issue? What are some of the implications for Christian theism regarding how these questions are answered?
5. What are some advantages of each view? What are some difficulties that you believe each view faces? Can you think of any further objections to the views discussed in this chapter? Can you think of any further arguments in favor of the views discussed in this chapter? Do you think it is adequate to hold a view that avoids contradiction but leaves a great deal of mystery?

Suggestions for further reading

Selected premodern sources

Augustine, *City of God* 5.9.
Boethius, *The Consolation of Philosophy* 5.2–6
Anselm, *De Concordia: The Compatibility of God's Foreknowledge, Predestination, and Grace with Human Freedom* 1–2.
Thomas Aquinas, *Summa contra Gentiles* 1.44–71.
William Ockham, *Predestination, God's Foreknowledge, and Future Contingents*. 2nd ed. Translated with Introduction, notes, and appendices, by Marilyn McCord Adams and Norman Kretzmann (Indianapolis, IN: Hackett, 1983).
Luis de Molina, *On Divine Foreknowledge: Part IV of the Concordia*. Translated by Alfred J. Freddoso (Ithaca, NY: Cornell University Press, 1988).

Selected modern/contemporary sources

Beilby, James K. and Paul R. Eddy, eds. *Divine Foreknowledge: Four Views* (Downers Grove, IL: InterVarsity, 2001).
Cobb, Jr., John B. and Clark Pinnock, eds. *Searching for an Adequate God: A Dialogue between Process and Free Will Theists* (Grand Rapids, MI: Eerdmans, 2000).

Craig, William Lane. *The Only Wise God: The Compatibility of Divine Foreknowledge and Human Freedom* (Grand Rapids, MI: Baker, 1987).

Erickson, Millard. *What Does God Know and When Does He Know It?* (Grand Rapids, MI: Zondervan, 2003).

Hasker, William. *God, Time, and Knowledge* (Ithaca, NY: Cornell University Press, 1989).

Leftow, Brian. "Timelessness and Foreknowledge." *Philosophical Studies* 37/140 (1991): 309–25.

Perszyk, Ken, ed. *Molinism: The Contemporary Debate* (New York: Oxford University Press, 2011).

Pike, Nelson. "Divine Omniscience and Voluntary Action." *Philosophical Review* 74 (1965): 27–46.

Pinnock, Clark, Richard Rice, John Sanders, William Hasker, and David Basinger. *The Openness of God: A Biblical Challenge to the Traditional Understanding of God* (Downers Grove, IL: InterVarsity Press, 1994).

Plantinga, Alvin. *God, Freedom, and Evil* (Grand Rapids, MI: Eerdmans, 1977), 66–73.

Plantinga, Alvin. "On Ockham's Way Out." *Faith and Philosophy* 3 (1986): 235–69.

Rogers, Katherin A. *Perfect Being Theology* (Edinburgh: Edinburgh University Press, 2000), 71–91.

Teske, Roland J. "Omniscience, Omnipotence, and Divine Transcendence." *The New Scholasticism* 53/3 (1979): 280.

Wierenga, Edward. "Omniscience," in *The Oxford Handbook of Philosophical Theology*, ed. Thomas P. Flint and Michael C. Rea (New York: Oxford, 2009), 129–44.

Zagzebski, Linda. *The Dilemma of Freedom and Foreknowledge* (New York: Oxford University Press, 1991).

5

Can God Do Anything?

Can God do anything and everything? Does God always get what he wants? These questions relate to ongoing controversies over the extent and exercise of divine power. Some have questioned whether it is coherent to say that God is all-powerful (omnipotent). Even if the concept of divine omnipotence is internally coherent, other questions arise regarding the exercise of God's power, that is, relative to divine providence, minimally defined as God's action to bring about his purposes in the world. Specifically, does everything happen just as God has determined it would? Does God cause everything? These questions center on the debate over determinism.

Near one end of the spectrum, some theologians maintain that God acts only by persuasion; God's power is, by nature, limited to the extent to which God can persuade free creatures to cooperate with divine desires. On the other end of the spectrum, some theologians maintain theistic determinism, typically understood as the view that God causally determines everything to happen just as it does. Many other theologians maintain that God is omnipotent but grants significant freedom to creatures such that theistic determinism is false.

These views hold significant ramifications for understanding divine providence. The debate often centers on the relationship between divine sovereignty and creaturely freedom. Some who defend divine sovereignty are critical of libertarian conceptions of human freedom, which they believe undermine divine sovereignty. Conversely, many advocates of libertarian freedom are critical of some conceptions of divine sovereignty, which they believe undermine genuine free will. Whereas some think divine sovereignty and human free will are incompatible, others maintain they can be held together consistently. Much depends on how sovereignty and free will are defined. This chapter introduces prominent contemporary perspectives on divine omnipotence and on the providential exercise of divine power, including a brief survey of some relevant biblical data.

The coherence of omnipotence?

The perfect or greatest being, it is often supposed, would possess the greatest possible power. Accordingly, the vast majority of Christian theists maintain that God is all-powerful (omnipotent). Some have claimed, however, that the concept of omnipotence is incoherent, at least if it means that "God can do everything."[1] If God is all-powerful, some claim, he should be able to do anything, including things like making a square circle. However, philosophers have long understood omnipotence in a way that defeats this objection. As Richard Swinburne argues, the assertion "God is omnipotent, that is, literally can do anything" requires the "obvious qualification that to be omnipotent a person need not be able to do the logically impossible."[2]

As C. S. Lewis explains it:

> [God's] Omnipotence means power to do all that is intrinsically possible, not to do the intrinsically impossible. You may attribute miracles to him, but not nonsense. This is no limit to his power. If you choose to say "God can give a creature free will and at the same time withhold free will from it," you have not succeeded in saying *anything* about God: meaningless combinations of words do not suddenly acquire meaning simply because we prefix to them the two other words "God can." ... It is no more possible for God than for the weakest of his creatures to carry out both of two mutually exclusive alternatives; not because his power meets an obstacle, but because nonsense remains nonsense even when we talk it about God.[3]

Omnipotence, then, only requires the "power to do what is logically possible."[4] Indeed, Ronald Nash explains, in "classical Christian discussions of omnipotence," it "was always understood to be compatible with certain limitations upon God's power. There are certain things that even an omnipotent God cannot do."[5] As Thomas Aquinas put it, "Power is said in reference to possible things" such that the "phrase, *God can do all things*, is rightly understood to mean that God can do all things that are possible."[6] Thus, with regard to logical impossibilities Aquinas

---

[1] Cf. Peter Geach, *Providence and Evil* (Cambridge: Cambridge University Press, 1977), 4.
[2] Swinburne, *The Coherence of Theism*, Rev. ed. (Oxford: Clarendon, 1993), 153.
[3] C. S. Lewis, *The Problem of Pain* (New York: HarperOne, 2001), 18.
[4] Swinburne, *The Coherence of Theism*, 180.
[5] Ronald Nash, *The Concept of God: An Exploration of Contemporary Difficulties with the Attributes of God* (Grand Rapids, MI: Zondervan, 1983), 37.
[6] Aquinas, *Summa Theologiae* I.25.3.

adds, "it is better to say that such things cannot be done, than that God cannot do them."⁷ Similarly, Swinburne explains, "It is no objection to A's omnipotence that he cannot make a square circle. This is because 'making a square circle' does not describe anything which it is coherent to suppose could be done."⁸

However, J.L. Mackie influentially claimed that, other than logical impossibilities, "there are no limits to what an omnipotent thing can do."⁹ Yet, this raises paradoxes of omnipotence, including the famous question of whether God can create a rock so heavy that he cannot lift it. Whichever way one answers this question, it seems, there is something that God cannot do. Either God cannot create such a rock or God can create such a rock but then God cannot lift it. Some defenders of divine omnipotence have claimed that this supposed dilemma is really "just an incoherent act-description."¹⁰ Further, omnipotence defenders claim, the very question, if it is to have any significance, smuggles in a self-contradiction; "the paradox of omnipotence must begin by presupposing that God is omnipotent."¹¹ As such, George Mavrodes explains, saying God cannot create such a rock does not amount to any limitation on divine omnipotence because the "supposed limitation turns out to be no limitation at all, since it is specified only by reference to another power which is itself infinite."¹² Accordingly, Mavrodes argues, this and other paradoxes of omnipotence do not succeed "because they propose, as tests of God's power, putative tasks whose descriptions are self-contradictory. Such pseudo-tasks, not falling within the realm of possibility, are not objects of power at all. Hence the fact that they cannot be performed implies no limit on the power of God, and hence no defect in the doctrine of omnipotence."¹³

Some have thought omnipotence should be defined, then, as "the possession of all logically possible powers which it is logically possible for a being with the attributes of God to possess."¹⁴ Once one understands

---

⁷Aquinas, *Summa Theologiae* I.25.3.
⁸Swinburne, *The Coherence of Theism*, 159.
⁹J. L. Mackie, "Evil and Omnipotence," *Mind* 64/254 (1955): 201.
¹⁰Thomas V. Morris, *Our Idea of God: An Introduction to Philosophical Theology* (Notre Dame, IN: University of Notre Dame Press, 1991), 74.
¹¹Nash, *Concept of God*, 48.
¹²George Mavrodes, "Some Puzzles Concerning Omnipotence," *The Philosophical Review* 72 (1963): 223.
¹³Mavrodes, "Some Puzzles Concerning Omnipotence," 223.
¹⁴Anthony Kenny, *The God of the Philosophers* (Oxford: Clarendon, 1979), 98.

omnipotence as limited by that which is logically possible, it follows that God cannot do two mutually exclusive things. Further, most Christians theists understand God's omnipotence to mean that God cannot do anything that contradicts his very essence. For example, on the premise that God is unfailingly good and never breaks his promises, it follows that God's action would be in line with, and thus restricted by, any promise or promises that God makes. If this is so, the exercise of divine power would not be limited in the sense of God lacking any power, but it would be limited to that which is logically possible and compatible with God's own nature and covenantal promises.

The view that God can choose to limit his own action is often referred to as divine *self-limitation*. While some prefer to avoid the language of divine self-limitation, others have embraced it as an effective way to communicate the idea that, without in any way diminishing God's power, God's free choices—relative to the way the world is ordered and/or relative to promises that he makes—set parameters with regard to God's "future" action. As Tom Morris notes, this understanding reveals another way to answer the rock paradox. One might say that God could create a rock that he cannot lift since he could "create an ordinary stone and promise never to move it."[15] If, as many Christian theists believe, God *must* always keep his promises, God (morally, at least) could not move the stone. As Katherin Rogers puts it, "God cannot break His promises, because that would be wicked."[16] This kind of moral restraint would not undermine divine omnipotence because it does not entail any lack of ability or sheer power. At the same time, *that* God is omnipotent provides assurance that God can indeed keep his promises; "unless he is sufficiently powerful, we cannot be confident that he will succeed" in keeping his promises.[17]

In this regard, Christian theists continue to debate the extent of divine freedom. The most prominent arguments on this issue center on whether God was free to create or not create and whether or not God is free to do evil. The latter debate over moral freedom asks "whether God's omnipotence gives him the power to sin."[18] Although a decidedly minority view, some Christian theists maintain that it might be coherent to say that

---

[15] Morris, *Our Idea of God*, 75.
[16] Katherin A. Rogers, *Perfect Being Theology* (Edinburgh: Edinburgh University Press, 2000), 99–100.
[17] Morris, *Our Idea of God*, 65–66.
[18] Michael Rea and Louis P. Pojman, "Classical Theistic Attributes: Introduction," in *Philosophy of Religion: An Anthology*. 7th ed, ed. Michael Rea and Louis P. Pojman (Stamford, CT: Cengage, 2015), 81.

God *could* do evil, even if (as most claim) God never would do any evil. This debate delves into technical ground that we cannot adequately survey here.[19] Here, it is sufficient to note that this debate is ongoing, but the vast majority of Christian theists maintain the traditional view that God, by nature, *cannot* do evil. This is closely related to a famous debate, known as the Euthyphro dilemma (named after Plato's dialogue, *Euthyphro*), over whether something is good because God wills it or God wills it because it is good. The traditional response to this is that goodness is itself grounded in God's nature such that it is neither the product of an arbitrary divine will nor a norm external to God. God is, on the traditional view, incapable of doing evil. To take one example, Thomas Aquinas argued: "To sin is to fall short of a perfect action ... which is repugnant to omnipotence" and is not power but pseudo-power. Therefore, though God possesses the sheer power to do any evil action, "God cannot sin, because of His omnipotence."[20]

Beyond the question of moral freedom, most Christian theists maintain that God freely chooses to do what he does and could choose to do otherwise.[21] Those who maintain that God cannot do anything evil, can still coherently maintain divine freedom relative to choosing which good things God does.[22] However, even some Christian theists who believe God chooses between good actions maintain that, because God is love and/or on the view that God must will whatever is best, it was necessary that God create some world.[23] Most Christian theists, however, maintain that God did not need to create this or any world

---

[19] Regarding the debate over divine freedom relative to evil, see R. Zachary Manis, "Could God Do Something Evil? A Molinist Solution to the Problem of Divine Freedom," *Faith and Philosophy* 28/2 (2011): 209–23; Bruce Reichenbach, *Evil and a Good God* (New York: Fordham University Press, 1982), 139–53; Kevin Timpe, *Free Will in Philosophical Theology* (New York: Bloomsbury Academic, 2014), 103–18; Keith Yandell, "Divine Necessity and Divine Goodness," in *Divine and Human Action: Essays in the Metaphysics of Theism*, ed. Thomas V. Morris (Ithaca, NY: Cornell University Press, 1988), 313–34.

[20] Aquinas, *Summa Theologiae* I.25.3.

[21] Rogers, however, while agreeing God acts freely, "lean[s] toward the view that God inevitably does the best, and this world is it," given the libertarian decisions of creatures. Rogers, *Perfect Being Theology*, 108. See the discussion of this issue in Robert M. Adams, "Must God Create the Best?" in *God and the Problem of Evil*, ed. William L. Rowe (Malden, MA: Blackwell, 2001), 24.

[22] See, for example, David Baggett and Jerry Walls, *Good God: The Theistic Foundations of Morality* (New York: Oxford University Press, 2011), 37, 104–5.

[23] For example, Tom Oord argues that God must create the world because God is love. See Oord, *The Nature of Love: A Theology* (St. Louis, MO: Chalice, 2010), 132.

but freely chose to create.²⁴ Thomas Morris characterizes this as the "firmly [though not unanimously] held traditional claim that God was free not to create any contingent things at all."²⁵ This view emphasizes God's freedom relative to supererogatory actions, that is, actions that go beyond any moral obligation.²⁶

Although most Christian theists have thought of God's goodness and love as necessarily diffusive, most have reasoned that, even without any world, God's love is diffusive in the form of God's intra-Trinitarian love relationship. Here, John Webster explains, "God's triune self-sufficiency means that his relation to created being is gratuitous."²⁷ Thus, "creation need not have been," but in "creating, God acts in accordance with his goodness."²⁸ Karl Barth put it this way, "God's loving is necessary" as "the essence and nature of God" yet "it is also free from every necessity in respect of its object." That is, God "would still be One who loves without us and without the world" and thus "needs no other" to be "the One who loves."²⁹

Although there is some disagreement regarding divine freedom, then, Christian theists generally agree that God cannot "do self-contradictory acts." If God could "do self-contradictory acts," Nash explains, there would be "no inconsistency in His *promising* eternal life to all who trust in Christ but actually condemning to everlasting damnation all who trust Christ."³⁰ Further, Christian theists generally agree that, as Rogers states, "whatever God does, His action is perfect, and is the source and standard for all value."³¹

---

²⁴Jeffrey E. Brower extends this to "most orthodox Jews, Christians, and Muslims" believe God could "have chosen to create a universe different from the actual one—or none at all." Brower "Simplicity and Aseity," in *The Oxford Handbook of Philosophical Theology*, ed. Thomas P. Flint and Michael C. Rea (New York: Oxford University Press, 2009), 107.

²⁵Morris, *Our Idea of God*, 177. So, also, J.P. Moreland and William Lane Craig, *Philosophical Foundations for a Christian Worldview* (Downers Grove, IL: IVP Academic, 2003), 519. However, on Roger's reading at least, Augustine and Anselm maintained that God must create the world. Rogers, *Perfect Being Theology*, 102–103. Cf. the discussion of divine freedom in Paul Helm, *Eternal God: A Study of God without Time* (New York: Oxford University Press, 1998), 171–94.

²⁶See Baggett and Walls, *Good God*, 104–5.

²⁷Webster, *God without Measure: Working Papers in Christian Theology*, vol. 1: God and the Works of God (New York: T&T Clark, 2016), 92.

²⁸Webster, *God without Measure*, 104.

²⁹Karl Barth, *Church Dogmatics*, ed. Geoffrey W. Bromiley and T. F. Torrance (Edinburgh: T&T Clark, 1957), 2/1, 280. Cf. Barth, *Church Dogmatics* 2/2, 166, 4/1, 213. However, there is ongoing disagreement among Barth scholars over whether (the mature) Barth viewed the God–world relationship as necessary in some way.

³⁰Nash, *Concept of God*, 40.

³¹Rogers, *Perfect Being Theology*, 105.

God is omnipotent and always gets what he really wants

While most Christian theists agree that God is all-powerful, there are numerous conceptions of how God exercises that power in relation to creatures. In this regard, many classical theists maintain that God is all-powerful and the entire history of the world is the result of divine determinism. On this view, nothing takes place apart from God's efficacious will. For some who hold this view, anything less than determinism amounts to a denial of divine sovereignty.

On determinism, every event is caused by prior factors such that it must occur just as it does.[32] Determinism is, by definition, incompatible with libertarian free will, which may itself be minimally defined as the kind of free will that is incompatible with determinism. Most Christian determinists, however, maintain that humans are morally responsible for their actions and possess a kind of "free will" that is compatible with causal determinism, which is thus called compatibilist free will.[33] To consistently hold that determinism is compatible with free will, many compatibilists define free will as the freedom to do what one wants. That is, Steven B. Cowan and James S. Spiegel explain, to say one has "free will" means "that the person has the ability to do what she wants to do" and is "not coerced by external forces against her will."[34]

Theistic compatibilists believe humans are free to do what they want but what they want is causally determined by God, whether directly or indirectly.[35] Many theistic compatibilists believe that God causally determines every event, including all creaturely decisions and actions. On this view, nothing occurs except that which God has causally determined.

---

[32]More specifically, "causal determinism is the thesis that the course of the future is entirely determined by the conjunction of the non-relational past and the laws of nature." Timpe, *Free Will in Philosophical Theology*, 8.

[33]There are different varieties of compatibilism. The description here refers to what is sometimes called broad compatibilism, which is the view that determinism is compatible with free will *and* moral responsibility. On various forms and contemporary issues regarding compatibilism see the essays in Kevin Timpe, Meghan Griffith, and Neil Levy, eds. *The Routledge Companion to Free Will* (New York: Routledge, 2017).

[34]Cowan and Spiegel, *The Love of Wisdom: A Christian Introduction to Philosophy* (Nashville, TN: B&H, 2009), 237.

[35]Hereafter, unless otherwise specified, I use the word compatibilists to refer to Christian compatibilists.

This does not mean that humans lack agency or genuine causal power; many here distinguish between God as the primary cause of everything on a different plane of causation and creaturely causation as secondary causes of events.[36] Along these lines, Webster maintains, "to attribute all created effects to God as omni-causal is not to rob creatures of their proper action, because what God in his perfect wisdom, power and goodness causes is creatures who are themselves causes."[37]

Many theologians trace Christian theistic determinism back to Augustine (354–430). However, scholars disagree over just how to understand Augustine's view in this respect, with considerable debate over whether Augustine changed from an indeterminist to a determinist over the course of his career.[38] As Eleonore Stump puts it, "Historians of philosophy read Augustine on free will so variously that it is sometimes difficult to believe they are reading the same texts."[39] Helm—along with many others—maintains that, at least in his later writings, Augustine held to causal determinism of a compatibilist kind.[40] There is also considerable disagreement over how to understand Thomas Aquinas's views on this matter. Some maintain that Aquinas was a determinist, perhaps of the kind that would be called

---

[36]Here, there are three main theories of how creaturely objects might have "the power to cause effects." The first, adopted by many theistic compatibilists, is concurrentism, which maintains that "it is God and the created being together which operate to produce an effect." Rogers, *Perfect Being Theology*, 116. Beyond this view, on one side is occasionalism, the view, "the only agent (with the possible exception of free rational creatures) is God. It is not the fire, but God, which causes the cotton to turn to ash." The world behaves in "a regular fashion" because God causes events with law-like regularity. Rogers, *Perfect Being Theology*, 115. On the other end of the spectrum is "mere conservationism," the view that "God merely keeps things in existence, and the things act and hence produce effects on their own." Rogers, *Perfect Being Theology*, 113.

[37]Webster, *God without Measure*, 112.

[38]One common view is that early in his writing career (e.g., in his work *On Free Choice of the Will*), Augustine adopted something like what we now call libertarian free will and later (prompted by the controversy with Pelagius) shifted his view to determinism of a kind something like what we now call compatibilism.

[39]Eleonore Stump, "Augustine on Free Will," in *The Cambridge Companion to Augustine*, ed. Eleonore Stump and Norman Kretzmann (Cambridge: Cambridge University Press, 2006), 124.

[40]Helm, "The Augustinian-Calvinist View," in *Divine Foreknowledge: Four Views*, ed. James K. Beilby and Paul R. Eddy (Downers Grove, IL: InterVarsity, 2001), 162n3. Rogers agrees: "Augustine is certainly a *compatibilist*." Rogers, *Perfect Being Theology*, 7. Cf. also Jesse Couenhoven, who notes that Augustine revised his views while exhibiting "a fundamental continuity and consistency for much of his career," yet concludes that "Augustine the bishop was one of the first theological compatibilists." Jesse Couenhoven, "Augusine of Hippo," in *The Routledge Companion to Free Will*, ed. Kevin Timpe, Meghan Griffith, and Neil Levy (New York: Routledge, 2017), 247. Conversely, David Hunt maintains Augustine was not a compatibilist. "Response to Helm," in Divine Foreknowledge: *Four Views*, 196.

compatibilist today.[41] Others interpret Aquinas as maintaining libertarian freedom.[42]

With regard to Protestant theology, there is also some disagreement about Martin Luther's view. Many believe Luther was a strong determinist based particularly on the strong statements he makes in his dispute with Erasmus, such as "'free-will' belongs to none but God only" and "'free-will' is an empty term whose reality is lost" (relative to human depravity) and God "moves and works of necessity even in Satan and the ungodly."[43] There is less confusion over John Calvin's view. Calvin advocated double predestination, the view that God unilaterally decrees the salvation of those whom he has elected and the eternal damnation of those he has not. In Calvin's view, God determines even the mental actions of humans. Calvin writes, the "internal affections of men are not less ruled by the hand of God than their external actions are *preceded* by his *eternal decree*" and, as such, "God performs not by the hands of men the things which He has decreed, without *first working* in their hearts the *very will* which *precedes* the acts they are to perform."[44]

Relative to Protestant theology, the label Calvinist is often used to refer to determinism, in contrast to Arminianism, which often stands as a label for indeterminism (the contrary of determinism)—despite the fact that both Calvinism and Arminianism are far richer traditions that should not be reduced to this single point. While some have argued that Calvin was not a compatibilist, per se, Helm maintains that "clearly the consensus view is that he was."[45] However, others have argued that applying today's categories to Calvin is anachronistic. Whatever one concludes, in this regard, theistic determinism was further developed and articulated in technical fashion by many Calvinist Protestant Scholastics.[46]

---

[41]Cf. Reginald Garrigou-Lagrange, *God: His Existence and His Nature*, 5th ed., trans. Dom Bede Rose (St. Louis, MO: Herder, 1936), 2:538–39; Helm, "Augustinian-Calvinist View," 163.

[42]See, for example, Eleonore Stump, *The God of the Bible and the God of the Philosophers* (Marquette, WI: Marquette University Press, 2016), 44n40, 23–24n14.

[43]Martin Luther, *The Bondage of the Will*, trans. J.I. Packer and O.R. Johnston (Grand Rapids, MI: Baker, 2003), 137, 148, 204. Elsewhere, Luther writes, "All we do, however it may appear to us to be done mutably and contingently, is in reality done necessarily and immutably in respect of God's will." Luther, *Bondage of the Will*, 80.

[44]John Calvin, "Defence of the Secret Providence of God," in *Calvin's Calvinism: Treatises on the Eternal Predestination of God and the Secret Providence of God*, trans. Henry Cole (London: Wertheim and Macintosh, 1857), 2:23 (emphasis original).

[45]Helm, "Augustinian-Calvinist View," 162n3.

[46]Richard A. Muller contends that there is more complexity in modern reformed thought than the compatibilism versus libertarianism distinction encapsulates. *Divine Will and Human Choice: Freedom, Contingency, and Necessity in Early Modern Reformed Thought* (Grand Rapids, MI: Baker Academic, 2017), 31.

Beyond its grounding in the Christian tradition, some believe theistic determinism is most consistent systematically with strict classical theism. Helm argues, "The existence of an omniscient, timelessly eternal God is logically inconsistent with the libertarian freedom in any of his creatures."[47] Richard Plantinga, Thomas R. Thompson, and Matthew Lundberg, further, contend that if God is "outside of the world in eternal timelessness" and "God's will and plan toward the world" are "absolutely immutable," then the relationship between God and the world is "one characterized by determinism. So conceived, whatever God timelessly wills toward creation will, as an inexorable cause, work its way out in the world."[48]

Yet, the strict classical theist Katherin Rogers rejects determinism—in keeping with her understanding of Anselm—and is primarily motivated to do so by the problem of evil, the number one objection raised against determinism. Indeed, Rogers contends that determinism "seems to lay the ultimate responsibility for the existence of evil on God."[49] She writes: "If God could have prevented all the moral evil in our world by controlling everyone's choices without infringing on anyone's freedom," as compatibilists maintain God could, "why does he not do so?"[50]

Some determinists maintain that God causally determines all events and thus does cause evil, but it is not evil for God to cause evil because God causes evil for good purposes (see Chapter 6). Other determinists, motivated by the desire to say God does not cause evil at all, maintain that while all of history is causally determined, God causes some things while permitting other things to be determined by the chain of cause and effect. For instance, Paul Helm argues, while "God ordains everything which comes to pass—even the evil actions and omissions of human beings," humans "are nevertheless accountable to God for their actions and omissions."[51] Further, Helm argues, God "does not causally determine everything in the sense that he is the efficient cause of everything, though everything that happens has sets of efficient or deficient causes in a way consistent with compatibilist accounts of human actions. Nevertheless, nothing happens that God is unwilling should happen."[52]

---

[47]Helm, *Eternal God*, 144.
[48]Richard Plantinga, Thomas R. Thompson, and Matthew Lundberg, *An Introduction to Christian Theology* (Cambridge: Cambridge University Press, 2010), 100.
[49]Rogers, *Perfect Being Theology*, 101. Cf. Kenny, *God of the Philosophers*, 86–87.
[50]Rogers, *Perfect Being Theology*, 8.
[51]Helm, "Augustinian-Calvinist View," 165.
[52]Helm, "Augustinian-Calvinist View," 177.

For Helm, God "positively governs all acts that are not evil" and God "governs all other acts, evil acts, by permitting them."⁵³ Accordingly, Helm argues, "God ordains evil" not by positively causing it but "by willingly permitting it."⁵⁴ Thus, Helm insists, "God is not the cause of evil actions" and "God could not positively govern evil acts."⁵⁵ Put differently, "God does not and cannot will evil actions, but he may nevertheless know that they will occur and be willing for them to occur" for some "highest and holiest reasons."⁵⁶ Thus, Helm maintains, "the Augustinian says that the removal of God's hand led to the encroachment of evil," which "God is not and could not himself be the author of, though he willingly permits it."⁵⁷

Yet, Craig argues, given determinism, "divine permission" does not make sense. On Helm's view, Craig argues, "Since free creatures' decisions are indirectly caused by God, he is still implicated in evil."⁵⁸ Hunt likewise argues, if "universal causal determinism is true," as Helm believes, then—despite Helm's claims—it seems to follow that God is "the ultimate cause of *all* our actions (and not just of our good actions)."⁵⁹ Since, on Helm's view, God "created the initial state of the universe and the causal rules by which one state is succeeded by another state," unless God "created *something* with the power to make an undetermined contribution to reality [contra determinism], God is the sufficient cause of absolutely everything—including our sins."⁶⁰

Rogers adds regarding Augustine's view, which she considers deterministic, "though perhaps we can stop short of saying that God 'causes' the sin, in the final analysis it is 'up to' God whether or not the sin occurs," which nevertheless "seems to lay the ultimate responsibility for the existence of evil on God."⁶¹ In this regard, she follows Anselm instead, who maintains that creatures do "evil deeds owing only to the exercise of their own

---

⁵³Helm, "Augustinian-Calvinist View," 178.
⁵⁴Helm, "Response to Craig," in *Divine Foreknowledge: Four Views*, 159.
⁵⁵Helm, "Augustinian-Calvinist View," 176.
⁵⁶Helm, "Augustinian-Calvinist View," 176.
⁵⁷Helm, "Augustinian-Calvinist View," 177.
⁵⁸Craig, "Response to Helm," in *Divine Foreknowledge: Four Views*, 205. David Bentley Hart adds, "if an action is causally necessitated or infallibly predetermined, its indeterminacy with regard to its proximate cause in no way makes it free." "Providence and Causality: On Divine Innocence," in *The Providence of God*, ed. Francesa Aran Murphy and Philip G. Ziegler (New York: T&T Clark, 2009), 41.
⁵⁹Hunt, "Response to Helm," 198 (emphasis original).
⁶⁰Hunt, "Response to Helm," 198 (emphasis original).
⁶¹Rogers, *Perfect Being Theology*, 101.

characteristically free will," in contrast to views that maintain "God is the Creator and author also of evil works and, by inference, unjustly punishes the wicked."[62] Putting their criticism more strongly, Plantinga, Thompson, and Lundberg argue that this view of "classical theistic determinism was largely what provoked the most general protest of modern atheism."[63]

Beyond the problem of evil (discussed further in Chapter 6), given theistic determinism as Helm explains it, "nothing happens that God is unwilling should happen."[64] This, however, raises the problem of divine unfulfilled desires. As John Piper frames the problem, "What are we [determinists] to say of the fact that God wills something that in fact does not happen?"[65] While not all determinists agree, in Piper's view Scripture teaches that God desires to save everyone.[66] Yet, Piper also believes, "There is nothing beyond God's own will and nature which stops him from saving people."[67] To reconcile God's will to save everyone and will to not save everyone, Piper posits two wills in God, along the lines of the traditional distinction between God's revealed and hidden wills. Piper writes: "God wills not to save all, even though he is willing to save all, because there is something else that he wills more [the full manifestation God's glory], which would be lost if he exerted his sovereign power to save all."[68]

However, for Piper's appeal to a greater good to succeed, the greater good and lesser good must be incompatible in some way that even God *could not* determine that both obtain. Indeterminists argue, however, that if God causally determines the mental actions of humans (as Calvin appears to maintain, see above), then it seems God could *immediately* make every mind in the universe humbly and joyfully recognize "the full range" of God's glory. If so, there would be no incompatibility between God actually saving everyone and everyone fully recognizing God's glory. David Baggett and Jerry Walls critique compatibilism, in this regard, saying "it's only the elect

---

[62]Anselm, *De Concordia: The Compatibility of God's Foreknowledge, Predestination, and Grace with Human Freedom* 1.7.

[63]Plantinga, Thompson and Lundberg, *An Introduction to Christian Theology*, 100.

[64]Helm, "Augustinian-Calvinist View," 177.

[65]Piper, "Are There Two Wills in God?" in *Still Sovereign: Contemporary Perspectives on Election, Foreknowledge, and Grace*, ed. Thomas R. Schreiner and Bruce A. Ware (Grand Rapids, MI: Baker, 2000), 123.

[66]Piper, "Two Wills," 108.

[67]"How Does a Sovereign God Love? Reply to Thomas Talbott," *The Reformed Journal* 33/4 (1983): 10.

[68]Piper, "Two Wills?" 123. Cf. Paul Helm's view in Chapter 6.

who can actually receive salvation, so no offer of salvation to the non-elect is a genuine offer .... to describe such an empty offer as a genuine one is worse than euphemistic."[69]

Some determinists, however, maintain universalism—the view that everyone will ultimately be saved. Regarding election, the highly influential theologian Karl Barth (1886–1968) proclaims that God's "first and last word is Yes and not No."[70] Alongside Barth's commitment to God's sovereign will as the prime cause to which all other causes are subordinate and his position that all are elect in Christ, many scholars take this statement (and others) to amount to universalism.[71] Whatever one concludes regarding Barth's position, the determinist universalist has no problem maintaining both that God causally determines history *and* that God wants to save everyone.[72]

God has maximal persuasive power but cannot determine history

In contrast, some theologians sharply criticize the traditional doctrine of omnipotence and deterministic views of providence. Charles Hartshorne claims:

> The notion of an all-arranging, chance-excluding Providence is doubly tragic; it is cruel, for it compels us to try to imagine that our worst tortures are deliberately contrived for our own or someone's good by an allegedly all-loving being, and it is dangerous, for it suggests that we need not use our own resources to avert evil where possible and to help others in danger and privation.[73]

---

[69]Baggett and Walls, *Good God*, 72.

[70]Barth, *Church Dogmatics*, II/2, 13. Cf. Barth, *Church Dogmatics*, III/3, 105.

[71]For example, Oliver Crisp argues that Barth's doctrine of election either leads to "a form of necessary universalism" such that all humans *must* be saved or it is "incoherent." Oliver Crisp, "I Do Not Teach It, but I Also Do Not [Not] Teach It: The Universalism of Karl Barth," in *All Shall Be Well: Explorations in Universalism and Christian Theology from Origen to Moltmann*, ed. Gregory MacDonald (Eugene, OR: Cascade, 2011), 307.

[72]Conversely, some Christian theists maintain universalism and indeterminism. See, for example, John Hick, *Evil and the God of Love* (London: Collins, 1966); Thomas B. Talbott, *The Inescapable Love of God* (Parkland, FL: Universal, 1999).

[73]Hartshorne, *Reality as Social Process* (New York: Hafner, 1971), 107. Cf. Hartshorne, *Omnipotence and Other Theological Mistakes* (Albany: State University of New York Press, 1984).

Hartshorne further criticizes compatibilism, maintaining that "power to cause someone to perform by his own choice an act precisely defined by the cause is meaningless."[74]

On Hartshorne's process theism, conversely, all minds possess some creative, undetermined, power such that God *cannot* possess or be in control of all the power in the world. On this view, God is not omnipotent in the sense of having "all the power that exists united into one individual power."[75] Rather, Hartshorne explains, God is "the greatest possible power," but nevertheless "one power among others" whose influence is limited according to the willingness of creation to respond as God wishes.[76]

On this view, God does not "act" in the traditional sense of direct causation (aka strong actualization). God acts via persuasion, never coercion or causal determinism.[77] In Hartshorne's view, since an effect is only partially determined by its cause, determinism is not possible.[78] For Hartshorne, individuals "can only be influenced, they cannot be sheerly coerced."[79] God may choose his action or reaction, but his choice does not and *cannot* overrule others' choices. God's will is the most powerful will among other wills but no will, not even God's, can unilaterally determine events. God is the persuasive mover of all, possessing the greatest power that is compatible with the free agency of all others. God works to order the world so as to prearrange "the course of events so far as it would be friendly to do so."[80] Yet, such prearrangement is complicated by God's lack of foreknowledge and severely limited by the nature of social reality. Indeed, since the world is part of God's being, in Hartshorne's process view, "by sympathetic union with our volitions God wants, not by choice, what we choose to want."[81]

God might be said to be "omnipotent," then, only in a severely qualified sense.[82] God has the greatest power that is compatible with all creaturely agents, which cannot be encroached upon. As such, God's power is *essentially* limited and, if omnipotence is defined as possessing (*essentially*) unlimited

---

[74]Hartshorne, *The Divine Relativity: A Social Conception of God* (New Haven, CT: Yale University Press, 1964), 135.
[75]Hartshorne, *Man's Vision of God and the Logic of Theism* (Hamden, CT: Archon, 1964), 30.
[76]Hartshorne, *Divine Relativity*, 138.
[77]See Hartshorne, *Divine Relativity*, xvii, 138.
[78]Hartshorne, *Divine Relativity*, 141.
[79]Hartshorne, *Man's Vision*, xvi.
[80]Hartshorne, *Man's Vision*, 105.
[81]Hartshorne, *Man's Vision*, 291.
[82]Hartshorne, *Omnipotence*, 26.

power, then this view denies divine omnipotence. Here, as Hartshorne puts it, "There is as much that God cannot make us do or be as there is that we cannot make him do or be."[83]

From the process perspective, David Ray Griffin similarly maintains that most "problems of Christian theology" stem from "the traditional doctrine of divine omnipotence." He believes, "we must fully surrender this doctrine if we" are to hold that God is "unambiguously loving."[84] Given omnipotence of the kind defined as the power to do anything that is logically possible, Griffin argues, "God could intervene to prevent any specific instance of evil" without any loss to creatures, by determining all events while making individuals think that they possess significant free will.[85] Given that God does not do so, Griffin concludes that God must not be omnipotent in the traditional sense. Griffin maintains, instead, that God has "perfect power, with 'perfect' defined as the 'greatest conceivable.'"[86]

Advocates of more traditional conceptions of omnipotence tend to claim that the process God is weak and impoverished and not worthy of worship. Here, critics contend, not only does God often not get what he wants, but also God is incapable of bringing about his ultimate purpose and there is no guarantee that history will move in a positive direction.[87] Griffin claims, in response, "traditional theism's idea of omnipotence" does not provide an adequate "standard" for saying "the power of process theism's God is imperfect, finite, or limited."[88]

Although not identifying himself as a process theologian, Thomas Jay Oord takes a strikingly similar view to that of Griffin. Oord argues that God lacks the power to prevent evil because he is *uncontrolling* love. Oord contends, a "God who can veto any specific act should veto acts of genuine evil. Not to do so means God is morally culpable."[89] Further, "if God does not care enough to prevent genuinely evil occurrences while having the

---

[83] Hartshorne, *Man's Vision*, 293.

[84] David Ray Griffin, "Critique of the Free Will Defense," in *Encountering Evil: Live Options in Theodicy*, ed. Stephen T. Davis (Louisville, KY: Westminster John Knox, 2001), 96.

[85] David Ray Griffin, "Creation out of Nothing, Creation of Chaos, and the Problem of Evil," in *Encountering Evil*, 117.

[86] David Ray Griffin, "Rejoinder," in *Encountering Evil*, 139. Cf. David Ray Griffin, *God, Power, and Evil: A Process Theodicy* (Louisville, KY: Westminster John Knox, 2004), 251-74.

[87] See, for example, Stephen T. Davis, "Critique of Process Theodicy," in *Encountering Evil*.

[88] Griffin, "Rejoinder," 139.

[89] Thomas Jay Oord, *The Uncontrolling Love of God: An Open and Relational Account of Providence* (Downers Grove, IL: IVP Academic, 2015), 141.

power to do so, God is not love."[90] On Oord's essential kenosis approach, conversely, "God does not essentially possess all power" and cannot coerce creatures.[91] Oord's view is thus quite similar to, and subject to the same kinds of criticisms as, the process view.

God is omnipotent and grants significant power to creatures

Many Christian theists maintain that God is both omnipotent in the sense that he *could* determine everything and that God does not causally determine history but freely grants significant power and libertarian free will to creatures, within limits. To distinguish this view from both determinism and the merely *persuasive* indeterminism discussed in the last section, I will refer to this position as sovereignty indeterminism.

Many advocates of sovereignty indeterminism claim this view is biblically supported (see the later discussion) and was the prevalent view in the patristic tradition. Richard Swinburne claims, "All Christian theologians of the first four centuries believed in human free will in the libertarian sense, as did all subsequent Eastern Orthodox theologians, and most Western Catholic theologians from Duns Scotus (in the fourteenth century) onwards."[92] Defenders of this view also point to numerous advocates later in the tradition, including Anselm (1033/34–1109), Philip Melanchthon (1497–1560), and Arminius (1560–1609).

In this respect, Rogers adopts what she understands to be Anselm's view, wherein "the free choice is the one that originates solely with the chooser. If it is caused by anything outside the will of the one choosing then it isn't really free."[93] Yet, she notes: "Any systematic philosophy of God which incorporated

---

[90] Thomas Jay Oord, "Matching Theology and Piety: An Evangelical Process Theology of Love" (PhD diss., Claremont Graduate University, 1999), 345.
[91] Oord, "Matching Theology and Piety," 314.
[92] Swinburne, *Providence and the Problem of Evil* (Oxford: Clarendon Press, 1998), 35. Paul Gavrilyuk, further, notes that "the common core of patristic theodicy" held that God was not culpable for creatures' "free evil choice" because "God did not causally determine these choices." "An Overview of Patristic Theodicies," in *Suffering and Evil in Early Christian Thought*, ed. Nonna Verna Harrison and David G. Hunter (Grand Rapids, MI: Baker Academic, 2016), 6, 4.
[93] Rogers, *Perfect Being Theology*, 101. Cf. Anselm, *De Concordia: The Compatibility of God's Foreknowledge, Predestination, and Grace with Human Freedom* 1.7, 3.1, 3.5.

free choice on the part of creatures would have to hold that God is somehow affected by and responsive to something outside Himself."⁹⁴ In this and other regards, Rogers recognizes, the strict classical theist "system of perfect being theology" that she affirms "would flow more smoothly" on a "compatibilist account," but "libertarianism allows for a more satisfactory theodicy than does compatibilism."⁹⁵

There are numerous nuanced accounts of sovereignty indeterminism, ranging from those of strict classical theists like Rogers, moderate classical theists such as William Lane Craig, and open theists such as Clark Pinnock, with significant differences between them. For the purposes of this book, I will survey the open theist and Molinist versions of this view.⁹⁶ Before doing so, however, here I will briefly treat some prominent criticisms that apply to both.

First, some argue that libertarian accounts of free will—and there is more than one kind—are incoherent because they (appear to) offer an account of creaturely decisions as "uncaused cause[s]."⁹⁷ There are various responses to this objection. Some believe that agents cause their acts but such causation is reducible to event-causality.⁹⁸ Others appeal to a view known as agent causation—the view that free agents themselves are irreducible causes of some events.⁹⁹ In this regard, Craig argues that "libertarians do not consider an agent's freely choosing something to be an instance of an agent's causing its own choice, for that would lead to an infinite regress of causes. Rather, an agent's freely willing something is just an action of the agent, not an effect of the agent" and no effect is produced without God's "simultaneous concurrence."¹⁰⁰

Indeterminism has also been accused of placing undue value on creaturely freedom and being motivated by the desire for human autonomy. In the view of many sovereignty indeterminists, however, God does not grant creaturely

---

⁹⁴Rogers, *Perfect Being Theology*, 37–38.
⁹⁵Rogers, *Perfect Being Theology*, 137.
⁹⁶For an alternative account see Bruce R. Reichenbach, *Divine Providence: God's Love and Human Freedom* (Eugene, OR: Cascade, 2016).
⁹⁷See Dennis W. Jowers, "Conclusion," in *Four Views on Divine Providence*, ed. Dennis W. Jowers (Grand Rapids, MI: Zondervan, 2011), 245.
⁹⁸See Laura W. Ekstrom, "Event-Causal Libertarianism," in *Routledge Companion to Free Will*, 62–71.
⁹⁹See Meghan Griffith, "Agent Causation," in *Routledge Companion to Free Will*, 72–85.
¹⁰⁰Craig, "Response to Helseth," in *Four Views on Divine Providence*, 57. Note Walter J. Schultz's recognition that "agents do not decide to decide" in "'No-Risk' Libertarian Freedom: A Refutation of the Free Will Defense," *Philosophia Christi* 10/1 (2008): 187. See also David Bentley Hart's contention that "God imparts to the creature its own dependent actuality" such that one is "able to impart actuality to potentialities." "Providence and Causality," 41.

freedom merely for its own sake but free will is an instrumental value that is granted for some higher value or values, at least one of which is often identified as love. As Stephen T. Davis sees it, "God wanted to create a world in which created rational agents (e.g., human beings) would decide freely to love and obey God."[101] In Wolfhart Pannenberg's view, further, in granting creaturely freedom, God manifests "a form of love that lets the creatures have their own existence."[102]

Many sovereignty indeterminists maintain that the higher value or values that freedom makes possible (e.g., love) require at least freedom to act within some non-capricious limits in a context where relatively predictable effects follow from causal actions (sometimes referred to as nomic regularity or law-like regularity).[103] If God consistently grants libertarian free will of this kind, it follows that there are some states of affairs that God, although omnipotent, cannot actualize because they are contingent upon creatures' free decisions. As Brian Leftow puts it, "It is not due to lack of power in anyone that nothing but its agent can cause an incompatibilistically free action."[104] If God consistently grants creatures libertarian free will, the exercise of his power would thereby be self-limited to "anything logically possible *that does not require creaturely cooperation.*"[105] As John Sanders understands it, God "does not limit his power or abilities, but does restrain the exercise of his power or the scope of his activities" and this "divine self-restraint" is "the restraint of love in concern for his creatures."[106] Against this background, the following two sections turn to a discussion of open theist and Molinist conceptions of sovereignty indeterminism.

God is omnipotent but uncertain about the future

Many open theists affirm sovereignty indeterminism.[107] As Pinnock describes the open theist form of this view, although God "could control

---

[101] Davis, "Free Will and Evil," in *Encountering Evil*, 74.
[102] Wolfhart Pannenberg, *Systematic Theology* (Grand Rapids, MI: Eerdmans, 1991), 1:438.
[103] Michael Murray refers to this as "free and effective choice." *Nature Red in Tooth and Claw: Theism and the Problem of Animal Suffering* (New York: Oxford University Press, 2008), 136–41.
[104] Brian Leftow, "Omnipotence," in *The Oxford Handbook of Philosophical Theology*, ed. Thomas P. Flint and Michael C. Rea (New York: Oxford University Press, 2009), 191.
[105] Richard Rice, *Suffering and the Search for Meaning* (Downers Grove, IL: IVP Academic, 2014), 52.
[106] Sanders, *The God Who Risks*, Rev. ed. (Downers Grove, IL: IVP Academic, 2007), 241.
[107] One notable exception being Thomas Jay Oord.

everything," God "chooses not to do so ... for the sake of the freedom that love requires."[108] In this regard, Greg Boyd holds, though omnipotent, "God limits the exercise of his power when he creates free agents" because it is logically impossible to "meticulously control free agents."[109]

As such, creatures "sin by rejecting God's plans and, to some extent, by thwarting his will."[110] Yet, Boyd maintains, "God is always able to bring an eternally prepared good purpose to events that are brought about by our free will."[111] While holding that God cannot know creatures' future free decisions, Boyd maintains that God has "perfect anticipation," sufficient to ensure that God's overarching purposes unfold. To ensure that evil does not finally triumph, Boyd maintains, God can use his "perfect anticipation" and then "simply exclude" any "possible story lines that could not result in God's bringing good out of evil."[112]

Whereas Boyd holds that human freedom is irrevocable, within limits, Boyd further maintains that God "can and does at times unilaterally intervene and work in a coercive way to bring about a certain state of affairs."[113] Indeed, Boyd maintains, "God sometimes overrules an agent's decisions, despite his general covenant not to do so."[114] Some have referred to this as selective determinism, which seems at odds with Boyd's axiom that "God cannot revoke" the "free will of agents" but God "must work around the irrevocable free will of humans and angels."[115] In this regard, Boyd explains that creatures "possess a [finite] domain of self-determination that God has covenanted not to coerce" such that "under ordinary circumstances" God must "stop short of coercion."[116] After this "irrevocable gift of self-determination" is "spent," however, "God is under no obligation to refrain from intervening on the agent's freedom."[117] Accordingly, "God at times predestines certain

---

[108] Pinnock, "Constrained by Love: Divine Self-Restraint according to Open Theism," *Perspectives in Religious Studies* 34/2 (2007): 149.

[109] Boyd, "God Limits His Control," in *Four Views on Divine Providence*, 191.

[110] Boyd, "Response to Helseth," in *Four Views on Divine Providence*, 72.

[111] Boyd, "Response to Craig," in *Four Views on Divine Providence*, 139.

[112] Boyd, "God Limits His Control," 207.

[113] Gregory A. Boyd, "Response to John Piper," quoted in *Four Views on Divine Providence*, 216.

[114] Gregory A. Boyd, *Satan and the Problem of Evil* (Downers Grove, IL: InterVarsity Press, 2001), 191.

[115] Boyd, "Response to Helseth," 71; Boyd, "God Limits His Control," 191. On "select determinism" see Jason A. Nicholls, "Openness and Inerrancy: Can They Be Compatible?" *Journal of the Evangelical Theological Society* 45/4 (2002): 640.

[116] Boyd, *Satan and the Problem of Evil*, 183, 196–197.

[117] Boyd, *Satan and the Problem of Evil*, 191.

acts of wicked individuals" but only after they have "resolved their own characters."[118]

This presupposes that "God can sometimes know what agents will freely choose under certain conditions."[119] Yet, critics question the effectiveness of this "settled character" hypothesis to account for the biblical data. Further, critics maintain, such a hypothesis could only be helpful relative to God knowing what already existing creatures will do—it provides no help in explaining how God could providentially and certainly guide the world to bring about his purposes with regard to large-scale events and timelines. Here, critics ask, given open theism, how could God be certain that evil will not continue forever or arise in the future? Boyd proposes that, in the afterlife, human wills are "irrevocably solidified" so that they no longer could depart from God's will.[120] On this view, "while love must be freely chosen, it does not have to be eternally chosen in a libertarian sense. Rather, the purpose of libertarian freedom is provisional, intended eventually to lead us to a much greater, eternally solidified form of compatibilistic freedom."[121]

Eschatologically and otherwise, many critics of open theism believe it cannot maintain a sufficiently robust concept of divine providence and sovereignty and thus amounts to a weak form of sovereignty indeterminism, in contrast to what Thomas Flint calls "the traditional theological claim that God is the all-knowing, sovereign, providential lord of the universe."[122] Craig claims, "It is impossible to have a biblically sound doctrine of providence on the open view."[123] Further, some object that open theism struggles to maintain certainty that God's ultimate purposes will not be thwarted, believing the avenue of selective determinism undermines the kind of *consistently* granted freedom that is necessary for higher values (e.g., love). In this regard, Craig contends, Boyd's "open theology is forced to revert to Calvinistic determinism to account for God's providence and thus actually winds up destroying human freedom."[124]

---

[118]Boyd, *Satan and the Problem of Evil*, 122.
[119]Boyd, "God Limits His Control," 194.
[120]Boyd, "God Limits His Control," 194.
[121]Boyd, "God Limits His Control," 194. Here, Boyd uses the phrase "compatibilistic freedom" but what he describes seems consistent with the sourcehood view of libertarian freedom. See Timpe, *Free Will in Philosophical Theology*, 83–101.
[122]Flint, *Divine Providence: The Molinist Account* (Ithaca, NY: Cornell University Press, 1998), 3.
[123]Craig, "Response to Boyd," in *Divine Foreknowledge: Four Views*, 58.
[124]Craig, "Response to Boyd," in *Divine Foreknowledge: Four Views*, 58.

Some opponents further believe that selective determinism exacerbates the problem of evil, raising questions like, if God could "simply exclude" those "possible story lines that could not result in God's bringing good out of evil," as Boyd maintains, why would God not simply exclude all possible story lines that result in evil or at least decrease instances of horrendous evil? If the open theist responds that God can only exclude some storylines, how could he be sure to "exclude" the right ones if he lacks certain knowledge of what creatures would freely do in given situations? Open theists often maintain, in this regard, that God is akin to a master chess player who can outmaneuver opponents no matter how they freely decide to move.[125] Craig argues, conversely, that the God of open theism is a "Not-So-Grand Master" who "will churn up a lot of unforeseen, unnecessary, and pointless suffering as he plays the game."[126] Boyd responds: "An infinitely intelligent God can anticipate and prepare for events that *might* and *might not* take place just as effectively as for events that will *certainly* take place."[127]

God is omnipotent and will finally accomplish his purpose

In contrast to open theism, many sovereignty indeterminists believe that God does possess exhaustive definite foreknowledge and that this allows one to consistently hold a more robust conception of divine providence—wherein God will certainly accomplish his ultimate, good purposes—while holding that God consistently grants libertarian freedom to creatures. Molinism is one prominent way of holding this view.

On Craig's understanding of Molinism, God does not always get what he wants yet God does maintain exhaustive providential sovereignty. On this view, God *consistently* grants libertarian freedom to humans, defined as "the absence of external causal constraints determining one's action."[128] Further, God possesses "middle knowledge" such that "by knowing how persons would freely choose in whatever circumstances they might be, God

---

[125] See Greg Boyd, "The Open-Theism View," in *Divine Foreknowledge: Four Views*, ed. James K. Beilby and Paul R. Eddy (Downers Grove, IL: InterVarsity, 2001), 44–45.
[126] Craig, "God Directs All Things," in *Four Views on Divine Providence*, 88.
[127] Boyd, "Response to Craig," in *Four Views on Divine Providence*, 136 (emphasis original).
[128] Craig, "Response to Boyd," in *Four Views on Divine Providence*, 226.

can, by decreeing to place just those persons in just those circumstances, bring about his ultimate purposes through free creaturely decisions."[129] In this way, God "can plan a world down to the last detail and yet do so without annihilating creaturely freedom, since God has already factored into the equation what people would do freely."[130]

To some, this view of providence sounds too close to determinism, particularly with respect to the way Craig (and others) sometimes speak of divine providence as if God can just place anyone in whatever circumstances he wants such that they would do as he wants. Yet, insofar as God consistently grants libertarian free will, things are not so simple. Every situation and event is inseparably connected to antecedent conditions and events, which hold massive implications for every subsequent situation and event. Accordingly, for God to actualize some situation he otherwise would desire might require actualizing unacceptably undesirable antecedent conditions or future events, or both.

On Molinism, God's providence takes into account the entire history of the universe—from beginning to end—such that what God can bring about, or actualize, is limited to what Molinists call feasible worlds (or actualizable worlds), which are those possible worlds (referring to the entire history of any logically possible world) that God can bring about without contravening creatures' free decisions. On this view, God sometimes has unfulfilled desires because God works with and around what he knows free creatures *would freely do* in any given situation. Accordingly, "the Molinist can explain" God's unfulfilled desires "in terms of the wrong counterfactuals [of creaturely freedom] being true" while maintaining that God's "plans will ultimately be achieved" and "God has morally sufficient reasons for permitting the evils in the world."[131]

Here, the Molinist claims an advantage over open theism relative to maintaining the certainty of God's accomplishing his ultimate purpose and God's taking the *most preferable* actualizable route to accomplishing that ultimate purpose. Yet, some opponents criticize Molinism and think its view of sovereignty is deficient because "eternally and necessarily, God cannot create a world where creaturely freedom and love are possible and everything happens according to his will."[132] Molinists maintain this just amounts to an

---

[129] Craig, "God Directs All Things," 82.
[130] Craig, "God Directs All Things," 82.
[131] Craig, "God Directs All Things," 87–88.
[132] Paul Kjoss Helseth, "Response to Craig," in *Four Views on Divine Providence*, 233–34.

objection to libertarian free will, which requires that God cannot causally determine all creatures to always *freely* do what God wants. Because God consistently grants such freedom, God does not always get what he wants, but God will certainly accomplish his ultimate purpose.

Some biblical data relevant to omnipotence and providence

Is God omnipotent?

Most theists agree that Scripture teaches that God is omnipotent. Jeremiah 32:17 states: "Nothing is too difficult for" God (cf. 32:27; Job 42:2; Ps 147:5). Similarly, an angel tells Mary, "nothing will be impossible with God" (Luke 1:37) and Jesus states, "with God all things are possible" (Matt 19:26; cf. Mark 10:27; 14:36; Luke 1:37). Scripture further teaches that God "upholds all things by the word of His power" (Heb 1:3; cf. Rom 1:20; Eph 1:19). Further, Revelation 19:6 explicitly declares: "For the Lord our God, the Almighty [*pantokrator*, literally all-powerful], reigns" (Rev 19:6; cf. 1:8).

Yet, some maintain, Scripture does not "affirm that God can do [absolutely] anything" but asserts "that there are things God cannot do. God cannot lie, for example, or swear by a being greater than Himself" (Heb. 6:18, 13).[133] Such Scriptures, omnipotence defenders maintain, are consistent with God being omnipotent in the sense that he possesses the power to do all that is logically possible and consistent with his divine attributes. The most prominent debate is over the relationship of divine sovereignty and human freedom.

The debate over divine sovereignty

Scripture repeatedly speaks of God as the creator and sustainer of the universe, who is sovereign over all that occurs (cf. Rom 11:36). God alone is the one who "speaks and it comes to pass" (Lam 3:37). Psalm 115:3 declares, God "does whatever he pleases" (cf. 135:6; Job 42:2). Nebuchadnezzar came to the realization that God "does according to His will in the host of heaven

---

[133] Nash, *Concept of God*, 39.

and among the inhabitants of earth; And no one can ward off His hand or say to Him, 'What have You done?'" (Dan 4:35). Indeed, God himself maintains, "Just as I have intended so it has happened, and just as I have planned so it will stand …. For the Lord of hosts has planned, and who can frustrate it? And as for His stretched-out hand, who can turn it back?" (Isa 14:24, 27). Further, God declares "the end from the beginning" and proclaims, "my purpose will be established, And I will accomplish all My good pleasure" (Isa 46:10; cf. Acts 2:23–28).

Moreover, a number of Proverbs describe strong providential divine action, saying things like: "The lot is cast into the lap, but its every decision is from the Lord" (Prov 16:33); "The mind of man plans his way, but the Lord directs his steps" (Prov 16:9); "Many plans are in a man's heart, but the counsel of the Lord will stand" (Prov 19:21; cf. 20:24). Likewise, Jesus says things like, not a sparrow "will fall to the ground apart from your Father" (Matt 10:29). Moreover, Acts 13:48 states that when some Gentiles heard the gospel, "as many as had been appointed to eternal life believed" (Acts 13:48). Ephesians 1:4–5 adds, God "chose us in Him before the foundation of the world … In love He predestined us to adoption as sons through Jesus Christ to Himself, according to the kind intention of His will" (Eph 1:4–5). Further, God "predestined" or planned all things "according to His purpose" and "works all things after the counsel of His will" (Eph. 1:11).

Many determinists believe these and other texts affirm that God's will is efficacious and always undefeated. Some open theists argue such texts may refer to some things God (selectively) determines and/or directs according to his present knowledge of people's character but should not be taken to refer to all occurrences. Since the previous chapter includes a focus on the kinds of open theist interpretations of Scripture that would also apply to the questions of this chapter, this section focuses on determinist versus indeterminist readings more broadly.

Sovereignty indeterminists who affirm exhaustive definite foreknowledge interpret the above texts (and other similar ones)—as referring to God's purpose that has "already factored into the equation what people would do freely."[134] On this view, one can straightforwardly affirm that "the counsel of the Lord will stand" (Prov 19:21) and "Man's steps are ordained by the Lord" (Prov 20:24) in an indeterministic fashion. Further, one might interpret Proverbs 16:9 to mean that humans freely do some things (e.g., the "mind

---

[134] Craig, "God Directs All Things," 82.

of man plans his way") and God also does some other things to direct the outcome, without determining human wills ("the Lord directs his steps"). This kind of divine action is sometimes referred to as weak actualization, when God brings about something in a way that depends upon the free decisions of others, in contrast to strong actualization, when God causes something independent of the free decisions of others.

Perhaps the most oft-cited passage regarding sovereignty and determinism is Romans 9–11. Many determinists take the phrase "Jacob I loved, but Esau I hated" (Rom 9:13) to mean that God unconditionally elected Jacob and unconditionally damned Esau. This view, they believe, is further reinforced in Romans 9:15–16, where it says, "For He says to Moses, 'I will have mercy on whom I have mercy, and I will have compassion on whom I have compassion.' So then it does not depend on the man who wills or the man who runs, but on God who has mercy." Further, Romans 9:17–18 speaks of God hardening the heart of Pharaoh, saying: "So then He has mercy on whom He desires, and He hardens whom He desires." Then, Paul states: "You will say to me then, 'Why does He still find fault? For who resists His will?'" (Rom 9:19). Determinists argue this indicates that God's will *cannot be* resisted. Paul then references the potter and clay imagery, saying "does not the potter have a right over the clay, to make from the same lump one vessel for honorable use and another for common use?" (Rom 9:20–21).

Sovereignty indeterminists, however, believe such texts teach a strong view of divine providence but do not teach determinism. They contend that the context in Romans and the OT passages to which Paul alludes throughout Romans 9–11 themselves provide evidence for indeterminism. For example, the phrase "Jacob I loved, but Esau I hated" (Rom 9:13), often misunderstood as a reference to Jacob and Esau before they were born, is actually a post-exilic quotation from Malachi 1:2–3 in the context of God's steadfast, gracious treatment of Israel long after Edom (Esau's descendants) had perished. Further, Romans 9:15–16—"I will have mercy on whom I have mercy"— quotes from Exodus 33:19, in the context of the golden calf rebellion, wherein God bestowed undeserved mercy on Israel of his own sovereign will. Yet, indeterminists maintain, the people had a choice to come to the Lord's side or not (Exod 32:26). Further, many indeterminists read the reference to Pharaoh (Rom 9:17–18) in the context of the Exodus narrative, which states *both* that Pharaoah hardened his heart (e.g., Exod 8:15, 32) and that God hardened Pharaoh's heart (e.g., Exod 9:12). Indeterminists often understand this to mean that Pharaoh made his own free decisions to obstinately oppose God and God acted in a way that, indirectly (via weak actualization), hardened Pharaoh's heart, without violating Pharaoh's free will.

Indeterminists further note that Jeremiah 18:1–10 employs the potter and clay imagery in the context of God's conditional response to his people, maintaining that he will relent if his people repent (18:7–10). Regarding vessels for honorable or common use (Rom 9:20–21), indeterminists highlight that Paul elsewhere exhorts, "if anyone cleanses himself … He will be a vessel for honor" (2 Tim 2:21; cf. 1 Theses 4:3–4). Indeterminists also point to other statements in Romans that they believe indicate indeterminism, such as "Behold then the kindness and severity of God; to those who fell, severity, but to you, God's kindness, if you continue in His kindness; otherwise you also will be cut off. And they also, if they do not continue in their unbelief, will be grafted in, for God is able to graft them in again" (Rom 11:22–23; cf. Rom 10:9). The debate between determinists and indeterminists with regard to how best interpret these and other passages continues on, including a great deal more complexity than can be adequately surveyed here.

The debate over human freedom

The debate over human freedom runs parallel to the debate over divine sovereignty. Numerous passages describe human choice. For example, God proclaims, "I have set before you life and death, the blessing and the curse. So choose life in order that you may live" (Deut 30:19; cf. 11:26–28; 30:15; 2 Chron 15:2; Jer 18:7–10; 21:8). Likewise, Joshua stated, "choose for yourselves today whom you will serve" whether Yahweh or pagan gods (Josh 24:15; cf. 1 Kings 18:21). Further, God proclaims judgment against his people because they "chose that in which" God "did not delight" (Isa 65:12; cf. Ps 78:22). Elsewhere, Paul states, "If you confess with your mouth Jesus as Lord, and believe in your heart that God raised Him from the dead, you will be saved" (Rom 10:9; cf. Acts 16:31; Heb 3:8–12). Accordingly, Christ proclaims, "I stand at the door and knock; if anyone hears My voice and opens the door, I will come in to him and will dine with him, and he with Me" (Rev 3:20; cf. John 1:12; 3:16–18; 8:31–32). Many indeterminists take texts like these to be suggestive of libertarian free will. In this regard, Craig maintains that 1 Corinthians 10:13, which states that God "will provide the way of escape" from temptation, implies that relative to situations wherein "one succumbs to temptation … God had provided a way of escape that one could have taken," indicating "libertarian freedom."[135]

---

[135]Craig, "Response to Helm," in *Divine Foreknowledge: Four Views*, 202.

Compatibilists tend to agree that such texts exhibit human freedom of some kind, but they maintain that human freedom does not exclude determinism. Humans can do what they want but what they want is itself causally determined and these texts might just describe humans doing what they want, indicating nothing against the compatibilist perspective. In this regard, compatibilists frequently appeal to passages like Genesis 50:20, where Joseph states of his brothers' selling him into slavery, "you meant evil against me, but God meant it for good in order to bring about this present result, to preserve many people alive" (cf. 45:5). Here, advocates say, is evidence of compatibilism. Joseph's brothers willed evil against God but God willed it for good. Compatibilists similarly appeal to Philippians 2:12–13, "work out your salvation with fear and trembling; for it is God who is at work in you, both to will and to work for *His* good pleasure." In such texts (and others), compatibilists claim, human free will (secondary causation) acts in subordination to God's overarching deterministic will (primary causation). Many indeterminists, however, maintain that nothing in such texts (and others like them) indicates causal determinism and such texts merely assert that God's providential actions, which do not preclude human libertarian freedom, can bring good out of evil (Gen 50:20) and work out the salvation of those who respond positively to God's free gift (Phil 2:12–13). Further, the indeterminist maintains, if God did causally determine the events of history, he would not need to determine that Joseph be sold into slavery in order "to preserve many people alive" (Gen 50:20).

Indeterminists, further, point to biblical data suggesting that God sometimes has unfulfilled desires. God's will is sometimes unfulfilled because creatures reject or resist God's desires (Isa 66:4; Ezek. 18:23; Matt 23:37; Luke 7:30).[136] Whereas God "longs to be gracious" to his people and "waits on high to have compassion," they were "not willing" (Isa 30:18). Later, God proclaims, "I will choose [*bāḥar*] their punishments" because "I called, but no one answered; I spoke, but they did not listen. And they did evil in My sight and chose [*bāḥar*] that in which I did not delight [*ḥāpēṣ*]" (Isa 66:4; cf. 65:2, 12; Jer. 19:5; Pss. 78:22; 81:11–13). Human rejection of God's will also appears in Luke 7:30; "the Pharisees and the lawyers rejected God's purpose [*boulē*] for themselves" (cf. Mark 7:24).[137] Further, Jesus frequently specifies those who do "the will" [*thelēma*] of the Father, indicating that not everyone

---

[136]See the extensive discussion in Peckham, *The Concept of Divine Love* (New York: Peter Lang, 2014), 205–8, 236–41, 372–78, 577–82.
[137]Evidently, H. J. Ritz notes, "the Βουλη of God can be hindered." "Βουλη," *EDNT*, 224.

does God's will (Matt 7:21; 12:50; 18:14; Mark 3:35; John 6:40; cf. Matt 6:10; Matt 23:37; John 7:17). Moreover, indeterminists argue, God's very patience suggests unfulfilled desires (cf. Rom 2:4; 2 Pet 3:15). Many indeterminists also maintain that God genuinely "desires [*thelō*] all men to be saved" (1 Tim. 2:4; cf. Ezek 18:32; 2 Pet 3:9), but, most Christian theists agree, other texts teach that some will not be saved (cf. John 3:18; 1 John 2:17; Heb. 10:36; Rev 2:1; 9:20–21; 16:9–11).[138]

The indeterminist maintains that God's unfulfilled desires suggest that indeterminism is true. The determinist, conversely, appeals to the traditional distinction between God's so-called revealed and hidden wills. The determinist, further, maintains that the indeterminist account undermines divine sovereignty of the kind taught by Scripture. Indeterminists, conversely, argue that determinism does not adequately account for the kind of free will that is taught in Scripture. In this regard, some advocates of sovereignty indeterminism with exhaustive foreknowledge maintain that their view can do justice to the data regarding divine sovereignty and human freedom (including divine unfulfilled desires) in a way that other views cannot. Alongside the debate over divine sovereignty, the debate over how to understand Scripture relative to free will continues unabated.

Conclusion

This chapter has introduced some prominent contemporary approaches to divine omnipotence and prominent views of the providential exercise of divine power, along with a brief survey of some relevant biblical data. The following chapter turns to the related issue of the problem of evil.

Study questions

1. Can God do anything and everything? Is it coherent to say that God is omnipotent or all-powerful? What are some implications of how one answers these questions relative

---

[138] Regarding the debate on this, however, see Robin Parry and Christopher Partridge, eds. *Universal Salvation? The Current Debate* (Grand Rapids, MI: Eerdmans, 2003), 55–76.

to divine sovereignty, providence, and the problem of evil? How do these questions relate to the debates over divine freedom?
2. What are some of the implications of divine self-limitation? Is this a coherent concept? How does it relate to the discussion over divine omnipotence and providence?
3. Does God always get what he wants? How do you evaluate the various perspectives on divine providence? Do you think God causally determines history? Is determinism the view most compatible with strict classical theism? What do you think of the debate between compatibilists and libertarians over how to define free will? Can God have unfulfilled desires if determinism is true?
4. How do you think one should evaluate the views of divine providence surveyed in this chapter? What role does the data from Scripture play in the way you think of divine sovereignty and human freedom? What do you make of differing interpretations of the Christian tradition and ambiguity over what view some prominent theologians held relative to divine power, sovereignty, determinism, and providence? What are some of the implications for Christian theism regarding how these questions are answered?
5. What are some good reasons for affirming each view? What are some of the strongest objections to each view? Can you think of any further difficulties with any of the views discussed in this chapter? Can you think of any further advantages of views discussed in this chapter? What are some practical implications of the various views?

Suggestions for further reading

Selected premodern sources

Augustine, *On Free Choice of the Will*.
Augustine, *The Enchiridion*, chapters 95–97, 100–106.
Augustine, *On Grace and Free Will*.
Anselm, *De Concordia: The Compatibility of God's Foreknowledge, Predestination, and Grace with Human Freedom*.

Thomas Aquinas, *Summa Theologiae* I.22–25.
Martin Luther, *The Bondage of the Will*.
John Calvin, *Concerning the Eternal Predestination of God*.
Jacob Arminius, *A Declaration of the Sentiments of Arminius*.

Selected modern/contemporary sources

Barth, Karl. *Church Dogmatics*. ed. Geoffrey W. Bromiley and T. F. Torrance (Edinburgh: T&T Clark, 1957, 1960), 2/1, 490–607, 3/3, 3–289.

Flint, Thomas P. *Divine Providence: The Molinist Account* (Ithaca, NY: Cornell University Press, 2006).

Griffin, David Ray. *God, Power, and Evil: A Process Theodicy* (Louisville, KY: Westminster John Knox, 2004).

Hartshorne, Charles. *Omnipotence and Other Theological Mistakes* (Albany: State University of New York Press, 1984).

Jowers, Dennis W., ed. *Four Views on Divine Providence* (Grand Rapids, MI: Zondervan, 2011).

Mavrodes, George. "Some Puzzles Concerning Omnipotence." *The Philosophical Review* 72 (1963): 221–23.

Muller, Richard A. *Divine Will and Human Choice: Freedom, Contingency, and Necessity in Early Modern Reformed Thought* (Grand Rapids, MI: Baker Academic, 2017).

Murphy, Francesca Aran and Philip Gordon Ziegler, eds. *The Providence of God* (New York: T&T Clark, 2009).

Reichenbach, Bruce R. *Divine Providence: God's Love and Human Freedom* (Eugene, OR: Cascade, 2016).

Sanders, John. *The God Who Risks: A Theology of Divine Providence*. Rev. ed. (Downers Grove, IL: IVP Academic, 2007).

Schreiner, Thomas R. and Bruce A. Ware, eds. *Still Sovereign: Contemporary Perspectives on Election, Foreknowledge, and Grace* (Grand Rapids, MI: Baker, 2000).

Timpe, Kevin. *Free Will in Philosophical Theology* (New York: Bloomsbury Academic, 2014).

Walls, Jerry L. *Does God Love Everyone?* (Eugene, OR: Cascade, 2016).

Ware, Bruce, ed. *Perspectives on the Doctrine of God: Four Views* (Nashville, TN: B & H, 2008).

6

Is God Entirely Good?

If God is omnipotent and entirely good (omnibenevolent), why is there so much evil? As the Enlightenment skeptic David Hume (1711–1776) famously framed the problem of evil: "Epicurus's old questions are yet unanswered. Is he [God] willing to prevent evil, but not able? Then he is impotent. Is he able, but not willing? Then he is malevolent. Is he both able and willing? Whence then is evil?"[1] More recently, the atheist philosopher J. L. Mackie contended that the premise "evil exists" is logically incompatible with the premises that "God is omnipotent" and "wholly good."[2] This framing of the problem is known as the logical problem of evil. Many philosophers have argued that this perceived dilemma can only be escaped by denying either God's goodness, omnipotence, or existence.

In recent decades, however, many philosophers have come to the conclusion that the logical problem of evil can be effectively answered by a free will defense (discussed further below). As such, emphasis in the debate has shifted from the logical problem of evil to what is called the evidential problem of evil. Put simply, the evidential problem of evil claims that the kind and amount of evil in this world renders it improbable that an all-powerful and entirely good God exists.[3] In addition to the logical and evidential problems, which are framed as philosophical problems, many people struggle with the religious or existential problem of evil, which relates to how people might deal with their experiences of suffering and evil. This chapter focuses on the philosophical forms of the problem.

In this discussion, philosophers typically distinguish between moral evil and natural evil. Moral evil is evil that results "from the free actions

---

[1]Hume, *Dialogues Concerning Natural Religion* (Edinburgh: Blackwood and Sons, 1907), 134.
[2]See J. L. Mackie, "Evil and Omnipotence," *Mind* 64/254 (1955): 201–202.
[3]For an introduction to the evidential problem of evil, see William L. Rowe, ed. *God and the Problem of Evil* (Malden, MA: Blackwell, 2001), 121–233.

of personal beings" and natural evil is evil "that cannot be ascribed to the free actions of" creatures.[4] In its broad sense, "any response to the problem of evil from the perspective of Judeo-Christian religious belief, broadly construed," might be called a theodicy.[5] The term "theodicy" comes from the Greek roots for God (*theos*) and righteousness (*dikē*). Some philosophers distinguish between a theodicy and a defense, defining a defense as offering only what "God's reason [relative to evil] might possibly be" and a theodicy as attempting to actually answer "why God permits evil."[6]

A successful defense or theodicy must account for all kinds of evil but there is disagreement about what kind of account, if any, is adequate given the amount of horrendous evil in the world. Many approach the issue on the premise that God must have some morally sufficient reason for acting as he does relative to evil and that any such reason must meet at least two conditions. First, it must sufficiently outweigh the evil (the outweighing condition). Second, the outweighing good must be such that God could not achieve it otherwise (the necessity or only-way condition). This chapter introduces prominent contemporary approaches to the philosophical problem of evil, followed by a brief survey of some relevant biblical data.

Determinist approaches to the problem of evil

Many theistic determinists maintain that God is not the author of evil, either in the sense that when God causes evil he does not do so with evil intentions or in the sense that he does not cause any evil at all. Paul Helm takes the latter view, maintaining that God "positively governs all acts that are not evil" and "governs all other acts, evil acts, by permitting them."[7] Yet, some theologians question whether language of divine permission makes sense on determinism (see Chapter 5). Further, some maintain that even if God

---

[4]Alvin Plantinga, *The Nature of Necessity* (Oxford: Clarendon, 1974), 191.
[5]Stephen T. Davis, "Introduction," in *Encountering Evil: Live Options in Theodicy*, ed. Stephen T. Davis (Louisville, KY: Westminster John Knox, 2001), xi.
[6]Alvin Plantinga, *God, Freedom, and Evil* (Grand Rapids, MI: Eerdmans, 1977), 28. In this chapter, I tend to use the broader definition of theodicy.
[7]Helm, "The Augustinian-Calvinist View," in *Divine Foreknowledge: Four Views*, ed. James K. Beilby and Paul R. Eddy (Downers Grove, IL: InterVarsity, 2001), 178.

does not directly cause evil, it follows from theistic determinism that God indirectly causes evil and is thus "still implicated in evil" in that God "sets up causally determining circumstances that make" the "evil action of creatures … inevitable for the creatures."[8] Yet, if compatibilism is true, Jerry Walls argues, "God could have created a world in which all persons *freely* did only the good at all times."[9]

Some determinists maintain that God determines that evil occurs in order to bring about some greater, outweighing good. John Calvin, for instance, favorably quotes Augustine's statement that God "knew that it pertained to his most omnipotent goodness to bring good out of evil things rather than not to permit evil things to be" and "so ordained the life of angels and men" accordingly.[10] Helm writes, further, "God ordains evil because it is logically necessary for his goal of the greater good."[11] Many theistic compatibilists maintain that the greater good is God's glory. This is sometimes called the divine glory defense/theodicy.[12] On this view, in John Piper's words, "the greater value is the manifestation of the full range of God's glory in wrath and mercy (Rom. 9:22–23) and the humbling of man so that he enjoys giving all credit to God for his salvation (1 Cor. 1:29)."[13] Some determinists, however, have serious misgivings about divine glory defenses. For instance, John S. Feinberg worries that "a theology that says evil in our world is justified, because God uses it to bring himself glory" may evoke the reaction that God "is morally repugnant."[14]

Apart from this kind of objection, other critics contend that this kind of greater good defense only works if God's glory, or some other sufficiently

---

[8]Craig, "Response to Helm," in *Divine Foreknowledge: Four Views*, ed. James K. Beilby and Paul R. Eddy (Downers Grove, IL: InterVarsity, 2001), 205.

[9]Walls, "Why No Classical Theist, Let Alone Orthodox Christian, Should Ever Be a Compatibilist," *Philosophia Christi* 13/1 (2011): 82.

[10]Augustine, *On Rebuke and Grace* 10.27, quoted in John Calvin, *Institutes of the Christian Religion* 3.23.7, trans. Ford Lewis Battles, ed. John T. McNeill (Philadelphia, PA: Westminster Press, 1960), 2:956.

[11]Helm, "God, Compatibilism, and the Authorship of Sin," *Religious Studies* 46/1 (2010): 122.

[12]See Daniel M. Johnson, "Calvinism and the Problem of Evil: A Map of the Territory," in *Calvinism and the Problem of Evil*, ed. David E. Alexander and Daniel M. Johnson (Eugene, OR: Pickwick, 2016), 43–48.

[13]Piper, "Are There Two Wills in God?" in *Still Sovereign: Contemporary Perspectives on Election, Foreknowledge, and Grace*, ed. Thomas R. Schreiner and Bruce A. Ware (Grand Rapids, MI: Baker, 2000), 124.

[14]Feinberg, *The Many Face of Evil: Theological Systems and the Problems of Evil*, Rev. and Expanded ed. (Wheaton, IL: Crossway, 2004), 187.

great good, depends upon the causation of evil. Yet, critics argue, God's glory could itself not be increased and, given compatibilism, God could immediately make it the case that creatures are aware of his glory to the maximum possible degree.[15] Further, Walls maintains, if God "must display justice by punishing evil in order fully to manifest his glory," then "God needs evil or depends on it fully to manifest his glory," which "undermines not only God's goodness, but his sovereignty as well."[16] Yet, some determinists respond, what right has the clay to accuse the potter? God has the right to determine the world to be any way he decrees; God is the standard of goodness itself so anything he does is, by definition, good. Some worry, however, that such a view might entail, or at least imply, that goodness is merely the result of an arbitrary divine will.

Apart from this approach, many determinists maintain there is some inscrutable reason that God operates as he does. As Martin Luther wrote: "If I could by any means understand how this same God, who makes such a show of wrath and unrighteousness, can yet be merciful and just, there would be no need for faith."[17] Some determinists argue, further, that humans are not in a position to know what God's reasons might be relative to evil. This line of argument, which can be affirmed also by those who deny determinism, has come to be known as skeptical theism (discussed below).

In all this, while determinists offer various other technical and nuanced arguments, two of the most prominent responses to the problem of evil are: (1) the appeal to some outweighing, greater good for which evil is purportedly *necessary* (e.g., the divine glory defense as a species of *felix culpa* arguments—see below) and (2) the appeal to inscrutability or skeptical theism.[18]

Skeptical theism

Skeptical theism does not involve any skepticism relative to the existence of an entirely good and all-powerful God. Rather, the skeptical theist is

---

[15]See, further, John C. Peckham, *Theodicy of Love: Cosmic Conflict and the Problem of Evil* (Grand Rapids, MI: Baker Academic, 2018).

[16]Walls, "Why No Classical Theist," 75.

[17]Martin Luther, *The Bondage of the Will*, trans. J.I. Packer and O.R. Johnston (Grand Rapids, MI: Baker, 2003), 101.

[18]For additional nuanced arguments, see David E. Alexander and Daniel M. Johnson, eds. *Calvinism and the Problem of Evil* (Eugene, OR: Pickwick, 2016).

skeptical with regard to the human capacity to be aware of and understand God's reasons relative to the kind and amount of evil in this world. That is, skeptical theists maintain we have no good reason to believe that we are in a position to know and/or understand what God's reasons might be relative to the evil in this world.[19]

As Alvin Plantinga explains it: "If God is good and powerful as the theist believes, then he will indeed have a good reason for permitting evil; but why suppose the theist must be in a position to figure out what it is?"[20] Indeed, Plantinga contends: "Perhaps God has a good reason, but that reason is too complicated for us to understand. Or perhaps He has not revealed it for some other reason."[21] Even as a doctor has a good reason for giving a five-year-old a shot but the five-year-old may not be able to fathom how there could be any "justifying reason" for this, "given the gulf between God's knowledge and our knowledge, it seems unreasonable to expect that we could know the God-justifying reason for every case of evil, even if such a reason were to exist."[22] Stephen T. Davis similarly comments, given "God's transcendence and our cognitive limits, we would expect that there will be evils that we cannot explain (but God can) and goods so great that we cannot comprehend them (although God can)."[23]

This relates closely to what philosophers call noseeum arguments, which basically claim: If I cannot see x, there must be no x.[24] Some argue that we cannot see any morally sufficient reason that God might have relative to evil, therefore God must not have any morally sufficient reason. Yet, skeptical theists maintain, the fact that I do not see what God's morally sufficient reason might be does not render it probable that God has no such reason. As Stephen Wykstra explains, even as one might not see "tiny flies" or "noseeums" that are indeed present but so small that you "no see 'um," one might not be in a position to know or understand God's reasons but they may indeed be there.[25]

---

[19]For more on this, see Justin P. McBrayer and Daniel Howard-Snyder, eds. *The Blackwell Companion to the Problem of Evil* (Malden, MA: Wiley Blackwell, 2013), 377–506. See, further, Trent Dougherty and Justin P. McBrayer, eds. *Skeptical Theism: New Essays* (New York: Oxford University Press, 2014).

[20]Alvin Plantinga, "Reply to the Basingers on Divine Omnipotence," *Process Studies* 11/1 (1981): 28.

[21]Plantinga, *God, Freedom, and Evil*, 10.

[22]Gregory E. Ganssle and Yena Lee, "Evidential Problems of Evil," in *God and Evil*, ed. Chad Meister and James K. Dew (Downers Grove, IL: InterVarsity, 2013), 18–19.

[23]Stephen T. Davis, "Free Will and Evil," in *Encountering Evil: Live Options in Theodicy*, ed. Stephen T. Davis (Louisville, KY: Westminster John Knox, 2001), 88.

[24]See Stephen J. Wykstra, "Rowe's Noseeum Arguments from Evil," in *The Evidential Argument from Evil*, ed. Daniel Howard-Snyder (Bloomington: Indiana University Press, 1996), 126–50.

[25]Wykstra, "Rowe's Noseeum Arguments," 126.

Critics maintain that skeptical theism does not provide an adequate response to the problem of evil. For instance, Bart Ehrman claims that appeals to "mystery" amount to "an admission that there is no answer."[26] Further, some maintain, even if appeals to inscrutability succeed as a logical defense, it would be helpful for Christian theists to go beyond skeptical theism and attempt to supply "suitable reasons that might explain God's permission of actual evils."[27]

Process theodicy and finitist approaches

Process and other finitist approaches often defuse the problem of evil by denying the traditional doctrine of omnipotence. On finitism, as I use it here, God does not possess the power to prevent evil and thus could not be culpable for failing to do so. Accordingly, Charles Hartshorne maintains, the problem of evil is a "false problem" that stems from "a faulty or non-social definition of omnipotence."[28]

David Ray Griffin advocates his own nuanced process theodicy, maintaining that if God has the power to do all that is intrinsically possible, as omnipotence is traditionally defined, then "God could intervene to prevent any specific instance of evil" and would be morally wrong to not prevent every instance of evil.[29] Griffin thus believes "we must fully surrender" the "traditional doctrine of divine omnipotence" in order to maintain that God is entirely good and "unambiguously loving."[30] Similarly, Thomas Jay Oord proposes an essential kenosis theodicy wherein God lacks the power to prevent evil because such power is incompatible with what Oord understands to be God's nature of self-emptying, uncontrolling love. With

---

[26]Ehrman, *God's Problem: How the Bible Fails to Answer Our Most Important Question—Why We Suffer* (New York: HarperOne, 2008), 13.

[27]Michael Murray, *Nature Red in Tooth and Claw: Theism and the Problem of Animal Suffering* (New York: Oxford University Press, 2008), 35.

[28]Charles Hartshorne, *Reality as Social Process* (New York: Hafner, 1971), 41.

[29]David Ray Griffin, "Creation out of Nothing, Creation of Chaos, and the Problem of Evil," in *Encountering Evil*, 117.

[30]David Ray Griffin, "Critique of the Free Will Defense," in *Encountering Evil*, 96. See, also, David Ray Griffin, *God, Power, and Evil: A Process Theodicy* (Louisville, KY: Westminster John Knox, 2004), 251–310.

Griffin, Oord contends that a "God who can veto any specific act should veto acts of genuine evil. Not to do so means God is morally culpable."[31] Oord maintains, however, that "God does not essentially possess all power" and is thus not culpable for failing to prevent or mitigate evil.[32]

In finitist approaches, then, the perceived dilemma in the problem of evil is resolved by denying divine omnipotence, as traditionally understood. Critics of this view, however, maintain it is not a viable option for Christian theists because it rejects the traditional view of divine omnipotence, undermines divine sovereignty, does not appear to cohere with the biblical accounts of God working miracles to prevent the kinds of evils we see in the world today, and lacks sufficient grounds to assure that evil will ever be finally and fully defeated. Further, Bruce Reichenbach contends that even the process "God could exercise his persuasive causation to a greater extent to limit horrendous evils."[33]

Protest or anti-theodicy

Some Christian theists maintain that the project of theodicy itself is problematic. As John K. Roth puts it, "most theodicies" actually "legitimate evil."[34] Approaches to theodicy, the anti-theodicist maintains, tend to make evil an instrumental good or attempt to downplay or explain away evil. Conversely, a "theodicy of protest believes" that strong "emotions" of protest against evil "are in many cases justified" and should be expressed as challenges to God's goodness.[35] Roth himself believes that God exists and that God is all-powerful but he maintains that God is not really entirely good after all. Rather, Roth claims, "God is everlastingly guilty" for "fail[ing] to use" his power "well enough."[36] This, he thinks, is the only way to deal

---

[31] Thomas Jay Oord, *The Uncontrolling Love of God: An Open and Relational Account of Providence* (Downers Grove, IL: IVP Academic, 2015), 141.
[32] Thomas Jay Oord, "Matching Theology and Piety: An Evangelical Process Theology of Love" (PhD diss., Claremont Graduate University, 1999), 314.
[33] Bruce R. Reichenbach, "Evil, Omnipotence, and Process Thought," in *The Problem of Evil: Selected Readings*, ed. Michael L. Peterson (Notre Dame, IN: University of Notre Dame Press, 2017), 323.
[34] Roth, "A Theodicy of Protest," in *Encountering Evil*, 17.
[35] Roth, "Theodicy of Protest," 18.
[36] Roth, "Theodicy of Protest," 14.

truthfully with the problem of evil. For the vast majority of Christian theists, this approach is not a viable option because it challenges God's goodness.

The free will defense

The free will defense, particularly as articulated by Alvin Plantinga, is widely viewed as the most successful defense against the logical problem of evil to date.[37] As William Rowe puts it, "the logical problem of evil has been severely diminished, if not entirely resolved" as a "result of Plantinga's work."[38] The free will defense maintains that evil is the result of the misuse of creaturely free will. God granted some creatures a kind of free will that is incompatible with determinism and it is thus not possible for God to determine that all beings freely do what God desires. That is, as Katherin Rogers puts it, "God can no more make a controlled free being than He can make a round square."[39]

Plantinga maintains that a world with "significantly free" creatures "is more valuable, all else being equal, than a world containing no free creatures."[40] Yet, "to create creatures capable of moral good," God "must create creatures capable of moral evil; and He can't give these creatures the freedom to perform evil and at the same time prevent them from doing so."[41] Some free creatures "went wrong in the exercise of their freedom" and "this is the source of moral evil" but it "counts neither against God's omnipotence nor against his goodness; for He could have forestalled the occurrence of moral evil only by removing the possibility of moral good."[42]

Free will defenses, in some form, have long been advocated by Christian theists, perhaps most famously by Augustine in his early work *On Free Choice of the Will*.[43] As Paul Gavrilyuk explains: "Relatively early among patristic theologians, a broad agreement emerged that the free will of some

---

[37] See Plantinga, *The Nature of Necessity*; Plantinga, *God, Freedom, and Evil*.
[38] William Rowe, "Introduction to Part II: The Logical Problem of Evil," in *God and the Problem of Evil*, ed. William L. Rowe (Malden, MA: Blackwell, 2001), 76.
[39] Rogers, *Perfect Being Theology* (Edinburgh: Edinburgh University Press, 2000), 101.
[40] Plantinga, *God, Freedom, and Evil*, 30.
[41] Plantinga, *God, Freedom, and Evil*, 30.
[42] Plantinga, *God, Freedom, and Evil*, 30.
[43] Augustine is also associated with *felix culpa* approaches to the problem of evil and, like many other classical theologians, viewed evil as a privation of being (rather than an entity in itself) such that evil is a privation of good (*privatio boni*). However, this view does not itself amount to a defense or theodicy.

rational creatures accounted for the actualization of evil. The Creator could not be held responsible for the free evil choices that rational creatures made, since God did not causally determine these choices."[44]

Critics have sometimes objected that an omnipotent God should be able to create a world in which free beings only do good.[45] However, Richard Swinburne responds, "A God who gives humans such free will necessarily brings about the possibility [of evil], and puts outside his own control whether or not that evil occurs. It is not logically possible," then, "that God could give us such free will and yet ensure that we always use it in the right way."[46]

Yet, given divine foreknowledge, might God have simply chosen to create only those creatures who would freely choose only the good? Plantinga answers that, if—as the free will defense maintains—what creatures freely do is not up to God, it might be the case that any world (in the sense of the entire history of a universe) including significantly free creatures *that God could actualize* would include evil. Or, it might be the case that any world that God could actualize that contains significantly free creatures contained far less good and/or so few creatures that God is justified in preferring this world.[47]

Other critics object, if God has the power to prevent evil, he should always prevent evil.[48] The free will defender responds that this amounts to the claim that God should not consistently respect free will, the truth of which depends on whether God is morally justified in consistently granting free will. Perhaps free will is necessary for some outweighing value or values. Yet, some critics persist, what about evils that it seems God could prevent without undermining such free will? For instance, it seems God could effectively warn of some impending evil via a dream without undermining free will. Some free will defenders might claim that doing so undermines the extent of epistemic distance and freedom needed for moral goodness or some other value. However, God is portrayed in Scripture as communicating with people via dreams and if God could do so then why could he not do so now? The free will defender might respond that such instances were special cases.

---

[44]Gavrilyuk, "An Overview of Patristic Theodicies," in *Suffering and Evil in Early Christian Thought*, ed. Nonna Verna Harrison and David G. Hunter (Grand Rapids, MI: Baker Academic, 2016), 4.
[45]Mackie, "Evil and Omnipotence," 209–10.
[46]Swinburne, *Is There a God?* Rev. ed. (New York: Oxford University Press, 2010), 86.
[47]See Plantinga, *Nature of Necessity*, 189–90.
[48]See, for example, Griffin, "Creation out of Nothing," 117.

Critics argue, further, that free will is not worth the cost of all the evil in this world. Free will defenders respond that free will may be necessary for moral goodness, love, or some other sufficiently outweighing value. Further, some critics contend that the free will defense does not account for natural evil. As William Rowe puts it: "Natural disasters (floods, earthquakes, hurricanes, etc.) bring about enormous amounts of human and animal suffering. But it is obvious that such suffering is not proportionate to the abuses of free will by humans."[49] However, Plantinga claims, it is possible that what we call "natural evils" are themselves the result (even if only indirectly) of the free will decisions of creatures, including perhaps "non-human persons" such as "Satan and his cohorts."[50] If this is possible, free will defenders argue, the free will defense does extend—at least at the level of defense—to the problem of natural evil. This dovetails with cosmic conflict approaches, discussed further below.

Open theism

Open theists often concur with the main elements of the free will defense, but argue further that God is not culpable for evils because he did not know with certainty that they would occur. That is, Richard Rice explains, since future "free decisions" are "not there to be known," God is not only "not responsible for these decisions" but "God cannot be blamed for not knowing them, not preventing them or not warning us about them."[51] Voicing the problems other approaches face that he believes open theism eludes, Greg Boyd asks, "how are we to understand God's giving freedom to creatures whom he is certain ahead of time (let alone has predestined ahead of time) will use it to commit atrocious acts on innocent people and eternally damn themselves to hell?"[52] Open theists take the position that God created this world in hope that it would turn out far better than it has and "God did everything possible to minimize the chance that anyone would rebel."[53] This, approach, open theists claim, provides a much more straightforward

---

[49]Rowe, "An Exchange on the Problem of Evil," in *God and the Problem of Evil*, 136.
[50]Plantinga, *The Nature of Necessity*, 192.
[51]Rice, *Suffering the Search for Meaning* (Downers Grove, IL: IVP Academic, 2014), 104.
[52]Greg Boyd, "The Open-Theism View," in *Divine Foreknowledge: Four Views*, ed. James K. Beilby and Paul R. Eddy (Downers Grove, IL: InterVarsity, 2001), 46.
[53]Rice, *Suffering*, 102.

response to the question regarding why God did not simply create only those beings he foreknew would always freely do good or otherwise prevent evils he foreknew.

Critics doubt, however, whether open theism's suggestion that God might not be culpable for that which he does not foreknow actually helps with regard to the problem of evil. Presumably, critics note, an omnipotent God with comprehensive present knowledge could stop any evil just before it would occur and thus may need a good reason for not preventing evil just as much as the God who possesses exhaustive definite foreknowledge. If so, critics contend, open theism provides no unique advantage and has the significant disadvantage of denying the traditional view that God has exhaustive definite foreknowledge and thus (among other things) struggles to account for the certainty of a final eschatological defeat of evil.[54]

Felix culpa and the greater good

Some approaches maintain that evil is necessary for some greater good. The philosopher Gottfried Leibniz (1646–1716), who coined the term "theodicy," maintained that God could not create anything but the best and, hence, this world must be the best possible world.[55] If so, the evils in this world must be necessary for some greater good or goods. Leibniz's approach has been widely criticized, especially his claim that this is the best possible world. As Stephen Davis notes, "better worlds than this world certainly seem conceivable."[56] Further, there might be no such thing as a best possible world. As Plantinga states: "Perhaps for any world you pick, there is a better" one.[57] In addition, Plantinga criticizes the assumption that God can create just any world he pleases—particularly with respect to possible worlds that contain significantly free beings—calling this Leibniz's lapse.[58]

Long before Leibniz's version of the greater good approach, however, the idea that it is actually fortunate that evil occurred because it brings about some greater good was voiced by many prominent Christians. This view is

---

[54]See the discussion in Chapter 5.
[55]See Gottfried Leibniz, *Essays on Theodicy*.
[56]Davis, "Free Will and Evil," in *Encountering Evil*, 75.
[57]Plantinga, *The Nature of Necessity*, 168.
[58]Plantinga, *God, Freedom, and Evil*, 44.

often labeled *felix culpa*, which means "happy fault." The concept of *felix culpa* is often traced to Ambrose of Milan (337–397), who taught the Fall "did us more good than harm" and in this and other respects, significantly influenced Augustine.[59] Thomas Aquinas (1225–74) later wrote, in this respect, "God allows evils to happen in order to bring a greater good therefrom" and thus "we say: 'O happy fault, that merited such and so great a Redeemer!'"[60]

John Hick's soul-making theodicy, while non-traditional in many respects, is a recent, prominent version of *felix culpa* theodicy. Rejecting the traditional view of the Fall of humanity, Hick maintains that humans began as "immature creature[s]" who had to develop by "living in a challenging and therefore person-making world."[61] Hick contends that morality and spirituality and love relationship can only be had via a process of development, which requires creaturely freedom and distance from God within a world like ours with all its ambiguity, suffering, and evil. Such things are needed for soul-making. Evil is thus necessary for good. Hick has called this an Irenaean theodicy, claiming that "Irenaeus suggests that man was created as an imperfect, immature creature who was to undergo moral development."[62] While he notes that the soul-making theodicy "cannot, as such, be attributed to Irenaeus," Hick considers Irenaeus the "patron saint" of this "type of theodicy" presented by later thinkers, "the greatest of whom" was "Friedrich Schleiermacher."[63]

Hick's soul-making theodicy would explain why God does not intervene to prevent evils. Yet, critics of the soul-making theodicy contend that the degree of epistemic distance from God that Hick's theodicy assumes cannot be necessary for authentic love relationship given that children can love their parents without first being set at such a distance and/or given the apparent proximity between God and some biblical characters. Further, Davis comments, "surely an omnipotent being … could have made us grow and learn in a much less painful, harsh, and destructive world."[64]

---

[59]In Latin, Ambrose wrote, "*Amplius nobis profuit culpa, quam nocuit.*" Ambrose, *De Institutione Virginis*, 17, 104. The phrase also appears in the Liturgical Hymn the *Exultet* (also known as the Paschal Proclamation), which some believe was written by Ambrose. Augustine wrote: "For He judged it better to bring good out of evil, than not to permit any evil to exist." Augustine, *The Enchiridion* (or *On Faith, Hope, and Love*), 27 (*NPNF1* 3:246).

[60]Thomas Aquinas, *Summa Theologiae* III.1.3.

[61]John Hick, "An Irenaean Theodicy," in *Encountering Evil*, 39.

[62]Hick, *Evil and the God of Love* (London: Macmillan, 1966), 220.

[63]Hick, "An Irenaean Theodicy," 40.

[64]Davis, "Critique of Irenaean Theodicy," in *Encountering Evil*, 60.

J. L. Schellenberg adds, "there must remain an infinite number of ways of growing into wholeness and fulfillment in God" without the "horrors" of this world.[65]

Richard Swinburne sets forth his own *felix culpa* defense, which he calls a "higher-order goods defense."[66] Building on the free will defense, Swinburne's higher-order goods defense posits "the good of [freely] performing certain sorts of good action" such as "those done in the face of evils," such as "showing sympathy," "helping the suffering, and showing courage of a certain sort," all of which "cannot be done unless there is pain and suffering … to which they react."[67] These are, he contends, part of a "logical straightjacket of goods which cannot be realized without actual or possible evils."[68] Recognizing that some think there are "too many, too various, and too serious evils to justify bringing about the goods which they make possible," Swinburne stresses that "each evil or possible evil removed takes away one more actual good."[69]

Yet, critics of *felix culpa* approaches claim, if every evil is necessary for some outweighing good, evils themselves would appear to amount to instrumental goods. As Davis puts it, "those theists who hold that all evil helps lead to a greater good deny that [gratuitous or] 'genuine evil' exists. They implicitly affirm that all evil is only apparent."[70] Karl Barth adds, if "sin is understood positively" as "counterbalanc[ing] grace" and "indispensable to it, it is not real sin."[71] If so, Kevin Diller comments, "we can no longer condemn evil and injustice as wholly antithetical to what is good."[72]

---

[65]Schellenberg, "Stalemate and Strategy: Rethinking the Evidential Argument from Evil," in *God and the Problem of Evil*, 165.

[66]See Swinburne, "Some Major Stands of Theodicy," in *God and the Problem of Evil*, 250, 251. Notably, Plantinga also recently set forth a *felix culpa* theodicy. See Alvin Plantinga, "Supralapsarianism or 'O Felix Culpa,'" in *Christian Faith and the Problem of Evil*, ed. Peter van Inwagen (Grand Rapids, MI: Eerdmans, 2004), 1–25.

[67]Richard Swinburne, "Some Major Strands of Theodicy," in *God and the Problem of Evil*, ed. William L. Rowe (Malden, MA: Blackwell, 2001), 250. For a fuller account, see Richard Swinburne, *Providence and the Problem of Evil* (Oxford: Clarendon Press, 1998).

[68]Swinburne, "Strands of Theodicy," 251.

[69]Swinburne, "Strands of Theodicy," 258.

[70]Davis, "Critique of Process Theodicy," 134. Hick himself "reluctantly" admits that this involves "some kind of instrumental view of evil." *Evil and the God of Love*, 239.

[71]Karl Barth, *Church Dogmatics*, ed. Geoffrey W. Bromiley and T. F. Torrance (Edinburgh: T&T Clark, 1960), 3/3, 333.

[72]Kevin Diller, "Are Sin and Evil Necessary for a Really Good World?" in *The Problem of Evil: Selected Readings*, ed. Michael L. Peterson (Notre Dame, IN: University of Notre Dame Press, 2017), 402.

Further, critics question how *felix culpa* approaches could be compatible with the traditional Christian view that evil will finally be eradicated. Whatever evil is constitutive of good would need to continue in the eschaton if such goods are to continue. The *felix culpa* proponent may argue, however, that the relevant evils are only necessary for some greater good in a *developmental* sense—that is, only necessary with regard to the process of their development such that evils could be discontinued after the benefit is achieved. Critics, however, doubt whether there are sufficiently outweighing goods that are indeed *developmentally* necessary and even if there are such goods, whether *all* the evil in the world is necessary to develop them.

Cosmic conflict approaches

Some approaches maintain that there is a cosmic conflict between God's kingdom and the demonic realm. Given that God is omnipotent, no creature could oppose God at the level of sheer power. As such, a cosmic conflict is only possible to the extent that God grants creatures—including celestial beings such as angels—free will to oppose God and his kingdom. Cosmic conflict approaches thus tend to build on the free will defense while positing that evils in this world stem not only from humans' free decisions but also from the free decisions of celestial beings, namely, the devil and his minions, who oppose God's kingdom. As C. S. Lewis puts it, "this universe is at war," though not "a war between independent powers" but a "rebellion" and "we are living in a part of the universe occupied by the rebel."[73]

Cosmic conflict approaches are based on the traditional view that Satan and his angels rebelled against God's government and thus fell from the moral perfection they possessed when God created them. As David Bentley Hart puts it, the world is under the "mutinous authority of angelic and demonic 'powers.'"[74] Kevin Vanhoozer adds, "The world is now under the dominion of the powers of darkness" and, as such, "the world resists and rejects God's authoritative rule."[75]

On one understanding of the nature of this cosmic conflict, Satan has slanderously alleged that God and his government are not fully good and

---

[73]Lewis, *Mere Christianity* (New York: HarperOne, 2001), 45.
[74]*The Doors of the Sea: Where Was God in the Tsunami?* (Grand Rapids, MI: Eerdmans, 2005), 65.
[75]Kevin J. Vanhoozer, *Faith Speaking Understanding* (Louisville, KY: WJK, 2014), 100.

just (see, for example, the case of Job). Such a cosmic dispute based on charges against God's character cannot be settled by sheer power because no display of power can defeat an allegation against one's character; only a demonstration of character can do that. The cosmic conflict, then, is a cosmic courtroom drama, within which Christ himself—via the cross and otherwise—provides conclusive demonstration of God's justice and character of unselfish love.[76]

Toward answering the devil's slanderous allegations before the heavenly court, God agrees to parameters within which Satan might make his case. For a finite being to make any such case against the omnipotent God, there must be consistent parameters or non-unilateral rules of engagement. That is, the finite being must be granted some limited jurisdiction within which to operate, which God covenants not to transgress. Such covenantal rules of engagement limit (morally) the exercise of God's power to eliminate or mitigate evils that fall within the enemy's temporary jurisdiction. This amounts to a kind of divine self-limitation but one that is not simply decided by God alone; the parameters are agreed upon before the heavenly council or court in the context of the cosmic courtroom drama.

Yet, critics ask, why would God create the devil in the first place and why would God choose to grant and respect the freedom of evil celestial agencies?[77] Cosmic conflict advocates maintain, with the free will defense, that there is some great value possible only if significant creaturely free will is consistently maintained. This includes the significant free will and power of celestial beings who have chosen to exercise their free will in opposition to God and are granted the space to do so within the covenantal rules of engagement, with ramifications for even (so-called) natural evil.

Some criticize cosmic conflict approaches, however, as not really dealing with "natural evils" at all, but claiming instead that evil in nature itself stems from moral evil. Michael Tooley maintains "though it is possible that earthquakes, hurricanes, cancer, and the predation of animals are all caused by malevolent supernatural beings, the probability that this is so is extremely low."[78] Cosmic conflict advocates maintain, however, that this approach does not require the view that celestial beings directly cause natural evils, but only that such evils take place in the context of a conflict wherein even the laws

---

[76]See Peckham, *Theodicy of Love*.
[77]See Jeffrey Burton Russell, *Mephistopheles* (Ithaca, NY: Cornell University Press, 1990), 300.
[78]Michael Tooley, "The Problem of Evil," in *The Stanford Encyclopedia of Philosophy* (Fall 2015 edition), http://plato.stanford.edu/archives/fall2015/entries/evil/, accessed 7/6/18.

and processes of nature might be affected and divine action relative to moral and natural evils might be limited by the rules of engagement.[79] As such, it might be that when God does not prevent some horrendous evil, doing so would have either: (1) been against the rules, (2) undermined free will of the kind necessary for love and/or some other great value or values, and/or (3) resulted in greater evil or less flourishing of goodness relative to the entire history of the world.[80]

Perhaps the most prominent criticism of this view is the claim that a cosmic conflict is not plausible. Particularly since the Enlightenment, many scholars believe there are no such things as Satan and demons. However, Plantinga responds, whether one finds a cosmic conflict perspective "implausible will of course depend on what else one believes: the theist already believes in the existence of at least one non-human person who is active in history: God. Accordingly the suggestion that there are other such persons ... may not seem at all implausible to him."[81] Further, advocates note that the vast majority of Christians throughout the ages have believed in a conflict between God and demonic agencies. As Paul Gavrilyuk explains, "the common core of patristic theodicy" included the view that "God is not the author of evil" but the "misuse of angelic and human free will is the cause of evil."[82] Jeffrey Burton Russell adds, "the devil has always been a central Christian doctrine, an integral element in Christian tradition."[83] As such, Russell maintains, "To deny the existence and central importance of the Devil in Christianity is to run counter to apostolic teaching and to the historical development of Christian doctrine."[84] Greg Boyd, further, points to what he calls a "nearly universal intuition of cosmic conflict" across the cultures of the world.[85]

---

[79]See, e.g., Plantinga, "Supralapsarianism or 'O Felix Culpa,'" 15–17. See also, among others, Greg Boyd, *Satan and the Problem of Evil: Constructing a Trinitarian Warfare Theodicy* (Downers Grove, IL: InterVarsity Press, 2001), 242–318; "Natural Evil: A 'Free Process' Defense," in *God and Evil*, ed. Chad Meister and James K. Dew (Downers Grove, IL: InterVarsity, 2013).

[80]See Peckham, *Theodicy of Love*, 107–109.

[81]Plantinga, "Self-Profile," in *Alvin Plantinga*, ed. James E. Tomberlin and Peter van Inwagen (Dordrecht: D. Riedel, 1985), 43.

[82]Gavrilyuk, "An Overview of Patristic Theodicies," 6.

[83]Jeffrey Burton Russell, *Satan: The Early Christian Tradition* (Ithaca, NY: Cornell University Press, 1981), 226.

[84]Russell, *Satan*, 225.

[85]Greg Boyd, *God at War: The Bible and Spiritual Conflict* (Downers Grove, IL: IVP Academic, 1997), 18.

Critics, however, claim that cosmic conflict approaches undermine divine sovereignty and may lend support to some form of cosmic dualism—the view that good and evil are eternal and in perpetual conflict.[86] Cosmic conflict advocates, however, explicitly reject dualism—maintaining that the devil and his cohorts are finite, created beings with only limited and temporary jurisdiction that God grants. While God temporarily operates within the parameters of the cosmic conflict, advocates maintain, God remains the omnipotent sovereign who will finally exercise his power to fully and finally eradicate evil.

Some biblical data relevant to the problem of evil

The problem of evil is voiced prominently in the Bible. Isaiah states, "Justice is far from us, and righteousness does not overtake us; we hope for light, but behold, darkness, for brightness, but we walk in gloom .... We hope for justice, but there is none" (Isa 59:9, 11; cf. Hab 1:4). Ecclesiastes 3:16 adds: "I have seen under the sun that in the place of justice there is wickedness." Given the evil in this world, biblical authors repeatedly raise major questions about God's justice and hiddenness, such as "Why has the way of the wicked prospered? Why are all those who deal in treachery at ease?" (Jer 12:1; cf. Mal 2:17; Pss 10:5, 13; 94:3–7).[87] Malachi 2:17 adds, "Where is the God of justice?" (cf. Hab 1:13; Ps 94:3–7).

Christian theists note various streams of data relevant to the problem of evil, only a small fraction of which will be surveyed here. For one thing, despite the questions raised by evil in the world, Scripture consistently maintains God's utter and complete goodness. The "LORD is righteous in all His ways and kind in all His deeds" (Ps 145:17). "There is no unrighteousness in Him" (Ps 92:15). God "will do no injustice" (Zeph 3:5). "God is Light, and

---

[86]See, for example, Miguel A. De La Torre and Albert Hernández, *The Quest for the Historical Satan* (Minneapolis, MN: Fortress, 2011), 212.

[87]The problem of divine hiddenness—including questions as to why God does not make himself known more explicitly than he does—has become a major issue of discussion in recent literature. See, for example, Daniel Howard-Snyder and Paul K. Moser, eds. *Divine Hiddenness: New Essays* (New York: Cambridge University Press, 2002). This chapter will focus on the problem of evil but many of the approaches to the problem of evil also hold significant implications relative to divine hiddenness.

in Him there is no darkness at all" (1 John 1:5). Indeed, "God cannot [even] be tempted by evil" (James 1:13; cf. Hab 1:13). God's "work is perfect, for all His ways are just; a God of faithfulness without injustice, righteous and upright is He" (Deut 32:4). Accordingly, the song goes forth in Revelation 15:3, "Great and marvelous are Your works, O Lord God, the Almighty; Righteous and true are Your ways, King of the nations!" (cf. Rev 19:1–2).

Further, in light of Scripture's claims, there are a number of approaches that most Christian theists do not consider viable options. First, given the view that Scripture maintains that God is wholly righteous, many Christian theists maintain that protest or anti-theodicies are not viable options. Whereas there is biblical warrant for deeply and passionately lamenting and protesting the evil and injustice in the world, Christian theists maintain that God is not to be blamed. Second, given that Scripture upholds divine omnipotence and portrays God as intervening in miraculous ways (e.g., providing food and drink, healing maladies, calming storms, and even raising the dead), most Christian theists reject the view that God lacks the kind of power necessary to prevent the evils in the world and thus reject finitism as inadequate. Further, most Christian theists maintain that God possesses exhaustive definite foreknowledge and thus do not consider open theism a viable approach. Moreover, critics note, even without foreknowledge, an omnipotent God with comprehensive present knowledge could anticipate and prevent instances of evil just before they would occur. As such, the biblical data suggests to most Christian theists that the problem of evil cannot be resolved by rejecting or qualifying any of the premises: (1) God is omnibenevolent, (2) God is omnipotent, (3) God is omniscient with exhaustive foreknowledge, or (4) there is evil in this world.

Numerous Christian theists believe that Scripture supports the free will defense. Stephen T. Davis contends, the free will defense "is a theodicy that grows out of the witness of the Christian scriptures."[88] However, much hinges upon how one understands Scripture regarding free will (see Chapter 5). Something like the free will defense might help make sense of instances where divine action appears to be restricted, such as when Christ "could do no miracle there except that He laid His hands on a few sick people and healed them. And He wondered at their unbelief" (Mark 6:5–6; cf. 9:23–24, 28–29). This and other instances in Scripture appear to somehow connect divine action to faith (Matt 17:20; Mark 9:23–24) and/or prayer (Mark 9:29;

---

[88] Davis, "Free Will and Evil," 89.

cf. Mark 11:22–24), without reducing the explanation as to why God acts as he does to such factors (cf. Matt 26:39; Luke 22:32). Free will defenders claim that these and other instances make a great deal of sense if indeterminism is true.

As seen above, however, some theists maintain that God causally determines evil, but does so with good intentions. If so, the KJV rendering of Isaiah 45:7—"I form the light, and create darkness: I make peace, and create evil" (*rāʿaʿ*)—might be straightforwardly taken as indicating that God causes evil. However, critics note that modern translations rightly tend to translate *rāʿaʿ* not as "evil" but—in keeping with its semantic range—"calamity" and that this (and other similar texts) is about God bringing appropriate disciplinary judgment, not moral evil (e.g., the NASB reads, "forming light and creating darkness, causing well-being and calamity").

Whether maintaining that God directly causes evil or not, many determinists appeal to a greater good defense, with many appealing to the divine glory defense—the view that evil is somehow necessary to the manifestation of God's glory (also a kind of *felix culpa* defense). Scripture says much about God's glory and can be taken as speaking of some undesirable events as for God's glory (for example, the man born blind in John 9, the Exodus, the crucifixion, and others). Indeterminists maintain, however, that even the view that such events took place for God's glory does not entail that they were determined to take place or necessary for God's glory. What took place might have been the most preferable avenue available *for God* given creatures' free decisions and/or other divine commitments. For instance, many indeterminists maintain, blindness does not itself increase God's glory but might be an occasion for God's glory to be manifested. Yet, the very need to manifest God's glory in such a way would, indeterminists maintain, actually provide evidence of indeterminism.

Some theists find biblical support for *felix culpa* arguments in Scripture's counsel regarding God bringing good out of evil. Aquinas writes, "God allows evils to happen in order to bring a greater good therefrom; hence it is written (Rom. 5:20): 'Where sin abounded, grace did more abound.'"[89] In this regard, many quote Romans 8:28, "And we know that God causes all things to work together for good to those who love God, to those who are called according to His purpose." Some take this text (and others like it) to mean that God works in such a way that each evil amounts to a greater good

---

[89] Aquinas, *Summa Theologiae* III.1.3.

that could not have been achieved without that evil. However, others read this text differently, as an expression of how God can bring good out of evil with reference to his accomplishing his entirely good overarching purpose, without entailing that God needed such evil or that it is better that such evil takes place. As Rice puts it, "This [text] does not mean that everything is ultimately good. Nothing makes it good that bad things happen. What it means is that God works for good, no matter what happens."[90]

Scripture also often speaks of suffering as producing goods such as perseverance, character, and hope (Rom. 5:3–4; cf. 1 Pet 4:12–14; 2 Cor 12:8–10). Some might appeal to such texts as supportive of something like Swinburne's higher-order goods defense, Hick's soul-making theodicy, or another *felix culpa* view. However, critics of *felix culpa* approaches maintain that the fact that God *can* bring good out of suffering does not entail that the suffering was necessary for greater good.

Relative to soul-making approaches, critics think the view that God could not create mature, loving humans except through the evil in this world runs counter to the traditional view of the Fall and the traditional view that God will resurrect humans and transform their natures, "in the twinkling of an eye," at glorification (1 Cor 15:52; cf. 53–55; Phil 3:20–21). Perhaps the greatest issue some critics have with *felix culpa* approaches is the view that, in Swinburne's words, "each evil or possible evil removed takes away one more actual good."[91] This, critics believe, runs counter to Paul's rejection of the view: "Let us do evil that good may come" (Rom. 3:8; cf. 6:1).

In this and other regards, however, Christian theists can appeal to skeptical theism and may find support for some appeal to inscrutability in the book of Job (e.g., Job 38:1–4; 42:1–3) and elsewhere (e.g., Isa 55:8–9). In Job 38, God interrupts Elihu's speech and "answered Job out of the whirlwind," asking, "Who is this that darkens counsel by words without knowledge?" (Job 38:1–2). Further, "Where were you when I laid the foundation of the earth? Tell *Me*, if you have understanding" (Job 38:4; cf. Job 11:7; 38:33). Plantinga comments, God "attacks Job's unthinking assumption that if he, Job, can't imagine what reason God might have, then probably God doesn't have a reason at all" by "pointing out how limited Job's knowledge is."[92] Although Job "can't see what God's reason might be," it "doesn't follow that probably

---

[90] Rice, *Suffering*, 99.
[91] Swinburne, "Strands of Theodicy," 258.
[92] Alvin Plantinga, *Warranted Christian Belief* (New York: Oxford University Press, 2000), 497.

God doesn't have a reason."⁹³ Peter van Inwagen adds, "If anyone insists that he has good reason to believe that nothing of any great value depends on the world's being" as it is, "we must ask him why he thinks he is in a position to know things of that sort. We might remind him of the counsel of epistemic humility that was spoken to Job out of the whirlwind."⁹⁴

Cosmic conflict advocates also appeal to Job for support for their position, particularly the cosmic dispute before the heavenly council in Job 1-2. Beyond Job and other passages that evince a cosmic courtroom drama (e.g., Zech 3:1-2; Psalm 82; Daniel 10:12-13), proponents contend that evidence of the cosmic conflict can be found all over Scripture. One prominent instance is the temptation narrative wherein Christ is "tempted by the devil" (Matt 4:1), who seeks to be worshiped and claims to have the jurisdiction to give Christ "all the kingdoms of the world and their glory" (Matt 4:8-9; cf. Luke 4:6). Here, Joel B. Green comments, "we discover that the world of humanity is actually ruled by the devil."⁹⁵ Further, proponents contend, the gospels are replete with instances of the cosmic conflict, including many instances of demon possession and the overarching motif of conflict between Christ's kingdom and the domain of the "ruler of this world" (John 12:31), the devil. Christ himself appears to blame the devil for the evil in this world when he states in the parable of the wheat and the tares, "an enemy has done this!" (Matt 13:28). As Brian Han Gregg notes, "the conflict between God and Satan is clearly a central feature of Jesus' teaching and ministry."⁹⁶

This conflict appears throughout the OT and as a central feature of NT teaching. For example, Ephesians 6:11-12 exhorts: "Put on the full armor of God, so that you will be able to stand firm against the schemes of the devil. For our struggle is not against flesh and blood, but against the rulers, against the powers, against the world forces of this darkness, against the spiritual *forces* of wickedness in the heavenly *places*" (cf. Col 2:15, Rom. 8:38; 13:12; 2 Cor 10:3-5). Further, Revelation 12:9-10 depict Satan as "the great dragon" and "the serpent of old who is called the devil and Satan, who deceives the whole world," the "accuser of our brethren" (Rev 12:9-10; cf.

---

⁹³Plantinga, *Warranted Christian Belief*, 497.

⁹⁴Van Inwagen, "The Problem of Evil, the Problem of Air, and the Problem of Silence," in *God and the Problem of Evil*, 219.

⁹⁵*Luke*. NICNT (Grand Rapids, MI: Eerdmans, 1997), 194.

⁹⁶Brian Han Gregg, *What Does the Bible Say about Suffering?* (Downers Grove, IL: IVP Academic, 2016), 66. Cf. Peckham, *Theodicy of Love*.

20:2; Gen 3:1–5). Whereas, some critics maintain that, in the twenty-first century, the biblical data should not be taken as describing the reality of such supernatural beings. Garrett DeWeese contends that rejecting the reality of "spiritual beings" entails that one "dismiss totally the worldview of both the Old and the New Testaments, and indeed of Jesus himself."[97] The discussion continues about how to reconcile the God of Scripture with the kind and amount of evil in this world.

Conclusion

This chapter introduced prominent contemporary approaches to the philosophical problem of evil, followed by a brief survey of some relevant biblical data. We now turn to the all-important doctrine of the Trinity.

Study questions

1. What is the relationship between divine omnipotence, omniscience, and omnibenevolence relative to the problem of evil? Do you think denying any of the three "omnis" is a viable option for a Christian theist? Do you think Christian theists should attempt to find logical explanations to resolve the conceptual problem or do you agree with anti-theodicy approaches that doing so amounts to justifying evil?
2. Which of the approaches to the logical and evidential problems of evil do you find the most compelling? Do you find more than one approach to the problem of evil to be viable? Is there any combination of approaches that you think would be stronger than any approach by itself? Do you come to the same conclusion of which approach or approaches are preferable when they are considered specifically with regard to the logical or evidential problems, respectively?

---

[97] Garrett DeWeese, "Natural Evil: A 'Free Process' Defense," in *God and Evil*, ed. Chad Meister and James K. Dew (Downers Grove, IL: InterVarsity, 2013), 63.

3. How do you think one should decide between possible approaches to the logical and evidential problems of evil? What role does the data from Scripture play in the way you approach the problem of evil? How does the Christian tradition affect your view? What is at stake for Christian theism relative to the problem of evil? Is it important for Christian theists to go beyond skeptical theism? Why or why not?
4. What are some of the strengths of each approach to the problem of evil? What are the biggest weaknesses of, and objections to, each view? Can you think of any further difficulties with any of the views discussed in this chapter? Can you think of any further advantages of views discussed in this chapter?
5. Which view do you think has the most promise regarding the problem of natural evil? How do you think the related problem of selective miracles is best approached? Do you think any approach or approaches might also helpfully address the problem of divine hiddenness? Do any of these approaches provide the conceptual resources that you find helpful in thinking of these issues?

Suggestions for further reading

Selected premodern sources

Augustine, *On Free Choice of the Will*.
Augustine, *The Enchiridion*, chapters 10–16; 24–29; 95–103.
Boethius, *The Consolation of Philosophy* 4.
Anselm, *On the Fall of the Devil*.
Thomas Aquinas, *Summa Theologiae* I.2.3; I.48–49.

Selected modern sources

Leibniz, Gottfried. *Essays on Theodicy*.
Hume, David. *Dialogues Concerning Natural Religion* X; XI.

Selected recent/contemporary sources

Alexander, David E. and Daniel M. Johnson, eds. *Calvinism and the Problem of Evil* (Eugene, OR: Pickwick, 2016).

Boyd, Gregory A. *Satan and the Problem of Evil: Constructing a Trinitarian Warfare Theodicy* (Downers Grove, IL: InterVarsity Press, 2001).

Davis, Stephen T., ed. *Encountering Evil: Live Options in Theodicy* (Louisville, KY: Westminster John Knox, 2001).

Gatumu, Kabiro wa. *The Pauline Concept of Supernatural Powers: A Reading from the African Worldview*. Paternoster Biblical Monographs (Milton Keynes: Paternoster, 2008).

Griffin, David Ray. *God, Power, and Evil: A Process Theodicy* (Louisville, KY: Westminster John Knox, 2004).

Harrison, Nonna Verna and David G. Hunter, eds. *Suffering and Evil in Early Christian Thought* (Grand Rapids, MI: Baker Academic, 2016).

Hick, John. *Evil and the God of Love* (London: Macmillan, 1966).

Lewis, C.S. *The Problem of Pain* (New York: HarperOne, 2001).

Mackie, J.L. "Evil and Omnipotence," *Mind* 64/254 (1955): 200–12.

Meister, Chad and James K. Dew, eds. *God and Evil* (Downers Grove, IL: InterVarsity, 2013).

Peckham, John C. *Theodicy of Love: Cosmic Conflict and the Problem of Evil* (Grand Rapids, MI: Baker Academic, 2018).

Peterson, Michael, ed. *The Problem of Evil: Selected Readings* (Notre Dame, IN: University of Notre Dame Press, 2017).

Plantinga, Alvin. *God, Freedom, and Evil* (Grand Rapids, IN: Eerdmans, 1977).

Rice, Richard. *Suffering the Search for Meaning* (Downers Grove, IL: IVP Academic, 2014).

Stump, Eleonore. *Wandering in the Darkness: Narrative and the Problem of Suffering* (New York: Oxford University Press, 2010).

Swinburne, Richard. *Providence and the Problem of Evil* (Oxford: Clarendon Press, 1998).

7

How Can God Be One and Three?

The doctrine of the Trinity maintains that there is one and only one God in three distinct (fully) divine persons. Yet, how can God be one and three? Does God have parts? Some have claimed that the Trinity doctrine amounts to contradiction. Christian theists maintain, however, that the doctrine is not contradictory because God is one in a different sense than God is three. As such, while there may be mystery, there is no contradiction in the doctrine of the Trinity.

While Christian theists agree that there is one God in three persons, some disagree over just how to understand the threeness and oneness of God. Specifically, there are diverse views regarding how to conceive of God as three persons. Some maintain that the only distinctions between the persons are eternal relations of origin; the Father is unbegotten, the Son is eternally begotten by the Father, and the Spirit eternally proceeds from the Father (or from the Father and Son). Much of this discussion revolves around the Nicene Creed. Further, traditional Christian theism maintains that the Trinitarian persons are ontologically equal and that there can be no gradations of divinity. While Trinitarians reject the claim that the Son and/or Spirit are ontologically subordinate to the Father (subordinationism), some have recently claimed that the Son is eternally subordinate to the Father in a functional—rather than ontological—manner.

Closely related to the Trinity doctrine is the classical doctrine of divine simplicity, which maintains that God has no parts. While there is more than one way to conceive of divine simplicity, some believe that the strict conception of divine simplicity raises significant problems for the Trinity doctrine, raising questions such as If God is absolutely simple, how could there be any genuine distinction between the persons of the Trinity?

This chapter begins with a discussion of the coherence of the basic Trinity doctrine, followed by a discussion of the patristic conception of the Trinity and a brief survey of some contemporary disputes among Trinitarians who share a high regard for the traditional Trinity doctrine.[1] Finally, this chapter concludes with a brief survey of relevant biblical data, focused on the basic Trinity doctrine, and a brief discussion of the related dispute over divine simplicity.

Is the Trinity coherent?

How can God be one and three? To understand this, it is important to first understand the basic claims of the Trinity doctrine. Minimally, Christian theism holds that there is one and only one God in three distinct (fully) divine persons.[2] The minimal Trinity doctrine thus affirms:

(1) There is one and only one God (the oneness/unity of God).
(2) There are three united persons of the Trinity (the triunity of God).
(3) The three persons are not numerically identical to each other; the Father is not the Son or Spirit, the Son is not the Father or Spirit, and the Spirit is not the Father or Son (the distinctness of the three persons).[3]
(4) The three persons are fully divine and thus coequal and coeternal; the Father is God, the Son is God, and the Holy Spirit is God (the full divinity of the persons).[4]

The minimal doctrine of the Trinity thus affirms (1) God's oneness/unity, (2) God's triunity, (3) the distinctness of the three persons, and (4) the full divinity of the persons.

---

[1] Due to the complexity of the issue and sheer amount of data to consider, I have elected to limit this final chapter to primarily a discussion of those views shared by Christian theists who affirm at least the minimal doctrine of the Trinity outlined in this chapter.

[2] In Nicene terms, there is one God—three hypostases, yet one ousia (homoousios). As John Calvin put it, "Say that in the one essence of God there is a trinity of persons; you will say in one word what Scripture states, and cut short empty talkativeness." Calvin, *Institutes of the Christian Religion* 1.13.15, trans. Ford Lewis Battles, ed. John T. McNeill (Philadelphia, PA: Westminster Press, 1960), 1:128.

[3] Numerical identity refers to the kind of identity wherein: If A and B are numerically identical, it follows that they are the same *in every respect*.

[4] The Athanasian Creed states: "So the Father is God: the Son is God: and the Holy Spirit is God. And yet they are not three Gods: but one God." Philip Schaff, *The Creeds of Christendom* (New York: Harper & Brothers, 1890), 2:67.

These four affirmations exclude a number of views that Christians have traditionally viewed as heresies, the most prominent of which are tritheism, modalism, and subordinationism. Tritheism is the view that there are three gods. It is thus a form of polytheism that overemphasizes the threeness of God to the exclusion of divine oneness (contra theses 1 and 2). Modalism (aka modalistic monarchianism), conversely, overemphasizes the oneness of God by holding that God is only one person who manifests himself in different modes of appearance and thus only appears to be three persons (contra thesis 3). As Michael Rea explains, "If modalism were true, then the terms 'Father,' 'Son,' and 'Holy Spirit' would be analogous to terms such as 'Superman' and 'Clark Kent.'"[5]

Subordinationism is the view that the Son and/or Spirit are subordinate by nature (ontologically subordinate) to the Father (contra thesis 4). The most prominent form of subordinationism is Arianism, which teaches that the Son was created at some time in the past and, as created, the Son is not of the same substance (*homoousios*) as the Father but of a different, lesser, substance (*heteroousios*). The Son, then, is not fully divine and not eternal (contra thesis 4). This heresy is named after Arius of Alexandria (*c.* 250–336), whose views were condemned at the Council of Nicea, especially the claim that "there was a time when he [the Son] was not."[6] Other forms of subordinationism include semi-Arianism, which maintains the Son was begotten or made *at some time* in the past, adoptionism, which claims Jesus was a mere human adopted as the Son of God, and various views claiming the Holy Spirit is ontologically subordinate in some fashion.

Contra subordinationism, the traditional Trinity doctrine maintains that there can be no gradation of divinity; "there is none like" Yahweh, nor "any God besides" Yahweh (1 Chron 17:20). The three "divine persons share the same divine essence."[7] That is, the three Trinitarian persons are consubstantial (*homoousios*), or one in essence. If being divine entails possession of all essential divine attributes, then one cannot be partially divine any more than one can be a little bit pregnant. As Tom McCall puts it regarding the view of the Cappadocian father Gregory of Nyssa (335–*c.* 395), "the Father does not have A+ divinity, while the Son has A divinity and the Spirit is relegated to

---

[5]Rea, "The Trinity," in *The Oxford Handbook of Philosophical Theology*, ed. Thomas P. Flint and Michael C. Rea (New York: Oxford University Press, 2009), 407.
[6]See Philip Schaff, *The Creeds of Christendom* (New York: Harper & Brothers, 1978), 29.
[7]R.T. Mullins, "Hasker on the Divine Processions of the Trinitarian Persons," *European Journal for Philosophy of Religion* 9/4 (2017): 183.

A– divinity. There is only one divinity (on pain of polytheism), and either you have it or you don't."[8]

How, then, can God be one and three without contradiction? Affirming God's "oneness" and "threeness" would be inconsistent only if one affirms that God is one and three *in the same respect*. Yet, even as there is no inconsistency in affirming that a three-leaf clover is one clover and three leafs, affirming that God is one in some respect and three in another respect is perfectly consistent. It must be stressed here that all analogies of the Trinity of which I am aware are woefully inadequate. I do not refer to the three-leaf clover here as an analogy of the Trinity. I merely raise the three-leaf clover as a clear demonstration that it is consistent to maintain that one thing is both three and one in different respects. Accordingly, one can consistently affirm that God is one substance and three persons.

One might think there is a contradiction here, however, if one thinks what it means to be a person excludes the possibility that more than one person could be one substance. For example, some think of a person as a physically individuated *being* in the way that humans are such that three persons must be three beings. However, Trinitarians do not view the three distinct divine persons as distinct beings but mean by "persons" something else (discussed further below) that is compatible with the ontological unity of the three persons in one substance. The persons of the Trinity transcend the physical and creaturely limitations of mere humans.

Further, one might think that saying the Father *is* God, the Son *is* God, and the Holy Spirit *is* God requires that there are three gods. However, this conclusion does not account for the distinction between the "is" of predication and the "is" of identity. Saying "Clark Kent is Superman" is an example of the "is" of identity. Clark Kent is identical to Superman—Kent and Superman are numerically the same man. Clark Kent = Superman. Conversely, saying "Superman is strong" is an example of the "is" of predication. "Superman" is not identical to "strong" but the word "strong" is something true about—or correctly predicated of—Superman.

When Trinitarians say the Father *is* God, the Son *is* God, and the Holy Spirit *is* God they mean this in the sense of the "is" of predication.[9] It is true

---

[8]Thomas H. McCall, "Trinity Doctrine, Plain and Simple," in *Advancing Trinitarian Theology: Explorations in Constructive Dogmatics*, ed. Oliver D. Crisp and Fred Sanders (Grand Rapids, MI: Zondervan, 2014), 51.

[9]See Paul Copan, "Is the Trinity a Logical Blunder? God as Three and One," in *Contending with Christianity's Critics: Answering New Atheists & Other Objectors*, ed. Paul Copan and William Lane Craig (Nashville, TN: B&H, 2009), 212. Cf. Keith Yandell, "How Many Times Does Three Go into One," *Philosophical and Theological Essays on the Trinity*, ed. Thomas McCall and Michael C. Rea (New York: Oxford University Press, 2009), 151–68.

of the Father that he is fully divine, that is, God. However, it is not true that the Father is God in the sense of the "is" of identity. What is meant by the term "Father" is *not* identical with everything meant by the term God. A true statement about God using the "is" of identity would be: God *is* the Trinity or God is the Father, Son, *and* Spirit. As such, there are three divine persons but there are not three gods. The Father is God *but not by himself*; the Father is God in *essential* unity with the Son and Spirit.

Accordingly, for the minimal doctrine of the Trinity to be consistent with monotheism, it need only be the case that the three "divine persons are related in such a way that there is only one God, and not three Gods."[10] This simply requires an understanding that God transcends creaturely limitations such that the three persons of the Trinity are ontologically united as one being in a way that may be beyond human comprehension but that does not entail any contradiction. God is one and three in different, non-contradictory, respects such that the triune God is one and only one substance in three distinct, fully divine, persons.

Retrieving the classical doctrine of the Trinity?

Many contemporary Trinitarians advocate for the retrieval of the classical conception of the Trinity, which some identify with the patristic doctrine that revolves around the Nicene Creed. Initially adopted by the near-unanimous consensus of bishops at the Council of Nicea (325) and expanded at the Council of Constantinople (381), the Nicene-Constantinopolitan Creed states:

> I believe in one God the Father Almighty; Maker of heaven and earth, and of all things visible and invisible.
> And in one Lord Jesus Christ, the only-begotten Son of God, begotten of the Father before all worlds [God of God], Light of Light, very God of very God, begotten, not made, being of one substance [essence] with the Father; by whom all things were made; who, for us men and for our salvation, came down from heaven, and was incarnate by the Holy Ghost of the Virgin Mary, and was made man; and was crucified also for us under Pontius Pilate; he

---

[10] Mullins, "Hasker on the Divine Processions," 183.

suffered and was buried; and the third day he rose again, according to the Scriptures; and ascended into heaven, and sitteth on the right hand of the Father; and he shall come again, with glory, to judge both the quick and the dead; whose kingdom shall have no end.

And [I believe] in the Holy Ghost, the Lord and Giver of Life; who proceedeth from the Father [and the Son]; who with the Father and the Son together is worshiped and glorified; who spake by the Prophets. And [I believe] one Holy Catholic and Apostolic Church. I acknowledge one Baptism for the remission of sins; and I look for the resurrection of the dead, and the life of the world to come. Amen.[11]

With regard to the patristic doctrine of the Trinity, however, it has long been customary to posit that Eastern (Greek) and Western (Latin) approaches differ regarding how to understand the threeness-in-oneness of God. As the story goes, the West (e.g., Augustine) emphasized and started from the unity of nature (oneness) in the Trinity, then attempted to explain how the one God could be three; the East (e.g., the Cappadocian Fathers) emphasized and started from the threeness of the Trinitarian persons and thereafter attempted to explain how they could be one God. However, much recent scholarship has strongly questioned this hypothesis, sometimes called the "de Régnon thesis."[12] For instance, Stephen Holmes has recently sought to "demonstrate that the patristic inheritance, East and West, essentially spoke with one voice" regarding the Trinity.[13] Holmes contends, "The doctrine of the Trinity received from the fourth century" contains "no fundamental difference between East and West."[14]

Holmes maintains that much recent work on the Trinity badly "misunderstands and distorts" the doctrine.[15] This he attributes to departures from the "patristic" doctrine, which—as Holmes understands it—teaches that the "divine nature is simple, incomposite, and ineffable," consisting of "three divine hypostases that are instantiations of the divine nature: Father,

---

[11]Quoted from the Anglican *Book of Common Prayer*, in Philip Schaff, *The Creeds of Christendom* (New York: Harper & Brothers, 1890), 2: 58–59.

[12]The "de Régnon thesis" is believed to stem from the work of Théodore de Régnon in his *Études de théologie positive sur la Sainte Trinité* (1892). Yet, recent scholarship maintains that de Régnon's own views have been mishandled. See Kristin Hennessy, "An Answer to de Régnon's Accusers: Why We Should Not Speak of 'His' Paradigm," *Harvard Theological Review* 100/2 (2007); Michael René Barnes, "De Régnon Reconsidered," *Augustinian Studies* 26, (1995).

[13]Holmes, *The Quest for the Trinity: The Doctrine of God in Scripture, History and Modernity* (Downers Grove, IL: IVP Academic, 2012), 144.

[14]Holmes, *The Quest*, 146.

[15]Holmes, *The Quest*, xv.

Son, and Holy Spirit."[16] These three exist "really, eternally, and necessarily," and "are distinguished by eternal relations of origin—begetting and proceeding—and not otherwise," such that other than language referring to such "relations of origin," everything "that is spoken of God ... is spoken of the one life the three share, and so is indivisibly spoken of all three."[17]

In Holmes's view, the classical/patristic doctrine of the Trinity requires affirmation of disputed doctrines such as divine simplicity, timeless eternity, the eternal generation of the Son, and the eternal procession of the Spirit (see the discussion below).[18] The debate over divine simplicity is discussed at the end of this chapter. First, we turn to some contemporary disputes among Trinitarians. The debates below are bound up with differing views regarding the extent to which the Trinity as revealed in relation to the world—known as the economic Trinity—corresponds to the Trinity apart from the world (*in se*)—known as the immanent Trinity.

Some Trinitarians emphasize the "vast distinction between God's actions in the world [the economic Trinity] and God's eternal being [the immanent Trinity]."[19] Yet, many also employ what theologians call "Rahner's Rule," which, as Karl Rahner writes, starts "out from the proposition that the economic Trinity *is* the immanent Trinity and vice versa."[20] While theologians understand both Rahner's Rule and the distinction between the economic Trinity and immanent Trinity in various ways, many advocates of classical Trinitarian doctrine fear that Rahner's Rule lends itself to a myriad of problems, including "an economizing of God and a deflationary historicizing of triunity."[21] Many theologians agree that we cannot know what God is like apart from revelation, itself only accessible within the economy. However, some fear that, in John Webster's words, "attention to God's outer acts" may be "thought to license talk of God as some sort of magnified historical agent acting on the same plane as other such agents."[22]

---

[16]Holmes, *The Quest*, 146. Cf. Khaled Anatolios, *Retrieving Nicea: The Development and Meaning of Trinitarian Doctrine* (Grand Rapids, MI: Baker Academic, 2011).

[17]Holmes, *The Quest*, 146.

[18]See Holmes, *The Quest*, 112, 146.

[19]Fred Sanders, *The Triune God* (Grand Rapids, MI: Zondervan, 2016), 144.

[20]Karl Rahner, *Theological Investigations: Volume XVIII: God and Revelation* (New York: Crossroad, 1983), 114 (emphasis original).

[21]Sanders, *The Triune God*, 150.

[22]Webster, *God without Measure: Working Papers in Christian Theology*, vol. 1: God and the Works of God (New York: T&T Clark, 2016), 8.

In this regard, Trinitarians hold various views regarding the extent to which God's revelation in the economy corresponds to God's inner being.

The debate over conceptions of divine triunity

There is some debate among Trinitarians over just how to conceive of the triunity of the divine persons. Some stress divine unity while others stress distinctness of the three persons. This is often framed as a dispute between Western or Latin patristic conceptions, which purportedly emphasized divine oneness, and Eastern or Greek patristic conceptions, which purportedly emphasized divine threeness. As noted above, however, recent scholarship has called this framework into serious question.

Distinct from the historical debate over patristic views of the Trinity, some employ the labels "Latin Trinity" and "Social Trinity" to distinguish between the competing contemporary approaches that emphasize divine oneness and threeness, respectively.[23] Alternatively, Thomas Morris distinguishes between "*singularity theories of the Trinity,* which attempt to stress the unity of the divine nature, without falling into modalism, and *social theories of the Trinity,* which attempt to highlight the diversity or distinctness of the three persons, without falling into polytheism."[24]

Singularity or Latin theories

The so-called singularity or Latin theories maintain that the persons of the Trinity share one unitary faculty of reason, will, and consciousness. Holmes contends this view is the Eastern *and* Western patristic doctrine, wherein the "divine nature is simple" and "incomposite" such that there is only "one cognition, one wisdom, and one perception within the Trinity."[25] On this view, the Trinitarian persons are not "persons" in what Holmes characterizes as the modern sense, wherein "personality" requires "self-

---

[23]See Thomas McCall and Michael Rea, "Introduction," in *Philosophical and Theological Essays on the Trinity,* ed. Thomas McCall and Michael C. Rea (New York: Oxford University Press, 2009), 1–2.
[24]Thomas V. Morris, *Our Idea of God: An Introduction to Philosophical Theology* (Notre Dame, IN: University of Notre Dame Press, 1991), 176–77.
[25]Holmes, *The Quest,* 145.

determination," "volition," "self-awareness," and "cognition."²⁶ Rather, the Trinitarian "persons" share one singular faculty of cognition, volition, and self-awareness. Here, Phillip Cary contends, in Nicene orthodoxy there "is only one will in God;" the Trinitarian persons "have but one will as they have but one being. Otherwise they would not be one God."²⁷ Likewise, Holmes contends, the "East and West alike are united in insisting on the unity of the divine will and knowledge."²⁸

In Holmes's view, any conception of the Trinity as three centers of consciousness (e.g., social Trinity views) is "a simple departure from … the unified witness of the entire theological tradition."²⁹ Rather, Holmes contends, the Trinitarian persons are distinguished only by the "eternal relations of origin—begetting and proceeding;" everything else "spoken of God … is spoken of the one life the three share, and so is indivisibly spoken of all three."³⁰

Critics of singularity theories, however, think this view comes too close to modalism and does not have a robust enough conception of the distinctness of the Trinitarian persons.³¹ Some contend, further, that singularity theories appeal to apophaticism (negative theology) in a way that reduces the Trinitarian claim to something like "within the one God there are three 'somewhats,' three something-or-others."³² Moreover, singularity theories are typically bound up with the controversial doctrine of divine simplicity, which some believe is incompatible with the Trinity doctrine (see the discussion later in this chapter). Some object, further, that singularity theories do not provide a context for personal, I–Thou, relationships of love within the Trinity, raising questions regarding how God could be love (if love must be personally relational) apart from the creation of some world. Morris refers to this as "the problem of the lonely God."³³ Advocates respond by

---

²⁶Holmes, *The Quest*, 144.

²⁷Cary, "The New Evangelical Subordinationism: Reading Inequality into the Trinity," in *The New Evangelical Subordinationism?*, ed. Dennis W. Jowers and H. Wayne House (Eugene, OR: Pickwick, 2012), 6.

²⁸Holmes, *The Quest*, 144. Cf. Gregory Nazianzen, *Orations* 31.14 (*NPNF2* 7:322).

²⁹Holmes, *The Quest*, 195.

³⁰Holmes, *The Quest*, 146. This entails, but may not be entailed by, the traditional view that each Trinitarian person is operative in each of God's external works (sometimes called the doctrine of indivisible or inseparable operations, often referred to by the Latin phrase *opera trinitatis ad extra indivisa sunt*).

³¹See Morris, *Our Idea of God*, 180–82.

³²Dale Tuggy, *What Is the Trinity* (CreateSpace, 2017), 62. Tuggy himself is a critic of the Trinity doctrine.

³³See Morris, *Our Idea of God*, 183.

conceiving of love in a way that does not require such personal relationality. Critics maintain that such a conception amounts to less than the "goodness of a full and perfect love."[34]

Relational or social theories

Accounting for divine love is one major motivation of many relational or social theories.[35] As Morris defines it, "A social theory represents the Trinity as a community of three distinct persons, each with a distinct center of consciousness and will, yet all existing with the others in as close a relation of harmony and love as it is possible to stand in."[36] There are various social theories, some of which employ a social analogy wherein "the divine persons are relevantly like a family, a supremely unified community of monarchs, or three human persons whose interpersonal relationships are so strong as to be unbreakable."[37] Whereas some advocates "conceive of the divine persons as distinct substances who share a generic divine nature which they hold together in common," others maintain there is one and only one divine substance.[38] For instance, William Hasker views the persons of the Trinity as "distinct centers of consciousness" with a "single concrete divine nature."[39]

Some opponents contend that social theories are (1) incompatible with the ecumenical creeds, (2) entail "that God is not a person," (3) compromise "adequate doctrines of omniscience and omnipotence," or (4) amount to tritheism and thus "a kind of polytheism."[40] This last charge of tritheism is the most oft-discussed concern.[41] In this regard, some who adopt this view nevertheless avoid the label "social Trinity" (sometimes preferring

---

[34]See Morris, *Our Idea of God*, 183.
[35]See, for example, Richard Swinburne, *The Christian God* (New York: Clarendon, 1994), 177–78; Catherine Mowry LaCugna, *God for Us: The Trinity and Christian Life* (New York: HarperCollins, 1991); Thomas F. Torrance, *The Trinitarian Faith* (Edinburgh: T&T Clark, 1989); John D. Zizioulas, *Being as Communion: Studies in Personhood and the Church* (Crestwood, NY: St. Vladimir's Seminary Press, 1985).
[36]Morris, *Our Idea of God*, 177.
[37]McCall and Rea, "Introduction," 2.
[38]McCall and Rea, "Introduction," 2–3.
[39]William Hasker, *Metaphysics and the Tri-Personal God* (New York: Oxford University Press, 2013), 25, 251.
[40]See the discussion in McCall and Rea, "Introduction," 4–6. Cf. the essays on both sides of the issue in McCall and Rea, eds. *Philosophical and Theological Essays on the Trinity*.
[41]For a response to such criticism, see Tom McCall, "Social Trinitarianism and Tritheism Again: A Response to Brian Leftow," *Philosophia Christi* 5/2 (2003): 405–30.

"relational Trinity") because some social theories seem to undermine the essential oneness/unity of the Trinity.[42]

Many advocates of relational or social theories attempt to avoid tritheism by claiming that the persons of the Trinity somehow interpenetrate one another and thus coinhere in one substance. This is typically referred to as perichoresis.[43] As Millard Erickson puts it, in the Trinity "there are three wills but the three, in the pattern known as perichoresis, always agree."[44] Critics like Dale Tuggy argue that "perichoresis-talk seems firmly stuck at the metaphorical level" and that perichoresis "metaphors simply hide an unintelligible claim."[45] Advocates respond that, absent actual contradiction, the inability to precisely define how perichoresis works is not a sufficient reason to dismiss it since many other claims regarding God's nature end up in mystery (without contradiction) at some point.[46]

In order to avoid the charge of polytheism, the relational or social theory advocate needs to maintain that there is some "monotheism-securing relation between the divine persons."[47] That is, there must be some relation between the persons such that the persons together are one and only one God. For instance, Cornelius Plantinga, Jr. advocates for what he calls a "strong of social theory of the Trinity," in which the "Father, Son, and Spirit" are "viewed as distinct centers of consciousness" and maintains that the "Father, Son, and Spirit must be regarded as tightly enough related to each other so as to render plausible" the claim to monotheism.[48] In this regard, William Lane Craig has employed the analogy of the mythical Cerberus, the three-headed watchdog of Hades in Greek mythology, contending that Cerberus would have three centers of consciousness while being only one

---

[42]See Thomas H. McCall, *Which Trinity? Whose Monotheism?* (Grand Rapids, MI: Eerdmans, 2010), 236–41; Thomas H. McCall, "Relational Trinity: Creedal Perspective." Pages 113–37 in *Two Views on the Doctrine of the Trinity*, ed. Jason S. Sexton (Grand Rapids, MI: Zondervan, 2014).

[43]See, for example, Swinburne, *The Christian God*, 184.

[44]Millard Erickson, *Who's Tampering with the Trinity* (Grand Rapids, MI: Kregel, 2009), 135.

[45]Dale Tuggy, "The Unfinished Business of Trinitarian Theorizing," *Religious Studies* 39 (2003): 170, 171. Tuggy claims both social Trinity and Latin Trinity approaches are inconsistent and unintelligible.

[46]Tuggy might respond that he has shown claims regarding perichoresis to be inconsistent. Advocates of perichoresis, however, believe otherwise.

[47]McCall and Rea, "Introduction," 5.

[48]Cornelius Plantinga, Jr., "Social Trinity and Tritheism," in *Trinity, Incarnation, and Atonement: Philosophical and Theological Essays*, ed. Ronald J. Feenstra and Cornelius Plantinga, Jr. (Notre Dame, IN: University of Notre Dame Press, 1989), 22. Plantinga, Jr. claims, further: "A Person who extrapolated theologically from Hebrews, Paul, and John would naturally develop a social theory of the Trinity." "Social Trinity and Theism," 27.

dog.[49] Critics object, however, that Craig's view makes God consist of parts (a mereological Trinity), an objection that hinges on how one views divine simplicity.[50]

While social theorists agree that God is one, they offer various proposals regarding just what the monotheism-securing relation might be. These include "Being the only members of the same kind," "Being the only members of the community that exists necessarily and that is necessarily sovereign over all that is not divine," "Being the only members of the divine family," "Enjoying perfect love and harmony of will with one another," and "Being necessarily mutually interdependent, so that no divine person can possibly exist apart from the other divine persons."[51] In this regard, the relational or social theory advocate can argue that they need not know just what the monotheism-securing relation is but can simply posit that there is such a triune relationship, the ontology of which may be—at least at present—beyond human understanding.

Apart from tritheism, critics maintain that social theories rely on a faulty modern concept of person and, in this and other ways, deviate from the patristic tradition.[52] For his part, conversely, McCall thinks that "Trinitarian theology should insist on an understanding of persons that is consistent with the New Testament portrayal of the divine persons, that is, as distinct centers of consciousness and will who exist together in loving relationships of mutual dependence."[53] Further, McCall maintains that such a "robust sense of person" need not lose "continuity with the tradition."[54]

---

[49]William Lane Craig, "Toward a Tenable Social Trinitarianism," in *Philosophical and Theological Essays on the Trinity*, 98. Cf. Yandell's proposal in Yandell, "How Many Times Does Three Go into one."

[50]Cf. the objections in Daniel Howard-Snyder, "Trinity Monotheism," in *Philosophical and Theological Essays on the Trinity*, 118–22. Further, Craig thinks his model leaves "whether the persons of the Trinity are parts of God" as an "open question." William Lane Craig, "Another Glance at Trinity Monotheism," "Toward a Tenable Social Trinitarianism," *Philosophical and Theological Essays on the Trinity*, 129. For Craig, "The crucial fact is that these individuals [the Trinitarian persons] compose one unique, indivisible individual which is a substance." Craig, "Another Glance," 130.

[51]McCall and Rea, "Introduction," 3.

[52]Holmes, *The Quest*, 199.

[53]McCall, *Which Trinity? Whose Monotheism?* 236.

[54]McCall, *Which Trinity? Whose Monotheism?* 238. Elsewhere, McCall argues that some traditionally categorized as advocates of so-called Latin Trinitarianism (e.g., Augustine, Richard of St. Victor) make claims that seem to affirm elements of social Trinitarianism. For instance, McCall argues that Augustine himself "views the divine persons as distinct agents with will and consciousness." McCall, "Social Trinitarianism and Tritheism Again," 410.

Relative identity theories

A lesser known approach to the threeness-in-oneness problem is called relative Trinitarianism. This approach relies on rather technical distinctions about relative identity to claim that the Trinitarian persons are "numerically the same but not identical" such that "it is possible that the divine persons are genuinely distinct but yet, by virtue of their consubstantiality, one and the same God."[55] One version of this, set forth by Jeffrey Brower and Michael Rea, uses the analogy of a statue that is also a pillar.[56] The statue and pillar are different things—at least in that the statue could erode while leaving the pillar—but share one material constitution so that most would identify the statue and pillar as one and only one object. "Brower and Rea say that Father, Son, and Holy Spirit [though immaterial] are to be understood as doing something analogous to sharing the same matter." Here:

> The divine essence plays the *role* of Aristotelian matter and each of the three person-constituting properties ('Fatherhood,' 'Sonship,' and 'Spiration,' for example) play the role of form. Thus, as in the case of the statue and the pillar, the persons of the Trinity stand in the relationship of numerical sameness without identity: they are one and the same God, but different persons.[57]

Like social theories, this "view posits three divine persons who are really distinct" but unlike *some* social theories, this "view also insists that there is one divine individual substance" and denies "that the Trinity is composed of parts."[58] Although this is not a very widespread option, this is one serious alternative in the contemporary conversation. The complexities of this approach, however, preclude further discussion of views regarding its strengths and weaknesses here.

---

[55] McCall and Rea, "Introduction," 10.
[56] Jeffrey E. Brower and Michael C. Rea, "Material Constitution and the Trinity," in *Philosophical and Theological Essays on the Trinity*, 263–82.
[57] McCall and Rea, "Introduction," 12.
[58] McCall and Rea, "Introduction," 12.

The debate over eternal generation and procession

Eternal generation and eternal procession are typically taken to mean that the Son is timelessly generated or timelessly begotten by the Father and the Spirit timelessly proceeds from the Father (or from the Father and the Son). While some advocates contend otherwise, many scholars hold that divine temporality is incompatible with eternal generation.[59] For Gregory of Nazianzus, as understood by Holmes: "The Father begets the Son and spirates the Spirit, impassibly, timelessly and incorporeally."[60] Augustine likewise writes, the Father "begot him [the Son] timelessly in such a way that the life which the Father gave the Son by begetting him is co-eternal with the life of the Father who gave it."[61] Given eternal generation, one can both affirm that there was no time when the Son was not, excluding Arianism, and that the Son is "begotten" and thus distinguished from the Father and Spirit while being inseparable from the Father and Spirit and of one substance (ousia).

The Nicene Creed is widely taken to assert the traditional doctrines of eternal generation and procession. However, some Trinitarians reject eternal generation and procession, either rejecting this aspect of the Creed or interpreting the Creed differently.[62] Kevin Giles, however, argues that rejection of eternal generation is a "doctrinally dangerous" move that "reject[s] a theological idea enshrined in the creeds and confessions."[63] Critics, nevertheless, contend that eternal generation and procession lack biblical warrant.[64] Millard Erickson, for one, claims "the concept of

---

[59] See Mullins, "Hasker on the Divine Processions of the Trinitarian Persons." Cf. Paul Helm, "Eternal Creation," *Tyndale Bulletin* 45/2 (1994): 321–38. Hasker, however, is representative of those who affirm divine temporality and eternal generation and procession. See Hasker, *Metaphysics and the Tri-Personal God*, 214–25. Cf. Swinburne, *The Christian God*, 182–85.

[60] Holmes, *The Quest*, 112. See Gregory, *Or.* 29.2.

[61] Augustine, *The Trinity* 15.47, trans. Edmund Hill (Brooklyn, NY: New City, 1991), 432. Cf. Augustine, *The Trinity* 15.26.47 (*NPNF1* 3:225).

[62] Before recently affirming eternal generation, Wayne Grudem previously employed the latter strategy. Cf. Wayne Grudem, *Systematic Theology* (Grand Rapids, MI: Zondervan, 1994), 254 fn. 38.

[63] Giles, *Jesus and the Father: Modern Evangelicals Reinvent the Doctrine of the Trinity* (Grand Rapids, MI: Zondervan, 2006), 240.

[64] See, for example, John Feinberg, *No One Like Him: The Doctrine of God* (Wheaton, IL: Crossway, 2001), 489–92. See also R.T. Mullins, "Divine Temporality, the Trinity, and the Charge of Arianism," *Journal of Analytic Theology* 4 (2016): 281–83.

eternal generation does not have biblical warrant and does not make sense philosophically. As such, we should eliminate it from theological discussions of the Trinity."[65] Similarly, John Feinberg explicitly rejects the "doctrines of eternal generation and procession," claiming they "are shrouded in obscurity as to their meaning, and biblical support for them is nowhere near as strong as supposed."[66] Further, Feinberg contends, "everyone grants that" Christ "must be Son in some metaphorical sense. Even the doctrine of eternal generation doesn't allow him to be Son in the literal sense that we use the term. So, if the term is used metaphorically, why must we demand that the metaphor means the doctrine of eternal generation?"[67]

For his part, Giles concedes that the "biblical support is not strong" for "differentiating the Father, Son, and Spirit on the basis of origination."[68] He thus appeals to the patristic tradition as "the key" to the "meaning" of the Trinity doctrine.[69] Others, however, have attempted to make a case that eternal generation is biblically warranted.[70] Conversely, Paul Helm maintains that "those who formulated the doctrine of the Trinity in terms of the begetting of the Son and the processing of the Spirit were influenced by Neoplatonism" and asks, "do these claims [regarding eternal generation] not take us far from the New Testament, and give rise to unnecessary speculation?"[71]

Critics also contend that this view might entail subordinationism. For instance, J. P. Moreland and William Lane Craig contend, "although creedally affirmed, the doctrine of the generation of the Son (and the procession of the Spirit) is a relic of Logos Christology which finds virtually no warrant in the biblical text and introduces a subordinationism into the Godhead which anyone who affirms the full deity of Christ ought to find very troubling."[72] Conversely, advocates contend that eternal generation and procession refer only to the personhood of the Son and Spirit, leaving the essence of

---

[65]Erickson, *Who's Tampering*, 251.
[66]Feinberg, *No One Like Him*, 492.
[67]Feinberg, *No One Like Him*, 492.
[68]Giles, *Jesus and the Father*, 239, fn 166.
[69]Giles, *The Eternal Generation of the Son* (Downers Grove, IL: IVP Academic, 2012), 37.
[70]See the essays in Fred Sanders and Scott R. Swain, eds., *Retrieving Eternal Generation* (Grand Rapids, MI: Zondervan, 2017), 29–146.
[71]Helm, "Of God, and of the Holy Trinity: A Response to Dr. Beckwith," *The Churchman* 115/4 (2001): 351.
[72]J.P. Moreland and William Lane Craig, *Philosophical Foundations for a Christian Worldview* (Downers Grove, IL: IVP Academic, 2003), *Philosophical Foundations*, 594. Cf. Erickson, *Who's Tampering*, 184, 252; Helm, "Of God," 350.

Son and Spirit ungenerated and thus avoiding subordinationism.[73] Critics, however, wonder how this does not amount to the conclusion that Father, Son, and Spirit have different essences or natures—being distinctly and essentially unbegotten, begotten, and spirated. Advocates of the eternal processions believe the Trinitarian persons share one substance while being "distinguished by eternal relations of origin—begetting and proceeding—and not otherwise."[74]

The doctrine of the eternal procession of the Spirit is further complicated by the dispute over whether the Spirit eternally proceeds from the Father alone or from the Father and the Son. The latter view—the *filioque*—was inserted into the Niceno-Constantinopolitan Creed by the West, modifying the phrase regarding the Holy Spirit, "who proceedeth from the Father" to "who proceedeth from the Father and the Son." Affirmed in most Western creedal churches, the filioque is rejected by The Eastern Orthodox Church and others, being one of the principal reasons for the East–West Schism of 1054. In this regard, Feinberg notes: "If my rejection of the doctrines of eternal generation and eternal procession are correct, then there are really no grounds for a controversy over whether the Spirit proceeds just from the Father or from Father and Son. To the extent that the split between the Eastern and Western churches resulted from this dispute, the split was totally unnecessary."[75] Many advocates, conversely, claim that the doctrines of eternal generation and procession are fundamental to the Trinity doctrine.

The debate over functional subordination within the Trinity

As noted above, the traditional Trinity doctrine rejects ontological subordination of the Son or Spirit as heretical. However, many Trinitarians maintain that the Son is *functionally* subordinate to the Father, at least within the context of the incarnation. These typically understand John 14:28—"The Father is greater than I"—and other texts regarding Jesus's posture of submission to the Father as referring only to Christ's *function* within the incarnation or plan of redemption more broadly.

---

[73]See, for example, Giles, *Jesus and the Father*, 240.
[74]Holmes, *The Quest*, 146.
[75]Feinberg, *No One Like Him*, 492.

Whether there is functional subordination and how to understand it has been the subject of considerable recent debate (especially among Evangelicals), particularly regarding whether Christ's functional subordination is temporary or eternal. Taking the latter view, Bruce Ware and Wayne Grudem maintain that, while the Trinitarian persons are ontologically equal, Christ and the Spirit are eternally functionally subordinate to the Father.[76] There is, then, an eternal functional hierarchy wherein the Son and Spirit submit to the Father's commands—sometimes called eternal relations of submission and authority (ERAS). Many others, such as Millard Erickson and Gilbert Bilezikian, maintain that the Father, Son, and Spirit are ontologically equal and also share equal authority such that submission of the Son and Spirit is temporary and functional "for the purpose of executing a specific mission of the triune God."[77]

Many critics of eternal functional subordination believe it "contains an implicit ontological subordination."[78] Kevin Giles, a most persistent and ardent critic, contends that if Christ's "subordination is eternal, it is not a role or functional subordination," but "an ontological status that cannot be otherwise," a "hierarchical ordering in the eternal or immanent Trinity" that amounts to "subordinationism."[79] He believes, further, "the eternal subordination of the Son in authority" has "no historical support at all, or any theological merit."[80] While supported in some Evangelical circles, the eternal subordination view has recently been the subject of strong, persistent criticism by numerous Evangelical theologians—some of whom (like Giles) have questioned its orthodoxy.[81] Erickson, however, thinks that each of the competing views of functional

---

[76]See, for example, Bruce Ware, "Tampering with the Trinity: Does the Son Submit to His Father?" *Journal for Biblical Manhood and Womanhood* 6/1 (2001); Bruce A. Ware, *Father, Son, and Holy Spirit: Relationships, Roles, and Relevance* (Wheaton, IL: Crossway, 2005); Grudem, *Systematic Theology*; Wayne Grudem, *Evangelical Feminism* (Wheaton, IL: Crossway, 2006). Cf. Robert Letham, *The Holy Trinity: In Scripture, History, Theology, and Worship* (Phillipsburg, NJ: P&R, 2004).

[77]See, for example, Erickson, *Who's Tampering*, 20; Gilbert Bilezikian, "Hermeneutical Bungee-Jumping: Subordination in the Godhead," *Journal of the Evangelical Theological Society* 40/1 (1997): 60.

[78]Erickson, *Who's Tampering*, 257. Cf. Cary, "The New Evangelical Subordinationism."

[79]Kevin Giles, "The Trinity without Tiers," in *The New Evangelical Subordinationism*, 283–84, 285. See also, Erickson, *Who's Tampering*, 257; Bilezikian, "Hermeneutical Bungee-Jumping," 63. Conversely, see Robert Letham, "Reply to Kevin Giles," *Evangelical Quarterly* 80/4 (2008).

[80]Giles, *Jesus and the Father*, 240.

[81]Debate erupted on the internet in summer 2016. Soon after, Ware and Grudem changed their position on eternal generation. On this, see Kevin Giles, *The Rise and Fall of the Complementarian Doctrine of the Trinity* (Eugene, OR: Cascade, 2017).

subordination "falls within the boundaries of traditional orthodoxy. Neither view has ever been condemned by an official body of the church."[82]

In this debate, both sides claim that Scripture and tradition are on their side. Grudem contends that eternal functional subordination is biblical and "has been the historic doctrine of the church" and that opponents "should also have the honesty and courtesy to explain to readers why they now feel it necessary to differ with the historic doctrine of the church as expressed in its major creeds."[83] Critics, however, note that statements drawn from tradition to support eternal functional subordination appear to refer to eternal generation, not functional subordination and that the tradition is incompatible with eternal functional subordination. Further, Erickson maintains, the "view of the eternal equality of authority of the three persons has been the dominant view of church theologians of the past."[84]

Notably, if functional subordination—whether eternal or temporary—is taken to mean that the Son's *divine* will is subordinated to the Father's will, then it is incompatible with singularity theories, which maintain the Father, Son, and Spirit share one, singular, faculty of willing. Phillip Cary claims, the Son and Father "have but one will as they have but one being. Otherwise they would not be one God. Such are the logical consequences of Nicaea, which orthodox trinitarianism understands but evangelical subordinationists do not."[85] Yet, Giles, while adamantly opposing the view that there are "three wills" in God, nevertheless allows that "a temporal voluntary subordination of the Son, that all agree took place in the incarnation, is no problem."[86]

Biblical data relevant to the Trinity doctrine

Despite taking various positions on the debated issues above, Trinitarians agree that there is one and only one God in three distinct (fully) divine persons. Further, Tom McCall writes, "Christians have been Trinitarians because they have been convinced that the revelation of God in Jesus Christ

---

[82]Erickson, *Who's Tampering*, 257.
[83]Grudem, *Evangelical Feminism*, 422.
[84]Erickson, *Who's Tampering*, 81. So, also, Bilezikian, "Hermeneutical Bungee-Jumping," 60.
[85]Cary, "The New Evangelical Subordinationism," 6.
[86]Kevin Giles, "The Trinity without Tiers," in *The New Evangelical Subordinationism*, 283.

demands it."[87] Fred Sanders adds, "The doctrine of the Trinity is in fact well-grounded in the gospel and well attested in the scriptures."[88] Further, Sanders states, "The church has always confessed the doctrine of the Trinity as something to be believed on the grounds of revelation alone as recorded in Scripture alone. The church should continue to do so."[89]

Given the limited space and scope of this chapter, this section focuses attention on biblical data relevant to grounding the minimal Trinity doctrine, without attempting to adjudicate the debates among Trinitarians regarding relations between the Trinitarian persons. The following sections thus survey some relevant biblical data regarding the four affirmations of the minimal Trinity doctrine—(1) God's oneness/unity, (2) God's triunity, (3) the full divinity of the persons, and (4) the distinctness of the three persons. This will be conducted by way of four questions that, if answered affirmatively, amount to affirmation of the minimal Trinity doctrine.[90]

Is there only one God?

Scripture directly teaches the oneness of God. Deuteronomy 6:4 explicitly affirms monotheism, saying, "Hear, O Israel! The Lord is our God, the Lord is one!" Deuteronomy 4:35 declares further, Yahweh "is God; there is no other besides Him." According to 2 Samuel 7:22, there "is none like" Yahweh "and there is no God besides" Yahweh. Elsewhere, Yahweh himself says, "I am the LORD, and there is no other; Besides me there is no God" (Isa 45:5; cf. 37:20; 44:6; 2 Kings 19:19; Ps 83:18; 86:10). This basic tenet of Hebrew faith is repeatedly reinforced by emphasis on the uniqueness of God and the forbidding of worship of anyone other than Yahweh (cf. Deut 4:39; 5:7–9).

Further, in the NT Jesus affirms and quotes Deuteronomy 6:4, "The Lord our God is one Lord" (Mark 12:29; cf. 12:32) and elsewhere refers to "the *one and only* God" (John 5:44). James 2:19 also explicitly affirms the oneness of God: "You believe that God is one. You do well; the demons also believe, and shudder." Likewise, 1 Corinthians 8:4 teaches, "there is no God but one" (cf. 1 Tim 1:17). Trinitarians take these and other texts to affirm that there is one and only one God.

---

[87] McCall, *Which Trinity? Whose Monotheism?* 231.
[88] Sanders, "Redefining Progress in Trinitarian Theology: Stephen R. Holmes on the Trinity," *Evangelical Quarterly* 86/1 (2014): 9.
[89] Sanders, *The Triune God*, 155.
[90] Space permits only brief mention of some selected verses here, all of which should be read and carefully interpreted in their own context.

Is there "threeness" relative to the one God?

Numerous so-called Trinitarian formulas speak of the Father, the Son, and the Holy Spirit. Foremost among these is the great commission stated by Jesus himself: "Go therefore and make disciples of all the nations, baptizing them in the name of the Father and the Son and the Holy Spirit" (Matt 28:19). Notably, the word "name" is singular here, which many have taken as indicating the unity of the Father, Son, and Holy Spirit.[91]

Other Trinitarian formulas include:

"Now there are varieties of gifts, but the same Spirit. And there are varieties of ministries, and the same Lord. There are varieties of effects, but the same God who works all things in all persons" (1 Cor 12:4–6).

"The grace of the Lord Jesus Christ, and the love of God, and the fellowship of the Holy Spirit, be with you all" (2 Cor 13:14).

"There is one body and one Spirit, just as also you were called in one hope of your calling; one Lord, one faith, one baptism, one God and Father of all who is over all and through all and in all" (Eph 4:4–6).[92]

… "the foreknowledge of God the Father, by the sanctifying work of the Spirit, to obey Jesus Christ" (1 Peter 1:2).[93]

Additionally, John 14–16 is packed with references to the interrelationship of Father, Son, and Holy Spirit. Further, each Trinitarian person is depicted at Christ's baptism: Jesus is baptized, the "Spirit of God" descends "as a dove" and the Father declares, "This is my beloved Son, in whom I am well-pleased" (Matt 3:16–17). Overall, Roderick K. Durst finds "seventy-five triadic order passages" in the NT wherein all three persons of the Trinity are mentioned within a range of one to five verses.[94] Durst concludes, "the quantity of divine triadic instances is so profound and in such a diversity of orders that it constitutes a qualitative *matrix*

---

[91] Craig Blomberg contends: "The singular 'name' followed by the threefold reference to 'Father, Son, and Holy Spirit' suggests both unity and plurality in the Godhead. Here is the clearest Trinitarian 'formula' anywhere in the Gospels." *Matthew*. NAC (Nashville, TN: B&H, 2001), 432.

[92] Here, as in many other instances in the NT, the word "Lord" is taken by biblical scholars to be a reference to Jesus.

[93] The overwhelming consensus of textual critics is that the Trinitarian formula in the KJV of 1 John 5:7 (the so-called Johannine comma, based on the Textus Receptus) is not original (likely a marginal scribal gloss), since it does not appear in early manuscripts.

[94] Roderick K. Durst, *Reordering the Trinity: Six Movements of God in the New Testament* (Grand Rapids, MI: Kregel, 2015), 68.

of Trinitarian consciousness. Trinity is how the New Testament authors inadvertently thought and viewed reality."[95]

Evidence for the Trinity is also apparent in the OT, particularly in light of the NT. Some Trinitarians point to hints at the plurality of God in statements by God such as "Let us make man in Our image" (Gen 1:26; cf. 3:22; 11:7). Stronger support comes from the many passages that indicate the "Angel of the LORD [Yahweh]" is himself Yahweh, which many scholars take as referring to the pre-incarnate Christ. To take just one example, just after the "angel of the LORD" appears to Moses in the burning bush, God Himself calls from the midst of the bush, suggesting that in some cases the angel of Yahweh is, in fact, Yahweh (Exod 3:2, 4; cf. Gen 16:7–13; Gen 22:11; 32:28; Hos 12:3–5; Ex 23:20–23; Judges 13:13–22; Isa 63:7–14; cf. Psalm 110:1).

In what might be the clearest OT reference to the Trinity, Isaiah 63 mentions Yahweh, the "angel of His presence" from Exodus, and "His Holy Spirit," saying: "He [Yahweh] became their Savior. In all their affliction He was afflicted, and the angel of His presence saved them; In His love and in His mercy He redeemed them, And He lifted and carried them all the days of old. But they rebelled and grieved His Holy Spirit" (Isa 63:8–10; cf. Gen 1:2; Eph 4:30). Regarding the "angel of His presence," J. Ridderbos comments, "the reference is to the Angel of the LORD who is Himself God and is also distinguished from God."[96]

While recognizing Scripture refers to the Father, Son, and Holy Spirit, however, some critics dispute that Scripture teaches Father, Son, and Spirit are distinct and/or (fully) divine. This brings us to the last two questions.

Are the Father, the Son, and the Holy Spirit (fully) divine?

The full divinity of the Father is generally unquestioned but some call into question the (full) divinity of the Son and/or the Spirit. Regarding the divinity of Christ, Trinitarians point to numerous passages. Foremost among these is John 1:1–3: "In the beginning was the Word [referring to Christ], and the Word was with God, and the Word was God. He was in the beginning with God. All things came into being through Him, and apart from Him nothing came into being that has come into being." Michael Horton comments on

---

[95] Durst, *Reordering the Trinity*, 66 (emphasis original).
[96] J. Ridderbos, *Isaiah* (Grand Rapids, MI: Regency, 1985), 557.

this passage, the "Word is simultaneously distinct from God the Father ('was with God') and one in essence with the Father ('was God')."[97] This passage also indicates that the Son already existed "in the beginning" (cf. Micah 5:2; Gal 4:4) and did not himself come into being since "apart from Him nothing came into being that has come into being" (John 1:3).

Later, in John 20:28, Thomas addresses Jesus as "My Lord and my God" (John 20:28). Moreover, Jesus accepted worship (John 9:38; cf. Matt 2:11; 14:33; 28:9, 17; Luke 24:52; Heb 1:6; Rev 5:8–14), indicating his claim to be fully divine since only God should be worshiped (Exod 34:14; cf. Matt 4:10; Luke 4:8; Rev 19:10). Indeed, in Hebrews 1:6, the Father commands, "Let all God's angels worship him."

Further, Trinitarians believe Colossians 2:9 indicates the full divinity of Christ, saying, "in Him all the fullness of Deity dwells in bodily form" (Col 2:9; cf. Phil 2:6). Just before this, Colossians 1:15–20 declares Christ:

> the image of the invisible God, the firstborn of all creation. For by Him all things were created, both in the heavens and on earth, visible and invisible, whether thrones or dominions or rulers or authorities—all things have been created through Him and for Him. He is before all things, and in Him all things hold together. He is also head of the body, the church; and He is the beginning, the firstborn from the dead, so that He Himself will come to have first place in everything. For it was the Father's good pleasure for all the fullness to dwell in Him, and through Him to reconcile all things to Himself, having made peace through the blood of His cross; through Him, I say, whether things on earth or things in heaven (Col 1:15–20).

Trinitarians argue that the language of firstborn, here, cannot consistently be taken to mean Christ's existence had a beginning because the passage further states that "all things have been created through Him and for Him. He is before all things" (Col 1:16–17). Trinitarians typically interpret language of Christ as firstborn (*prototokos*) and the "only begotten" or "one of a kind" (*monogenes*) Son, not as referencing Christ coming into being—on pain of contradiction with passages that indicate Christ's pre-existence (John 1:1–3; Col 1:16–17; cf. Mic 5:2; Rev 22:13)—but as figurative, covenantal language, referring to Christ's unique status as the covenantal Messiah ("anointed one") and Son of God (cf. Luke 1:35).[98] Christ fulfilled the covenant promises of

---

[97]Horton, *The Christian Faith* (Grand Rapids, MI: Zondervan, 2011), 275.

[98]Most NT scholars believe *monogenes* does not derive from language of birth (*gennaō*) but from language about being one "of a kind". See, for example, Leon Morris, *The Gospel according to John*. NICNT (Grand Rapids, MI: Eerdmans, 1995), 93. However, even if derived from *gennaō*, *monogenes*

the king who would usher in God's everlasting kingdom—see Daniel 2 and also the connection to the Davidic covenant wherein God says of David, "I also shall make him My firstborn" (Ps 89:27; cf. Isa 9:6).

Hebrews 1 includes similar language referring to Christ's covenantal, Messianic role in the plan of salvation. Hebrews 1:2–3 teaches that through the Son, God "made the world" and the Son "is the radiance of His [God's] glory and the exact representation of His [God's] nature, and upholds all things by the word of His power" (Heb 1:2–3). Trinitarians contend that no one could be the "radiance" of God's "glory and the exact representation of His nature" except one who is himself God. Further, Hebrews 1:5–6 states, "to which of the angels did He ever say, 'You are My Son, Today I have begotten You'? And again, 'I will be a Father to Him and He shall be a Son to Me'? And when He again brings the firstborn into the world, He says, 'And let all the angels of God worship Him'" (Heb 1:5–6; cf. Ps 2:7; 2 Sam 7:14, about David). Like Colossians 1:15, these verses cannot consistently refer to Christ coming into being because that would contradict other passages that teach Christ is eternal (e.g., John 1:1–3; Rev 22:13) and, in Hebrews 1:5–6, the angels already exist but Colossians 1:16–17 teaches that angels were created by Christ who is "before all things" such that Christ preexisted the angels. Hebrews 1:5–6, then, seems to refer to Christ coming into the world in the plan of salvation such that this "firstborn" language is of Christ as the Messiah of the covenant promise—the son of David—covenantal heir to the throne and to "birthright" privileges.

Hebrews 1:8–9 further indicates Christ's divinity, quoting Psalm 45:6–7 as a reference to Christ, saying: "But of the Son He says, 'Your throne, O God, is forever and ever, And the righteous scepter is the scepter of His kingdom. You have loved righteousness and hated lawlessness; Therefore God, Your God, has anointed You with the oil of gladness above Your companions'" (Heb 1:8–9; cf. Ps 110:1). Here, "God" (the Father) anoints "God" (the Son). In this regard, according to Luke 1:35, Christ is called the "Son" because of the incarnation—being conceived of the Holy Spirit and born of Mary, but pre-existing this birth as a human (cf. Gal 4:4). Jesus was not a mere human adopted as God's son (contrary to adoptionism) but "the Word became flesh" (John 1:14).

Some think language of sonship indicates Christ is subordinate to the Father. However, many Trinitarians argue that while Christ does lower

---

might be taken to refer to Christ's first-century incarnation since he was born of a woman. *Monogenes* might also be taken as covenantal language as indicated above.

himself relative to his role in the plan of redemption (cf. Phil 2:5–11), sonship language itself need not be taken to indicate subordination. First, given Christ's eternal preexistence (cf. John 1:1–3; Col 1:16–17; Rev 22:13), Christ's sonship is drastically different from that of any mere human. Mere human sons are subordinate to their fathers and mothers while they are children because they are young children, under their parents' authority. However, Christ is not younger than the Father. Further, even human sons do not remain permanently subordinate to their fathers so, many Trinitarians maintain, it is a false inference to maintain that sonship entails subordination. A son might become his father's boss in the workplace or his caretaker in his father's old age. Even in Scripture, sons are not necessarily subordinate to their fathers or mothers. David is frequently called the "son of Jesse" but not as an indication that he, as king, would be subordinate to his father Jesse.

If the Son is not, by nature, subordinate to the Father, Christ's statement in John 5:22–23 makes perfect sense: "All will honor the Son even as they honor the Father." Such a view likewise dovetails with the fact that Christ shares a throne with the Father and that throne is referred to as "the throne of God and of the Lamb" (Rev 22:1, 3). Indeed, "Son" language itself is often taken as indicating the full divinity of Christ. In this regard, Christ's own Father–Son language was understood by his opponents as a claim to divinity. They sought to kill him because he "was calling God His own Father, making Himself equal with God" (John 5:18).

In many other instances, Christ himself spoke in ways that many take to be direct or indirect claims to his divinity. He spoke of "His angels" (e.g., Matt 13:41) and "My kingdom," which "is not of this world" (John 18:36; cf. 8:23). He claimed "authority" to "forgive sins" (Mark 2:10), authority which belongs to God alone (Mark 2:7; Luke 5:20–21). Further, Jesus made claims like, "I and the Father are one" (John 10:30) and "He who has seen Me has seen the Father" (John 14:9). Indeed, many scholars believe Christ claims to be Yahweh, the great "I AM" of Exodus 3:14, when he declares, "Truly, truly, I say to you, before Abraham was born, I am" (John 8:58; cf. Mark 1:2–3). Further, in Revelation 22:13, Christ makes the striking claim, "I am the Alpha and the Omega, the first and the last, the beginning and the end" (cf. 1:8, 18), indicating Christ's eternality. Accordingly, Christ rightly shares the throne with the Father and the throne is referred to as "the throne of God and of the Lamb" (Rev 22:1, 3). Not only did Christ have no beginning but his "kingdom will have no end" (Luke 1:33; cf. Dan 2:44; 7:14; Isa 9:7; Heb 1:8; Rev 11:15).

Trinitarians also believe that Scripture teaches the (full) divinity of the Holy Spirit. In Acts 5:3, Peter says, "Ananias, why has Satan filled your heart to lie to the Holy Spirit" and then in parallel in Acts 5:4, Peter adds, "You have not lied to men but to God." Trinitarians understand this as indicating that the Holy Spirit is God (in the sense of an "is" of predication). Not only does the Holy Spirit share a name with the Father and Son (Matt 28:19), Scripture also attributes to the Holy Spirit divine attributes, referring to the Spirit as "the eternal Spirit" (Heb 9:14), indicating omniscience by saying the Spirit "knows" and "searches all things, even the depths of God" (1 Cor 2:10–11), and seemingly indicating omnipresence in that, according to Christ, the Father gave Christ's followers "another Helper, that He [the Holy Spirit] may be with you forever" (John 14:16; cf. Ps 139:7), even as they separately took the gospel message to the ends of the earth. Further, Trinitarians believe this indicates that the "Helper," the Holy Spirit—"the Spirit of truth" (John 14:17; cf. 15:26)—would take Christ's place with the apostles and go with them to the ends of the earth as they evangelized the world (cf. Acts 1:4–5).

Moreover, the NT quotes words that the OT attributed to God and attributes them to the Holy Spirit. For instance, just prior to quoting words spoken by God in Isaiah 6, Paul says, "The Holy Spirit rightly spoke through Isaiah the prophet to your fathers" (Acts 28:25). Likewise, Hebrews 3:7 introduces a quotation of God's words from Psalm 95:7 by saying, "as the Holy Spirit says." Notably, some of the words of God attributed to the Holy Spirit here are "your fathers tested and tried *Me*" and "saw what *I* did" (emphasis mine, cf. Exod 16:7). While there is less biblical data regarding the divinity of the Spirit, Trinitarians understand this to be a byproduct of progressive revelation, noting that emphasis on the Spirit comes late in the history of redemption and thus is explicitly reported "late" in the canon of Scripture.

Are the Father, the Son, and the Spirit distinct persons?

Does Scripture teach that the Father, the Son, and the Spirit are distinct persons? This fourth question can be separated into two questions: (1) Do the Father, Son, and Spirit have attributes only persons have? (2) Are the Father, the Son, and the Spirit distinct from one another?

Few question that the Father and the Son are portrayed in Scripture as persons but some have questioned the personhood of the Holy Spirit.

Here, Trinitarians contend that Scripture teaches the Holy Spirit possesses attributes only persons possess and acts in ways that only persons can act. For example, the Holy Spirit:

reveals, searches, and knows the thoughts of God (1 Cor 2:10–11)
speaks (Acts 8:29; cf. 10:19–20; 28:25; 1 Tim 4:1; Heb 3:7)
teaches (Luke 12:12; cf. John 14:26)
testifies or bears witness (John 15:26; cf. Rom 8:16)
intercedes (Rom 8:26–27; cf. 15;16; Tit 3:5)
forbids or allows (Acts 16:6–7)
calls to ministry and sends out (Acts 13:2–4)
gives gifts to whom he wills—indicating he has a will (1 Cor 12:11)
guides (Acts 8:29)
possesses a name with the Father and Son (Matt 28:19)
can be lied to and tested (Acts 5:3–4, 9)
can be "grieved" (Eph 4:30; cf. Isa 63:10; Heb 10:29).

Trinitarians contend that a mere power or force cannot be grieved, cannot will and give gifts, cannot speak, search, teach, testify, forbid or allow, or intercede; only a person can. They take this and other evidence as teaching that the Holy Spirit is a person.

This brings us to the second question of this section: Are the Trinitarian persons *distinct* from one another? Some critics contend that even if the Holy Spirit is a person, "Holy Spirit" may just be another name for the person of the Father and/or Christ or otherwise just be the Spirit of the Father and/or Son. In contrast, Trinitarians maintain that Scripture teaches that the Father, Son, and Spirit are *distinct* persons.

For example, at Christ's baptism, each person appears as distinct (Matt 3:16). Scripture further depicts the Father and Son as sharing distinct I–Thou relations and conversations such as Christ's prayer to the Father in Gethsemane, "My Father, if it is possible, let this cup pass from Me, yet not as I will, but as You will" (Matt 26:39). Further, according to John 17:24, the Father and Son shared an I–Thou love relationship before the foundation of the world (John 17:24; cf. 3:35; 5:20). Whereas the Father and the Son willed that the Son would die on the cross as part of the plan of redemption, only the Son willed that he *himself* would die (cf. John 10:17–18). Indeed, Christians have traditionally been very careful to recognize the distinctness in that the Son died on the cross but the Father and Spirit did not; the Spirit descends on the Son like a dove, the Father and/or Son did not; the Father says "this is My beloved Son," not the Son or Spirit.

Further, Christ speaks of the Spirit as "another" distinct from himself (John 14:16) who would "teach" the apostles further (Luke 12:12; John 14:26). Christ even says, "It is to your advantage that I go away; for if I do not go away, the Helper will not come to you, but if I go, I will send Him to you" (John 16:7). The distinctions between the persons are further explicit in descriptions of the sending of the Holy Spirit. The Holy Spirit is sent by the Father and is, therefore, not Himself the Father. The Spirit is sent by the Son from the Father; thus, the Holy Spirit is not the Father or the Son. This is explicit in the juxtaposition of John 14:26 and John 15:26. In John 14:26, Jesus says: "But the Helper, the Holy Spirit, whom the Father will send in My name, He will teach you all things, and bring to your remembrance all that I said to you." In John 15:26, Jesus says: "When the Helper comes, whom I will send to you from the Father, that is the Spirit of truth who proceeds from the Father, He will testify about Me" (cf. the standard of valid testimony that required the testimony of others, John 5:31). This distinction between persons is further apparent when Jesus says that one who "speaks a word against" himself (the Son) can be "forgiven," "but whoever speaks against the Holy Spirit, it shall not be forgiven him, either in this age or in the age to come" (Matt 12:32). Trinitarians take this and other biblical evidence as indicating that the Father is not the Son or Spirit; the Son is not the Father or Spirit; the Spirit is not the Father or Son.

Relative to this and other biblical data, Trinitarians conclude that Scripture affirms: (1) God's oneness/unity, (2) God's triunity, (3) the full divinity of the persons, and (4) the distinctness of the three persons. Taken together, these affirmations amount to the minimal Trinity doctrine: there is one and only one God in three distinct (fully) divine persons.

The debate over divine simplicity

Questions regarding the Trinity doctrine overlap in some respects with the debate over the doctrine of divine simplicity, a matter of considerable dispute among Christian theists. Divine simplicity is well attested in the Christian tradition but has been rejected or heavily qualified by many recent philosophers and theologians.[99] Among those who affirm divine simplicity,

---

[99] See, for example, Alvin Plantinga, *Does God Have a Nature?* (Marquette, WI: Marquette University Press, 1980). Cf. Morris, *Our Idea of God*, 113–18; R.T. Mullins, "Simply Impossible: A Case against Divine Simplicity," *Journal of Reformed Theology* 7 (2013): 181–203.

there are varying accounts of what it means. Strict classical theists advocate for a strict kind of divine simplicity, which maintains there are no genuine distinctions (except, perhaps, regarding the Trinity) in God.[100]

Strict simplicity

As Thomas Williams explains it, divine simplicity means that God is "in no way a composite. In particular, God does not have a variety of features or attributes that are distinct from God's nature and from each other."[101] Williams elaborates: "If God is one thing and his wisdom or goodness is something else, then God depends on something other than himself to be what he is, in violation of his perfect self-sufficiency or 'aseity.'" Instead, strict classical theists maintain, "God just is—is identical with, is one and the same as—his wisdom, his goodness, his power, and so forth; and since identity is transitive, all those attributes are really identical with each other."[102]

As Katherin Rogers explains Aquinas's view, as she understands it, divine simplicity means "there is absolutely no multiplicity or composition in God. All the qualities which we attribute to God are identical to one another and to God Himself."[103] As James Dolezal puts it, leaning heavily on Aquinas: "The doctrine of divine simplicity teaches that (1) God is identical with his existence and his essence and (2) that each of his attributes is ontologically identical with his existence and with every other one of his attributes."[104]

Although he is not sure that it "actually reflects most tradition-based (Latin) versions" of divine simplicity, Tom McCall refers to this view as "strict simplicity," which he summarizes as holding:

> God is simple in the sense that within God (i) there is no composition whereby God is made up of parts or pieces that are ontologically prior to or more basic than God; (ii) there is no metaphysical or moral complexity of any kind; (iii) there are no genuine distinctions within God, and (iv) everything

---

[100]See, for example, James Dolezal, *God without Parts: Divine Simplicity and the Metaphysics of God's Absoluteness* (Eugene, OR: Pickwick, 2011). Cf. Steven J. Duby, *Divine Simplicity: A Dogmatic Account* (New York: T&T Clark, 2016).

[101]Thomas Williams, "Introduction to Classical Theism," in *Models of God and Alternative Ultimate Realities*, ed. Jeanine Diller and Asa Kasher (New York: Springer, 2013), 96.

[102]Williams, "Classical Theism," 96.

[103]Rogers, *Perfect Being Theology*, 19.

[104]Dolezal, *God without Parts*, 2.

in God is identical (divine properties are identical with one another, and the divine persons are all identical with the divine essence).[105]

As such, "the only distinctions that we can posit are those that we must admit are merely provisional and from our side."[106]

Objections to the doctrine of divine simplicity

Numerous objections have been raised against the doctrine of divine simplicity. Alvin Plantinga has argued that divine simplicity amounts to the view that God has only one property and that God himself is a property. Yet, Plantinga thinks it is obvious that God has more than one property and that God could not himself be a property because properties cannot act (create) or be personal. First, to say "God has but one property," Plantinga argues, "seems flatly incompatible with the obvious fact that God has several properties; he has both power and mercifulness, say, neither of which is identical with the other."[107] Second, Plantinga contends, "if God is identical with each of his properties, then, since each of his properties is a property, he is a property." Yet, "no property could have created the world; no property could be omniscient, or, indeed, know anything at all. If God is a property, then he isn't a person at all but a mere abstract object; he has no knowledge, awareness, power, love or life. So taken, the simplicity doctrine seems an utter mistake."[108]

Advocates of divine simplicity typically claim these objections are based on a misunderstanding of divine simplicity and that God should not be thought of as possessing properties at all. As Rogers puts it, the "major problem with the contemporary debate is that almost all participants misunderstand the classic doctrine of simplicity," which maintains that "strictly speaking God neither *has* properties nor *is* He a property ... however unified and exalted. God is simply act."[109] As such, Rogers maintains, "The mistake is in failing to see that God is not a property but an act."[110]

---

[105]McCall, "Trinity Doctrine, Plain and Simple," 54–55.
[106]McCall, "Trinity Doctrine, Plain and Simple," 52.
[107]Plantinga, *Does God Have a Nature*? 47. Cf. the criticisms of simplicity, so construed, and suggestion of simplicity of a different kind, in Hoffman and Rosenkrantz, *The Divine Attributes*, 82.
[108]Plantinga, *Does God Have a Nature*?, 47.
[109]Rogers, *Perfect Being Theology*, 27. cf. Dolezal, *God without Parts*, 29–30.
[110]Rogers, *Perfect Being Theology*, 25.

R.T. Mullins, however, finds this implausible, asking, "How can a person be an act?"[111] Further, noting that strict simplicity is incompatible with God having "accidental properties" such as being "our *Creator, Redeemer,* and *Lord*," Mullins contends, "Defenders of divine simplicity must reconcile this with a Bible that has no qualms predicating accidental properties of a God who is intimately and radically related to creatures."[112] Alan Padgett adds, "This doctrine [of divine simplicity] seems more at home in a Neoplatonic theology, such as Plotinus's, than in the Biblical theology of a dynamic God passionately involved in history."[113]

Along similar lines, many contend that strict simplicity raises difficulties for divine omniscience—particularly relative to how to account for God's timeless and simple knowledge of a temporal, changing, and complex world. Rogers responds, in defense, that "both God and the solution to this problem are simple. God knows all He knows in a single act. Aquinas systematizes this view nicely when he explains that God knows all things in knowing Himself, because in knowing Himself He knows the myriad ways in which He could be imitated."[114] The adequacy of this response, however, hinges (in part) upon the previously discussed debate over whether timeless omniscience is sufficient. In this regard, Mullins claims, "One cannot have divine simplicity without timelessness and immutability."[115] If so, to be consistent, those who reject divine timelessness and strict immutability will also have to reject divine simplicity, at least of the strict kind.

Beyond these objections, Mullins argues that strict simplicity is incompatible with divine freedom and amounts to a modal collapse such that *everything is necessary*.[116] Further, Mullins avers, such a view would "make God's essential nature dependent on creation," undermining aseity.[117] Dolezal, while advocating strict simplicity, takes this objection seriously and responds that he does not have an adequate explanation as to *how* strict simplicity can be compatible with divine freedom but believes the two should

---

[111] Mullins, "Simply Impossible," 201.
[112] Mullins, "Simply Impossible," 200 (emphasis original).
[113] Alan Padgett, *God, Eternity, and the Nature of Time* (Eugene, OR: Wipf & Stock, 2000), 134. For his part, Mullins agrees that "divine simplicity is derived from Greek philosophy." Mullins, "Simply Impossible," 190. However, he notes "one should not reject divine simplicity on this ground alone" since that would be to "commit the genetic fallacy." Mullins, "Simply Impossible," 191.
[114] Rogers, *Perfect Being Theology*, 30.
[115] Mullins, "Simply Impossible," 181.
[116] Mullins, "Simply Impossible," 196.
[117] Mullins, "Simply Impossible," 196.

be held together.[118] McCall adds that Mullins's objection "is a very serious objection, and it deserves serious consideration."[119] Indeed, McCall notes, this and other "criticisms deserve serious and sustained engagement."[120]

Finally, the most relevant objection for our purposes in this chapter is the claim that divine simplicity is incompatible with the doctrine of the Trinity.[121] Specifically, if God is absolutely simple, how can one account for the claim that God is three distinct persons? In this regard, the doctrine of divine simplicity was used against the Trinity doctrine by Eunomius in the fourth century and many believe it played a significant role in many Christological controversies in the patristic age and beyond. Today, McCall notes, "Many theologians take it to be obvious that the doctrine of divine simplicity is not consistent with the doctrine of the Trinity."[122] For example, Richard Plantinga, Thomas Thompson, and Matthew Lundberg maintain that "the affirmation of divine simplicity has been the biggest reason why the Trinity has been presented as an impenetrable mystery of faith" and is why many "tend to have a unipersonal view of God—typically associated with the Father."[123] On their view, divine simplicity has "no real biblical basis and has in fact worked to defeat the resources of a full-fledged trinitarianism."[124]

Conversely, McCall notes that in the "Christian tradition," which held simplicity and the Trinity together over the centuries, divine simplicity is employed many times "as support for the doctrine of the Trinity."[125] While McCall himself does not reject divine simplicity, he does fear that *strict* simplicity "truly may be inconsistent with trinitarian theology. If there are no distinctions within God, then the divine persons cannot be distinct. But if the divine persons cannot be distinct, then we do not have any doctrine of the Trinity."[126]

---

[118]See Dolezal, *God without Parts*, 210–12. Specifically, Dolezal states, "Though we discover strong reasons for confessing both simplicity and freedom in God, we cannot form an isomorphically adequate notion of *how* this is the case." Dolezal, *God without Parts*, 210 (emphasis original).

[119]McCall, "Trinity Doctrine, Plain and Simple," 59.

[120]McCall, "Trinity Doctrine, Plain and Simple," 53–54.

[121]Mullins argues it seems to be incompatible with an adequate conception of the incarnation. See Mullins, "Simply Impossible," 200–201.

[122]McCall, "Trinity Doctrine, Plain and Simple," 42.

[123]Richard J. Plantinga, Thomas R. Thompson, and Matthew D. Lundberg, *An Introduction to Christian Theology* (Cambridge: Cambridge University Press, 2010), 104.

[124]Plantinga, Thompson, and Lundberg, *An Introduction to Christian Theology*, 104.

[125]McCall, "Trinity Doctrine, Plain and Simple," 43.

[126]McCall, "Trinity Doctrine, Plain and Simple," 57.

In this regard, Dolezal recognizes that "it is a challenge to understand how there can be a real identity between the essence, which is one, and the divine persons, which are three. *Prima facie* it seems to contravene the law of identity."[127] To avoid contradiction, Dolezal appeals to the analogical nature of language. McCall, however, thinks that this move does not suffice to avoid the problem for strict simplicity.[128] Yet, McCall believes, "there are at least two versions of the doctrine [of divine simplicity] that are consistent with the doctrine of the Trinity" and which may elude some or all of the other criticisms. These he calls formal and generic simplicity.[129] Both agree with strict simplicity that "there is no composition whereby God is made up of parts of pieces that are ontologically prior to or more basic than God," while differing from strict simplicity in other respects.[130]

Formal simplicity

Rather than claiming there are no genuine distinctions in God at all, formal simplicity maintains that there are no distinctions within God except formal distinctions, which are neither real distinctions (in the technical sense) nor merely conceptual distinctions.[131] As Mullins puts it, "two things are formally distinct" if "there is some extramental feature in reality that makes them distinct, yet they are coextensive and inseparable."[132] In contrast to a real distinction, McCall explains, "a formal distinction is not a distinction between different things of the same essence or different things of different essences, nor is it a distinction between separable parts of the same thing."[133] In contrast to a conceptual distinction, on the other hand, a formal distinction "isn't something invented by us for our convenience or ease of reference."[134] As such, "two entities are formally distinct if the distinction is genuine (that is, it is within the thing itself and not merely rational or mental) but not between two different essences or between separable parts

---

[127] James E. Dolezal, "Trinity, Simplicity and the Status of God's Personal Relations," IJST 16/1 (2014): 88.
[128] McCall, "Trinity Doctrine, Plain and Simple," 58.
[129] McCall, "Trinity Doctrine, Plain and Simple," 44.
[130] McCall, "Trinity Doctrine, Plain and Simple," 55.
[131] This and the following sections rely heavily on McCall's clear and concise definitions and explanations in McCall, "Trinity Doctrine, Plain and Simple."
[132] Mullins, "Simply Impossible," 184.
[133] McCall, "Trinity Doctrine, Plain and Simple," 52.
[134] McCall, "Trinity Doctrine, Plain and Simple," 52.

or pieces of the same thing."[135] A formal distinction, then, requires that two aspects of something are "really identical" and "really inseparable" yet "genuinely distinct on account of distinctions found in themselves."[136]

John Duns Scotus advocated this view, maintaining (in McCall's words) that "the divine attributes are formally distinct from one another" and "formally distinct from the divine essence" and "the divine persons are formally—though not 'absolutely'—distinct from the divine essence."[137] For Scotus, "the divine persons are 'fully real, subsistent entities' who are, in the words of Richard Cross, 'necessarily interdependent.'"[138] This view of divine simplicity avoids modalism by maintaining that the three Trinitarian persons "are genuinely distinct" while avoiding polytheism by maintaining the persons are "really—even logically—inseparable."[139] McCall concludes that formal simplicity "offers an account of irreducible distinction-within-inseparability" that "supports the doctrine" of the Trinity.[140]

Generic simplicity

Generic simplicity maintains that there are genuine distinctions within God such that God has more than one property. Yet, "the divine attributes are mutually and necessarily coextensive" such that "whatever is properly predicated of the divine nature is a sort of unbreakable package."[141] That is, "all essential divine attributes are mutually entailing and coextensive."[142] There are, then, "distinct properties within the divine essence" but these are "not, strictly speaking, parts of God" because they are inseparable.[143]

According to McCall, Gregory of Nyssa advocated this view, which "draws an important distinction between the divine nature (which is simple) and the divine persons who subsist in that nature."[144] Gregory of Nyssa writes, "Things that are identical on the score of being [οὐσίας] will not all

---

[135]McCall, "Trinity Doctrine, Plain and Simple," 52.
[136]McCall, "Trinity Doctrine, Plain and Simple," 52.
[137]McCall, "Trinity Doctrine, Plain and Simple," 52.
[138]McCall, "Trinity Doctrine, Plain and Simple," 52–53. McCall is quoting the last part from Richard Cross, *Duns Scotus on God* (Aldershot: Ashgate, 2005), 154–55.
[139]McCall, "Trinity Doctrine, Plain and Simple," 53.
[140]McCall, "Trinity Doctrine, Plain and Simple," 56–57.
[141]McCall, "Trinity Doctrine, Plain and Simple," 50.
[142]McCall, "Trinity Doctrine, Plain and Simple," 55.
[143]McCall, "Trinity Doctrine, Plain and Simple," 50.
[144]McCall, "Trinity Doctrine, Plain and Simple," 47.

agree equally in definition on the score of personality [ὑποστάσεων]."[145] As such, Gregory affirms the doctrine of divine simplicity "but he denies that it erases all distinctions. The genuine *personal* distinctions are not distinctions of *nature*."[146] McCall concludes that generic simplicity also appears to be "consistent with the doctrine of the Trinity," but some might view it as merely "an account of divine unity rather than simplicity (preferring to reserve the label 'simplicity' for more robust versions)."[147]

Maintaining divine simplicity?

While some disagree regarding which version of divine simplicity is best, many classical theists maintain that God must be simple because, as Rogers puts it, a "perfect being must be unlimited, but to be composite or complex is to be limited."[148] The classical worry is, "if God can be thought to have any sort of parts at all then He can be thought to be corruptible," he can be taken apart "at least *in intellectu*" and is dependent on such "parts" in a way that compromises divine aseity.[149] Dolezal claims, in this respect: "Anything composed of act and potency must be caused to exist by an agent extrinsic to it and must also be liable to change, improvement, dissolution, or annihilation."[150] Edward Feser even claims, "To deny that there is anything simple or noncomposite would entail atheism, because it implicitly denies that there really is anything having the ultimacy definitive of God."[151] David Bentley Hart agrees, saying, "It seems obvious to me that a denial of divine simplicity is tantamount to atheism" and "all the dominant intellectual traditions of the major theistic faiths are more or less unanimous" in affirming "the simplicity of God."[152]

Conversely, many philosophers and theologians maintain that divine simplicity need not be affirmed but only a robust account of divine unity is needed, perhaps akin to what McCall calls generic simplicity. As Plantinga,

---

[145]Gregory of Nyssa, *Against Eunomius*, I. 19, PG 45: 320B; *NPNF2* 5: 56, quoted in McCall, "Trinity Doctrine, Plain and Simple," 47.

[146]McCall, "Trinity Doctrine, Plain and Simple," 47 (emphasis original).

[147]McCall, "Trinity Doctrine, Plain and Simple," 55–56.

[148]Rogers, *Perfect Being Theology*, 25.

[149]Rogers, *Perfect Being Theology*, 25. Cf. Anselm, *Proslogion* 18.

[150]Dolezal, *God without Parts*, 41.

[151]Feser, *Five Proofs of the Existence of God* (San Francisco, CA: Ignatius, 2017), 190.

[152]David Bentley Hart, *The Experience of God: Being, Consciousness, Bliss* (New Haven, CT: Yale University Press, 2013), 127.

Thompson, and Lundberg put it, "the Bible certainly does speak of the oneness or unity of God," but "its content is not the metaphysical simplicity of Greek theism."[153] Moreland and Craig add: "Divine simplicity is a doctrine inspired by the neo-Platonic vision of the ultimate metaphysical reality as the absolute One."[154] They see the claim that God is "an undifferentiated unity, that there is no complexity in his nature or being" as "a radical doctrine that enjoys no biblical support and even is at odds with the biblical conception of God in various ways."[155] Thus, they maintain, "we have no good reason to adopt and many reasons to reject a full blown [or strict] doctrine of divine simplicity."[156] Yet, they think a "modified doctrine of divine simplicity might be useful" with respect to maintaining that "God is not composed of mind and body" but is "pure mind. As such, God is remarkably simple in that such an immaterial substance is not composed of pieces, or separable parts in the way that a material object is."[157]

Further, John Cooper contends that the "strong version [of divine simplicity] is not required by classical theism. Its source is Neoplatonism, where the One is beyond all differentiation and distinction."[158] In Cooper's view, strict simplicity "implicitly denies any genuine distinctions among the persons of the Trinity, the divine attributes, God's essence and existence, and God's nature and freedom. It therefore contradicts much that Christian theology affirms."[159] Cooper affirms, instead, a moderate doctrine of divine simplicity, maintaining that since "God is not created or dependent on anything outside himself, he is not composed of principles, properties, or constituents more basic than himself. Thus he is ontologically (not logically) simple." This "rules out composition but not complexity in God—genuine distinctions among the persons of the Trinity, God's attributes, his essence and existence, and his nature and freedom."[160]

For many advocates of strict classical theism, however, strict simplicity is the most fundamental perfection of God, which entails and is entailed by other perfections of strict classical theism. For instance, Dolezal ties strict simplicity to divine aseity and timelessness, arguing that if God had

---

[153] Plantinga, Thompson, and Lundberg, *An Introduction to Christian Theology*, 104.

[154] Moreland and Craig, *Philosophical Foundations*, 524.

[155] Moreland and Craig, *Philosophical Foundations*, 524.

[156] Moreland and Craig, *Philosophical Foundations*, 525.

[157] Moreland and Craig, *Philosophical Foundations*, 525–26.

[158] John W. Cooper, *Panentheism: The Other God of the Philosophers* (Grand Rapids, MI: Baker Academic, 2006), 326.

[159] Cooper, *Panentheism*, 326.

[160] Cooper, *Panentheism*, 327.

"parts" then God would somehow depend on those parts—undermining strict aseity.[161] Further, some argue, if God were temporal, God would have temporal parts.[162] However, opponents of strict simplicity note that one need not affirm the strict kind of aseity at work here. Further, Mullins argues that the view God has temporal parts assumes a theory called perdurantism (worm theory), wherein temporal things have temporal parts, but advocates of divine temporality tend to affirm the alternate theory of endurantism, which maintains that the whole of any temporal object is present at each moment of time, such that "there simply is no such thing as temporal parts."[163]

Apart from this, both opponents and advocates see strict simplicity as fundamental to strict classical theism. For example, Nash explains:

> If a being is simple, then it has no parts. If a being has no parts, then it cannot change (since there is nothing for it to lose or gain). If a thing cannot change (is immutable), then it must be pure actuality in the sense that it cannot possess any potentiality. 'Before' and 'after' would be inapplicable to such a being, a point which entails that any simple being must also be timeless. It would appear that the Thomistic concept of God cannot do without the property of simplicity.[164]

For his part, Nash thinks Christian theists need not be beholden to the Thomistic concept of God and thus concludes that the doctrine of divine simplicity "can be safely eliminated from the cluster of divine attributes."[165] Further, Plantinga, Thompson, and Lundberg maintain, "if the traditional notion of divine simplicity can be trumped by a more biblical notion of divine oneness or unity, then the way is open for also rethinking" immutability and timeless eternity, which "depend on simplicity as their linchpin."[166]

Conclusion

This chapter has discussed the coherence of the basic Trinity doctrine, the patristic conception of the Trinity, and some contemporary issues among

---

[161] Dolezal, *God without Parts*, xvii.
[162] Cf. Williams, "Classical Theism," 96.
[163] R.T. Mullins, *End of the Timeless God* (New York: Oxford University Press, 2016), 27.
[164] Ronald Nash, *The Concept of God: An Exploration of Contemporary Difficulties with the Attributes of God* (Grand Rapids, MI: Zondervan, 1983), 22.
[165] Nash, *Concept of God*, 114.
[166] Plantinga, Thompson, and Lundberg, *An Introduction to Christian Theology*, 104.

Trinitarians, followed by a survey of some relevant biblical data regarding the basic Trinity doctrine. The chapter concluded with a brief overview of the contemporary debate over divine simplicity. We now turn to some concluding reflections on the doctrine of God.

Study questions

1. How might you respond to someone who claims the Trinity doctrine is inconsistent? How would you respond to questions like How can God be one and three? Is it possible to hold a consistent doctrine of the Trinity that avoids tritheism, modalism, and subordinationism? Why does the Trinity doctrine matter?
2. How do you think one should decide between various Trinitarian views relative to the persons of the Trinity, eternal relations of origin, and functional subordination? What role does the data from Scripture play in the way you think of these issues? What do you make of differing interpretations of the Christian tradition relative to these issues? What are some of the implications for Christian theism regarding how these questions are answered?
3. What are some of the strengths of each view regarding these disputed issues? What are some weaknesses of each view? Can you think of any further difficulties with any of the views discussed in this chapter? Can you think of any further advantages of views discussed in this chapter?
4. Do you think the doctrine of divine simplicity is consistent with the Trinity doctrine? How is your answer to this question affected by which conception of divine simplicity is in mind and which view of the Trinitarian persons is held? Is it important that a Christian theist affirm divine simplicity? Why or why not?
5. What is the relationship between the way one approaches the differing perspectives on divine attributes in previous chapters and how one conceives of the Trinity? What are the implications relative to divine simplicity?

Suggestions for further reading

Selected premodern sources

Augustine, *The Trinity*.
Gregory of Nyssa, *On Not Three Gods*.
Gregory Nazianzen, *Orations* 27–33.
Anselm, *Monologion* 17; 42–62.
Thomas Aquinas, *Summa Theologiae* I.3; I.27–43.
John Calvin, *Institutes of the Christian Religion* 1.13.

Selected modern/contemporary sources

Anatolios, Khaled. *Retrieving Nicea: The Development and Meaning of Trinitarian Doctrine* (Grand Rapids, MI: Baker Academic, 2011).

Crisp, Oliver and Fred Sanders, eds. *Advancing Trinitarian Theology: Explorations in Constructive Dogmatics* (Grand Rapids, MI: Zondervan, 2014).

Dolezal, James. *God without Parts: Divine Simplicity and the Metaphysics of God's Absoluteness* (Eugene, OR: Pickwick, 2011).

Erickson, Millard. *Who's Tampering with the Trinity* (Grand Rapids, MI: Kregel, 2009).

Feenstra, Ronald J. and Cornelius Plantinga, Jr., eds. *Trinity, Incarnation, and Atonement: Philosophical and Theological Essays* (Notre Dame, IN: University of Notre Dame Press, 1989).

Giles, Kevin. *The Eternal Generation of the Son* (Downers Grove, IL: IVP Academic, 2012).

Hasker, William. *Metaphysics and the Tri-Personal God* (New York: Oxford University Press, 2013).

Holmes, Stephen. *The Quest for the Trinity: The Doctrine of God in Scripture, History and Modernity* (Downers Grove, IL: IVP Academic, 2012).

Jowers, Dennis W. and H. Wayne House, eds. *The New Evangelical Subordinationism? Perspectives on the Equality of God the Father and God the Son* (Eugene, OR: Pickwick, 2012).

LaCugna, Catherine Mowry. *God for Us: The Trinity and Christian Life* (New York: HarperCollins, 1991).

McCall, Thomas H. *Which Trinity? Whose Monotheism?* (Grand Rapids, MI: Eerdmans, 2010).

McCall, Thomas H. and Michael C. Rea, eds. *Philosophical and Theological Essays on the Trinity* (New York: Oxford University Press, 2009).

Mullins, R.T. "Simply Impossible: A Case against Divine Simplicity." *Journal of Reformed Theology* 7 (2013): 181–203.

Plantinga, Alvin. *Does God Have a Nature?* (Marquette, WI: Marquette University Press, 1980).

Sanders, Fred. *The Triune God* (Grand Rapids, MI: Zondervan, 2016).

Tanner, Kathryn. *Jesus, Humanity, and the Trinity* (Edinburgh: T&T Clark, 2001).

Torrance, Thomas F. *The Christian Doctrine of God: One Being Three Persons* (New York: T&T Clark, 2001).

Zizioulas, John D. *Being as Communion: Studies in Personhood and the Church* (Crestwood, NY: St. Vladimir's Seminary Press, 1985).

Epilogue: Concluding Reflections

This book has introduced and surveyed some prominent contemporary Christian perspectives regarding who God is and what God is like. We are now in a position to briefly engage two related questions: (1) What are we to make of the doctrine of God in light of this survey of various ways of answering these questions? (2) Where do we go from here?

Regarding the first question, we can see from the material in the previous chapters that how one answers any of the big questions regarding the doctrine of God holds significant implications for how the other big questions might be answered. On the one hand, many advocates of strict classical theism maintain that strict conceptions of aseity, simplicity, timeless eternity, immutability, and impassibility are mutually entailing. That is, a proper understanding of, say, strict simplicity or strict timelessness or strict impassibility entails a strict understanding of the other divine attributes—and some maintain that this package either entails or strongly lends itself to determinism. Conversely, if strict impassibility is mutually entailing relative to strict immutability, timeless eternity, strict simplicity, and pure aseity, then if God is passible—even in a qualified sense—God cannot be *strictly* immutable, timeless, simple (in the strict sense), or pure actuality. As such, one who rejects strict impassibility or strict timelessness or strict simplicity will thereby depart from strict classical theism, with significant implications regarding how to conceive of the God–world relationship.

In this respect, we've seen that some critics of classical theism—particularly of the strict variety—depart from the strict classical theist package of attributes in all or nearly all respects. However, the doctrine of God need not be approached as if it requires a binary decision between strict classical theism and its opposite. Christian theists offer various robust accounts of the doctrine of God, many of which may broadly be characterized as forms of moderate classical theism. Just what approach to the doctrine of God one favors is closely connected to how one navigates the interrelationship of philosophy, theology, and biblical studies. As noted in Chapter 1, one's metaphysical framework (macro-level) is closely related to one's doctrinal system (meso-level) and understanding of Scripture (micro-level). How to decide what approach to the doctrine of God to adopt depends on the way one understands and employs Scripture, tradition, philosophy, and experience.

This brings us to the question of where we go from here. There are, of course, many differing perspectives regarding the way forward. Just as I have not attempted to adjudicate between the positions surveyed within this book, I will not attempt to adjudicate here between differing views about just how the doctrine of God should be approached and conceptualized. However, there is broad agreement among many Christian theists that, whatever else we might say, our theological judgments should meet the standard of biblical warrant. As Alan Padgett puts it, "Theology will *always* take its sources in special revelation and the Word more seriously than even the best developed theories based upon them. All such models will have to be taken as provisional and partial."[1] In this and other respects, we should remember that God is always greater than we can fully grasp and the doctrine of God should be approached with the humility appropriate to the recognition that we are mere creatures attempting to understand what we can about the Creator of all.

With regard to the issues and questions surveyed in this book, much hinges on how one approaches theological method—particularly relative to the theological interpretation of Scripture. In this regard, some advocate that Scripture must be read through the lens of a (strict) classical metaphysical framework. Others think doing so would be a mistake—methodologically and otherwise. Still others prefer a critical appropriation of classical metaphysics, with differing opinions regarding just what to depart from and what to retrieve. Here, as noted in Chapter 1, many continue to perceive "a pervasive tension in Christian thought between 'the God of the philosophers and the God of the Bible', between God as 'wholly other' and God as a partner

---

[1] Alan Padgett, "The Trinity in Theology and Philosophy: Why Jerusalem Should Work with Athens," in *Philosophical and Theological Essays on the Trinity*, ed. Thomas McCall and Michael C. Rea (New York: Oxford University Press, 2009), 334.

in interpersonal relationships, between God as the absolute, ultimate source of all being and God as the dominant actor on the stage of history"—with many conceptions of God attempting to locate themselves somewhere along the spectrum of views in this regard.[2] In my view, the commitment to the standard of biblical warrant that most Christians share requires that even one's metaphysical framework should be normed and intentionally subjected to correction by Scripture. Here, it seems to me, theologians should continue to pay more and more attention to the richness of the biblical data, especially the overarching narrative of Scripture regarding the God–world relationship and the history of redemption.

While Christian theologians who do so may nevertheless disagree over just how to answer the big questions about the doctrine of God, I am confident that intentional, close attention to Scripture—interpreted theologically in a methodologically rigorous way—is always valuable for the task of theology. Perhaps other areas and topics of theology proper warrant more attention than they have traditionally received in systematic treatments of the divine nature and attributes. For example, Scripture portrays God as a covenantal God, a concept that I believe holds significant implications for every aspect of the doctrine of God and which may require more attention to divine attributes featured prominently in the Bible such as divine love, goodness, holiness, faithfulness, truthfulness, justice, righteousness, grace, mercy, compassion, jealousy/passion, and many others. This, however, is a topic for further study of a more constructive nature.[3]

For now, my hope is that the survey of some prominent positions in this book might serve readers well as an orientation to the main contours of the contemporary debates among Christian theists over the doctrine of God, providing an introduction and background for deeper study of these and other questions; a starting point from which one may enter and engage in the ongoing quest to better understand the God who is beyond *comprehensive* understanding; the God of Christian faith who is who he is irrespective of our opinions, "who is and who was and who is to come, the Almighty" (Rev 1:8).

---

[2]William Alston, *Divine Nature and Human Language* (Ithaca, NY: Cornell University Press, 1989), 147.
[3]The exploration of a view I call covenantal theism is the topic of another book, tentatively titled *The God of Love: A Canonical Theology of Divine Attributes* (Baker Academic, forthcoming).

Glossary

Definitions are tricky things. Words mean what they are used to mean and, particularly in theology, words have a variety of meanings. This glossary attempts to offer some basic definitions of some technical terminology used in this book but the reader should understand that philosophers and theologians use these terms in various nuanced ways.

Accidental properties accidental (or contingent) properties are properties that something might possess or might not possess or might possess at one time and not possess at another

Accommodative language language that accommodates the limits and understanding of the intended audience

Actualizable worlds (aka feasible worlds) those possible worlds (referring to the entire history of any logically possible world) that God can bring about without contravening the free decisions of creatures

Adoptionism (aka dynamic monarchianism) the view that Jesus was a mere human who was adopted as God's son

Analogical language (of God) language relative to God that holds some similarity to how God actually is but is also quite dissimilar to how God is in himself

Anthropomorphic language describing God in human form or as having human characteristics that God does not have

Anthropopathic language describing God as having human passions or emotions (*pathos*)

Anti-theodicy an approach to the problem of evil that claims that attempts at theodicy amount to justifications of evil

Apophatic theology (aka negative theology) a way of approaching theology that speaks of God in terms of what should not be said about God; operates via the way of negation

Arianism the view that the Son was created by the Father at some time in the past. Not to be confused with semi-Arianism, which is the view that the Son was begotten by the Father at some time in the past

Aseity self-existent, existing of oneself (*a se*); existence is not derived from or dependent on anything else; sometimes taken in a strong sense to mean that God is not dependent on anything in any way whatsoever

Atemporality (aka timelessness) of God variously understood but often meaning that God's being is incompatible with time (where time is conceived as the succession of moments or events); utterly outside time; there is no temporal before or after from God's perspective

Attributes, Communicable attributes that humans can possess in some lesser way than God

Attributes, Incommunicable attributes that only God can possess, which cannot be extended to humans

Beneficence the doing of good

Biblical warrant a standard requiring that one's claims are adequately grounded in Scripture

Boethian solution (relative to foreknowledge) claims that the problem of divine foreknowledge and human freedom can be resolved by maintaining eternalism such that divine knowledge is not actually prior to the events God eternally knows; also known as the atemporalist solution

Canonical related to viewing Scripture as a unified, divinely commissioned, corpus that is to function as the supreme norm or rule of faith and practice

Causal determinism the view that all events are determined to occur just as they do by prior causes

Christian theism belief in the one, triune God who is the creator of everything other than himself and the sustainer of the world

Classical theism the classical conception of God, traditionally holding that God, as the perfect being, is necessary, self-sufficient, simple, eternal, immutable, impassible, omnipotent, omniscient, and omnibenevolent

Communicable attributes attributes that humans can possess in some lesser way than God

Compatibilism the view that determinism is compatible with free will and/or moral responsibility

Compatibilist free will the view that humans possess a kind of free will and/or moral responsibility that is compatible with causal determinism; regarding free will, compatibilists claim that humans are free to do what they want but what humans want to do is causally determined by some external factor or factors

Contingent properties contingent (or accidental) properties are properties that something might possess or might not possess or might possess at one time and not possess at another

Cosmic conflict the view that maintains there is a supernatural conflict between God's kingdom and the demonic realm

Cosmic conflict approaches (to the problem of evil) approaches to the problem of evil that posit that evils in this world are partially due to a supernatural conflict between God's kingdom and the demonic realm

Cosmic dualism the view that good and evil are eternal principles in perpetual conflict, not to be confused with cosmic conflict approaches, which reject such dualism

Counterfactual a conditional that is contrary to fact, typically used of a conditional statement where the condition is false, such as if Gandalf had possessed the ring, he would have been corrupted by it

Counterfactuals of creaturely freedom (CCF) counterfactuals about decisions that creatures would make given different states of affairs; usually used in reference to what any given free agent would choose to do in a given situation

Defense (relative to the problem of evil) a response to the problem of evil that offers some possible way in which evil in the world is compatible with God being omnipotent and omnibenevolent

de Régnon theory the theory that the western patristic view of the Trinity focused on God's oneness and the eastern patristic view of the Trinity focused on God's threeness

Determinism the view that every event is caused by prior factors such that it must occur just as it does

Determinism, Theistic the view that God causally determines everything that occurs, whether directly or indirectly (excludes libertarian free will of creatures)

Disquotation principle (relative to theories of truth) the principle that T is true is equivalent (or at least functionally equivalent) to the state of affairs T; that is, the statement "T is true" amounts to T such that what makes it true that snow is white is the fact that snow is white

Divine glory defense a defense relative to the problem of evil that maintains that God determines evil because it is necessary for the greater good of God's glory

Doctrine of God (aka theology proper) the study of God's nature, attributes, and relation to the world

Economic Trinity refers to the Trinity as the Trinity appears in relation to the world (i.e., in the economy)

Efficacious grace grace that is sufficient and effective to accomplish God's goal, typically used relative to human salvation

Endurantism the view that maintains that the whole of any temporal object is present at each moment of time

Epistemic distance refers to conceptual space between God and humans such that humans can form their own beliefs relative to God and the things of God

Epistemology refers to the study of knowledge; the branch of philosophy that investigates the origin, nature, methods, and limits of human knowledge (from Greek: *episteme*, meaning knowledge)

Equivocal language (of God) refers to language that means something totally different about God than what it means in reference to creatures

Essential properties those properties that something must possess, without which that thing would not exist or be the kind of being that it is

Eternal having no beginning or end; sometimes used as equivalent to timeless or atemporal but not necessarily so

Eternal generation the view that the Son is eternally generated or begotten by the Father; often understood to mean that the Father timelessly begets the person of the Son

Eternalism a view of the nature of time that holds that the past, present, and future all exist and there is no privileged time that is objectively "now," in contrast to presentism; sometimes also known as the block theory of time wherein the universe is thought to be a four-dimensional space–time manifold

Eternal procession (of the Spirit) the view that the Spirit eternally proceeds or is eternally "spirated" by the Father or by the Father and the Son

Euthyphro dilemma the dilemma of whether God (or the gods) loves or wills something because it is good or whether it is good because God (or the gods) loves or wills it. If the former, there appears to be a standard of goodness external to God and if the latter, it appears as if goodness might be arbitrarily decided by God. Named after a dialogue partner of Socrates in Plato's *Euthyphro*

Everlasting without beginning or end, typically conveying temporality without beginning or end

Evidential problem of evil the problem of evil framed as a problem of probability or plausibility given the kind and amount of evil in the world; that is, it is claimed that the kind and amount of evil in the world renders it unlikely that an all-powerful (omnipotent) and entirely good (omnibenevolent) God exists

Exhaustive definite foreknowledge (EDF) refers to the concept that God knows the entirety of the future (exhaustive, from the end to the beginning) and in precise detail (definite)

Existential problem of evil the problem of evil relative to how people might be affected by and cope with their experiences of suffering and evil

ex nihilo out of nothing, typically used in reference to the traditional Christian belief that God created the universe out of nothing, that is, without being dependent on any preexisting material

Fallacy of necessity the fallacy of confusing necessity of consequence with necessity of the thing consequent. For example, confusing the claim "*Necessarily*, if Henry is a bachelor, Henry is unmarried" (necessity of consequence) with the claim "Henry is *necessarily* unmarried" (necessity of the thing consequent)

Feasible worlds (aka actualizable worlds) those possible worlds (referring to the entire history of any logically possible world) that God can bring about without contravening the free decisions of creatures

felix culpa a Latin phrase appearing in the Christian tradition that can be translated "happy fault," often used in reference to the claim that evil is *necessary* for some greater good or goods and thus it is good that evils occur

Finitism the view that God does not possess the power to prevent evil (and thus could not be culpable for failing to do so)

Foreknowledge knowledge of the future beforehand

Foreknowledge, Simple the view that God directly knows the future without the combination of any parts of knowledge (i.e., "simple" rather than "complex" foreknowledge)

Free will defense a defense against the logical problem of evil, which claims that insofar as God grants creatures free will of a kind that is incompatible with determinism, God cannot determine that those creatures freely never do evil. Accordingly, if God has a morally sufficient reason for granting creatures such free will, God could be omnipotent and omnibenevolent and evil could yet occur because of the free decisions of creatures

Functional subordination the view that the Son and/or Spirit voluntarily submitted to the Father relative to a role in the plan of salvation

God–world relationship the relationship between God and everything else (the world).

Greater good defense a defense relative to the problem of evil that maintains that God permits or determines evil because it is necessary for some outweighing (greater) good or goods

Growing block theory of time a view of the nature of time that holds that the present *and* past exist, but the future does not yet exist. This holds a view of reality as a space–time block that is growing as time progresses

Hellenization thesis the theory that the Christian tradition was corrupted by a Hellenized (Greek) conception of God.

Hypothetical knowledge (of future free decisions) knowledge of what a creature would freely do in a given circumstance

Immanence (of God) refers to God being in close proximity to humans; God being "with us"

Immanent Trinity refers to the Trinity as the Trinity is apart from the world (God in Godself (*in se*); the intra-Trinitarian relationship)

Immutable changeless, unchanging, or incapable of change (in some respect); the strong view of utter immutability maintains that God does not change *at all*

Impassible without passions (in some or all respects); taken in an unqualified sense it means cannot be affected by anything outside oneself; sometimes meant in a qualified sense where God has emotions but those emotions are self-determined or simply that God cannot be overwhelmed by suffering

Incommunicable attributes attributes that only God can possess, which cannot be extended to humans

Incompatibilist freedom free will that is not causally determined by external factors (aka libertarian free will)

Incorporeal bodiless, having no body (*corpus*); sometimes used to convey the idea that God cannot occupy space

Indeterminism the contrary of determinism; the view that history is not entirely causally determined to occur just as it does

Latin theories of the Trinity (aka singularity theories) approaches to the Trinity that emphasize the unity of the divine nature, claiming there is only one center of consciousness in the Trinity, without falling into modalism

Libertarian free will free will that is not entirely causally determined by external factors. That is, free will of the kind that is incompatible with determinism (aka incompatibilist freedom)

Logical problem of evil the claim that the premises (1) God is omnipotent, (2) God is omnibenevolent, and (3) evil exists are not logically compatible

Macro-level of theological conceptualization consists of the overarching philosophical presuppositions relative to the nature of reality (ontology), knowledge (epistemology), God, and the world, which impinge upon how one views and interprets everything else (aka macro-hermeneutical principles)

Merism a reference to something by its two poles such as saying "heaven and earth" to convey "the universe" or "high and low" to convey "everywhere" or "the end from the beginning" to convey "all" of something

Meso-level of theological conceptualization consists of one's doctrinal commitments and how they interrelate to the macro- and micro-levels (aka meso-hermeheutical principles)

Metaphysical framework one's overarching views regarding the nature of ultimate reality, particularly relative to questions concerning existence, the nature of being, the nature and properties of beings, space and time, causality, and others; or, the way one views reality and the relationship between realities

Metaphysics the branch of philosophy that addresses first principles, largely focused on ontology (the study of being) and holding massive implications for epistemology; sometimes refers to that which is beyond the physical realm

Micro-level of theological conceptualization the level of interpretation of individual texts and passages of Scripture (aka micro-hermeneutical principles)

Middle knowledge knowledge of what anyone would freely do in any given circumstances; knowledge of "would" counterfactuals

Modalism the view that there exists only one person who is God, manifesting himself in three different modes in history; Father, Son, and Spirit are not three persons but merely three modes of the singular divine person

Molinism a theological system wherein God knows the future by way of middle knowledge coupled with God's natural and free knowledge; named after Luis de Molina

Monotheism the belief that there is one and only one God

Monotheism-securing relation a phrase referring to some kind of relation between the three divine persons of the Trinity such that there is one and only one God

Moral evil evil that results from the free actions of non-divine persons

Natural evil evil that is not the result of the free actions of non-divine persons

Necessary being a being whose existence is necessary (e.g., God is a necessary being; it is necessary that God exist; it is impossible that God not exist or God exists in every possible world)

Necessity of consequence refers to the necessity of the relationship of two things that must go together. Regarding foreknowledge, it corresponds to the conclusion that, since God's knowledge is infallible, it is necessarily true that whatever God believes about the future will come to pass

Necessity of the thing consequent refers to the necessity of some specific thing or event that is the consequence of some other thing or event

Negative theology (aka apophatic theology) a way of approaching theology that speaks of God in terms of what should not be said about God; operates via the way of negation

Neoplatonism refers to a strand of Platonic philosophy originating in the Greco-Roman world in the third century (largely associated with Plotinus [c. 204–270] and those who followed his philosophical trajectory), which is typically believed to have significantly influenced Augustine and many other theologians in the patristic age and beyond

Noseeum arguments arguments labeled by philosophers that claim something like "if we cannot see God's reasons for something (usually relative to evil), then there must not be any such good reasons"

Numerical identity refers to the kind of identity wherein "if A and B are numerically identical, it follows that they are the same *in every respect*"

Ockhamism (relative to foreknowledge) an approach that maintains God's knowledge of the future free decisions of creatures does not render those decisions necessary or in any way less than genuinely free

Omnibenevolence (of God) God is entirely good and always wills only good

Omnicausality (of God) the view that God causes everything

Omnipotence all-powerful, typically defined as possessing the power to do anything that is logically possible (and compatible with God's other perfect attributes)

Omnipresence being present everywhere (in some sense)

Omniscience all-knowing, having knowledge of everything that it is possible for one to know; God knows everything there is to know (e.g., all facts, all true propositions, the knowledge content of all states of affairs)

Ontology the study of being (from Greek: *ontos*, meaning being); the branch of philosophy (metaphysics) that studies the nature of being

Open theism a concept of God that affirms many of the classical attributes of God but holds that the future is open to God and God does not exhaustively know the future

Panentheism literally "all in God;" the view that the world is part of God's being ("in God") but God is more than the world

Pantheism literally "all [is] God;" the view that God and the world are identical

Patristic tradition typically refers to the first few centuries of the Christian tradition after the first-generation apostles, often identified as roughly the first five to eight centuries after the Apostolic Age

Perdurantism (aka worm theory) the view that temporal things have temporal parts that "perdure" throughout time; that is, different parts of temporal things exist as spread over time somewhat analogous to the way a worm is spread out through dirt

Perfect being the being who is the greatest in any and every conceivable way

Perichoresis (relative to Trinity doctrine) the view that the persons of the Trinity interpenetrate one another and thus coinhere in one another

Possible world refers to the entire history or timeline of any logically possible universe; that is, a possible world is a comprehensive conception of the way *all* things might be, inclusive of the entire history of some logically possible universe

Potentiality (aka potency) the potential of a substance to change or become in some way; potency involves the capacity to change; it is a concept rooted in Aristotelian metaphysics

Predestination a term that is often taken to mean that God determines beforehand just what occurs and is thus often associated with determinism; it may also be used by indeterminists to refer to God's plan or purpose that takes into account things God foreknows but does not causally determine

Presentism a view of time that holds that only the present exists, the past has passed away, and the future is not yet; it is the intuitive view of many people, in contrast to eternalism and the growing block theory of time

Privatio boni the privation (or lack) of good

Problem of evil the problem of reconciling God's goodness and/or existence with evil. *See* Evidential problem of evil; Existential problem of evil; Logical problem of evil

Process theism (aka process theology) a conception of God as "in process" such that God is growing along with the world, which is part of God's being

Process theodicy the process theology approach to the problem of evil, which claims that God does not have the power to prevent evils and thus cannot be culpable for them

Protest theodicy an approach to the problem of evil that protests evil and may claim that God is not good because he ordains or permits evil and that any theodicy amounts to justifying evil

Providence God's sustenance and governance of the world, including action to bring about divine purpose(s) in the world, beginning with God's creation of the world

Pure act (*actus purus*) the view that God is pure act denies that God has any potentiality or passive potency; God's essence is his existence and God is pure Being; a concept based on Aristotelian metaphysics

Rahner's rule the saying that the economic Trinity is the immanent Trinity

Relational theories of the Trinity approaches to the Trinity that emphasize the three persons of the Trinity as each having a distinct center of consciousness; sometimes used to distinguish itself from the connotations of some social theories that seem to undermine the essential oneness/unity of the Trinity, emphasizing instead that there is only one divine substance

Relation of reason refers to the view that the universe is really related to God but God is not really related to the universe; the universe depends on God but God is completely independent from the universe such that God cannot be affected by it at all

Relative identity theory of the Trinity a theory of the Trinity wherein the persons of the Trinity are different, yet share one constitution such that the persons are distinct yet there is one individual substance that is not composed of parts

Religious problem of evil the problem of evil relative to how people might deal with their experiences of suffering and evil, particularly relative to their posture toward religion

Selective determinism the claim that God causally determines some things that he predicts will occur

Self-limitation (of God) God's promise to act in this or that way which morally restricts his future action

Self-sufficiency (of God) denotes that God does not need anything relative to his existence or essential nature

Semi-Arianism the view that the Son was begotten (generated) by the Father at some time in the past

Sempiternal eternal in a temporally everlasting way, rather than timeless

Settled character hypothesis the theory that God could infallibly predict what someone would do based only on his present exhaustive knowledge, which includes knowledge of that person's character

Simple foreknowledge the view that God directly knows the future (e.g., without the combination of kinds of knowledge; "simple" rather than "complex" foreknowledge)

Simplicity denotes that God is non-composite, not composed of parts; the strict version maintains there are no genuine distinctions in God and thus God does not (strictly speaking) possess properties in addition to, or genuinely distinct from, the divine essence

Singularity theories of the Trinity (aka Latin theories) approaches to the Trinity that emphasize the unity of the divine nature and claim there is only one center of consciousness in the Trinity, while denying modalism

Skeptical theism an approach to the problem of evil which maintains that humans should not expect to be in a position to know or understand God's reasons relative to the evil in this world

Social Trinity variously understood but typically used to describe approaches to the Trinity that emphasizes the three persons of the Trinity as each having a distinct center of consciousness

Soul-making theodicy an approach to the problem of evil which claims (in brief) that the evil in our world is necessary for the making of human souls that are capable of love

Sovereignty the view that God is the supreme ruler over everything

Sovereignty indeterminism the view that God is both omnipotent in the sense that he *could* determine everything and that God does not causally determine history but freely grants significant power and libertarian free will to creatures, within limits

Strict classical theism an understanding of classical theism that affirms the tenets of classical perfect being theology, taken in a strong or strict sense

Strong actualization refers to God causing something directly, apart from any contribution by the actions of others

Subordinationism the view that the Son and/or Spirit are subordinate (less than) by nature (ontologically) to the Father

Succession relative to time, succession refers to the movement from one moment to the next, the temporal succession of past, present, and future

Supererogatory actions good actions that go beyond any moral obligation, beyond the "call of duty"

Systematic theology the study and articulation of an orderly and coherent account of theistic beliefs

Temporality (divine) the view that God experiences succession of moments (i.e., succession of past, present, and future)

Theistic determinism the view that God causally determines everything that occurs, whether directly or indirectly (excludes libertarian free will of creatures)

Theodicy broadly defined as any Christian response to the problem of evil in defense of the goodness and righteousness of God and more narrowly defined as a Christian response to the problem of evil that attempts to provide God's actual reasons for permitting evil; from the Greek roots for God (*theos*) and righteousness (*dikē*)

Theology   the study of God in relation to everything else

Theology proper (aka doctrine of God)   the study of God's nature, attributes, and relation to the world

Timelessness (aka atemporality) of God   variously understood but often meaning that God's being is incompatible with time (where time is conceived as the succession of moments or events); utterly outside time; there is no temporal before or after from God's perspective

Transcendence (of God)   conveys that God is beyond creaturely experiences and greater than and beyond the creaturely plane of existence

Trinity   the view that there is one and only one God in three distinct, (fully) divine persons

Trinity, Economic   refers to the Trinity as the Trinity appears in relation to the world (i.e., in the economy)

Trinity, Immanent   Refers to the Trinity as the Trinity is apart from the world (God in Godself [*in se*]; the intra-Trinitarian relationship)

Tritheism   the view that there are three gods; a kind of polytheism

Truth-maker   philosophical terminology for something that makes a true statement true

Universalism   the view that all will be saved

Univocal language (of God)   conveys that a word is used to mean exactly the same thing when used of God and humans (literally, "one voice")

Volitional   having to do with willing or making a choice

Way of eminence (*via eminentiae*)   the way of doing theology by predicating every great-making property to God in a maximal way

Way of negation (via negativa)   the way of doing theology that negates that which is thought to be limiting or less than proper for a perfect being

Weak actualization   refers to God bringing about something in a way that depends upon the free actions of others (in contrast to strong actualization, which refers to God causing something independent of any actions of others)

Would counterfactuals   counterfactuals regarding what would happen given a particular state of affairs (e.g., what a given creature would freely do in any given situation)

Index

accidental properties 10, 29–30, 40–1, 228
accommodative language 57–9, 96–7, 137
action, divine
    singular timeless act 71–4, 98
    theories of 152 n.36. *See also* causality, primary and secondary
actualizable worlds 166, 183
adoptionism 201, 221
Alston, William 15, 240–1
Ambrose of Milan 186
analogical language (of God) 58–9
anatomical imagery, language of 58–60
Angel of the LORD 219
angels, fallen. *See* demonic realm
Anselm 5, 12–13, 15–16, 28, 31, 76, 77, 78, 81, 100, 114, 118 n.48, 124, 125, 150 n.25, 154, 155–6, 160
anthropomorphic language 58, 63, 64 n.237, 96–7, 137
anthropopathic language 57–9, 63, 76
anti-theodicy. *See* evil, problem of, protest approach to
apophatic theology 6 n.10, 62, 207. *See also* way of negation
Aquinas, Thomas. *See* Thomas Aquinas
Arianism 62, 66 n.248, 201, 212
Aristotelian philosophy 8, 13, 15, 60, 62, 64 n.238, 65, 77
Aristotle 8 n.20, 12, 19, 29, 48, 54, 62, 113
Arminian theology 153
Arminius, Jacob 118 n.48, 123, 129, 160
aseity 6–7, 10, 51, 52, 96, 226, 228, 232
    biblical data on 56
    pure 10, 29–33, 43–4, 233–4
aspatiality, divine. *See* incorporeality
atemporality of God. *See* timelessness, divine
Athanasian creed 200 n.4
Augustine 12–13, 15, 19 n.78, 28, 61, 64–5, 76–8, 81, 114, 118, 150 n.25, 152, 155, 177, 182, 186, 204, 210 n.54, 212
Augustinian theology 13, 43, 61–2, 71–2, 76–7, 111, 155
Averroes 8 n.19
Avicenna 8 n.19

Baggett, David 149 n.22, 150 n.26, 156–7
Barr, James 96
Barth, Karl 6 n.10, 22 n.85, 46, 83–4, 150, 157, 187
Bartholomew, Craig 3 n.4
beneficence 54
best possible world 149 n.21, 185
biblical warrant 3, 241
Bilezikian, Gilbet 215
blessedness, divine 35
Bloesch, Donald 43
Blomberg, Craig 218 n.91
Boethian solution. *See* foreknowledge, Boethian approach to
Boethius 76–7, 78, 81, 118 n.48, 124, 125
Bonhoeffer, Dietrich 50
Boyd, Gregory A. 86 n.122, 116–17, 130–1, 133–4, 135–40, 163–5, 184, 190
Bray, Gerald 64
Brower, Jeffrey E. 150 n.24, 211
Brueggemann, Walter 54–5

Calvinist theology 111, 114, 134, 153, 164
Calvin, John 58 n.205, 76, 78, 114, 118 n.48, 129, 153, 156, 177, 200 n.2
Canale, Fernando 3 n.3, 91 n.168
Cappadocian fathers 201–2, 204, 212, 231–2
Carson, D.A. 9–10 n.27, 57
Cary, Philip 207, 216
Castelo, Daniel 45, 62, 64, 65, 66
cataphatic theology 6 n.10
causal determinism. *See* determinism
causality, primary and secondary 152, 171
Chalamet, Christophe 84
Childs, Brevard 3 n.4
Christology. *See also* Trinity and eternal generation of the Son
  divinity of Christ 219–22
  functional subordination 214–16
  heresies 62, 66 n.248, 74, 201, 212, 221
  Logos 213
  sonship 220–2
classical theism 4–20
  core 21
  criticism of 13–20
  moderate 13, 22, 86, 239–40
  modified 8–9, 13, 22, 86
  revised 8–9
  strict 9–13, 21, 28–35, 239–40
Clement of Alexandria 8 n.20, 44, 62, 62 n.226
communicable attributes 6 n.10
compassion, divine 30–1, 33, 35, 56–8, 91, 169, 171
compatibilism. *See* free will, compatibilist
compatibilist free will. *See* free will, compatibilist
concurrentism 152 n.36. *See also* causality, primary and secondary
Cone, James 15, 50
conservationism 152 n.36

constancy, divine. *See* immutability
contingent properties. *See* accidental properties
Cooper, John W. 8–9, 40, 70, 76, 233
cosmic conflict. *See* evil, problem of, cosmic conflict approaches to
cosmic dualism 191
Couenhoven, Jesse 152 n.40
Council of Constantinople 203
Council of Nicea 201, 203–4. *See also* Nicene creed
counterfactuals 128–32, 140
  would 128–9, 130–2, 140
covenantal, of God 42, 53, 98, 104, 148, 163, 189, 220–1, 241
Cowan, Steven B. 110 n.4, 151
Craig, William Lane 8 n.22, 9 n.26, 9 n.27, 48, 51 n.167, 54, 75 n.42, 82, 87, 89–90, 93–6, 99–102, 118–19, 121–3, 129–32, 134–5, 140, 155, 161, 164, 165–6, 177, 209–10, 213, 233
creation ex nihilo 51, 60, 86, 116
Creator-creature distinction 9, 19, 41, 43, 50–1, 62, 72, 93, 96
Creator, of God 1, 9, 16, 41, 63, 72, 89, 91–4, 101, 132, 167, 228
Creel, Richard 27 n.1, 74
Crisp, Oliver 157 n.71
Cross, Richard 231
Culpepper, Gary 33
Cyril of Alexandria 66 n.249
Cyrus 117, 134

Davies, Brian 9 n.27
Davis, Stephen T. 47, 73, 75, 86, 90–1, 162, 179, 185–7, 192
Demarest, Bruce 40–1
demonic realm 188–91, 195–6
de Régnon thesis 204
determinism. *See* determinism, theistic
determinism, selective. *See* selective determinism

determinism, theistic 73, 109–15, 145, 151–7, 176–78
  traditional view(s) 152–3, 160–1
devil. *See* Satan
DeWeese, Garrett 77, 196
dialectical theology 22, 46, 84
Dickens, Charles 128
Diller, Kevin 187
displeasure, divine 7, 35–7, 51, 56, 91
disquotation Principle 131
divine Glory Defense 177–8, 193
divinity of Christ. *See* Christology, divinity of Christ
divinity of the Holy Spirit. *See* Holy Spirit, divinity of
docetism 62
doctrine of God, definition of 1
Dolezal, James E. 9–10 n.27, 10, 29, 31–4, 43, 54, 57–8, 75–6, 226, 228, 230, 232–4
dualism, cosmic 191
Duby, Steven J. 29
Duns Scotus, John 77, 160, 231
Durst, Roderick K. 218–19

economic Trinity. *See* Trinity, economic
Ehrman, Bart 180
embodiment, divine 45, 59–60. *See also* anatomical imagery, language of
Emery, Gilles 30–1
emotions, divine 7, 32, 34, 36–7, 41–2, 45, 49–52, 55–63, 75–6
endurantism 234
Epicurus 175
epistemic distance 183, 186
equivocal language (of God) 59
Erasmus 153
Erickson, Millard 40 n.81, 209, 212–13, 215–16
essential kenosis 19 n.76, 39, 160, 180
essential properties 29–30
eternal functional subordination 214–16

eternal generation 199, 203, 205, 207, 212–14
eternalism 79–82, 89, 96, 111–12, 123–7. *See also* timelessness, divine
eternal procession of the Spirit 204, 205, 207, 212–14
eternal relations of authority and submission. *See* eternal functional subordination
eternal relations of origin. *See* eternal generation and eternal procession of the Spirit
eternity, divine 7, 11, 69–99. *See also* timelessness, divine and temporality, divine
Eunomius 229
Euthyphro dilemma 149
everlasting, of God. *See* eternity, divine and temporality, divine
evil
  gratuitous 187
  moral 175–6
  natural 175–6, 184
  problem of. *See also* theodicy
    biblical data regarding 191–6
    cosmic conflict approaches to 184, 188–91, 195–6
    determinist approach to 154–6, 176–8, 193
    evidential 175
    existential 175
    felix culpa approach to 177–8, 185–8, 193–4
    free will defense approach (*see* free will defense)
    greater good approaches 177–8, 185–8, 193–4
    higher-order goods approach (*see* higher-order goods defense)
    logical 175, 182
    open theist approach to 165, 184–5, 192
    process approach to 180–1, 192

protest approach to 181–2, 192
religious 175
skeptical theist approach to 178–80, 194–5
soul-making approach to 186–7, 194
exhaustive definite foreknowledge. *See* foreknowledge

faithfulness, divine. *See* goodness of God
fallacy of necessity 120–2
feasible worlds. *See* actualizable worlds
Feinberg, John 9–10 n.27, 47–9, 87, 177, 213–14
felix culpa. *See* evil, problem of, *felix culpa* approaches to
Feser, Edward 71, 232
Fiddes, Paul S. 37 n.63
filioque 214
finitism 157–60, 180–1, 192
Flint, Thomas P. 131 n.133, 164
foreknowledge, divine 9, 109–41, 183, 185
biblical data on 133–41
Boethian approach to 123–8
determinist approach to 110–15
Molinist approach to 128–32
Ockhamist approach to 119–23
open view of 115–19
simple 127–8
Thomistic understanding 113–14
traditional view(s) of 113–14, 118
Frame, John 9–10 n.27, 43 n.105, 83
freedom, divine 51–2, 60, 86, 115–16, 127, 148–50, 167, 228–9
free will
biblical data on 170–2
compatibilist 110–11, 114–15, 151–8, 161, 164, 176–8
libertarian 109–10, 115–16, 119–28, 130, 145–6, 151, 155–6, 158, 160–2, 164, 165–7, 182–4, 188
free will defense 182–4, 187, 188–9, 192–3

Ganssle, Gregory E. 70, 90, 100, 103, 124, 126, 179
Garrigou-LaGrange, Reginald 113 n.18, 113 n.19
Gavrilyuk, Paul 44, 60 n.217, 61–6, 160 n.92, 182–3, 190
Geach, Peter 146
Giles, Kevin 212, 213, 215, 216
God of the philosophers 12, 14–16, 54, 64, 240–1. *See also* Hellenization thesis
gods
of Greek mythology 63
of the ANE nations 133, 136
God-world relationship, definition of 1
González, Justo L. 50
goodness of God 54, 175–96. *See also* theodicy
biblical data on 191–2
necessary 148–50, 167
question of 175–96 (*see also* evil, problem of)
greater good defense 156, 177–8, 185–8
Greek philosophy. *See* Hellenization theory
Green, Joel B. 195
Gregg, Brian Han 195
Gregory of Nazianzus 207 n.28, 212
Gregory of Nyssa 201–2, 231–2
Griffin, David Ray 18, 159, 180–1
growing block theory of time 80
Grudem, Wayne 9–10 n.27, 49, 215, 216

Harnack, Adolf von. 60 n.217
Hart David Bentley 155 n.58, 161 n.100, 188, 232
Hartshorne, Charles 6, 16–21, 35–7, 157–9, 180–1
Hasker, William 86 n.122, 116, 118, 127, 208
Hellenization thesis 14–16, 18, 42, 43, 44, 49, 60–6

Helm, Paul 31, 33–4, 58, 70–4, 76, 78–9, 82 n.98, 86, 95–6, 110–12, 114–15, 118, 125–6, 141, 153–6, 176–7, 213
Helseth, Paul 135
Henry Carl F.H. 35
Hick, John 157 n.72, 186–7, 194
hiddenness, divine 191 n.87
higher order goods defense 187, 194
Hippolytus of Rome 60 n.217
Hoffman, Joshua 101 n.238, 116 n.34, 118
Holmes, Stephen 204–7, 212, 214
Holy Spirit 201, 204. *See also* Trinity and eternal procession of the Spirit
    divinity of 223
    functional subordination 214–16
    personhood of 224–5
homoousios 200 n.2, 201, 212
Horton, Michael 42, 83, 104, 111, 219–20
Hume, David 175
Hunsinger, George 22 n.85
Hunt, David 109, 118, 125, 127–8, 133, 136, 139, 152 n.40, 155
hypothetical knowledge. *See* middle knowledge

immanent Trinity. *See* Trinity, immanent
immaterial, of God. *See* incorporeality, divine
immutability, divine 6–7
    biblical data on 53–6
    ethical 35–9, 54
    qualified 8, 27, 39–53, 86
    utter (aka strict) 11, 28–35, 71, 75, 228
impassibility, divine 7–8, 98–9
    biblical data on 55–60
    external 27, 32–3
    internal 27–8, 32–3
    qualified 8–9, 11, 27–8, 39–46, 61

    sensational 27–8, 32–3
    strict 11, 14, 28–35, 44, 61, 71, 75, 113
    traditional view(s) 60–4
incarnation 44, 57, 66 n.249, 73–4, 87–9, 91–2, 105, 203, 214–16, 221, 229 n.121
incommunicable attributes 6 n.10
incompatibilist free will. *See* free will, incompatibilist
incorporeality, divine 11, 59–60, 101–2
indeterminism 51, 109–10, 115–32, 157–67, 193. *See also* determinism
Irenaeus 8 n.20, 186

Jowers, Dennis 161
Jüngel, Eberhard 38
Justin Martyr 44, 62, 118 n.48

Kärkkäinen, Veli-Matti 8, 13
Kenny, Anthony 147
kenoticism 38, 52
Kitamori, Kazoh 38
knowledge
    conceptualist account 118–19
    perceptualist account 118
Kretzmann, Norman 81–2

Latin theories of the Trinity. *See* Trinity, Latin theories
Lee, Yena 179
Leftow, Brian 5 n.6, 6 n.14, 7 n.15, 7 n.18, 8 n.20, 32, 82 n.96, 125, 162
Leibniz, Gottfried 185
Lewis, C.S. 146, 188
liberal theologies 22 n.86
libertarian free will. *See* free will, libertarian
Lister, Rob 8 n.22, 9–10 n.27, 41–4, 52 n.175, 55–7, 62, 64, 75
logical problem of evil. *See* evil, problem of, logical
Long, D. Stephen 13 n.41

love, divine 18, 36–8, 40, 49–50, 54–7, 150, 159–60, 162, 164, 166, 169, 180–1, 184, 186, 189–90, 207–8
Lundberg, Matthew D. 62 n.226, 154, 156, 229, 232–4
Luther, Martin 78, 118 n.48, 129, 153, 178

Mackie, J.L. 147, 175
Maimonides 8 n.19
Mavrodes, George 147
McCall, Thomas H. 201–2, 210, 216–17, 226–7, 229–32
McCann, Hugh 72, 73, 95, 96
McCormack, Bruce 22 n.85, 46, 55
McFague, Sallie 15, 100 n.230
Melanchthon, Philip 160
metaphysical framework, definition of 4
middle knowledge 128–32, 140, 165–6. *See also* Molinism
Middle Platonism 8 n.20
miracles 146, 181, 192–3
modalism 201, 207
Molina, Luis de 129–30
molinism 113 n.19, 128–32, 140, 165–7
  grounding objection 131
Molnar, Paul 22 n.85
Moltmann, Jürgen 14, 37–8, 61
moral evil. *See* evil, moral
Moreland, J.P. 9 n.26, 9–10 n.27, 48, 51 n.167, 54, 100–2, 213, 233
Morris, Thomas 21, 78, 87, 91, 95, 98, 138, 147–8, 150, 206–8
Muller, Richard A. 12, 40 n.81, 153 n.46
Mullins, R.T. 50, 57, 70, 73–4, 80–82, 84–5, 89–90, 92, 97–9, 101–2, 228, 230, 234
Murray, Michael 162 n.103

Nash, Ronald 7 n.18, 9 n.26, 9–10 n.27, 48, 54, 86, 146, 147, 150, 234
natural evil. *See* evil, natural
natural theology 17

necessity
  accidental 122–3
  divine 6
  temporal 122–3
necessity of consequence 120–2
necessity of the thing consequent 120–2
negative theology. *See* apophatic theology and way of negation
neoplatonism 8, 13, 15, 19 n.78, 61, 65, 77–8, 213, 228, 233
Nestorianism 62
Nicene creed 203–4, 207, 212, 214, 216
nomic regularity 162
noseeum arguments 179
numerical identity 200

occasionalism 152 n.36
Ockhamism. *See* foreknowledge, Ockhamist approach to
Oden, Thomas 47
Oliphint, K. Scott 9–10 n.27
omnibenevolence, divine 175–96
omnicausality 152
omnipotence 6, 9, 145–50. *See also* providence
  biblical data on 167 (*see also* providence, biblical data on)
  coherence of 146–50
  traditional view(s) of 146–50, 152–3, 158–60, 180–1
omnipresence 100–05
  biblical data regarding 103–5
  traditional view(s) of 101–2
omniscience 6, 9, 69, 109–41, 163, 228. *See also* foreknowledge
  biblical data on 132–41
omnisubjectivity 112
omnitemporality
  view of Craig 93–4, 99
  view of Ware, Horton, and Frame 83
oneness of God
  biblical data on 217
  coherence of 202–3

ontological argument 5
Oord, Thomas Jay 19 n.76, 39, 51, 52 n.176, 86 n.122, 149 n.23, 159–60, 180–1
open theism 9, 19, 22, 48, 52, 85–6, 115–19, 133–140, 162–5, 184–5

Padgett, Alan 47, 88, 92–4, 97, 228, 240
panentheism 14 n.50, 17–19, 35–9, 100. *See also* process theology
Pannenberg, Wolfhart 162
pantheism 17, 100
Parmenides 78
Parunak, H. Van Dyke 138
Pasnau, Robert 101–2
passibility, divine 9, 28, 98–9. *See also* impassibility, divine
    biblical data on 55–60
    qualified 9, 46–53, 66
    strong 14, 17, 35–9
    traditional view(s) 60–4
passion, divine. *See* passibility, divine
Peckham, John C. 4 n.5, 51–2
Pelagius 152 n.38
perdurantism (aka worm theory) 234
perfect being theology 5–8, 10–12, 17, 30
perichoresis 209
personhood, divine 202, 206–7, 210, 223–5
Philo of Alexandria 8 n.20, 62 n.226, 64 n.237
philosophical frameworks 3–4
Pike, Nelson 75, 122
Pinnock, Clark 19, 48, 52, 60, 86, 91, 115–16, 161–3
Piper, John 35, 156, 177
Plantinga, Alvin 9 n.26, 9–10 n.27, 49, 121–2, 131, 179, 182–5, 190, 194–5, 227
Plantinga, Jr., Cornelius 209
Plantinga, Richard J. 62 n.226, 154, 156, 229, 232–4

Plato 7, 8 n.20, 60, 78, 149
Platonic philosophy 8, 60, 62–3. *See also* Middle Platonism and neoplatonism
Plotinus 64 n.238, 78, 125, 228
Pojman, Louis 11, 15, 78
possible world semantics 6, 166, 185
potentiality (aka potency) 29, 32
prayer 16, 56, 74, 81, 192–3, 224
predestination 134–6, 153, 163, 64, 168–9. *See also* providence
presence, divine. *See* omnipresence
presentism 79–81, 89, 131
privatio boni 182 n.43
problem of evil. *See* evil, problem of
process theodicy. *See* evil, problem of, process approach to
process theology 6, 16–21, 35–7, 43–4, 85–6, 100, 115–16, 157–9, 180–1
promise-keeping, of God 40, 47, 54, 86, 148, 221
providence 145
    biblical data on 167–72
    determinist conception of 151–7
    molinist conception of 165–7
    open theist conception of 162–5
    process conception of 157–60
    sovereignty indeterminist conception of 160–7
    traditional view(s) of 152–3, 160–1
pure act (*actus purus*) 29–30, 32–3, 40, 43, 52, 76, 113, 227, 232–4. *See also* pure aseity

Rahner, Karl 205
Rahner's rule 205
Rea, Michael 11, 15, 78, 201, 211
regret, divine. *See* repentance, divine
Reichenbach, Bruce 181
relational theories of the Trinity. *See* Trinity, relational theories
relation of reason 34, 40, 72, 113
relenting, divine. *See* repentance, divine

religious problem of evil. *See* evil, religious problem of
repentance, divine 55, 138–9
responsiveness, of God 44, 53–5, 74–6, 88, 160–1
Rice, Richard 86 n.122, 115, 184, 194
Richard of St. Victor 210 n.54
Richards, Jay Wesley 3 n.2, 12 n.39, 13 n.41, 21, 41
Ridderbos, J. 219
Rogers, Katherin 3, 5–6, 7 n.17, 12 n.39, 13, 15–16, 20, 28–9, 33–5, 58, 64, 70–8, 80–1, 95, 101, 105, 111–12, 124–7, 136, 148, 149 n.21, 150, 152 n.36, 152 n.40, 154–5, 160–1, 182, 226–8, 232
Rosenkratz, Gary S. 101 n.238, 116 n.34, 118
Roth, John K. 181–2
Rowe, William 182, 184
rules of engagement 189–90. *See also* problem of evil; cosmic conflict approaches to
Russell, Jeffrey Burton 190

Sanders, Fred 13–14, 20, 205, 217
Sanders, John 86 n.122, 162
Satan 104, 153, 184, 188–91, 195–6
Schellenberg, J.L. 187
Schleiermacher, Friedrich 22 n.86, 186
Schultz, Walter J. 161 n.100
selective determinism 117, 134, 163–5, 168
self-limitation, divine 148, 162. *See also* promise-keeping
self-sufficiency (of God) 6, 10, 51, 52, 79. *See also* aseity
semi-Arianism 201
sempiternity. *See* everlasting
settled character hypothesis 117, 135, 163–4
Shults, F. LeRon 84
simple foreknowledge. *See* foreknowledge, simple

simplicity, divine 6, 71, 113, 225–34
  formal 11, 230–1
  generic 231–2
  strict (aka strong) 9 n.27, 11, 28–30, 78, 199, 205–6, 210, 226–30, 233
singularity theories of the Trinity. *See* Trinity, singularity theories
skeptical theism. *See* evil, problem of, skeptical theist approach to
social Trinity. *See* Trinity, social theories
Sonderegger, Katherine 44–5, 70, 105
sonship of Christ. *See* Christology, sonship
soul-making theodicy. *See* evil, problem of, soul-making approach to
sovereignty 130, 145, 151–7, 160–7. *See also* providence
  biblical data on 167–70
sovereignty indeterminism. *See* providence, sovereignty indeterminist conception of
spacelessness, divine. *See* incorporeality
Spiegel, James S. 110 n.4, 151
Stoicism 42, 46, 49, 61
Stott, John 50
strict classical theism. *See* classical theism, strict
strong actualization 158, 169
Stump, Eleonore 16, 71, 74, 81–2, 114, 152
Stumpff, Albrecht 64 n.237
subordinationism 199, 201, 213–15
suffering. *See* evil, problem of
suffering, divine. *See* passibility
supererogatory actions 150
Swinburne, Richard 9 n.26, 47, 87, 90, 101–2, 116–17, 146–7, 160, 183, 187, 194
sympathy, perfect divine 36–7
systematic theology
  definition of 2
  nature of 2–4

Talbott, Thomas B. 157 n.72
Taliaferro, Charles 49
temporality, divine 8, 9, 17, 43, 69, 85–94. *See also* timelessness, divine
  analogical 91–2
  biblical data regarding 94–9
  traditional view(s) 76–8, 80–1, 87
tensed facts 80, 111–12
Tertullian 66
theistic determinism. *See* determinism, theistic
theistic mutualism 9 n.27
theistic personalism 9 n.27
theodicy. *See* evil, problem of
  definition of 176
theological method 3–4, 240–1
theology, definition of 1
theopaschite terminology 65–6
Thomas Aquinas 1, 12–13, 15, 18, 28–30, 32, 53, 59 n.214, 61 n.222, 62, 72, 76–8, 81, 113–14, 118 n.48, 125, 146–7, 149, 152–3, 186, 193, 226, 228
Thompson, Thomas R. 62 n.226, 154, 156, 229, 232–4
time
  metaphysical 91–2
  nature of 7, 79–82, 234
  physical 91–2
timeless action. *See* action, divine, singular timeless act
timelessness, divine 7, 9, 11, 29–33, 69–79, 82–5, 90–1, 111–13, 123–7, 154, 205, 212, 228, 233–4. *See also* eternalism
  biblical data regarding 94–9
  relative 92–4
  traditional view(s) 76–8, 80–1, 87
Timpe, Kevin 151 n.32
Tooley, Michael 189
Torrance, T.F. 46, 91–2
transcendence, divine 43, 45, 51, 82–3, 93, 179

trinitarian formulas 218–19
Trinity 199–225, 229–30
  biblical data regarding 217–25
  classical doctrine 203–6, 210
  coherence of 200–3
  distinct personhood of Father, Son, and Spirit 223–5
  divinity of Trinitarian persons 219–23
  economic 205
  immanent 205
  Latin theories 206–8
  minimal doctrine 200
  relational theories 208–10
  relative identity theories 211
  singularity theories 206–8, 216
  social theories 206, 207, 208–10
  traditional view(s) of 203–6, 207, 210, 212–13, 214–16
tritheism 201, 208–9
Tuggy, Dale 207, 209

unfulfilled desires, divine 156, 166, 171–2
universalism 157
univocal language 58
unmoved Mover 19 n.77, 48, 62, 91, 113

Vanhoozer, Kevin J. 9–10 n.27, 42–3, 188
Van Inwagen, Peter 195
via eminenatiae. *See* way of eminence
via negativa. *See* way of negation

Walls, Jerry 149 n.22, 150 n.26, 156–7, 177, 178
Ware, Bruce 8 n.22, 9–10 n.27, 39–42, 59, 82–3, 102, 215
way of eminence (*via eminentiae*) 5, 17
way of negation (via negativa) 5, 6 n.10, 17
weak actualization 169
Webster, John 10, 32, 72, 150, 152, 205

Weinandy, Thomas 32, 33
Wesley, John 118 n.48
Whitehead, Alfred North 16 n.64
Wierenga, Edward 126
William of Ockham 77, 119–20
Williams, Daniel Day 36
Williams, Thomas 8, 11, 30, 31, 32, 70, 71, 90, 113, 226
Willis, John T. 55
will of God 156, 168–9, 171–2. *See also* unfulfilled desires, divine
revealed and hidden 156

Wolterstorff, Nicholas 8 n.22, 9 n.26, 47, 49, 53–4, 59–61, 69, 87–8, 94, 97, 99, 102
would counterfactuals. *See* counterfactuals, would
wrath, divine 50, 56, 58, 65 n.246, 66 n.249, 98, 177–8
Wykstra, Stephen 179

Yong, Amos 50

Zagzebski, Linda 112 n.14, 126 n.98

www.ingramcontent.com/pod-product-compliance
Lightning Source LLC
Chambersburg PA
CBHW062128300426
44115CB00012BA/1856